TONY ZALE THE MAN OF STEEL

THAD ZALE & CLAY MOYLE

Win By KO Publications
Iowa City

TONY ZALE THE MAN OF STEEL

THAD ZALE & CLAY MOYLE

(ISBN-13): 978-0-9903703-1-4

(hardcover: 50# acid-free alkaline paper)

Includes footnotes, appendix, bibliography, and index.

Fourth printing with revisions May 2015
www.TonyZale.org

Designed by Deb Zale

Manufactured in the United States of America.

Win By KO Publications
Iowa City, Iowa
winbykopublications.com

DEDICATION

Tony Zale The Man of Steel
spans eighty years and is dedicated to those
who aspire to accomplish their dreams in life.
The benchmark set by this world champion
in and out of the ring is formidable, but the *real* key
to success for the champion of these pages is about
what you give back. In the words of Tony Zale,
*"You receive far more from life by what
you give, rather than by what you get."*
Bless all of you who take the time to
read the message within these pages.

Thad Zale

CONTENTS

PROLOGUE BY HANK STRAM

Anthony Florian Zaleski was the epitome of a blue collar worker. He fully accepted the hard, dirty work of the steel mill, trained tenaciously and long at his sporting love, and never forgot the friends he made along the way or the city that meant the most to him. The respect and admiration that was returned lasted throughout his life. From his Golden Gloves days in Memorial Auditorium in Gary, Indiana, to his championship events in Chicago, Seattle, New York and Newark, his popularity emanated like ripples in a pond. His friends and his city were always at the center.

For me, growing up when he was coming into his own was a unique experience. I would go to the Roxy (Ridge) movie theater in Glen Park, Indiana, to watch the Pathe News sports segment to see the coverage of what Tony Zale had done in the ring. There was no television in those days. Don Dunphy would broadcast the fight on radio and a story about it would appear in the newspaper the next afternoon, but that was nothing like being able to actually see it on that screen at the show.

Kids of the 1930s and 40s were respectful of their parents, teachers, the folks in authority and sports heroes. They idolized winners from the ring, the football fields, or the baseball diamonds. Those athletes were revered as someone special who accomplished a great goal or gained success. They showed what was ultimately possible by really working to get to the top. You took pride in what they had accomplished.

I would come out of the theater deeply inspired by that man of medium stature, who happened to be from Gary, Indiana, my hometown too, who could fight the way he did in front of thousands. And his winning would make it even sweeter.

People say he was a fighter. But fighting was what he did, not what he was. He was something much more. He could be a terminator in the ring, but he was a caring, great person outside of the ring.

It's great to win a Super Bowl, World Series or be in the Final Four. But when you win those, you win them through commitment as a team. Tony became a champion on his own. He was truly a champion in the fullest sense. He was not flamboyant in any way. He didn't trash talk to hype the gate; he didn't use a fancy dance routine around the ring, nor was he a showboat. In the ring, he methodically put his skills together with his capabilities to always do his absolute best.

Integrity, dedication, and honesty were the blocks of his character mortared together by a magnificent ability, lightening quickness, and a fierce competitiveness. He would stand face to face, round after round with champion or challenger alike to give and take until it was over by decision or by knockout. He had a heart like a blow torch and hands like trip hammers.

Because of his interest in kids, he had a tremendous influence on youngsters of all ages during his career, and continued to inspire and work with them long after he retired from the ring.

At his funeral on March 24, 1997, his nephew said, "He was the finest piece of steel Gary will ever produce." And, it's true. But, will there be another as great as Tony Zale? Maybe one day, but not in the near future. Because finding someone in the world of boxing to accept the work ethic, the humility, the impeccable standards, the incredible determination and all those other personal traits that combine into a winner of this magnitude, is truly rare.

Hank Stram, Friend & Sportscaster
Pro Football Hall of Fame, Super Bowl IV Winning Coach
Former Kansas City Chiefs Head Coach
April 27, 1997

COACH HANK STRAM   KANSAS CITY CHIEFS

INTRODUCTION

My name is Thad Zale, but my friends call me Ted. I am the nephew of Tony Zale, one of the greatest Middleweight Champions of the world. Tony was the World Middleweight Champion from 1940 to 1947, and then again in 1948. He was the second middleweight in history to win back his title after losing it. Back in 1908, another Polish fighter, Stanley Ketchel, known as the Michigan Assassin, became the first. Tony's three epic battles against the better known and colorful Rocky Graziano are still considered among the greatest trilogies in boxing's long and illustrious history. They are representative of the some of the greatest middleweight fights of the 20th century.

This story actually begins near the end, in the summer of 1987. My wife Deb and I went with Tony and Philomena to dinner at one of their favorite Italian restaurants on the near northwest side of Chicago. It was during that intimate Italian dinner when Tony and Philomena asked me if I would be willing to take on the task of writing his biography. I was absolutely surprised by this request and completely honored.

Back in 1978 and 1979, Tony had helped in my preparation for the 1980 Olympic tryouts. The games were scheduled to take place in Russia in 1980, but participation of the United States was canceled by President Jimmy Carter due to Russia's invasion of Afghanistan. As a result of this training with my uncle, we grew very close. So close in fact, that my wife and I named our first born in his honor.

In making the commitment to Tony and Philomena to pen his life's story, I indicated that of course I had never written a book before. In my current occupation, I worked more than full time in the financial industry trying to make a living for my family. But before we parted ways that night, I promised to them both that I would work on it as diligently as possible.

Over the next seven years, I began to lay the foundation. I held interviews with Uncle Tony on his long weekends with us in Michigan. I interviewed my older cousins who saw his fights with both Graziano and Cerdan. I interviewed aunts, uncles, brothers, cousins, friends and any others that still could recall his championship years. They all had vivid memories of Tony Zale's boxing days.

Then, in the late fall of 1991, came the shocking news that Philomena was ill with cancer and she died shortly after its discovery. Uncle's feisty, loving caregiver, "Mighty Mouth," was gone. The task of his future care now became the concern of everyone in our family.

Uncle Tony survived for some five years after Philomena passed, as he continued to show us how to be right and do right. We continued to bring him to Michigan for all but his last few years. When his medical condition demanded more care and he became less mobile, we began to visit him regularly at a Portage, Indiana, nursing home. On these visits, we would usually bring along a classmate or two of our son or daughter. He loved the children and enjoyed receiving their group hugs. During the next five years, other cousins, nieces and nephews from the Zale, Kordys and Krecik families provided for his daily and weekly care.

The love we all shared for Uncle Tony cannot be put into words. For my part, I am finally able to complete "his" story thanks to my co-author, historian and boxing enthusiast, Clay Moyle. Many Tony Zale fans like Rinze Van Der Meer and Albert Stol of Arnhem, the Netherlands, my cousins Walter "Sonny" Zale, Lillian (Kordys) Lopez and Armand Lopez and my brothers have contributed their recollections to this book. Several of my relatives have passed over the years since I started this endeavor and their interviews are a part of his story. I sincerely hope you enjoy the Champ's journey from beginning to end.

FOREWORD

On March 20, 1997, Tony Zale left this world. It was about 1:00 in the afternoon when I received a call at my office from my cousin Jeanette who was with Tony in Portage, Indiana. She wanted me to know that he was doing poorly. Jeanette said the doctors had taken him off all medications. The end was near and hospice was now assisting him in his final hours. When I received this sad news, I asked Jeanette to hold and I quickly called Gus Latsis in Chicago, Tony's best friend. Gus and Tony were very close, like brothers, and had been best friends since the early 1940s.

As I updated Gus on Uncle Tony's current condition, we knew we were nearing the beginning of a sad chapter in our lives. I put Gus on hold and went back to the other line to speak to Jeanette. She told me the sorrowful news that Uncle Tony had passed. She sadly described that he had sat up in bed, looked at my cousins Helen, Jeanette, and Lillian, and said, "It is nice to see you all." He then laid back down, closed his eyes and he was gone. I switched back over to Gus to relay the sad news, and we both silently cried together. I clearly remember Gus then saying to me, "first my wife, and now my best friend." But after all, Tony Zale, that man of steel, was only human.

I quickly left my office and headed home, packed my bags, and left for Indiana. As I drove from Lansing, Michigan, I wondered what I would find when I arrived. I wondered what needed to be done to help my brother Ray and my cousins, Lillian, Helen, Jeanette, Danny and Paul prepare for Tony's funeral. What kind of honors would he be given? Who would bestow upon this champion the rightful conclusion to a life well spent? In the last couple of years of Tony's life, things weren't particularly easy. Of course, Tony never took the easy way. Life had been a constant challenge for him; a challenge to be a better person. He was also challenged to help others, to believe in God, and to live a right and honest life in accordance with the Ten Commandments. As I drove the three hours back to Indiana, back to his heritage as well as mine, I wondered how many would come to pay their last respects. How many Tony Zale fans were still left out there and how many remembered what he had accomplished in such an extraordinary career?

Tony was one of the last of the great boxers of his time. Most of those pre-1950 fighters were now gone. These were men who, as young boys, loved boxing, and not just the money. These were men who listened on the radio to Jack Dempsey fights and came alive with the adrenaline generated by the announcer's description of every punch and counter punch. Death is always bittersweet. Bitter because we miss a human presence in our lives. Sweet, because the ravages of disease can no longer pose a threat or bring hardship upon our loved one. We selfishly forget it is *their* life, and the Lord's. Parkinson's Disease took its toll on Tony in the later stages of his life. Parkinson's is a cruel disease that is a degenerative disorder of the central nervous system that typically impairs an individual's motor skills, speech, and other functions. Former heavyweight champion Muhammad Ali is a modern day example of how the body suffers its effects. This disease robbed Tony of some of his language skills as well as his ability to swallow. It had stolen the use of his legs a few years earlier, even though until the end, his body remained physically toned from all his road work during his sixties and seventies. Parkinson's also took away that glowing eye, the shine of life from a champion who had given and shown us so much.

As I arrived, my relatives were beginning to gather at the funeral home to make the final arrangements. I couldn't help but wonder how all of us would feel about the loss of our family treasure. I remember Ray, my brother sixteen years my senior, saying, "Tony's in a better place. He doesn't have to deal with the day to day breakdown of his body anymore." Tony's journey was 83 years long. His heart, which had always beaten so strongly, had now given way to old age.

It had been a month since we had journeyed to Northwest Indiana, and I wanted to remember Tony as he was the other times we had seen him. On that last visit, he still had the same old smile for us. I had brought with me a video of his third fight with Rocky, and also the Marcel Cerdan fight. I wanted us to watch them together. As usual, he was waiting in the hall for us. The children always greeted him with hugs and kisses. They just adored him, and he them. These young visitors brought back that old sparkle to his eyes.

As we viewed the first and second rounds of the Graziano fight, Tony leaned over to me and said, "You know, he wasn't the toughest I fought, but he got the best press." I replied that he sure did. The

'Rock-a-bye-Baby' was the darling of New York City. As we watched Graziano battle back in the second round after Tony had floored him in the first, I could see in his eyes, Tony still mentally fending him off. He used his right to block, parried with his left, and moved away from him trying to avoid getting caught with any punches. With the best right to the body of any fighter, Tony put Graziano down for the count in the third round. He finished him with his left hook that could have been patented. This fight wasn't Rocky's destiny, it was Tony's.

I leaned over to Tony and told him we loved him. He nodded without a blink. His eyes were fixed on that past fight, his third meeting with the bad boy from across the tracks. In the third round, Rocky comes out swinging and leaves himself open as Tony nails him with a left hook. Down he goes! Tony, with Rocky leaning against the ropes, shoots a right uppercut and then throws a left hook. Rocky staggers off the ropes. As Rocky throws his left jab, Tony steps in and nails him with a right to the ribs, just below the heart and then a left hook to the jaw. Rocky is down and out. It is a classic combination and to this day one of the most beautifully executed boxing knockouts you will ever see. The referee checked to make sure Tony had gone to a neutral corner, and he continued to count, but he had to know Rocky was finished. There was no way he was getting up from those punches. At the count of ten, Rocky was still out and Tony had reclaimed the middleweight championship. At that time he was only the second in history to accomplish that feat.

Tony won, but ironically, he was worried about his opponent. Rocky was not moving. His head hit the canvas so hard it caused an immediate concussion. They tried to revive him, but he was completely out. He was still breathing, although he wasn't responsive. Tony acknowledged the applause, but he was concerned. Was the Rock okay? They finally got him up, and he still wasn't responding well. It was time to take him to the hospital to be checked out.

I stopped the tape and talked to Tony. As we took him down the hallway past all his friends, many of the nursing home crew said, "Hi Tony." He responded to each and every one by name. The residents all knew him too, as most were from his era. They knew what he did back in the day. This was the Champ I knew. This was the man who gave me my inspiration for so many years of my youth.

When I lost my father, Tony's eldest brother Joe, at the tender age of eight, Uncle Tony became a beloved father figure, a person that I instantly respected and admired. I grew up knowing he was this "celebrity" type person to the world, but he was adored by me as my favorite uncle. The love I had for the man named Tony Zale was seen through the eyes of a young child.

Now, as I walked to the casket, flashbacks of my most vivid memories of him raced across my mind. A man so strong that he was nicknamed the "Man of Steel" by sports writers for his chiseled, iron-like physique from the years he spent working in the steel mills in Gary, Indiana. The man with whom I had formed much more than a familial bond was gone. I was strangely afraid and did not want to look at his lifeless body lying there before me. I didn't want to accept the fact that the Champ was gone. I didn't want to have to do this adult thing that I remembered "having" to do when I was eight years old. I already missed my friend, the man who at one time was on top of the world, "Uncle Tony, a Champion *of* the World."

I didn't know what to expect as I took that dreadful walk with my relatives into the room where Tony was lying in state. I was startled by the sight of the bump on the left side of his neck, cancer of the lymph nodes I guessed. I wanted to remember him as he was during our visits. It had been just over four weeks since we had seen him last, and now he seemed only a shell. He was pale and gaunt and this gland was swollen so dramatically. It seemed improbable, but then so is life sometimes. God had chosen this way to end it for the Champ. These next few days would speak volumes about our uncle and his personal mission.

The next day, we arrived at the funeral home early to say our personal good-byes to our Uncle Tony. I was surprised that there were 20 plus people there already. People in their fifties and sixties began streaming through the door and lined up to say goodbye to a man and to an era. We personally greeted each and thanked them for coming to honor our uncle. We had hoped Tony's two daughters from California would be able to say their final good-byes too, but they had neither the health, nor the ability to travel, even though they were offered flights at no expense by the Kordys family. Tony hadn't ever really developed the father-daughter relationship that I knew he would have liked. They had been stripped away from their father by an ugly divorce after he lost the championship in 1948 to Marcel Cerdan. If he saw his children once a year, he was lucky, and so were they. For him, the loss of his two daughters would always remain his worst defeat.

As the stream of mourners coming to pay their last respects continued, many shared with us their personal thoughts of what Tony Zale meant to them. He had taught most of them at some time or another, and some had even been in his corner watching him fight for his championships. Others had realized their own personal dream due to the impact of this man having been in their lives. They came to thank him in their own way. There were policeman, fireman, corporate executive officers, doctors, lawyers, electricians, plumbers, sanitation workers and a few directors of the board from the Mercantile Exchange who came to thank him. Tony had helped them all. Some had fought under his tutelage. Many of them were taught that famous smashing right to the body and left hook to the chin.

Some visitors didn't want to leave and stayed with us until after the doors closed, eagerly sharing their personal stories of Tony Zale. Yes, he was a great fighter and boxing coach. Yes, after the ring, he had devoted his life to kids by helping the inner city youth of Chicago make something of themselves. Yes, he helped them grow and understand that they had the Spirit within. He taught them that all things were possible if they believed in themselves. Instead of the old adage, "seeing is believing," Tony taught them that *if you believe in yourself first, then you will see good things come your way.* He gave them some skills in the ring, but more importantly, Tony encouraged them to stay in school and complete their education. He never took advantage of his opportunity as the "Champ" for monetary gain or to fill his ego.

In the mid 1930's, Tony was offered a boxing scholarship to the University of Wisconsin. Hoping to first get his family out of poverty and move them up to middle class status, he instead chose to become a professional fighter.

Tony always regretted his decision of not getting a college education before becoming a professional boxer. He was a great Golden Gloves champion and by the best of his recollection, had over 200 amateur bouts. He passed this aptitude on to the young men who idolized him and channeled his "no quit attitude" to encourage them in their studies rather than in the ring. He taught them that we are all cut from the same mold by God, but we all have different talents and abilities. We all have a different meaning in life and our journey is to do the best we can with our individual God-given skills. Getting an education first will provide you, once you are successful, with the necessary tools for "giving back to life." That was Tony's motto. That was Tony's life. All of the doctors, lawyers, friends and even current and former champions who attended knew what it was like to rise above life's hardships. They came to say goodbye to Tony. No matter the color of their skin, they all knew the difference he made in their personal lives.

Tony spent the years from 1949 to 1968 working for the Catholic Youth Organization (CYO) in Chicago, not earning much, but always giving more than he received. A friend from New York helped him move to the Big Apple to host at Gallaghers Steakhouse in 1968. The New Yorkers *really* knew how to treat him like the 'Champ' he was in the 1940s. They rarely took advantage of him. Then it was back to Chicagoland from late 1969 until his forced retirement in 1986 as head coach of the Chicago Parks District boxing program. Eventually, Tony's political allies in Chicago lost a key election in 1986 and as a result Tony would become one of the sacrificial lambs. So with new political bosses, he was replaced as head boxing coach. This was a crushing blow to the Champ. He compared his release to the disappointment he felt after losing his title to Marcel Cerdan in 1948.

Now, several nieces and nephews of the Cerdan family came to Gary, Indiana, from Paris, France, to say goodbye to Tony. I cannot imagine the difficulties they faced to arrive at the funeral home on time. No one in our family spoke French, so many hand signals and embraces surrounded our exchanges. The Cerdans loved Tony too. They knew that in 1948, when he lost to their Uncle Marcel, he was distracted and his mind wasn't on the fight. Tony's impending divorce, a right elbow that was spent and his age, marked the end of his great career and the continuation of Marcel's career as champion of the world. More than anything though, Tony's mental game was gone and beyond repair for that fight.

Tony was not flashy, nor one of the most famous fighters of all time, but he never tried to be. He was just Tony Zale, a man who lived well and died well. Like their Uncle Marcel, he was a champion of the world in one of the toughest sports of all - mano y mano.

Day two was to be as long as day one. An hour before I arrived at the funeral home, I had been rushing about to get a special photograph card of Tony printed which featured all of his fights on the back. As I set out the pictures with the fight history, I spoke to the people at the funeral home who had prepped him after his death. They had done such a good job of making his age weary features look so well in spite of the swollen lymph node. They proceeded to tell me how they could not believe how muscular Tony still was as well as how strong his legs appeared. Legs that had not been used much in the last two years still kept the muscular form that had been so well honed over the decades by this man of steel. Age had taken its toll on his mental side, and the Parkinson's had stolen his ability to move, but the body was still like aged steel. I wasn't surprised by this as Tony had continued to run well into his late seventies. After an episode one hot and muggy Chicago afternoon, his doctor had told him that running was taking too much of a toll on his body. For a fighter, and this fighter in particular, running to stay healthy was a way of life.

Again, I was surprised when I arrived at the funeral home to find several mourners paying respects to Tony before the family had arrived. We were forty-five minutes early for visitation and people were already streaming in. Today's visitation was scheduled from 1:00 to 8:00 pm. But that didn't happen. Instead, people were there from noon until 10:00 pm. Tony's best friend Gus Latsis, his children, and other Zale relatives greeted the mourners. Jack Sandner, a former student of Tony's and Chairman of the Chicago Mercantile Exchange, stayed with us throughout the visitation. At one time, Jack had wanted to quit school and become a professional boxer. Tony, after working with Jack on several occasions, convinced him to go back to school. He was good, he was a natural, but Tony saw his future in another arena. As you will read later, Jack helped repay Tony for the fatherly advice he provided and the example he set.

Tony moved back to Chicago to stay in 1970, thanks to the efforts of Ed Kelly, Chicago Parks Department Superintendent. Then in 1971, Mr. Kelly introduced the Special Olympics into the parks and recreational program. With the encouragement and support of John F. Kennedy's sister, Eunice Kennedy Shriver, Mr. Kelly and Tony wholeheartedly supported this program as an annual event. Tony immediately became an instructor, coach and judge. He indeed had an impact on every athletic event in which he would participate.

His friends from the Polish National Alliance (PNA) Silver Bell Club paid their respects. His friends from the Veterans of Foreign Wars came and said their prayers. His friends from the Elks Lodge paid their respects, with moving moments of silence in his honor.

I often wonder what would have happened if Tony hadn't lived up to his religious convictions. Where would the inspiration he provided to others have gone? All of them said that Tony had a direct impact on their lives. He taught them first and foremost about how to live, not just how to box. New stories with the same theme were heard. "If it had not been for Tony, I would have probably died on the streets of Chicago." Tony gave them clear and simple direction. He remembered how difficult it could be to live up to expectations, and to do the right thing. He wanted them first to believe in the Ten Commandments. Follow them without question. Love their families as they love themselves. And finally, get an education so they would have something to fall back on. Tony used his fists to demonstrate what one person could do when God was chosen as his or her co-pilot.

To be a prize fighter and eventually become a world champion was Tony's first goal in life. He achieved this in the greatest style that any fighter could have ever imagined. When it was over, and when the cheers and the applause were gone, Tony never forgot his roots and gave back to the young men and women who would follow.

Now, in 2014, some twenty-seven years after first being asked by my uncle to take on this labor of love, I am keeping the promise I made to him back then; a promise that has been rolling around in my mind for what seems like an eternity, this book being the end result.

With all that said, this is my uncle's story. The story of Tony Zale, the *real* man of steel.

THE ZALESKI CLAN

During some 123 years of captivity, a period of time known as "the patricians" from the eighteenth century until World War I, Poland found itself at the mercy of the neighboring countries Russia, Austria and Prussia. These countries pursued a common policy aimed at retaining the spoils of war while attempting to avoid conflict with one another.

In 1863, the Russians continued to suppress and control Poland.[1] The Russian Czar Alexander II was expected to assist Poland in its aim of becoming an independent nation, but instead the practices of the deceased Czar Nicholas continued to divide and conquer the Polish people. The rebellion of that year was fostered by the Russians so they could repress the nation further by creating chaos and upheaval, and then come to the rescue. Mandatory enrollment into the military meant the Zaleski family would be vulnerable and serving the Russians.

To survive as a family, they decided that they had to make a change. Poland and the town of Nowy Sącz, though their home, was now about to fall further under Russian control and they had to leave or suffer the consequences. Their farm and all that it meant to them was left behind. They took what livestock they could with all that they had saved and headed south before the Russians closed the border. They reached the outskirts of Budapest, Hungary, in 1864, and through sheer determination and effort, built their family stronger by working for others, doing carpentry, making leather goods for sale and saving enough to purchase some land to call their

---

1 World History at KMI/WhkmLa/Military/19 Century, Polish Rebellion of 1863-64.

own. Life was harsh and difficult, and the choice was to give up or go forward and build a life guided by their religious beliefs. To them, the choice was simple.

The Zaleski family was blessed with four strapping young boys by the late 1800's and each now had families of their own. Once again, the winds of war were stirring a flame within them that warned of impending danger. Their father explained to them how they could lose everything or make another choice. At his age, it made little sense to leave, but for each of his sons the time to leave with their young families was now. It would not be easy, but nothing of value came without a price.

The "Land of Milk and Honey," America, was of particular interest to the elder Zaleski. He had friends who made their way to this new world, and he wanted his grandchildren to be born with the spirit of religious freedom that this new land possessed. There was still enough time for them to make a move on their own terms, before they were forced out by circumstances beyond their control. The boys gathered their families and decided the four brothers would go to America first and send for their wives and children later. They would eventually settle near Detroit where a large Polish community existed. The brothers would work and save their earnings so they could send for their families, one by one. It would not be easy, but at least the families would be together on both sides of the ocean and would grow until they could be reunited.

Living and working together they were able to save and begin sending money back to the old country for their families. This continued, month after month, year after year, until they were all reunited. Or, that's what three of the brothers did. One of the four brothers found a romance in the new world, so when the others decided to move to Chicago where there was more work and better wages, that fourth brother stayed behind in Hamtramck, Michigan. Never again would the brothers be together as family.

Josef, born in 1870, was the oldest brother. In 1910, he returned to Budapest, Hungary, to ready his family for the trip to America. Jozef (Josef) Zaleski and his wife Kataryna (Catherine), born in 1875, prepared for departure. With their five children, Mary, Joseph Jr., Frank, John and Stephanie, they arrived in New York City on October 24, 1911. The family traveled by ship to New York on the Kaiser Wilhelm II from Bremen, Germany.

Kaiser Wilhelm II

At the outbreak of WWI, this particular ship was held in New York Harbor after it was confiscated by the U.S. Navy. It was re-named the U.S.S. Agamemnon. It was then used to transport troops back and forth across the ocean to Europe. In 1919, the U.S. Navy returned it to civilian hands. Thereafter, it then became known as the Monticello.

U.S.S. Agamemnon

Back in 1906, the city of Gary, Indiana, was founded along with United States Steel (USS) Gary Works. Many Eastern European immigrants were attracted to that area because of available jobs and ethnic neighborhoods. Josef wanted to begin a life outside of the congestion of Chicago. With brothers and friends, they built a two story home with four independent apartments. Josef hoped that his brothers would eventually bring their families to live in the other apartments. Although they appreciated the offer to settle in Gary, the brothers liked the big city. The Chicago community is where they had become comfortable. When the home's construction was complete, Josef Zaleski had a four-plex with a small mortgage. The Zaleskis lived in one and had three to rent. Little did they know, this would become a future Godsend.

In the early 1900's, Italians, Croats, Serbs, Poles, Czechs and Hunkies, a composite of Polish, Hungarian, Russian, and Slovak peoples, each had their own neighborhood in the new Gary. They were cheap labor, dependable and hardworking immigrants. They built U.S. Steel Gary Works with their sweat and blood. They also built houses of worship. For the Poles, it was St. Hedwig Catholic Church and School. The first building was outgrown and a new church and school was built to accommodate a growing city and ethnic population. The churches and the neighborhoods went hand in hand. They gave to God and they gave to their families. It was in this environment that a future champion named Anthony Florian Zaleski was born on May 29, 1913, in Gary, Indiana. He was the couple's sixth child, preceded by Mary (3-10-00), Joseph (9-17-02), John (8-12-04), Stephanie (10-29-08), and Frank (2-2-11).

On July 11, 1915, the Zaleski's seventh and last child was in the womb (Walter) and young Anthony had a chicken pox and measles combination. On that day, Josef took one of young Joseph's bicycles and peddled to the local pharmacy for Anthony's medicine. Joseph Jr. enjoyed building bikes and making changes to improve speed and durability. There were many bicycles for Josef to choose from that fateful day, but the one in particular that Josef had chosen to ride was a new 'coaster' bike Joseph had developed. Unfortunately, it had not yet been fitted with brakes.

As Josef peddled with ease, he probably was impressed with the speed he was gaining with little effort. Mechanically, this bike had little drag, so its peddling was smooth and easy as he was going faster and faster. As this father of seven approached an intersection, he could hear and see cars coming down the road. When he started braking, the simple back peddling motion did nothing to stop the bike and the next thing Josef saw were headlights approaching him quickly. There was nowhere else to go, and he braced for the impact. It was theorized that the first vehicle hit him broadside throwing him into the path of the second vehicle. Two Model T's trying to prove whose car was faster ended his life that day as Josef was pronounced dead at the scene.

To our knowledge, this is believed to be the first automobile-bicycle fatality recorded in Gary, Indiana. There was speculation among the Zaleski family about the involvement of alcohol in the accident because one of the reckless drivers owned a local tavern and was known by the Zaleski family to be a drinker. Regardless, in 1915, life insurance was not a thought for the Zaleskis. There was little or no savings, and after Josef's untimely death, all they had left was the roof over their heads. Catherine suddenly found herself a 40-year-old, nearly destitute widow with six children and a seventh on the way. Walter was born on August 13, 1915, only one month later.

As soon as possible after the birth of Walter, Catherine began cleaning and doing laundry for the doctor that attended to her fallen husband and helped in her delivery. She worked as long as it took to pay his bill and make a little extra money for the family.

Josef had always been told by his father how important it was to have a home. His father raised cows, horses and chickens and herded those animals with them as they traveled when they left Nowy Sacz, Poland.

Josef, too, had fashioned his family's life so that they could be self-sustaining, live off the land and support a small, affordable mortgage. When he and his brothers built his home, the apartment house was designed with the thought of supplementing the family by providing additional income, which it did. With those rents, he and Catherine had saved enough to build a barn, add a horse, another cow and several more chickens to feed their growing brood. Their garden also provided them with hearty vegetables and fruits.

Josef's death was a tragic loss, but the event brought the family closer. They joined together to find ways to fill the void created by the loss of the head of household. By choice and necessity, the four oldest children found part-time or full-time jobs earning a nickel to a dime per day to help provide for their family. Mary was able to appear older than she was and landed a full time job at Gary Screw and Bolt. She would come home with her hands cut from the sharpness of the steel. Stephanie worked part time at the local A & P grocery store. The oldest sons, Joseph and John, found work in the steel mills.

The Zaleskis struggled through the late 1910s and early 1920s as a result of their circumstances. The church continued to be the center of their outside life.

Unfortunately, Joseph and Anthony carried for life the unnecessary guilt of their father's death. Joseph felt guilty because it was his own bicycle that his father rode; and Anthony, because it was his medicine that their father was peddling to get. For years afterward, Anthony would see older gentlemen riding bicycles toward their homes. He would excitedly run inside and tell his mother, "Daddy's coming home!" If it had not been for their great faith in a higher power learned at home and through school at St. Hedwig, it would have been easy for this family to fall into despair. But that was not the case. The Zaleskis grew and adapted to a life without a father by accepting responsibility early and coming closer together in their faith in God. Their mother's undaunted faith gave her the will to see her family grow and succeed in life. No one could remember seeing her ill because she would never give in to sickness in spite of how miserable she might feel. This deep-rooted faith sustained her and was passed on to her children at every dinner prayer at home and each Sunday morning at St. Hedwig.

In 1918, three years after their father's death, Joseph and John, while employed in the steel mills, began discussing and practicing boxing. The two brothers would compare notes while listening to round by round accounts of fights on the radio. Both boys were enthusiastic about the sport and shared a thirst for knowledge about the "sweet science."

When they were able to save enough of their earnings, they bought their first radio from Goldblatts department store. All of the children would gather around the radio and listen to the action. In between rounds, it wasn't unusual to see John and Joseph rolling up the carpet and re-enacting the fight blow by blow for the rest of the family.

Though they did not know all the moves, they both knew they had natural ability. They honed their skills early in age by necessity and they would in time, pass those skills on to their younger brothers. Unbeknownst to them, Anthony adopted their styles and ultimately reached a level none of them could have ever imagined.

THE FORMATIVE YEARS

In the early days of most cities like Gary, ethnic neighborhoods were the norm. If you passed from a Polish to Italian neighborhood, you would be challenged. The Zaleski boys learned to defend themselves early and as they passed from neighborhood to neighborhood on their way home, they were treated with the respect they had earned. Joseph and John recognized they would have to practice their new art form to sharpen their skills so they built a ring inside the barn that housed their horse, cows and chickens. The smells were true country and all of the boys pitched in to keep the barn clean so that they could practice. It became a regular neighborhood hangout on weekends. Soon, the Zaleski boys held matches pitting different weight classes against each other. Over a couple of years, Joseph and John became so proficient with their skills that they began amateur careers. They both earned titles as "All Middle-State" amateur champions, comparable to today's "Golden Gloves." The daily lives of the Zaleski boys were filled by their involvement in church, work, school and boxing. The heritage was born and brother passed to brother skills that would eventually create a champion of the world.

Oldest brother Joseph became the hard puncher of the family. His proficiency at delivering a double left hook combination was passed to young Anthony. Brother John was the flashy one who discovered how ducking or slipping under a straight left gave you a wide open body shot. Anthony, young enough to watch how his older brothers moved in the ring, could identify the lethal combinations "right" to the body, "left" hook to the chin. When timed correctly, it meant an instant knockdown.

When the boys weren't training in their makeshift ring at home, they traveled to several of the local clubs to improve their skills.

Boxing clubs sprouted up in every ethnic neighborhood in the fast growing city of Gary. The competition and style varied from club to club and the Zaleski boys would work their way through every gym learning and discovering new combinations to add to their arsenals.

Anthony, too young to participate, would watch his brothers closely and pretend he was in the ring swapping leather. This imaging helped him see an opponent's moves and would allow him to counter and block traditional combinations. After watching Joseph and John dispatch opponents, he would dream of how he might have fought their fights. His mind would dissect every move and follow every block and counter move to gain points on a challenger. Throughout the 1920s, between school, church and chores, young Anthony watched his brothers and learned a skill that would pay great dividends in his future.

When Anthony was a first grader at St. Hedwig, he would stay inside during recess and practice his ABC's in Polish and English. Each child was given a small chalk board to practice on and when completed, they would be graded, the board erased and re-done the next day to show proficiency. Anthony finished both of his assignments and placed his chalk board on a table near his teacher's desk. As he headed toward the door to join his friends and classmates at recess, he noticed the class bully who was also working on his ABC's walking over to the teacher's table. The bully picked up Anthony's board, looked at it and began erasing Anthony's work.[2] Anthony immediately returned and asked him not to touch his board. The bully just laughed and walked back to his desk. Anthony, of course, took his chalk board and returned to redo what had been erased. When he completed his assignment, he took his board and once again set it on his teacher's table. As he walked to the door he looked back and the bully was also moving to the teacher's table, picking up Anthony's board and starting to erase it. Anthony this time yelled, "Leave my work alone," and the bully responded, "Make me." Anthony quickly came back to the bully, grabbed his board with his left hand and hit the bully on the chin with his right. In the few seconds that this took, their teacher came back into the room and shouted for them to "Stop!" It was too late though, as Anthony's right to the chin floored his first opponent and created more tears than he had ever seen.

Anthony, of course, was afraid that the nun was going to punish him and his eyes welled up, but she was kind, controlled, and understanding. She knew that Anthony would not have responded this way unless provoked. She first dealt with the bully sending him to the principal's office, and then sat Anthony down to explain what had happened. After his explanation, she asked where he had learned to throw a punch like that. Anthony told her about his brothers and watching them practice boxing at home. She then cautioned him about fighting in school and to always bring a problem like this to a teacher so that they could deal with it immediately. She also told Anthony that "with a punch like yours, you could be a champion one day." Anthony vowed at that moment to never fight outside of the ring and he would live up to that vow unless pressed to defend himself. He also learned to depend on the advice of those older and wiser than himself to help map his course in life's journey.

But as life would have it, a few years later, Anthony would find himself in a situation where this time he had no choice but to defend himself. One day, he was required to stay after school to make up some work due to his absence the day before. Normally, he would walk home with his brothers, since they had to go through several

---

2 Thad Zale interview of Tony Zale, September 1989.

ethnic neighborhoods to reach their home. Anthony's brothers told him they would come back to school for him so that he didn't have to walk home alone.

He finished his missed school work sooner than anyone expected. Unfortunately, rather than waiting for his brothers to come back, he thought he would start out to meet them on the path home. Little did he know, the Dawg Town Gang was waiting for someone just like him to show up unescorted through their turf. When they challenged him, Anthony put up his dukes and said, "I don't wanna fight. You're all bigger than me."

That didn't matter to the Dawg Town Gang. They proceeded to pummel him until they got him on the ground and started wailing on him mercilessly. The leader of the gang said, "You got enough?" The others chimed in for him to leave him alone saying, "He's had enough. He's bloody." As the leader got off Anthony and started walking away, up jumped Anthony and tackled him to the ground. He started punching the leader, bloodying his nose. The rest of the gang was startled and Anthony then jumped up and came after them. They all said he must be crazy, and ran off.

As luck would have it, from around the corner came John, Joseph and Frank. They were surprised to see their little brother chasing the Dawg Town Gang members, and followed in hot pursuit. When they finally caught up to Anthony, they were shocked at how angry he was. "Looks like you gave what you got," said his brother Joseph. Then they helped clean him up with their handkerchiefs and headed home. Anthony never would quit, no matter how bad of a beating he was taking.

In the 1920s, the summers of the young Zaleski brood were filled with fun and chores. Anthony's two oldest brothers, Joseph and John, were well on their way to becoming "All Middle-States Champions" in the featherweight and welterweight amateur divisions, respectively. These were comparable to today's "Golden Gloves Champions" and were the predecessor to this designaton.

They both worked in the steel mills and spent their spare time milking the cows, gathering eggs from their dozen hens, cleaning the barn and making sure their self-built ring and punching bags were always in use. Anthony helped and watched as his older brothers dispatched neighbor after neighbor. Soon, none of the local young boys around the area desired any ring time with Joseph and John, but preferred to watch them fight against each other. Anthony was exceptional from the very beginning and by his early teens, his older brothers did not desire ring time with him either. Brother John had one time caught a left to the body during a sparring session that convinced him he wanted no more of Anthony's game.

Young Joseph Zaleski

Anthony became so familiar with his brothers' styles that the brothers felt like they were fighting themselves. Instead of being matched against Anthony, they now preferred playing stick ball, swimming in Lake Michigan, fishing and crab catching at Burns Ditch. Campfires and boiled crabs always seemed to go together during the summer months after their chores were complete. The neighborhood kids also enjoyed these activities because they weren't being coaxed into the ring by young Anthony.

THE SPIRIT MOVES

The hardships of late 1929 and the 1930s brought about by the Great Depression are well documented in the history books and the Zaleskis were not immune to those difficulties. However, they were fortunate to have income from renters that helped them survive, providing the rents were paid on time. Living payday to payday was not uncommon. They were kept together by their mother Catherine (Mazur) Zaleski and the foresight of their father Josef. Now that Catherine assumed both roles of mother and father, the children lined up to help. Her policy was simple regimentation. They would pick up after themselves, help each other whenever needed, and seek direction from above through prayer, church and studies. She knew that the Lord's guidance would help them overcome their difficulties just as He had helped lead them to this land.

Josef was sorely missed, but there was no time to grieve. To survive they all had to pull together and find their strength from the New Testament in the example provided by Christ Jesus. They used the examples of Jesus' life from the Gospels of the New Testament and applied those experiences to how they would live. From the "Wedding Feast at Cana" to Our Lord's "Agony in the Garden," Catherine explained to her children how Jesus took a measured, balanced view of life and all of its experiences. He took all things in stride and turned the hardships to His advantage.

They also looked for ways to turn every difficulty they encountered to an advantage rather than dwelling on a negative. They were active in the St. Hedwig Catholic Church and School and drew strength from praying together as a community.

Top & bottom
(either way)
3rd Row - outside Rt to left - "Jaskulski" This boys father
accidently (by car) killed (Anthony Florian Zaleski's)
father when he was 2 yrs old! Leaving Tony's
mother with 6 children and one in the oven. She received
compensation for the breadwinner of the family.
This changed the entire structure in the Zaleski
household - making "Mary" - John - Joe go
to work at a very early age -
Picture taken in 1927

Please refer to the photo gallery in back of the book for roster of student names.

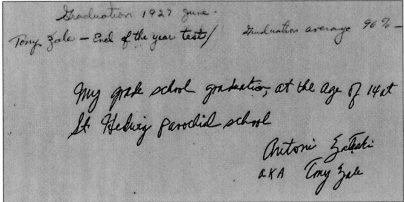

Graduation 1927 June.
Tony Zale — End of the year tests/ Graduation average 96 % —

My grade school graduation at the age of 14 at St Hedwig parochial school

Antoni Zaleski
aka Tony Zale

Praying together did not end at church. Each meal in the Zaleski home was blessed and included Bible study, if only a passage or two. The words and wisdom of the New Testament were taken to heart and their undivided belief in God and in themselves soared as they grew as a family. Through Catherine, the family strived to achieve small successes each and every day.

In the 1920s there weren't many ways out of the ethnic pockets and the prejudices that surrounded the cities. Sink or swim was the choice that many faced and this seems somewhat familiar to circumstances today. Education and sportsmanship through boxing provided an opportunity and a way out of poverty. The radio served as a primary source of entertainment. For young men and their families, listening to the radio was a way to reach out to the rest of the world. The radio provided an escape from the day to day struggles. The variety of shows of that era such as the Lone Ranger, Jack Benny, and Al Jolson entertained and brought smiles and laughter to otherwise troubled lives, if only for a few hours.

The Zaleski family would gather around the radio in the evenings after all the work was done and became recharged and fascinated with the Jack Dempsey and Gene Tunney "fights of the century." They would listen to the announcer's cryptic description of the action and during intermissions between rounds, would move the furniture to one side of the room, roll up the carpet and act out the blows they listened to so intently. Joseph and John were the most advanced in the art. They would jab and feign and hook as if they were engaging in the bout themselves. To them, it was more than mere sport; it was art in motion.

Though the boys would periodically act it out too well, there was never any malice intended. They would anxiously await the next round and anticipate the strategies each of the fighters would employ. Anthony never missed an opportunity to observe his brothers' moves and how to get an advantage over an opponent. When one strategy would not work, they changed their attack and used defense to bait the opponent into an error. Like a chess game, if one method did not work, they would move to a series of counter moves to clear the way for their attack. The concentration and the methods employed were not lost on Anthony. He would watch closely as his older brothers would demonstrate what to do and how to react and more importantly, how not to react. It provided the groundwork for what lay ahead for the future Champ.

On one occasion, Anthony and John traveled by train to watch their brother Joseph as he competed in an amateur tournament in Boston. In the finals, it appeared certain he would win the East Coast title after owning the Midwest title. He had knocked down the "hometown" favorite five times in three rounds, but lost on a split decision. Anthony could not believe it. His older brother had pummeled his opponent with everything, including the kitchen sink and he didn't win. Furthermore, he had not been hit by his opponent with one combination, so how could he have lost? Anthony was even more determined to watch his brothers even closer and find a knockout combination so this would never happen to him.

Sunday mass was the norm for the Zaleski Clan. It was an important event for the family, and they took it very seriously. On one particular Sunday, the parish priest delivered a sermon that was aimed at the Zaleski boys, as well as many other neighborhood young men. It seems these young pugilists were getting considerable press as they continued to participate and win boxing matches across the city and country.

For a priest who believed in "turning the other cheek," it was difficult to justify all of these Polish boys getting their names in the paper for beating up the Italians, Irish, Slovaks and Hunkies.

This type of reputation was not warranted by young Christian men. So his sermon admonished all boys embarking on this sport and delivered his own knockout blow.

"Stop fighting and getting your names in the paper, and start following the path of Jesus," said the priest. "Stop spending your talents on fighting and start working to convert this energy into spreading His word."

From that moment on, in an effort to disguise the fact that they were boxing, Joseph and John Zaleski began to fight under the names Joe Zale and Johnny Zale respectively. As soon as Anthony began fighting, he adopted that variation on the family name as well.

Tony Zale, for his part, always followed his brothers' example and as an eight year old, he would not let his religious beliefs get in the way.

Tony, even at this young age, had shown the ambition and the talent to follow in his brothers' footsteps in the boxing game and he was not about to change. He had copied his brothers' moves and added a few of his own. They had set the path for him.

That sermon was not wasted on them, though. Each of them became "men of God" in all they did in their lives and when the time came, the word would be spread with all of the vigor of their youth.

Photo Courtesy of
The Polish Community of Gary

St. Hedwig's first church was the spiritual center for Gary's south-side Polish community. Here parishioners gather for the funeral of a former parishioner. At left a band plays somber music for the occasion. (Courtesy St. Hedwig.)

Tony's formal debut in the ring didn't occur for some seven more years after that sermon. At Gary Froebel High School, known as the "Immigrant High,"[3] Tony excelled in his studies and enjoyed football and track and field. He was a speedy, tough halfback through his sophomore year and thought of playing football in college. The choice eventually boiled down to boxing or football, in his mind's eye. At the age of fifteen, after hundreds of rounds in his family's makeshift ring and at the local YMCA, Tony would have the chance to try out his skills against a "real" unknown opponent in a "real" ring in Chicago.

His debut was less than auspicious. He lost his first amateur bout after getting hit in the stomach by a more experienced fighter. That night, Tony would always remember how hard he had been hit in his solar plexus area during the first round and how his meal from earlier that evening had come up into his throat. Though his older brothers assured him he had competed well, he was still left with a nagging stomach ache and the memory that he had eaten too much before the fight.

---

3   Traces article, Spring 2007, page 18. By James B. Lane, a publication of the Indiana Historical Society.

The lessons learned were carried forward and in over 200 amateur bouts (only 95 officially recorded), he made use of body punches to bring down the guard of his opponents. He developed a combination that, in the words of Billy Soose whom he fought in 1940, "was like getting hit in the stomach with a hot poker and having it just left there. It hurt all the way to your toes."[4] That right to the body, as Tony perfected it, was so paralyzing that not many could recover from it.

Billy Conn was hit with that right to the body in 1942 and said, "In that third round after getting caught, I knew what Soose meant about that hot poker. I knew I had to stay away from him and dance but he caught me again in the fifth."[5] After that round, Conn's corner became very busy about what to do and how to avoid that now famous right-left Zale combination. It worked and Conn won the decision. Joe Louis, who had been watching from ringside, told Tony in the dressing room after the fight, "I thought you beat 'em."[6] Tony and Joe remained respectful friends for the rest of their lives from that day forward.

4 Jarrett, John, *Champ in the Corner. The Ray Arcel Story.* Gloucestershire, England, 2007.
5 *The Herald Tribune,* February 14, 1942, Sports Page, by Al Laney. Also, Tony Zale interviews with Billy Conn, November 14, 1977, The Cavalcade of Champions, Macleod Hall, Calgary Convention Center, Calgary Canada, reported by Tony Unitas.
6 Thad Zale interview of Tony Zale, September, 1988.

THE DECISION

From 1928 to 1932, Tony's amateur boxing career took off like a rocket. Fighting at least once per week and sometimes two or three bouts in one night, Tony began to hone his skills and deliver that devastating body punch. He had learned very well how it felt to be hit in the gut and thought that if he could perfect his style, he could drive a right to the body when his opponent's jab came forward. The timing of this counter punch was critical. Ducking under, or side stepping and slipping that right hand into the opponent's side just below the left rib cage and hitting near the kidney area would temporarily immobilize him. Adding a left hook to the jaw would then finish the job. It would take plenty of practice to perfect, but that happens when you fight every week. You must master both offensive and defensive skills, or find another line of work. What he learned from his older brothers was that you must have a good offense and a good defense. You need to quickly assess your opponent's weaknesses and determine how to block their attack, as well as most effectively deliver your own blows. If you do this consistently, you can be effective. Do it well enough, and maybe just maybe, you become a champion.

Tony brought home four amateur titles from welterweight up to middleweight and in 1932 he hoped to represent the United States in the Olympic Games. He lost in the finals because of an accidental head butt which opened a cut over his right eyebrow. It was deep enough to prompt the official to halt the bout and award his opponent a technical knockout, even though Tony led convincingly on points. He had looked forward to fighting in Los Angeles, California, and showing just how tough a young Polish boy could be. But it wasn't in the cards. He was unable to achieve his last amateur goal and lost to Carmen Barth of Cleveland, Ohio, who went on to win the gold.

CENTRAL ASSOCIATION AMATEUR ATHLETIC UNION

ANTHONY ZALE

is hereby granted registration for one year as an Amateur Boxer which may be suspended or revoked for cause at any time.

Representing UNATTACHED

Expiration date JUNE 7TH, 1934

This card **must** be presented to A. A. U. Boxing Inspector at time of weighing-in and physical examination.

Inspector will register date of contest on reverse side of this card.

Registration No.

554

✓ Anthony Zale

Signature of Boxer

DESCRIPTION OF BOXER

Full Baptismal Name ANTHONY ZALE

Residence Street No. 1932 DELAWARE STR.

City GARY State IND.

Place of Birth GARY, IND.

Date of Birth MAY 29-1913 Age 20

Nationality POLISH-AMERICAN

Occupation UNEMPLOYED

Employed by

Address Telephone

Height 5 Feet 9 Inches. Weight 155 Pounds. Color Eyes BROWN

Complexion LIGHT Color Hair BLONDE

Distinguishing Marks NONE

Any change in the above information must be reported at once.

DANIEL J. FERRIS,
Secretary National A. A. U.
Chairman National A. A. U., Registration Committee

ROY E. DAVIS,
Chairman, C. A. A. U.
Registration Committee

In 1934, Tony won the Chicago, Illinois, Golden Gloves Middleweight title. He and other young champions were set to meet the New York Champions in Madison Square Garden. Tony's coaches decided to move him up in weight class because a young fighter named Gus Lesnevich, his New York opponent, was considered unbeatable. So, they moved Tony up to light heavyweight to fight a young, hairy, barrel-chested southpaw named Melio Bettina. (Bettina would go on to win the World Light Heavyweight championship.) He beat Tony that night as an amateur. It was the best bout on the card according to those who attended. Later, Tony said, "He was too big for me and he beat me to a pulp. He won by hitting me in the kidneys. I learned from that. I later practiced jerking my elbows back at the right moment to crack my opponent on the wrists."[7]

Tony believed his extensive amateur career assured that he was conditioned and had developed an ability to take the hardest of punches and come back to finish an opponent. Running in the sand dunes of northern Indiana's Lake Michigan waterfront helped to create a solid muscled frame. Running in the sand also improved his foot speed. His willingness to push himself that extra mile, helped increase his endurance. It was thus scripted from an early age that he was to be a world champion; he just didn't know it yet.

New York City 1934

---

7 Jarrett, John, Champ in the Corner. The Ray Arcel Story. Stadia, Gloucestershire, England, 2007.

1934 Chicago Golden Gloves Boxing Team.

1934

It has been said that, "seeing is believing," but Tony began to understand that "if you believe, you will see." His older brothers assured him if he prioritized things, i.e., the Good Lord first, and then family, he could achieve anything in this land of opportunity. Having faith and adopting Christ's attitude as a guide would help him fulfill his life's goals. Two years after his loss in the Olympic Trials,

Tony's first test of this faith and attitude would come from a simple decision – do I turn pro or go to college on an athletic scholarship?[8] Ultimately, he chose to give up his amateur career and turn professional in an effort to help his family financially.

After Tony's loss from an eyebrow cut in the finals of the Olympic trials, his personal physician Dr. Danieleski suggested he have a bone reduction surgery that would shave some of the bony ridge from both eyebrows. This would help flatten that area and help Tony avoid future losses due to cuts. The greatest danger for the future Champ would be a layoff from the ring to allow the area to heal properly and the scar tissue to be formed and later massaged into place. If the healing process became complicated and the area infected, it might end his career permanently. Tony was willing to accept the risk and Dr. Danieleski performed the surgery in his office using all of his medical knowledge and expertise to make it a success. Tony never again suffered a technical knockout due to a cut over his eyes.

In the 1930s, life was anything but easy. The 'Great Depression' had a grip on everyone's life. For Tony, his decision to turn professional in 1934, rather than accept a scholarship to the University of Wisconsin, was based on the economics of the time. Rather than listen to his heart, he looked at all the struggles of those around him. He saw how difficult it was for his family when the rents didn't come on time. He knew how difficult it was for everyone around him when money was scarce. He knew at times, he went to sleep still hungry. But he also knew that his family had it better than most. At least, they raised some of their own food and had livestock to supplement their diet and provide food for sale at the market.

Brother John recognized that if Tony turned pro, they all might see a glimmer of hope and step out of poverty. He recognized Tony's talent early, and along with his help, they could make it together. John, a talented amateur champion, would be at Tony's side to make sure he was not taken advantage of, and would be given a lifetime percentage of Tony's income for his efforts.

But the professional ranks were far different from the amateurs. As an amateur, you would gladly take on all comers in your weight class at any time. In the pros, you had to move slowly through the

---

8 Thad Zale interview of Tony Zale interview, May 1988.

ranks, looking for fighters of equal or slightly greater skill or experience, so you could benefit from those experiences and continue to grow and polish your skills. Many fighters who did not enjoy the benefit of proper management found themselves up against men they had no business fighting. As a result of the beatings they suffered, they became discouraged and quit.

The great heavyweight champion Jack Dempsey was a prime example. Early in his career he was managed by an individual in New York known as "John the Barber." He attempted to put Dempsey in against fighters that Jack knew he wasn't ready to face yet, including Sam Langford.

Ultimately, Dempsey gave in and agreed to face a much more experienced professional fighter named John Lester Johnson, who broke a number of Dempsey's ribs and prompted him to retire from the ring for a period.

It was only later when he came under the skillful direction of his next manager, Jack Kearns, that he found himself on a path that led to a world championship.

Not fully comprehending how important management could be, John and Tony entered into a two-year agreement with a promoter and manager named Harry Shall in 1934. Harry had been his coach on the Chicago Golden Gloves amateur team that traveled to test the New Yorkers and had been the one that moved him up in weight class to fight Bettina.

But unfortunately for all, he viewed Tony as just another piece of meat, one to be chopped up and spit out to line his own pockets with money, and not theirs.[9]

So, between the summer of 1934 and February of 1935, Tony was matched in some 22 bouts, whether he was hurt, sick, or just worn out.

Torn muscles were over-trained and re-injured further, and John was powerless to protect him. They just didn't know what to do but follow the lead of their manager Harry Shall who they trusted because he said he "knew the business."[10]

---

9 Thad Zale interview of Dan Zale, nephew, May 10, 2000.
10 Thad Zale interview of Dan Zale, nephew, May 10, 2000.

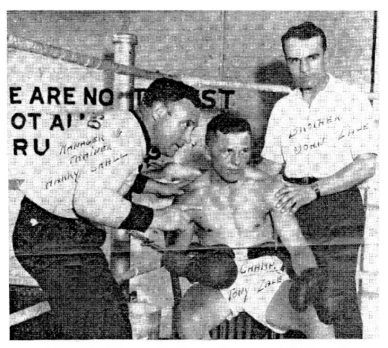

TRAINER   CHAMPION   BROTHER
HARRY SHALL   TONY ZALE   JOHN ZALE

Tony won 17 bouts, lost nine and drew one during this period. It wasn't the kind of performance he and his brother had planned. Because of this inexperienced and exploitive management, Tony, with John's prompting, retired from the ring. He then went on to toughen his body and heal his torn back and shoulder muscles.[11]

After this early retirement, Tony headed back to Gary and the steel mills. From July of 1935 through mid 1937, Tony requested every tough labor job the mills had to offer. From shoveling slag (cast-off, molten iron ore) around the blast furnaces, sniping cinders (scraping the walls of the blast furnaces) and lifting anything that weighed 50 pounds or more, Tony began to heal those torn muscles without further damaging them.

During that time frame, he strengthened his back, shoulders and legs to a finely chiseled physique. He also strengthened his resolve to get out of those mills and become a world champion. When he came back to the ring in the summer of 1937, a Chicago sportswriter was

---

11 Thad Zale interview of Tony Zale interview, July 1988.

Photo Courtesy of Calumet Regional Archives IU Northwest

surprised at his ashen color and sculpted body. He said that Tony looked like a new piece of steel off the line at the "Gary Steel Works," and the symbolism stuck. It was then, thanks to this reporter, that he became known in boxing circles as The Man of Steel from Gary, Indiana.

In the spring of 1937, Tony sought advice from three sources he trusted with his life – God, his brothers, and Henry Wilczek, a professional tailor and wrestler. Henry was the father of Hank Stram, a future professional football hall of fame coach.[12] (The Wilczek family's name was allegedly changed to Stram by the Barnum and Bailey Circus people when Henry performed in their show.)

As always, Tony's brothers, supported and believed he was ready for the pros again. Henry told Tony to pray to God and ask for His direction. Tony took his advice and headed to St. Hedwig Catholic Church to pray and make his covenant. That covenant was a simple commitment to his faith and a bond that he would live up to for the rest of his life. "Father, if I am permitted to become a champion of

---

12 Traces article, page 20, published in the spring of 2007, written by James B. Lane, a publication of the Indiana Historical Society.

the world, I will do everything within my power during and after my time in the ring to further belief in You."

So it was, with a "commitment for life," that Tony charted his course for the future. He would do this through prayer, a life-long pact to live simply, to obey the Ten Commandments and trust in family and close friends. Then, when his time as a champion ended, provide thanks and show gratitude by sharing his personal journey and lead others to God. Little did he know the path he chose would be far more difficult than he ever imagined.

With assistance from his brother John, Tony would begin training in earnest to resume his boxing career. It was agreed upon that John would still retain 10% interest in Tony for this commitment. Going back to gyms in the Northwest Indiana Region did not provide the competition that Tony and John were looking for to polish those needed skills. Frankly, many young professionals began refusing to enter the ring with Tony because of his deadly right to the body near the kidney area, and double left hook to the head combination. The bruised ribs and sore jaws created by this combination convinced many young men, opponents of Tony's, that there had to be an easier way to earn a living. It brought an end to their boxing aspirations.

When they couldn't find any other middleweights, Tony began sparring with light-heavyweights and heavyweights as well. They too, began shying away from him because of the hurt produced by the combination of his power and speed. It wasn't long before his reputation provided no sparring opportunities at all in the region's white only gyms. Tony and John decided that if he was to gain more experience and improve, he must begin joining the black gyms in the area.

As his reputation began to spread throughout Northwest Indiana and South Chicago, Tony became known in those gyms as the "Dark Town Destroyer."[13] It was another nickname, like The Man of Steel, that he did not feel comfortable with at any time during his career. The monikers that people placed on him were not important. Tony was a simple, shy and reserved man. His first goal was to become world champion. If others ascribed titles to him, he would not argue the point, only acquiesce to the description. He had a job, and the job was to be smart inside of the ring and dispatch his opponent as soon as possible.

---

13 Thad Zale interview of Tony Zale interview, October 1988.

During his amateur career, it was fight as many opponents as you could and learn from the experience of fighting against so many different styles. As a professional who was returning to the ring, after training in the black gyms, he finally began to be matched with fighters of similar experience and skill. He could learn and improve with each match, rather than get hurt and discouraged.

It was at this time that Tony and John finally met managers Art Winch and Sam Pian. Sam and Art had skillfully guided welterweight Barney Ross to three world titles and later "Fighter of the Year." They were two of the best fight managers and promoters around the Midwest and were well respected professionals. With John at his side, Tony heard from a fight promoter named Benny Ray that Art and Sam were looking for a good middleweight prospect. Benny had watched Tony fight several times over the years at Marigold Gardens Arena and realized what a quality middleweight prospect he was. They trusted Benny and knew he would steer them in the right direction. Tony and John were determined to make a good impression upon them.[14]

14 Thad Zale interview of Tony Zale. July 1988.

47

NEW MANAGEMENT

When Tony prepped in the locker room to train at Trafton's Gym, he knew he had to get Art and Sam's attention. He decided his first sparring match against a purported fifth or sixth level middleweight contender for the belt would be his "make or break" opportunity. With his brother John's help, he taped his hands and talked about visualizing the right to the body and left hook to the chin. John warned him to feel his opponent out for a round or two before landing the combination. Tony agreed.

After warming up and heavy bag work, it was Tony's turn as the "contender." During the first round, Tony saw the opening and did not hesitate. When his opponent shot out a left, Tony ducked in low, leading with his right just below the third rib near the kidney, and set the hook for the wipeout.[15] It worked, and the contender went down. Art and Sam looked at each other and smiled. Who was this man from Gary, Indiana, and where had he been? Hard and steel-like, he was crude, but someone they knew they could mold into a champion. Is this the kid who their buddy matchmaker Benny Ray had told them about? Benny had praised him for his knockout ability. It didn't take long for the word to spread.

Tony, John, Sam and Art sat down that afternoon to work out the details and left the finishing touches to the lawyers. Art and Sam signed Tony to a five-year contract on June 15, 1938, for $200.00 and a 50/50 split with Tony covering all the expenses.[16]

The Indiana steel mills would not see Tony shoveling slag or sniping cinders again. But they would place a claim to fame upon his new title as "The Man of Steel" from the U.S. Steel Gary Works. He

---

15 Thad Zale interview of Tony Zale. August 1988.
16 Thad Zale interview of Dan Zale, May 10, 2000.

would go back to shake hands and do exhibitions, but he would never shovel molten iron or scrape cinders off of the insides of a blast furnace. His journey was just beginning.

When Tony and John signed the contract with Art Winch and Sam Pian, they gave up the right to the training regimen Tony had followed for over 15 years. What he had been doing all those years was over-training and not letting his body heal. He would now have to follow their new regimen. In the past it was not unusual for Tony to spar 15 rounds and then go home and work out in the barn another 15 rounds on speed and heavy bags.[17] He simply did not know how to rest and he thought, "The more I train, the better I'll be."

As he learned how to rest under his new managers, he watched his own success catapult dramatically. They were teaching him how to build to a peak and be ready for every match without over doing it. Now, if only he could get used to the new regimen. They would have him fight only six to eight times a year, not bi-monthly. His opponents would be chosen by his managers based on their knowledge and experience. There would be no more mismatches for this soon-to-be champion.

ILLINOIS STATE ATHLETIC COMMISSION

NAME Tony Zaleski   Serial # 2764-B

ADDRESS 180 W. Randolph St.,

Chicago, Ill.

DATE OF BIRTH 24 yrs.   COLOR white

RING WEIGHT 160 lbs   LICENSE NO. 5493-B

LICENSE GRANTED 8-22-38   LICENSE EXPIRES 8-22-39

LICENSE SUSPENDED   LICENSE REVOKED

SUSPENSION LIFTED

MANAGER Sam Pian Lab. Test 5/2/39
NAME ZALE, Tony

---

17 Thad Zale interview of Tony Zale. August 1988.

Tony enjoyed the quiet clickety-clack of the South Shore Line as the train took him to the Chicago Loop and Trafton's Gym daily. It gave him time to think and see in his own mind's eye what the fellows in the gym and his managers had told him about his next opponent. Closing his eyes he could see the right hand lead coming at him and his counter left hook over it. He was ready to move in with another left hook, when suddenly a beautiful young lady lost her balance and fell into his lap. When she looked at him and apologized for losing her balance, he was immediately smitten. He couldn't remember when he had been hit any harder, but it wasn't his head or body that ached, it was his heart.[18] He didn't know her name, but he had seen her from a distance a few times. She was young and probably still in high school. He would have to ask his sisters for advice in the event she ran into him again. For now though, he had to go back and concentrate on an impending battle before he lost all sensibility.

By late December of 1939 and under his new management, Tony had a record of 38-14-2 with five consecutive knockouts. He was getting ready to spar at Trafton's Gym when the National Boxing Association Middleweight Champion, Al Hostak, his promoter Nate Druxman, and his manager Eddie Marino caused a stir at the gym that can only be described as bedlam. Hostak was looking for a tune-up bout with anyone that looked vulnerable. He, after all, had the fastest fists in boxing and no one to date had been able to stand up against his flurries.

Hostak and his manager were sizing up all the Chicago talent when Tony caught their eye. Tony entered the ring and was getting pummeled because he misjudged the timing of his sparring partner. It would take him a couple of rounds before he was able to measure and counter effectively.

Hostak liked the way Tony took a shot while ducking in. He told his manager that Tony was the one he wanted for a non-title fight, just a 10 round tune-up, before they headed back to the west coast. Hopefully this meant a good paycheck too.

After all, he successfully defended the title in New York and he was ready for a little fun and money from the Midwest. His manager

---

18 Thad Zale interviews of Jeanette Zale, January 18, 2000.

just wanted to know one thing. "Is that the best you've got around here, and could this kid draw a crowd?"[19]

They were all about to find out. On January 29, 1940, Tony Zale met Al Hostak, N.B.A. Middleweight Champion, for a non-title ten rounder. Chicago Stadium was packed. The draw was there and Al was getting 65% of the gate and a nice guarantee. All and all, he thought it would be an easy paycheck.

As the first round began, Al shot out quick jabs and Tony parried them away. Tony continued that for the entire round and occasionally traded lefts. The first round went to the Hostak. It was filled with three minutes of short jabs and counters. During that round, Tony was caught with a short right to the jaw that floored him for a no count.

Round two became a thriller when Tony ducked under the left and jammed a hard right to the ribs. Al gasped because he couldn't catch his breath. It was like fire. Who was this kid? When he instinctively shot a right cross, Tony was no longer there, having moved to his left. Round two went to Zale.

Round three started off the same way with Al working his left and setting up Zale for a knockout combination. Tony ducked under and side stepped the attack. Al took another shot, not quite as hard, and began to systematically try to take Tony apart. Tony countered, but Al was on the move with his reach and speed. Round three went to Hostak.

The fourth round was the same as the previous two and Al figured he had the fight in the bag. Between rounds four and five, Al told his trainers this was it. He was going to take Tony out in the next round.

Round five started with Al rushing Tony and throwing multiple combinations while aiming for a knock-out. But Tony parried everything that was thrown at him and Al looked frustrated. Tony bounced around the ring like a pinball from one corner to the next and waited for an opening between flurries. He didn't have a chance to throw any punches because Al kept hitting him. Rounds four and five went to Hostak.

Round six began with Hostak in a state of disbelief. How could this kid take all he had to give? Al had hit him with every

---

19 Jarrett, John, *Champ in the Corner. The Ray Arcel Story*. Stadia, Gloucestershire, England, 2007.

combination he knew and still Tony hadn't gone down. Nobody else had ever stood up to those punches before. Tony waited patiently and Al shot out a double jab. But just as he looked to do it again, Tony ducked under a left and delivered his own shot just under Al's heart. Before Al could react, a left hook caught him on the ear. What is that noise that is running through his head like a freight train? All he could do was backpedal and try to protect himself from more damage. Tony pursued, but in measured fashion, not over extending himself and keeping the pressure on. Round six belonged to Tony. Al was truly bewildered.[20]

Rounds seven, eight, and nine went the same way with Al continually being rocked and trying to stay away from Tony's punishing blows. Round ten followed the same pattern as the previous four, but Tony pursued Al to a greater degree in an attempt to press an opening if Al let down his guard. Finally, the fight came to a conclusion and a decision. Tony was named the winner by a unanimous decision. Al felt he'd been robbed in Chicago. He wanted a rematch in his own hometown. Yes, he thought to himself, it would be different in Seattle and at that time it would be with the Middleweight title on the line.

Al returned to Seattle livid with the prospect of getting this Zale kid in his part of the country. No more Chicago judges. Maybe Winch and Pian set him up at Trafton's. Maybe this kid was a "ringer." He chose the kid as an easy win for himself. Tony didn't look that good. Who had he fought? Didn't Tony quit because the game was too tough? A "Man of Steel," say the papers. Al thought to himself, we will see how much steel is in this guy when we get him out west. He wondered, how in heaven's name did he hit me like that. Al professed that never again will this upstart named Tony Zale hurt him. He figured he would get a couple of extra sparring partners he could work on and crush them as they tried to come inside. Al wondered if his own people might have helped set him up for failure. They should never have trusted Winch and Pian.[21]

Tony was really proud of what he accomplished. He had fought the N.B.A. Middleweight Champion and according to the three judges, beat him on all their scorecards. If he could just shorten up and go lower on that left hook a little more, he'd have it down at the

---

20 Thad Zale interview of Al Hostak, May 29, 1983.
21 Thad Zale interview of Al Hostak, May 29, 1983.

chin level. That would do it. Tony knew he could knock out Hostak, no matter how he countered. Slip under, bruise a rib or two and step in with a short left to the chin – not the ear. That is what he would have to practice even if he was nailed before he got the exact timing. He knew he could do it. Hostak was the perfect opponent because that left jab was always flicking away and measuring him. Just wait for the precise moment and end it completely. It's time to bring the championship home to Gary, Indiana. Mother would be so proud. It would be nice to let her relax a little and not have so many worries. Tony would be able to take care of her for a change instead of her taking care of everybody else. "Maybe even hire a cook. Maybe she'd like that!"[22]

But it was time to get back to work and Tony was back on the train headed for Trafton's Gym to continue working towards his goal of a world championship. He was thinking of all the training and sacrifices that it had taken him to reach this point when he noticed, through the window, that young lady who occupied some of his thoughts. She was boarding the train at the East Chicago, Indiana, station. So, she is from the Calumet Region, he thought to himself. He wondered if he should say hello as she walked by, but he hadn't discussed her with his sisters yet. She just had an air about her. It was something he couldn't explain, but he recognized something special about her, and it was a bit intimidating. He was almost afraid of her. If she walks by, I will speak to her. I wonder if she knows that I'm a boxer. Probably not, he thought.

As she made her way through the train, Adeline Richwalski had already decided to stop and talk to him if she saw him again. She knew who he was since she had read about the Hostak fight in the local newspaper. This was a chance for her to say hello. He stirred some excitement in her. After all, she already knew a football and basketball player, so why not a boxer?

As she walked toward him, his eyes met hers. He was really moved by her grace and her attitude. How could anyone be this beautiful? Tony shyly tried to look away, but her dark eyes just sucked him in deeper and left no room for escape. He tried to talk but nothing came out. She asked him if the seat next to him was taken and he coughed out a "no." Now, what would he say to her?

---

22 Thad Zale interview of Tony Zale, September, 1989.

Tony wondered what her story was. He had always seen her on the way into the Chicago loop, but never on his way home, except on that day she'd fallen into his lap. She said she didn't have a boyfriend and that she was concentrating on her musical studies. She was Polish too. He had heard of her family before since they owned one of the biggest coal yards around the area. She came from money. Why would she waste time with him? He was sure she could tell he was smitten with her.

Tony was sure glad she was never riding on the train on the way home. She really scared him the way she looked at him when they talked. His shyness prevented him from being more open with her. He needed some time to speak with his brothers and sisters for advice on what to do. They would know. But he needed to get back to concentrating on his next bout with Hostak.

Meanwhile, back home in Seattle, Hostak's manager and trainers were determined that their man wouldn't be defeated by Tony again. Al was a consummate professional and should have many good years left. He pounded Zale from one corner to the next and the guy had not only taken everything Al had to give, but came back to deliver more punishment than he'd received.

Had the Champion met his match? No, they were sure it wouldn't happen again. They would make certain of that. They'd get Al a couple of young middleweights with styles similar to Zale and let him practice on them. They were sure that would properly prepare him and he'd make short change of Zale when they met in Seattle.

BRINGING HOME
THE N.B.A. CHAMPIONSHIP

As a result of Tony's defeat of Hostak in late January of 1940, he had every reason to expect big things that year. By all indication, he was peaking at the right time and his timing was perfect. He was now under the skillful guidance of managers who knew what to do with this hard hitting Pole and how to turn him into a champion.

Al Hostak's loss to Tony reduced the demand for a middleweight title unification bout between himself and Ceferino Garcia, the New York State Athletic Commission champion. Further complicating matters was the fact that Garcia was under contract to New York based promoter Mike Jacobs, while Hostak was tied to Seattle promoter Nate Druxman. The two promoters and Hostak's manager, Eddie Marino, were unable to reach an agreement of the terms for a match between the pair. A unification bout between the two champions was out of the question for the immediate future. So instead of matching Garcia with Hostak, Jacobs matched him against Ken Overlin that coming May.

On February 3, 1940, it was announced that Hostak had broken his left hand in the fight with Tony and it had been set in a cast. He wouldn't be able to fight for at least eight weeks. So Tony was matched to face an Italian fighter named Enzo Iannozzi in Youngstown, Ohio, on February 29. Both men weighed 162 pounds.[23] Tony knocked him out in the fourth round of a scheduled ten-round affair.

A month later, on March 29, Tony was back in the ring in Chicago Stadium against the N.B.A.'s fourth ranked middleweight

---

23 *Portsmouth Times,* Tony Zale K.O.'s Foe, March 1, 1940.

contender, Ben Brown, a shifty boxer out of Atlanta, Georgia. He knocked the Irishman unconscious for the first time in Brown's career with a left hook in the third round.[24] Suddenly the press began calling Tony, a fighter who had looked like he was finished only four years earlier, the most improved fighter in the business and they began to look at him as a serious threat to capture the middleweight crown.[25]

Sam Pian attempted to secure a non-title match for Tony against the NYSAC champion, Ceferino Garcia, in June, but Garcia was already slated to face Overlin in May. Garcia's manager was hoping they would get a shot at the light-heavyweight champion Billy Conn, as long as they defeated Overlin. When Mike Jacobs came out on May 21 and promised the winner of the Garcia vs. Overlin bout a shot at the light-heavyweight title, any further discussion of a bout between Tony and Garcia came to an abrupt end. Overlin put the matter completely to rest on May 23 with a unanimous decision victory over Garcia to capture the NYSAC version of the World Middleweight Championship. Of course Overlin couldn't be considered the true world champion until he could defeat the N.B.A.'s titleholder. At least one reporter suggested that Overlin lacked sufficient firepower to contend with either Hostak or Zale.[26]

While Tony continued to wait for an opportunity to face Hostak for his title in Seattle, he was matched for another fight, this one against a Philadelphian named Baby Kid Chocolate. He knocked Chocolate out in the fourth round of their scheduled 10-round contest in Youngstown, Ohio, on June 12, 1940.[27] Ten days later, Sam Pian announced that after a month of negotiations, he had signed an agreement for Tony to fight Al Hostak in a Seattle's outdoor stadium on July 19, 1940, in a 15-round match for the N.B.A. Middleweight Championship of the World. The contract included a clause that should Tony win the fight, he would be required to grant Hostak a return bout within 60 days. Tony would have the right to choose as to whether or not that match would take place in Seattle or Chicago.

---

24 *Capital Times*, Brown Kayoed By Tony Zale in Third Round, March 30, 1940.

25 *Wisconsin State Journal*, Day, Zale Now Title Contenders, April 8, 1940.

26 *Daily Times-New*, Overlin's Title Empty until He Erases Hostak and Tony Zale, May 28, 1940.

27 *Steubenville Herald Star*, Tony Zale Kayoes Baby Kid Chocolate, June 13, 1940.

Zale, Hostak Sign

Tony Zale, contender for the N. B. A. middleweight title, at long last will get a coveted chance to become the Steel City's first recognized world's fistic champion.

Sam Pian, Zale's co-manager, announced in Chicago over the weekend that articles had been signed for the Gary battler to meet Al Hostak, recognized N. B. A. 160-pound king, in Seattle on July 19.

The Seattle bout will be the second between Zale and Hostak. The Gary battler scored one of the winter season's major fistic upsets when he decisively defeated Hostak in the Chicago Stadium.

According to Pian the articles for the Seattle title bout include a clause which will force Zale to give Hostak a return bout within 60 days should Tony triumph. Zale will have the say as to whether a return bout will be placed in Chicago or Seattle.

Zale expects to start roadwork here within the next few days, shifting to Trafton's gym in Chicago the first of next week and leaving for Seattle a week later.

Tony arrived in Seattle with Sam and Art on July 10, to complete his training for the contest. All three were confident that Tony would prove his non-title victory over Hostak hadn't been a fluke and they'd return to the Midwest with the title in-hand. Hostak was initially established as a 10-8 favorite to win the rematch and he declared that his hand was healed and he expected to knock Tony out in a hurry.[28]   The Champion was so confident he and his manager went so far as to say the man they'd really prefer to tackle was heavyweight champion Joe Louis.   Promoters Nate Druxman and Mike Jacobs were talking of matching him with the winner of the upcoming Ken Overlin and Billy Soose fight once he defeated Tony.

Al's chief sparring partner, a former N.B.A. middleweight titleholder named "Gorilla" Jones, claimed that Al was a much improved fighter and said he'd learned to protect himself inside, and was hitting shorter and sharper.[29]   By July 12, the Champion was already in fighting form, tipping the scales at the 160 pound middleweight limit.   "I feel right," Hostak said, "I know I've got a tough fight, knew it when I left Chicago last January, knew when I met Tony again I'd have to be ready. So I resolved to be ready this next time and I'm making good on it."   His manager, Eddie Marino, said that Al's mental attitude was just right and that his physical condition spoke for itself.[30]

Tony and his managers were just as confident about their victory and when interviewed by the Seattle press, Sam said, "You can discount all that chatter about Hostak breaking his hand on Zale and losing the fight back in Chicago as the result.   Zale had him licked long before he hurt his left duke. When Tony got up off the floor in the first round it broke Hostak's heart. He knew then and there that he didn't have any palooka in front of him. Tony got up and almost chased Hostak out of the ring. We hope his hand is good and strong as they report so when Zale gets through giving him a walloping there won't be any post-mortem crying about tough breaks and bad hands."[31]

As for Tony's hands, Winch said Tony spent 10 days chopping trees in the Wisconsin woods before they left the Midwest and he showed a Seattle reporter the calluses and ragged skin on Tony's hands to prove it.   "This Al is a great puncher but our Tony is going to give Seattle fans the surprise of their life," Winch said.[32]

As the local scribes began to get an opportunity to witness the separate sparring sessions of both fighters they offered their

---

28 *The Gallup Independent*, Bring on Louis, Say's Hostak – But First There's Tony Zale, July 13, 1940.
29 *Seattle Star*, Gorilla Rides With Al Any Way, July 12, 1940.
30 *Seattle Star*, Hostak at Fighting Weight, July 12, 1940.
31 *Seattle Times*, Zale Checks In For Big Fight, July 11, 1940.
32 *Seattle Star*, Tony Fit as Fiddle, Predicts He'll Win, July 10, 1940.

predictions on the likely outcome of the fight. Tacoma's sports writing dean, Elliot Metcalf, said it looked like Zale to him. A couple of local referees, Tommy Clark and Eddie Pinkman, said Hostak would win by a knockout.[33] *The Seattle Post Intelligencer's* Dick Sharp expressed his admiration for Tony's work against what he felt were excellent sparring partners in "Tiger" Al Lewis, Harry "Kid" Matthews and Tony Kahut every afternoon.[34] Another local scribe offered that he believed Al was in for the fight of his life when he entered the ring with Tony.[35]

The verbal warfare between the managers of both fighters began to heat up four days away from the fight when Al's manager, Marino, told a reporter that he and Al were both angry. "Those Chicago guys talk too much. What do they mean Zale had Hostak on the run (in their first meeting)? Didn't Al knock Tony down? Didn't Al have the best of the first four rounds, the rounds before Al breaks his hand? What do they mean Tony had him beat before he breaks his hand? We're angry, I tell you, and we're going to show 'em on Friday night," said Marino.

A moment later the same reporter ran into one of Tony's manager's, Sam Pian, who said, "Stick around a while and see Tony work. You're going to see the next middleweight champion of the world in action. Don't make a mistake and go picking your boy to win. He actually doesn't have a chance."[36]

Pian seemed to be doing everything he could to get the Champion's goat, going so far as to question Al's heart in the first fight with Tony. "Why I had a fighter named Barney Ross. He fought fifteen rounds for the world's championship with a broken hand. But he kept punching with the other. And he won the fight. He didn't give up and blow the decision," he told Royal Brougham of the *Seattle Post Intelligencer*.[37]

Tony's managers also called into question the amount of bandages the champion would be allowed to use on his hands for the fight. When the two men had fought in Chicago, Winch and an Illinois boxing commission inspector made Hostak remove all the bandages from his hands and start all over again. When the new

33 *Seattle Star*, Hostak-Zale Debate Hot; Work Ditto, July 13, 1940.
34 *Seattle Post Intelligencer*, Hostak, Zale Primed for 15 Round Title Bout Friday, July 14, 1940.
35 *Seattle Star*, Hostak vs. Zale…A Ring Epic, July 17, 1940.
36 *Seattle Star*, It's Steaming…Fact Is, It's Boiling…Hostak vs. Zale, July 16, 1940.
37 *Seattle Post Intelligencer*, The Morning After, July 16, 1940.

taping was approved, there was quite a bit less on Hostak's hands and that was one of the reasons blamed for breaking his left hand in the fight. Pian and Winch said they weren't going to stand for Al's hands being "loaded" for this fight. They were assured by George Adams, of the Washington State Athletic Commission, that he personally would oversee the taping with an inspector so there would be no chance of any violation of the rules.[38]

Zale Drills for Hostak

AP Wire Photo.

As the date of the fight between Tony and Hostak approached, Druxman was anticipating a crowd of approximately 17,000 and a gate of around $50,000 to view the men many considered the hardest punchers in the middleweight division. Former lightweight champion Benny Leonard was on hand to officiate the title bout.

The day before the fight, Dick Sharp said that ninety per cent of the boxing men who had been watching the two fighters work out

38 *Seattle Post Intelligencer*, Zale Handlers Complain To Ring Body, July 16, 1940.

over the past week seemed to believe that Al would have to knock Tony out in order to win. According to Sharp, the general opinion, including the judgment of numerous ex-fighters, trainers and others that always flocked to the training sessions, was that if the match went the distance, Tony would take the decision and the crown. But a large percentage of these individuals felt Al would be able to knock Tony out and he was established as a 10 to 6 betting favorite. But according to Sharp, if the final training sessions meant anything, Tony looked by far the sharper of the two. He thought Al looked listless in two rounds of sparring with "Gorilla" Jones, while Tony was "fast and snappy" against Harry "Kid" Matthews.[39]

On the morning of the fight, it was noted that while the Champion's hands were in good shape, he was going to be facing Tony after a six-month layoff. Tony had knocked out three opponents since their previous meeting. The Champion reportedly looked sluggish in his last heavy workout before the fight, while Tony demonstrated more stamina and vitality in his own workouts. Some observers felt Hostak's best chance of a victory was to seek an early knockout and the odds of a victory on his part had dropped to 8 to 6. Both men were expected to scale 159 pounds for the fight.[40]

Royal Brougham came out on the morning of the fight and wrote that something told him Hostak was facing a better man than

---

39 *Seattle Post Intelligencer*, Hostak Rules as Favorite, July 18, 1940.
40 *Oakland Tribune*, Hostak Choice To Keep Title, July 19, 1940.

(Freddie) Steele, when Steele crumbled under Hostak's punches in the bout that earned Al the title, and better than Solly Krieger. "It would be an easier way out for this ringsider to sidestep this one, and go on record with Delegate De Lacy, 'Present, but not voting.'" But here I am scrambling out there on the thin, precarious limb and (I hope I'm wrong) picking the winner and new champion: Tony Zale," wrote Brougham.[41]

In terms of physical characteristics, the fighters were nearly identical, both standing about 5' 10" and just about even in all of the other usual measurements, although Al had a 2 ½ inch reach advantage over Tony. Both fighters issued their final statements concerning the upcoming contest:

Tony: "I'm looking for a tough fight, but I beat him last time, and I think I can do it again. I'm sure I'm going to make the most of my chance."

Al: "I'm in shape and ready. I have been waiting for a chance to reverse that decision of the last fight, and I think I can win."[42]

On July 19, a disappointing crowd of less than 10,000 fans showed up at Seattle's Civic Stadium to view the N.B.A.'s version of the middleweight championship of the world contest between Tony and Al Hostak.[43] The official weights for the fight were reported as 158 pounds for Tony

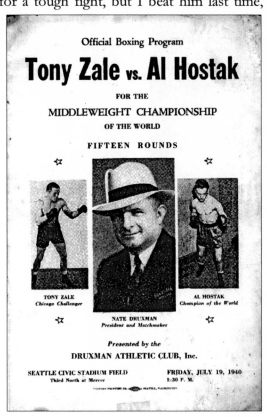

Official Boxing Program

Tony Zale vs. Al Hostak

FOR THE

MIDDLEWEIGHT CHAMPIONSHIP

OF THE WORLD

FIFTEEN ROUNDS

TONY ZALE
Chicago Challenger

AL HOSTAK
Champion of the World

NATE DRUXMAN
President and Matchmaker

Presented by the
DRUXMAN ATHLETIC CLUB, Inc.

SEATTLE CIVIC STADIUM FIELD
Third North at Mercer

FRIDAY, JULY 19, 1940
8:30 P. M.

WESTERN PRINTING CO. SEATTLE, WASHINGTON

41 *Seattle Post Intelligencer,* The Morning After, July 19, 1940.
42 *Seattle Post Intelligencer,* Boxers At Weight For Title Contest, July 19, 1940.
43 *The Charleston Gazette,* Seattle Scrap Fails to Draw, July 21, 1940.

and 158 ¾ pounds for the Champion.[44] Al looked nervous and drawn when he entered the ring, but once the opening bell rang, he seemed to shake off his nervousness and continually beat Tony to the punch, while skillfully avoiding punishment.

But Tony rallied in the second round and kept Al off with a stiff left jab. Al came back with lefts to the body, but Tony kept coming forward. Tony was faster in the third and refused to back up. Al landed some good blows, but Tony brushed them off and retaliated with some good blows of his own that seemed to take some of the steam out of the champion.

Al pulled himself together in the fourth round, but Tony continued to be the aggressor and had the best of the session. He took three of the first four rounds against the champion.[45]

Only in the fifth round did Tony appear to be in any trouble when Hostak landed a number of well-timed lefts and rights to the head that momentarily had the challenger in a groggy state and earned Hostak the laurels in that session.[46]

Tony recovered quickly though during the intermission and quickly resumed control of the fight in the sixth round. That session and the seventh went to Tony as he mercilessly poured blows in. Al rallied in the eighth and ninth rounds, but it was in the eighth that Al's eyes started to swell from Tony's punching. Al won the ninth round, but only because of a penalty suffered by Tony as a result of an accidental low blow.[47] The local crowd sensed that their Champion was in trouble. The tenth round was even, but Tony opened a cut under Hostak's left eye and both of the champion's eyes were badly swollen.[48]

After the tenth round, it appeared to some as though the champion appeared to be afraid to throw punches with the brittle hands he'd broken on previous occasions. His manager, Eddie Marino, said that the right hand appeared to be injured.[49] The first knockdown of the fight occurred in round 12 when Tony dropped

44 *Reno Evening Gazette*, Zale Takes Title From Al Hostak With TKO In Thirteenth,   July 20, 1940.
45 *Seattle Post Intelligencer*, Zale Annexes Middle Crown, July 20, 1940.
46 *The Daily Messenger*, Hostak KO'd by Zale 13th Round, July 20, 1940.
47 *Seattle Star*, Zale Is Real Champ, July 20, 1940.
48 *Reno Evening Gazette*, Zale Takes Title From Al Hostak With TKO In Thirteenth, July 20, 1940.
49 *Nevada State Journal*, Tony Zale Smashes TKO Over Al Hostak To Win Claims To Middleweight Diadem, July 20, 1940.

the champion for a count of nine with a right-hand punch to the kidney. It was the first knockdown the champion had ever suffered in his professional career.[50]

Early in the thirteenth and final round, Tony landed another hard right to the kidney and Hostak dropped to one knee, holding his side with one hand while holding a rope with the other hand to help remain upright. He climbed to his feet at the count of eight, but was quickly sent to the canvas for the third time as Tony found the range with another vicious body punch.[51] With Hostak wobbling on one knee, his manager waved the towel from the corner, and the referee, Benny Leonard, stepped in and ended the fight at the one minute and twenty second mark in that thirteenth round.[52] Afterward, Tony was relatively unmarked, and looked almost as fresh as he had when the fight started, while both of Hostak's eyes were nearly closed and he was bruised and battered. Leonard said of Tony, "He's a real fighter, a great new champion."

A very disappointed Hostak was quoted in his dressing room after the fight as saying that he would never fight again. Alex Shults of the *Seattle Times* said the former champion looked like a man in a dream state and not the shell of the man who had battered Freddie Steele into defeat two years prior to win the title. In Shults' view, Al knew he couldn't win before he entered the ring. On a side note, Shults reported that sometime during the fight, a souvenir-hunter entered Tony's dressing room and made off with his shoes as well as Sam Pian's hat and Art Winch's necktie. The new champion was forced to leave the stadium in his boxing shoes after the fight.[53]

Royal Brougham reported that Hostak looked sluggish, slow of foot, and that his normal timing and wallop was missing. He credited Tony and said that it was the deadliest kind of body punching that led to Al's downfall.[54] But Brougham also thought Al was a beaten man before the fight, when he heard him say, "Aw, let it go at that. I'll break my hand in the first punch anyway," as they were taping his hands in the dressing room. Still, Brougham said they could never

50 *Reno Evening Gazette*, Zale Takes Title From Al Hostak With TKO In Thirteenth, July 20, 1940.
51 *The Daily Messenger*, Hostak KO'd by Zale 13th Round, July 20, 1940.
52 *Reno Evening Gazette*, Zale Takes Title From Al Hostak With TKO In Thirteenth, July 20, 1940.
53 *Seattle Times*, Zale Captures Al's Crow In Sham Of Fight, July 20, 1940.
54 *Seattle Post Intelligencer*, Zale Takes Title From Champion In 13th Round, July 20, 1940.

say that Al didn't take his beating like a man. After the fight, Al's manager said his fighter's hands cracked up on him again and said he didn't think he should ever fight again.

Of Tony, Brougham said there was no wild whooping, no war dances of victory in the ring once the fight was stopped. Tony was just a fighter who had a chore to do, and did it. He did it in a thorough manner which makes one think that he is going to hang onto that title for quite a stretch. Tough, strong, a tremendous body puncher, he's a pretty good middleweight, wrote the scribe.[55]

Many years later, Tony would say that the championship fight against Al wasn't as difficult for him as their first fight had been. "Al, had the heart of a champion. But, I was at full strength (for the second fight) and he knew that he couldn't knock me out unless he brought a blackjack into the ring. In that second fight though, I began to know what a truly great fighter Al Hostak really was. No matter what I hit him with, he couldn't be put away. After a few rounds, the fight was mine, but he stayed in there and put up a battle anyway. He kept trying not just for the sake of trying, but because he really thought he still could win, because he didn't know how to quit. Al had the heart of a champion and simply would not quit. Some guys can never say die no matter how bad things are going against them, and Al Hostak was more like that than anyone I'd ever met," said Tony.[56]

Back home in Gary, Indiana, an impromptu celebration took place in the business section of the city when word reached the town that Tony had captured the middleweight crown as a result of the thirteenth round technical knockout. A large number of his followers paraded through that part of the city and the police were ultimately called out at dawn to quiet the blowing of horns and whistles in appreciation of the victory. City officials were already planning a homecoming celebration for the new champion.[57]

Sam and Art were elated that Tony had wrestled the N.B.A. version of the middleweight title away from Hostak. They indicated that any overtures to unify the title would need to come from both the New York and California groups that recognized Ken Overlin as the champion. "We've just won the biggest chunk of that

---

55 *Seattle Post Intelligencer*, The Morning After, July 20, 1940.
56 Boxing Illustrated, *The Greatest Man I Ever Fought*, October 1959.
57 *Hammond Times*, Gary Cheers Tony Zale's KO Triumph, July 21, 1940.

championship. Why should we let New York or anybody else tell us we've got to fight Overlin or anybody else at any terms other than the champion's end of the gate," they said.[58]

Although the clause in the contract they signed with Druxman prior to the title fight against Hostak required them to give Hostak a rematch should Al want one, there were many who suspected that Al might just choose to retire from boxing. The gate for the fight was reported as $27,000, far short of the $50,000 figure that Druxman had hoped for. Hostak received $10,000 for his work, while Tony received $3,000.[59]

Regardless of whom Tony fought next, Sam said he'd be a fighting champion and that after a rest of five weeks or so, their man would be back in action. They had promised Druxman an overweight match without the title at stake. There was some discussion of a possible fight against former middleweight champion Fred Apostoli.

58 *Port Arthur News*, Zale's Pilots To Await Offers, July 21, 1940.
59 *Oakland Tribune*, Overline Battle Zale's Next Hope, July 21, 1940.

TONY MEETS THE TALENTED BILLY SOOSE

Official Program

Their New World's Champion

Two of the smartest and most thought of men in the world of boxing are **ART WINCH** and **SAM PIAN,** Chicagoans who have been outstanding as a managerial unit since they broke into the limelight a dozen years ago with the flashy Earl Maestro. Since that time they've piloted Barney Ross to three world's championships, brought Davey Day to the top of the lightweight division and n o w have another title holder in that "Man of Steel" **Tony Zale** of Gary, Indiana, the boy from the mills, considered the greatest middleweight since Mickey Walker. Zale, who won the championship from Hostak, fights the tough and durable **Billy Soose** of Scranton, Pa. in Chicago's next big show at Mills Stadium — Wednesday, August 21st. It's a ten round affair backed by five good preliminaries.

BILL RAND, Promoter

Mills Stadium ❖ **Wed., August 21, 1940**

Price 10 Cents

On August 1, 1940, boxing promoter Bill Rand announced that he had signed Tony for a 10-round overweight contest to take place at Mill's Stadium in Chicago against Billy Soose. Soose, who turned 25 a day later, hailed from Pennsylvania and had enjoyed illustrious amateur and college careers before turning professional in early 1938. He was a three-time Golden Gloves winner as a collegiate champion at Penn State. He went 17-0, with 17 knockouts, over a two-year period while capturing the 1937 national intercollegiate title. Shortly thereafter, boxing officials enacted legislation in Pennsylvania to bar former Golden Glove winners from intercollegiate boxing because of Soose's success. Billy had been coached and mentored at Penn State by Leo Houck, a very successful professional fighter whose career spanned 24 years from 1902 to 1926.

Billy's winning ways continued as a professional, as he won 24 of his first 28 bouts, losing only to Johnny Duca, Charley Burley, and Georgie Abrams twice. Known more as a slugger in his amateur and collegiate days, Billy tore a tendon in the middle knuckle of his right hand and became more of a boxer thereafter, relying heavily upon the use of a great left hand.

Soose had surprised the boxing world on July 24, 1940, with a 10-round decision victory in his hometown over the reigning NYSAC middleweight champion Ken Overlin. It was a controversial decision with the two judges voting in Billy's favor, while the referee and the majority of the newspaper men at ringside gave the nod to Overlin. Regardless, it was an impressive performance by Soose and reflected poorly on Overlin who tired badly near the end of the fight and claimed he'd suffered an off night. It was a non-title bout as both men came in over the middleweight limit, Billy at 162 ¼ pounds and Overlin at 163.[60]

Tony's N.B.A. middleweight title wouldn't be at stake when he faced Soose on August 21, but the new champion was determined to make a good showing. On August 17, it was reported that Billy had looked impressive during his sparring sessions against Eddie Pierce and Nate Bolden at Trafton's Gym the prior day. He demonstrated that he had some power to go along with his shifty boxing style. Soose was being trained by highly respected Ray Arcel, who was so enthusiastic about the boxer's future that he quit working with light-heavyweight Billy Conn so he could concentrate his efforts on Soose.

---

60 *Titusville Herald*, Billy Soose Gets Decision By 3 to 2 Vote, July 25, 1940.

A number of folks who had seen Soose fight figured that Tony and his co-managers were taking on more than they bargained for in the classy fighter.[61]

On August 21, a crowd of 6,490 turned out and paid over $12,000 to view the action in Mill's Stadium where they witnessed a boxing version of the matador and the bull. Only in the first two rounds, when Tony was able to land a number of body punches along the line of those that he used to such great effect against Al Hostak, did he hold an advantage over his foe. Soose later said that Tony's right to the body hurt all the way to his toes.

But, once the third round began, Billy began to put his three to four inch height and reach advantages into play. He landed a right to Tony's jaw in the opening moments of the round and peppered him with long lefts throughout the remainder of that session. In fact, Billy won the third, fourth and fifth rounds on the strength of his left jabs, landing three blows to every one of Tony's. He landed his best blow of the fight in the sixth, a stiff left to the face that stopped Tony in his tracks. He also staggered Tony in the eighth round with two rights to the jaw that Tony would never forget. Billy could really dance and move inside the ring, not unlike another future heavyweight named Muhammad Ali.

Tony fought savagely in the last two rounds, looking for a knockout, but Billy kept himself well protected. The United Press scored the first two rounds to Tony and the remaining eight to Billy, who was awarded a unanimous decision over the champion. Only the fact that both men were over the middleweight limit of 160 pounds, with Billy at 162 and Tony 161, prevented the title from changing hands. Billy reportedly ran rings around the slower champion, seemingly hitting him at will after the second round.[62] He wisely remained on the move and avoided Tony's pet combination of a right to the body followed by a left hook to the jaw. It was a lesson in boxing, and unfortunately for Tony, he was on the receiving end most of the night. Tony was always willing to stand toe to toe with anyone, but Billy knew better.

Remarkably, young Billy Soose had defeated both middleweight champions within a one-month period, but failed to capture either title because the contests were each overweight bouts. It was

---

61 *The Vidette Messenger*, Zale's Foe Looks Good in Workout, August 17, 1940.
62 *Wisconsin State Journal*, Billy Soose Trims Tony Zale Easily, August 22, 1940.

believed that Zale and Overlin would be forced into a unification title fight, and that Soose would then face the winner. A number of Chicago writers who had witnessed Billy's defeat of Tony were already envisioning him as the first undisputed middleweight champion since Freddie Steele.[63]

While Soose would in fact go on to capture the NYSAC version of the middleweight crown on May 9, 1941, when he defeated Ken Overlin by way of a close 15-round unanimous decision, he and Tony never met in the ring again. He maintained that version of the middleweight title until that November when he gave it up to move up into the light-heavyweight division. He fought the last fight of his career on January 13, 1942, when he lost a decision to Jimmy Bivins, and subsequently enlisted in the United States Navy to serve his country during World War II. Still a young man when he was discharged four years later, Billy turned down an offer of one hundred thousand dollars to return to the ring for one fight. Instead, he retired to Lake Wallenpaupack, New York, where he lived out the rest of his life on his 525-acre resort called Billy Soose's Mountain Retreat. It included a restaurant, bar, marina, inn, and a ring for boxing and wrestling matches.

On May 29, 1983, Billy phoned Tony on the occasion of his 70th birthday. They reminisced about their fight against one another. Billy remembered well, the right to the body from Tony that Billy said felt like a hot poker being stuck into his side. Billy passed away of heart failure in September of 1998 at age 83. It would have been interesting to learn what would have happened had he and Tony met in the ring a second time.

In September of 1940, the Selective Training and Service Act was passed by the United States Congress and signed into law by President Franklin D. Roosevelt to enable the country to quickly build its military forces, if needed. The Act required that all men between the ages of 21 and 35 register with local draft boards. That October, Tony, along with a number of other notable boxers such as Joe Louis, Max and Buddy Baer, Pete Lello, and Davey Day, were registered for service.[64]

---

63 *Dunkirk Evening Observer*, Billy Soose Easily Takes NBA Champ Tony Zale, August 22, 1940.

64 *Port Arthur News*, Louis, Baer's And Others Register, October 16, 1940.

On November 3, Seattle boxing promoter, Nate Druxman, announced that he had signed Tony to fight former New York and California middleweight champion Fred Apostoli for a 10-round non-title bout in Seattle on November 19. Apostoli was already training in Seattle. Tony arrived on November 15 and planned to finish his training with a light workout on the 17th. Tony blamed his loss to Soose in August to being stale for the fight and said that he'd like to face him again with his title at stake, but his co-manager, Art Winch, said Soose's team was asking for too much money.[65]

Tony and Apostoli met on November 19 before a near capacity crowd in Seattle's Civic Auditorium and rewarded those in attendance with an action packed show from beginning to end. Tony weighed in at 161 ½ pounds, while Apostoli came in at 164 ¾ pounds for the non-title contest. Apostoli took an early lead in the beginning rounds, but Tony evened things up a bit in the middle rounds, flooring his opponent twice in the sixth round with right hand punches. Tony then took the seventh and eighth rounds before Apostoli came back and captured the ninth session. Fred was also winning the tenth and final round until Tony knocked him flat on his back seven seconds before the final bell and was awarded the decision in a rough and entertaining contest. *The San Antonio Light* newspaper, titled their sports page caption, "Zale Winner in Rough One," November 20, 1940.[66]

By mid-December, the NYSAC Middleweight Champion, Ken Overlin, had defeated Steve Belloise for the second time and the word was that Promoter Mike Jacobs was trying to put together a unification title bout between Overlin and Tony. Overlin had a difficult time beating Belloise in a split decision, and most thought Tony would have little trouble defeating him. But the talks broke down and instead, Sam Pian signed articles for Tony to fight the Wisconsin Middleweight Champion Tony "Martin" Cianciola of Milwaukee in the Milwaukee Auditorium on New Year's Day. He also signed on for Steve Mamakos in Chicago Stadium on January 10 in a pair of non-title bouts. Tony traveled to Milwaukee on December 27 to finish his training for the fight with Martin.

Tony and Martin fought before a crowd of 5,000 people on New Year's Day that produced a gate of $5,374. Because they already had

---

65 *San Antonio Light*, Apostoli and Zale Battle, November 19, 1940.
66 *San Antonio Light*, Zale Winner In Rough One, November 20, 1940.

a more lucrative match scheduled against Steve Mamakos only nine days later, Sam Pian said, "Tony was instructed not to risk injury, but to box and keep piling up points," against Martin. There were a few anxious moments for the Champion's managers in the opening round when Martin caught Tony with a right hand to the chin that sent him reeling backward into the ropes. This prevented him from falling down, but Tony came back and opened up a deep cut under one of Martin's eyes and had it partially closed by the end of the second round. He kept working on the eye over the next five rounds and the referee finally brought a merciful end to the bout at the end of the seventh round when it was clear that Martin could no longer see out of the eye and was in danger of being seriously hurt.[67]

With Martin out of the way, Tony turned his attention to Steve Mamakos and resumed his workouts on January 5. Mamakos, a Greek who had been fighting as a welterweight, was going to move up in weight and face his first middleweight opponent in this contest. He was fresh off a victory over Milt Aron. Chicago promoter Billy Rand was anticipating a good turnout for the match between the two men. A relative unknown only six months earlier, Mamakos had breezed into Chicago and surprised many by earning a draw against Aron, and then whipping him in a return match. The N.B.A. notified Tony that he needed to sign to defend his title very soon and Rand promised Mamakos that if he won, or made a good showing against Tony in their non-title bout on January 10, he would gain an opportunity to face him again with the middleweight title at stake. Should Mamakos fail to make a good showing, Rand said either Al Hostak or Billy Soose would get the chance.

The match between Tony and the tough Greek attracted a crowd of 11,064 spectators and drew a gate of $18,674. While Mamakos didn't earn a victory, losing by a split decision in 10 rounds, he demonstrated sufficient courage and stamina to earn the return engagement with the Champion that Rand had promised him if he made a good showing.

Tony knocked Mamakos down two times during the fight, in the fourth and ninth rounds, but on neither occasion did the Greek take a count, immediately bouncing back to his feet and resuming action with the Champion, and matching him punch for punch over much

67 *Chicago Daily News*, Zale Stops Cianciola in 8th Round, January 2, 1941.

of the contest.[68] Referee Frank McAdams scored the bout 55 to 45 and Judge William O'Connell 54 to 46 for Tony, while Judge Ed Hintz called the fight a draw. Rand wasted little time in signing the pair to a rematch for the N.B.A. middleweight title over 15 rounds to take place on February 21, 1941, in Chicago Stadium. It would be the first time Chicago had hosted a middleweight title fight since Mickey Walker fought Ace Hudkins there in 1928.

Tony promised to knock Mamakos out within eight rounds in the title contest. "Steve is one of the most rugged opponents I have ever faced," Tony said, "but he is only human and constant pounding on his chin will wear him down. I am confident I can knock him out inside of eight rounds."[69] Mamakos only laughed in response. "My chief asset is ruggedness," he said, "Zale couldn't knock me out before and I know he won't do it this time."[70] Mamakos believed that Tony would tire himself out in the early rounds and he'd finish him off by the eleventh round. Steve's trainer, Sam Buxbaum, said of him that he was a fighter built for 20-30-40-round fights. "He never wears down. I've never seen him tired, never heard him complain of needing rest. He just goes along at a steady pace and if nothing happens to him, he'll outlast any fighter in the game today."[71] At the afternoon weigh-in on the day of the fight, the Champion scaled 159 pounds to the challenger's 157 ½ pounds and Sam Pian predicted a knockout victory for his man.

A crowd of 14,306, the largest to see a fight in Chicago in three years, turned out and produced a gate of $37,450 to see Tony face Mamakos and an undercard that featured former champion Al Hostak against George Burnette. Bill Rand had promised Hostak a shot at the middleweight title if he made a good showing against Burnette. Tony came out strong in the first four rounds but suffered a terrific beating in the fifth stanza when he was knocked to the canvas and was staggering under a barrage of blows to the head as the bell rang. He was still groggy in the sixth, and the Greek closed his left eye in the eighth round. Mamakos held the edge as the pair entered the thirteenth round, but Tony landed a straight right hand

68 *Freeport Journal-Standard*, Zale Given Nod over Mamakos In Close Struggle, January 11, 1941.
69 *Alton Evening Telegraph*, Tony Zale Predicts an 8-Rounder With Mamakos, February 18, 1941.
70 *Chicago Tribune*, Mamakos and Zale to Finish Drills Today, February 19, 1941.
71 *Chicago Times*, The Barber Shop' February 20, 1941.

that shook the Greek and followed it with a left to the body and a right to the face that sent him crashing to the canvas. Mamakos was still on the floor at referee's count of six when the bell rang to end the round and saved him from being counted out. He appeared out on his feet as his seconds helped him to his corner.

Tony raced across the ring as the fourteenth round opened and caught the Greek in his own corner, where he landed a hard left, and then a big right that dropped his opponent for a count that he wasn't able to beat.[72] Although it had taken him fourteen rounds, Tony had made good on his promise to knock Mamakos out and retained his title in a hard fought battle. Tony always felt that Mamakos was one of the most underrated fighters he ever fought. While he always considered Hostak the greatest fighter he'd ever faced, with "lightning speed, power and ability to take a punch," he felt that Mamakos was the toughest.[73]

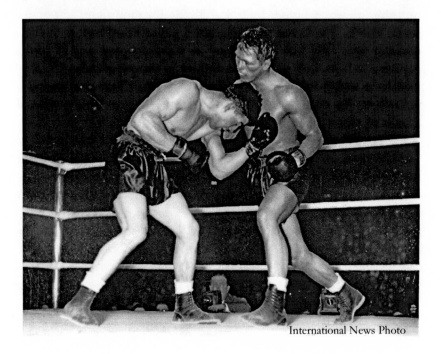

International News Photo

72 *Chicago Daily News*, Zale Wins K.O. In 14th Round, February 22, 1941.
73 *Unknown Chicago newspaper*, January 1973.

Tony's furious comeback and Hostak's impressive one-round knockout victory over Burnette set the stage for a third meeting between the pair and Rand made good on his promise, signing Tony and Al Hostak to fight for the N.B.A. middleweight title in Chicago Stadium in May of 1941.

CURTAINS FOR MAMAKOS

FEBRUARY 22, 1941

Photo Courtesy of AP Wire

Both Tony Zale and Steve Mamakos were down, but only Mamakos was counted out in their title fight last night at the Stadium. This picture shows Mamakos down in the fourteenth round, before he took the knockout count.

UNDISPUTED WORLD CHAMPION

In mid-April of 1941, it appeared that the fight between Tony and Hostak would be called off when Al's manager, Eddie Marino, demanded 20 percent of the purse for his fighter instead of the 12 ½ percent that Chicago promoter Bill Rand claimed they'd verbally agreed to previously. Rand and Zale's managers angrily pointed out that 12 ½ percent was all that Tony received when he fought for Al's title, but ultimately Sam and Art gave in and agreed to the adjustment in the fighters' shares so the fight could go on. The contract called for Tony to receive 35 percent and Al, 20 percent.[74]

As the date of the third fight between Tony and Al approached, the fighter's camps waged their verbal warfare in the press and argued over how much adhesive tape Al would be allowed to wrap around

---

74 *Racine Journal Times*, Tony Zale to Meet Hostak in Chicago, April 30, 1941.

his mitts. Voicing his opinion on the outcome of the fight, Art Winch said, "Hostak can't take it in the ribs and belly and that's just where Tony will hit him. Hostak won't last longer than the eighth round." The two fighters, while each expressing their confidence, were a bit more respectful of one another with their own comments. "I've defeated Hostak twice and am confident that I can do it again. He is a dangerous hitter, but I will be on my guard," said Tony. In response, Al said, "My broken hand has healed and I am in great condition. I am convinced that Zale can be hit, and this time I hope to hit him hard enough to settle all arguments."[75]

DAILY TIMES, CHICAGO, WEDNESDAY, MAY 28, 1941   **47**

Chicago turns out for Zale-Hostak title fight

By GENE KESSLER

Chicago goes overboard for a prize fight tonight. Promoter Bill Rand predicts a new-capacity crowd will see Tony Zale risk the world's middleweight championship in 15 rounds

'Hostile' Hostak vs. Man of Steel— Al Hostak (left) looks longingly at his left hand, which of Steel," last year. Zale's ability to "take it" is important   he fractured in first bout with Tony Zale (right), "Man factor in tonight's fight.

May 28, 1941, was another sweltering day that reached near 100 degrees in Chicago, and 15,087 fans showed up at Chicago Stadium and paid $48,475 to witness the Tony Zale and Al Hostak bout. This fight would be for the N.B.A. version of the middleweight championship of the world. The former champion, Hostak, received a big ovation when he was introduced, but the fans rocked the

75 *Chicago Times*, Jekyll – Hyde Ring Twinces, May 22, 1941.

building with their cheers when the announcer introduced the Champion.[76] Tony entered the ring no better than a 6-5 favorite with the betting fraternity, despite the fact that he had already defeated Al twice. Many believed that Hostak was such a heavy hitter that he would recapture the crown as long as his brittle hands held up.

It was clear from the beginning that Al's plan was to try and get to Tony and take him out early. He missed with a big right hand punch in the opening round and Tony countered with a hard right to the jaw. Al then landed a left and staggered Tony with a hard right, causing the tips of the Champion's gloves to touch the floor in order to stay on his feet. Al threw a vicious right hand swing to the jaw that missed and Tony clinched. Al was wild with another big right, and then landed to Tony's body.[77]

The *Chicago Times* sports editor, Marvin McCarthy, suggested that Hostak might have ended the fight right then and there had he been able to land just one more solid hit on the jaw before Tony's head cleared.[78] After receiving the body shot from Al, Tony came back and missed with a left hook, and a left lead, but then landed a hard right to Al's jaw as the latter backed away. Tony ducked under a left hook and missed with a jab and clinched. Al missed with a right uppercut and Tony landed two hooks, ducked under a left hand jab and was pounding on Al's ribs when the bell sounded to end the round.

Al missed with a left to start the second round and Tony landed a light jab to the face, hooked a left to the body and followed with another left to the same spot. Al landed a glancing left hook to the jaw, but Tony immediately hammered his unprotected ribs with hard rights and Al went down. He got up, but went down two more times from punches to his ribs, before briefly rallying and scoring with a right to Tony's head.

Tony then landed a hard right below Al's heart and the latter went down for a fourth time in the round, this time for a count of eight. He rose only to catch another right hand blow to the same spot and dropped for the fifth time. He gamely climbed to his feet for more but was knocked flat on his back by Tony for a sixth and final time in the round and he was counted out at the 2:32 mark as he

---

76 *Chicago Times,* Zale on Verge of K.O. Stops Hostak In Second, May 29, 1941.
77 *Chicago Tribune,* 15,087 Watch Stadium Bout; Gate Is $48,475, May 29, 1941.
78 *Chicago Times,* Birthday Brawl, May 29, 1941.

writhed on the floor, grimacing in pain.[79] It was a big night for Tony, who turned 27 years old at the stroke of midnight.

Although one might think it would be extremely disappointing to attend a middleweight championship fight and witness only five minutes and thirty-two seconds of action, sports writer Zyg Kaminski suggested that Hostak and Zale crowded more dynamic action into that period of time than a lot of fighters did in ten rounds. As far as Kaminski was concerned, it was one of the greatest fights he'd ever witnessed. He reported Tony's share of the purse as $16,966, and Hostak's as $9,695. Kaminski also reported that when newspapermen interviewed the Champion in his dressing room after the fight, the first thing he said was, "Now bring on Billy Soose."[80]

The loss that Tony suffered against Soose shortly after winning the title from Hostak obviously stuck in his craw. He was anxious to get another shot at Billy. Soose had recently defeated Ken Overlin for a second time in a hotly disputed decision and now owned the NYSAC version of the middleweight championship. A fight between Billy and Tony to unify the middleweight title seemed like a natural step, but there were several obstacles to overcome before such a match could be made. The first was that the contract Soose signed for the title fight with Overlin called for him to defend his title against either Overlin or his stable mate, Georgie Abrams, within 90 days of the date of his title fight with Overlin. Billy had a $5,000 forfeit on file with the commission guaranteeing such a defense. New York promoter Mike Jacobs would have to get the permission of Overlin's manager, Chris Dundee, before Billy could fight anyone else. The disappointing fight between Overlin and Soose figured to make a rematch between the pair difficult to sell to the fans.[81] Billy's manager, Paul Moss, said that Billy might fight Abrams in an overweight match, and then if that match drew a big enough crowd, seek another match with Overlin in Scranton, Pennsylvania in July.[82]

Meanwhile, Tony enjoyed a bit of a rest before his manager's matched him with Ossie "Bulldog" Harris in a non-title bout at Chicago Stadium on July 23, 1941. Harris, who was good enough to go ten rounds with Steve Belloise and Nate Bolden, and nine with

79 *Chicago Tribune*, 15,087 Watch Stadium Bout; Gate Is $48,475, May 29, 1941.
80 *Unknown newspaper source*, Aboard The Sports Special, May 30, 1941.
81 *Altoona Mirror*, Fans Believe Scrappers Were Even in Ability, May 10, 1941.
82 *Syracuse Herald*, Fight Offers Rain Down on Billy Soose, June 5, 1941.

Charley Burley, in his previous three contests, didn't fare as well with Tony. He knocked out Harris in less than two minutes after the opening bell. It was a right hand punch to the jaw that sent Harris over on his back and while he rolled over onto his stomach he was unable to rise before the count of ten. The punch to the jaw was setup by Tony with numerous rights to the body. A crowd of 3,800 viewed the match.[83]

The middleweight title picture was further clouded on July 30, 1941, when the NYSAC Champion, Billy Soose, lost a non-title bout to Georgie Abrams in New York's Madison Square Garden. Superman had his kryptonite and Soose had Abrams, a nemesis he just couldn't seem to overcome. It was the third time in three meetings that Billy had dropped a decision to Abrams. Despite the loss in front of a disappointing crowd, Mike Jacobs insisted that Billy would defend his title against Ken Overlin in September.

While the NYSAC continued to try and sort out their piece of the middleweight picture, Tony was signed to headline a show in Milwaukee's Juneau Park on August 16 in a non-title bout during the National Eagles convention. Initially, it appeared that Tony's opponent would be either George Burnette, Nate Bolden, or Tommy Yarosz, but ultimately a fighter out of Boise, Idaho, named Billy Pryor who could really only be classed as a journeyman, was selected.

The show was sponsored by the Pabst Brewing Company in conjunction with the convention and Pabst paid the fighters and the referee, former Heavyweight Champion Jack Dempsey. The fans were allowed to view the action at no charge. Although there was no official count taken, the local Milwaukee police department estimated that a record was set by a crowd of 135,000 people who attended this outdoor event. Jack Dempsey agreed with the figure, saying it reminded him of the time he fought Gene Tunney for the heavyweight title in Chicago. The previous largest boxing crowd was believed to be the 120,000 fans who attended the first heavyweight title fight between Jack Dempsey and Gene Tunney in Philadelphia, Pennsylvania. The main event of the Zale vs. Pryor fight turned out to be a mismatch and was considered a relatively dull affair despite the fact that Tony put Pryor down eight times before it was all over. Before the third round, both men were ordered to be more active by Fred Saddy, the head of the Wisconsin Boxing Commission.

---

83 *Helena Independent*, Champ Tony Zale Wins Over "Bulldog" Harris, July 24, 1941.

Tony put Pryor down for a count of four in the third round and another count of nine in the fifth session. Pryor was knocked down for two counts of eight in the seventh round, and then floored two more times in the eighth round for counts of eight and nine. In the ninth round he was floored two more times, the last time from a left hook, and he was finally counted out by Dempsey.[84]

On August 28, it was announced that Tony had signed to fight Georgie Abrams in Madison Square Garden on September 12 in a ten-round, non-title bout. But, on the date of the fight, word came out of New York that Tony would have to spend the night in a hospital rather than in a ring because he was suffering from a skin infection. What had initially appeared to be a minor skin ailment on his feet and legs suddenly got so bad that Tony went to see a doctor and wound up in the hospital where he was expected to remain for as long as a week. His feet and legs were badly swollen and covered with large blisters.

The cancellation of the fight was especially disappointing because it was going to be the first of a series of fights to take place that would lead to the unification of the middleweight title. If the fight was successful, Mike Jacobs planned to rematch Tony and Abrams for the N.B.A. championship in Chicago, and to have Billy Soose and Ken Overlin fight for the right to meet the winner.[85]

The groundwork for the unification of the title was laid only three days later though when Billy Soose fought Ceferino Garcia in Los Angeles in an overweight non-title bout. Soose had agreed to come in weighing no more than 165 pounds for the fight, while Garcia reportedly had to step on the scales with a roll of coins in each hand in order to exceed the 160 pound middleweight limit. Billy failed to make 165 pounds, instead weighing in at 169 ½ pounds. While Garcia's camp was unhappy with Billy's additional weight, they went ahead with the bout. Soose gave Garcia a boxing lesson in the early part of the fight, winning the first five rounds with ease, but Garcia came back and punished the Champion severely in rounds six and seven. He was hurting him badly in the eighth when the fight was stopped and ruled a draw because Soose's left eye was so badly cut.

---

84 *Milwaukee Journal Sentinel*, Boxing Takes the Title of State's Biggest Event, November 7, 1999.
85 *Capital Times*, Tony Zale in Hospital; Call off Abrams Go, September 12, 1941.

The referee ruled that the cut had been caused by a Garcia butt in the seventh round, while Soose said it occurred in the sixth round. Regardless, that was the reason given by the referee for calling the contest a draw, much to the disagreement of the fans in attendance.[86]

Afterward, it was learned that not only was Billy unable to make the agreed upon weight of 165 pounds, but he had a very difficult time getting down to the 169 ½ pound figure that he weighed in at. Remarkably, in October, Billy and his manager announced that he could no longer make the middleweight limit of 160 pounds and he would have to vacate the NYSAC version of the crown without ever having actually defended it.[87]

The N.B.A. immediately urged the NYSAC to recognize Tony as the only Middleweight Champion of the World in a step toward national boxing unity.[88] That wasn't about to happen. Once Soose appeared before the NYSAC, and formally abdicated his title, that group selected Soose's recent conqueror, Georgie Abrams. He would be their representative to fight Tony in Madison Square Garden on November 28, 1941, in a 15-round title bout that both groups sanctioned for the undisputed middleweight championship of the world.

As a result of the skin ailment, Tony ended up spending 16 days in the hospital instead of a week. By November 18, he was reportedly completely recovered and in excellent condition. He planned to enjoy a Thanksgiving feast with his family in Gary, Indiana, before traveling to New York for the fight.

Because of Tony's self-imposed desire to overtrain, he often ended up with some sort of ailment or sickness that was unexpected. By not allowing his body to re-build, he was constantly tearing it down, when he actually intended to build it up. Tony struggled with this unintentional overtraining throughout his career and even after he was Champ.

---

86 *Gettysburg Times*, Soose Eye Badly Cut, Gets Draw In Garcia Bout; Stopped In 8th, September 16, 1941.
87 *Waterloo Daily Courier*, Billy Soose to Abandon World's Middleweight Title, October 23, 1941.
88 *Warren Times-Mirror*, Asks N.Y. Solons to Recognize Tony Zale, October 27, 1941.

On the morning of the day of the fight, Abrams was named as an 8-5 favorite to defeat Tony and win the undisputed title. Despite the fact that Georgie was viewed as a light puncher, the smart guys figured his speed and boxing ability would carry him to victory over Tony. They figured this would be done in the same manner that Abrams beat Billy Soose 15 months earlier. However, it was noted that Abrams cut easily and had shown a tendency to tire in the closing sessions of ten-round contests.[89] One way or another, once the dust settled, there would be a single recognized middleweight champion for the first time since 1931. Mickey Walker gave up the title then and the New York State Athletic Commission and National Boxing Association sponsored separate tournaments to pick champions.

A crowd of 10,004 showed up in Madison Square Garden and generated a gate of $23,854 to view the battle for the undisputed middleweight championship of the world on November 28, 1941. The fans were rewarded with an entertaining and dominant performance by Tony Zale. Initially, it seemed as though the betting fraternity may have picked the right man when Abrams caught Tony off balance with a right to the chin and sent him crashing to the floor in the first round. Tony took the referee's count of nine and weathered the rest of the round without any further cause for

---

89 *Nevada State Journal*, Abrams, Zale Fight Tonight for World Middleweight Crown, November 28, 1941.

concern. It was in the second round that Tony really went to work, landing a number of hard rights to Abram's heart and bloodying his nose. He captured the third round as well with a vicious body attack and then landed two booming right hands to Abram's jaw in the fourth round that had many in the crowd wondering what was keeping Georgie on his feet. Tony also won the fifth round with ease.

Abrams was awarded the sixth round on a foul when one of Tony's body blows wandered a bit south of the border. Tony managed to open a deep cut over Abrams right eye in that round that half blinded him for the rest of the fight. In the eighth round, Abrams managed to land with a right to Tony's jaw that staggered him. Abrams then failed to take advantage of this opportunity, and in the ninth round, Tony returned the favor, landing right hand shots to Georgie's jaw that had him all but out on his feet by the end of the round.[90]

Abrams fought back gamely in round 10, opening a cut on Tony's left cheek, but Tony continued to attack the body and took both that round and the next. Abrams fought him on even terms in

---

90 *Syracuse Herald Journal*, Mike Jacobs Matches Fight Winner With Bill Conn, November 29, 1941.

the twelfth round, and the pair split the next two rounds in the view of United Press Staff Correspondent Jack Cuddy. Tony then came on strong in the final round and was pounding Georgie around the ring when the fight concluded.

Referee Billy Cavanaugh and Judges George Le Cron and Charlie Draycott were unanimous in their decisions to award the fight to Tony. The United Press scored the bout 10 rounds for Tony, four

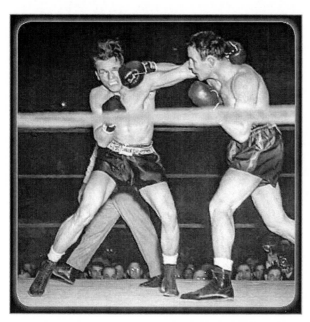

for Abrams and one even. Tony weighed in at 158 ¾ pounds for the fight, while Abrams came in at 159.[91]

In his dressing room afterward, Abrams said, "Zale is one of the toughest body punchers I ever fought and if I hadn't been in the best shape of my life, he might have splattered me all over the ring. After the first round, I came back to my corner and said to myself, 'This is easy, I'm going to win the middleweight title by a knockout.' Then in the second round, boom! And you saw what happened. He cut my left eye in the third round, and I never was able to see anything out of it from then on."

Tony expressed surprise that he hadn't been able to floor Abrams. "Those body punches were the same thing that finished Al Hostak and plenty of other guys," he said.[92]

---

91 *Syracuse Herald Journal*, Mike Jacobs Matches Fight Winner With Bill Conn, November 29, 1941.
92 *Nevada State Journal*, Zale Becomes Undisputed Middleweight Champion, November 29, 1941.

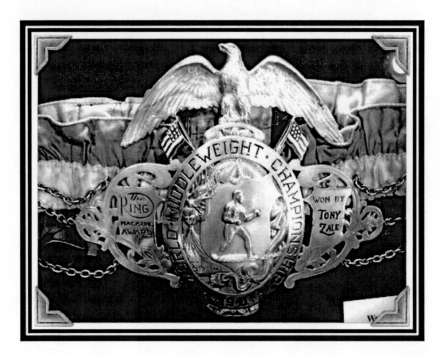

Mickey Walker, the last undisputed middleweight champion, attended the fight and said of Tony afterward, "He reminds me of Ace Hudkins. He's rugged, tireless, and a fine body puncher with very little boxing finesse."

Abrams had no defense for Tony's punishing body attacks and after the bout admitted he was lucky to escape a knockout.[93] The next day it was learned that Georgie suffered a hemorrhage of his right eye and initially it was thought that his chances of resuming his ring career were only fifty-fifty.[94]

93 *New Castle News*, Zale Defeats George Abrams, November 29, 1941.
94 *Kingsport Times*, Georgie Abrams Hurt in Tony Zale Fight, November 30, 1941.

International News Photo

Fortunately, after weeks of convalescence, Abrams experienced a complete recovery. He was able to fight again six months later, earning a ten-round decision over Steve Mamakos. This was before his Navy furlough was cancelled and he was called to serve his country during World War II. It was four years before Abrams was able to resume his ring career. Although he enjoyed some initial success upon his return to the ring and gave Sugar Ray Robinson one of his toughest fights in a split-decision loss in 1947, he ultimately retired in 1948. He had suffered four consecutive losses before retiring. The four years in the service of his country effectively robbed him of his prime as it did so many other fighters during that period. He never received another opportunity to fight for a world championship. He suffered from Alzheimer's late in life and passed away in the summer of 1994 at age 75.

BILLY CONN

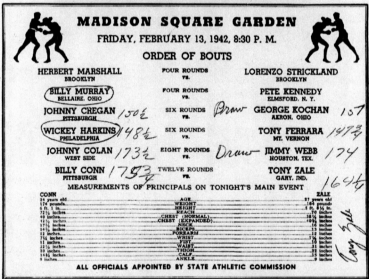

MADISON SQUARE GARDEN
FRIDAY, FEBRUARY 13, 1942, 8:30 P. M.
ORDER OF BOUTS

HERBERT MARSHALL BROOKLYN	FOUR ROUNDS vs.	LORENZO STRICKLAND BROOKLYN
BILLY MURRAY BELLAIRE. OHIO	FOUR ROUNDS vs.	PETE KENNEDY ELMSFORD. N. Y.
JOHNNY CREGAN *150½* PITTSBURGH	SIX ROUNDS *Draw* vs.	GEORGE KOCHAN *157* AKRON, OHIO
WICKEY HARKINS *148½* PHILADELPHIA	SIX ROUNDS vs.	TONY FERRARA *147¾* MT. VERNON
JOHNNY COLAN *173½* WEST SIDE	EIGHT ROUNDS *Draw* vs.	JIMMY WEBB *174* HOUSTON, TEX.
BILLY CONN *173¾* PITTSBURGH	TWELVE ROUNDS vs.	TONY ZALE *164¼* GARY, IND.

MEASUREMENTS OF PRINCIPALS ON TONIGHT'S MAIN EVENT

CONN		ZALE
24 years old	AGE	27 years old
174 pounds	WEIGHT	164 pounds
6 ft. 1 in.	HEIGHT	5 ft. 8½ in.
72½ inches	REACH	70 inches
40 inches	CHEST (NORMAL)	38½ inches
42½ inches	CHEST (EXPANDED)	40½ inches
17½ inches	NECK	16 inches
14½ inches	BICEPS	13 inches
12 inches	FOREARM	12 inches
7¾ inches	WRIST	7¾ inches
11 inches	FIST	11 inches
32½ inches	WAIST	31 inches
20 inches	THIGH	21 inches
14½ inches	CALF	15 inches
9 inches	ANKLE	9 inches

ALL OFFICIALS APPOINTED BY STATE ATHLETIC COMMISSION

In late November of 1941, contracts were signed for a match between Tony and former light-heavyweight champion Billy Conn to take place in Madison Square Garden on February 13, 1942. The length of the fight was still a point of contention at the time. Tony's managers preferred a ten-round fight, while Conn's manager, Johnny Ray, was asking for 15 rounds.[95]

Conn, aka "The Pittsburgh Kid," was 24 years old, and an extremely slick boxer with matinee idol looks. He turned professional a few months prior to his 17th birthday and over the course of the next five years put together an impressive resume that led to a fight with Tony's old Golden Gloves opponent Melio Bettina for the light-heavyweight championship of the world on July 13, 1939. Billy won a 15-round decision over Bettina to earn the title as a twenty-one year old. He successfully defended the title against Bettina on September 25, 1939, and against Gus Lesnevich twice, first on November 17, 1939, and then again on June 5, 1940. He also engaged in and won non-title bouts during that period of time with heavyweights Gus Dorazio, Henry Cooper, Bob Pastor, Lee Savold, Ira Hughes, Danny Hassett, Gunnar Barlund and Buddy Knox.

As a result of his growing popularity and the successes he enjoyed against a number of heavyweights, he received an opportunity to fight Joe Louis on June 18, 1941, for the heavyweight championship of the world. Billy was plenty tall enough for Louis at 6'1 ½", but he was much, much lighter than the champion. Louis had already won 17 straight title defenses and many were lauding him as one of the greatest heavyweights of all-time. Most knowledgeable fight fans gave Billy little chance against Louis. But Conn was an extremely confident fighter, and after he defeated Lee Savold, a top-10 heavyweight contender, on November 29, 1940, he officially relinquished his light-heavyweight title and announced his intention to fight heavyweights from then on.[96]

The fighters weighed in at noon on the day of the fight, and when Billy stepped on the scale it read 169 pounds. The fight's promoter, Mike Jacobs, immediately yelled out a figure of 174 pounds because he didn't want it known that Billy was that light, and the 174 pound figure was recorded as the official weight. Louis, who had planned to come in a bit lighter than usual in the hope of gaining

---

95 *Wisconsin State Journal*, Zale, Conn Sign for Winter Bout, November 30, 1941.
96 Kennedy, Paul, *Billy Conn – The Pittsburgh Kid*, Author House, Bloomington, IN, 2007.

some speed, weighed in at an even 200 pounds, but Jacobs yelled out a figure of 199 ½, so the papers reported a difference of 25 ½ pounds in weight between the fighters, instead of the actual 31 pound differential.[97] Jacobs, correctly anticipated that there would be a great amount of interest in a pairing between the two men and it drew a paid attendance of 54,487 to New York's Polo Grounds Stadium and generated a gate of $451,776.

To the shock of most of those in attendance, Conn was still on his feet at the end of twelve rounds. He had stunned the heavyweight champion of the world with his best punch of the fight in that last round, and was actually leading on points.[98] Billy had put on a boxing clinic, dancing around on his toes, moving this way and that, setting and unsetting, and proving an elusive target for Louis. Joe later said he felt like a man in a handcar trying to catch the Super Chief (train).[99]

At the start of the ninth round, Billy bound out of his corner, jabbed Joe in the mouth, grinned and said, "Joe, I got you." For the remainder of that round, and the next three, Billy bounced left hooks off Joe's head and jabbed him silly.[100] All he had to do was continue to fight the same way for the last three rounds and he'd win the decision. He would have been the new heavyweight champion of the world in one of the greatest upsets in boxing history.

Heading into the thirteenth round, the referee had him leading seven rounds to five, one judge had it seven to four, with one round even, and the other judge had it even.[101] But something had occurred in the twelfth round that gave Billy bigger ideas. Billy hurt Joe in that round, and he knew it. Winning was no longer enough, he was determined to knock out the champion.

While Billy sat on his stool awaiting the start of the thirteenth round, his manager, Johnny Ray, told him to box, keep away from Joe, and win by decision. But Billy replied, "I'm gonna knock him out." Ray threw up his hands and muttered, "You're on your own."[102]

---

97 Kennedy, Paul, *Billy Conn – The Pittsburgh Kid*, Author House, Bloomington, IN, 2007.
98 *Huntingdon Daily News*, Challenger Ahead On Points Is KO'd In 13th, June 19, 1941.
99 Louis, Joe, *'My Life Story*, Duel, Sloan and Pearce, New York, New York, 1947.
100 *Huntingdon Daily News*, Challenger Ahead On Points Is KO'd In 13th, June 19, 1941
       McConnell, J. Knox, The Boxer and the Banker, Vantage Press, New York, New York, 1984.
102 Kennedy, Paul, *Billy Conn – This Pittsburgh Kid*, Author House, Bloomington, IN, 2007.

In the early part of the round, Billy actually danced and jabbed as Johnny wanted him to, but then he attacked, landed a left hook, danced away and attacked again. Joe landed a hard right to the jaw, followed by a left hook and a right uppercut. Billy was stunned, but shook it off. Rather than become more cautious, Billy lost his temper and rushed Joe and engaged in a furious exchange. Billy threw a left hook that went wide, and Joe landed a right to the jaw that staggered Billy. "Now, now!" someone yelled from Joe's corner, and in the blink of an eye, a series of punches fell on Billy's jaw and he was sent crashing to the floor.[103] Billy tried to rise at the count of eight, but he wasn't able to make it in time and was counted out at the 2:58 mark of the thirteenth round.

Afterward, a relieved Joe Louis said, "Billy Conn is a great fighter with a lot of heart. He was much faster than I was and I had a hard time hitting him."[104]

Asked by the press why he'd gone for a knockout instead of playing it safe, Billy said, "After the twelfth, I thought I had him and I simply couldn't do anything else but go after him. Then it happened. What's the sense in being Irish if you can't be dumb."[105]

Joe Louis seemingly had little to gain and everything to lose when he'd agreed to fight Billy Conn. By failing to beat a light-heavyweight more convincingly he came under a substantial amount of criticism and there were a number of folks who claimed the fight was evidence that he'd begun to slip.

Six months later the shoe was on the other foot, when many in the press wondered why Billy and his manager would agree to fight the middleweight champion, Tony Zale. Some reporters felt that Tony had little chance of winning against the taller, heavier, and faster man, but others felt that accepting the fight was unwise on Billy's part, and that he had everything to lose, including the build-up he'd received for almost upsetting Joe Louis. But Mike Jacobs felt there would be a lot of interest in this fight as well, and estimated that it would produce a gate between 70,000 to 80,000 dollars.[106] The contract for the fight stipulated that Billy couldn't weigh any more

---

103 *Huntingdon Daily News*, Today's Sports Parade, June 19, 1941.
104 Kennedy, Paul, *Billy Conn – The Pittsburgh Kid*, Author House, Bloomington, IN, 2007.
105 *New York Herald Tribune*, Unknown article title, June 19, 1941.
106 *Charleston Gazette*, Conn-Zale Bout Puzzles Fans, December 3, 1941.

than 175 pounds, so in all likelihood, it was expected that he would have a weight advantage of somewhere in the range of 10-15 pounds.

In early January, Tony announced his intention to join the navy once the bout with Conn was concluded.[107] Two other champions, Joe Louis and Freddie Cochrane, were already in uniform, and Billy Conn had already completed his army physical examination.

At the end of January, Tony set a war of words in motion between the two fighters when he voiced the opinion that he would be able to knock out Conn when they met in the ring. He based that conviction on his own hitting ability and the reports he had received that Billy had looked sluggish in a January 28 bout against heavyweight Jay D. Turner.[108] When Conn was informed of this, he phoned the press and said he wanted to make the following announcement:

"The first time I see that mug on the street or in a movie or having a chocolate soda, I'm gonna walk up and knock his ears off. And you can tell him so. Who does he think I am one of those bums he's been lucky enough to get in the ring with? I'm promising right now, as soon as I see him, I'm goin' right to work. And when I finish he's gonna look like a plate of salami and eggs right here in Goldstein's Delicatessen in Pittsburgh. You can tell him for me that he's gonna be the first fighter ever to get hit – before he gets in the ring. I'm leaving for New York to start training for the fight right now. Only there ain't gonna be a fight if I catch up with that blowhard. At least there won't be a fight in the Garden. He won't be able to make it."[109]

When he learned of Billy's announcement, Tony responded in kind, "Who does that Conn think he is? Why doesn't he save all that energy until we get paid for it? He'll need it, I'm telling you. Joe Louis slowed him down so much that he had a tough time licking a couple of very ordinary heavyweights in the last six weeks. I know I can out hit him, and I think he knows it too. He's no super boxer. He can be tagged. Joe Louis proved that."[110]

Three days later, a reporter spoke with Tony beside a training ring in Stillman's Gym in New York City, and Tony reiterated his

107 *Syracuse Herald Journal,* Tony Zale Will Become a Sailor, January 7, 1942.
108 *Tuscon Daily Citizen,* Zale Say's He'll Knock Out Conn, January 31, 1942.
109 *Daily Times-News,* Billy Conn Pops Off By Telephone About Tony Zale, February 4, 1942.
110 *Laredo Times,* Tony Zale Peeved At Conn, February 5, 1942.

confidence in defeating Billy: "If I wasn't confident of beating Conn, I wouldn't have asked for the match. And after Conn's last two showings against heavyweight opponents, I'm almost positive," he said. Tony said he expected to weigh 162 pounds for the fight and when asked about his plans should he defeat Conn, he said that he'd go after Gus Lesnevich's light-heavyweight title. Asked if he'd also like a shot at Joe Louis, Tony said, "No, I won't try to fight Louis. I don't think I'd have too much chance with him. He's too heavy and hits too hard."[111]

While no one was laying any heavy bets on Tony, there were a few fight experts who said they wouldn't be surprised if Tony defeated Billy. Georgie Abrams' manager, Chris Dundee, was one of those parties. "Zale is a tough baby," Chris said, "He's fast, a good boxer, and a pretty fair puncher. He's always in shape and has been conditioning down in Hot Springs (Arkansas) for this bout. Conn takes a punch well and is rather hard to hit around the head, but he's easy to punch in the body. And this Zale is some body-puncher. What he did to my Abrams was a sight. Billy isn't going to like those midriff wallops Zale hands out."[112]

The two fighters wound up their training on February 11, Tony undergoing a light workout, while Billy, who promised to try for a knockout, punished three of his sparring partners in a tough workout. Jacobs promised a June rematch for Billy with Joe Louis, regardless of the outcome of his fight with Tony. The betting odds were 5-1 on Billy emerging the victor.

A crowd of 15,033 fans, including heavyweight champion Joe Louis in his army uniform, showed up in Madison Square Garden on February 13, and produced a gate of $48,000 to witness what was termed a drab bout between Tony and Billy Conn. Billy, who weighed 175 ¾ pounds to Tony's 164 ¼, walked away with the twelve-round decision victory, but it was Tony who earned the cheers and admiration from the crowd for his gutty performance.

Billy had a big advantage in height and reach, in addition to weight, and there was no doubt at all but that the decision belonged to him. The number one contender for the heavyweight title lost a lot of prestige for his failure to deck the middleweight champion, let alone knock him out. Billy had some trouble solving Tony's

111 *Wisconsin State Journal*, Zale Gives Conn 13-Pound Edge, February 8, 1942.
112 *Daily Times-News*, Conn Meets Tony Zale – But Why?, February 9, 1942.

crouching weaving style, but was administering a beating two-thirds of the way through the seventh round that had Tony on rubbery legs, seemingly on the verge of a knockout. But Tony, as tough as advertised, suddenly unleashed a smashing right to the heart and a hard left hook to the mouth. That slowed the bigger man to a walk, and brought a cascade of cheers from the crowd as Billy was then forced to fight on the defensive, while spitting blood for the remainder of the round.

Billy came back and hurt Tony in the ninth and eleventh sessions, but he was unable to put him away. Tony and he were pounding on one another with relatively even terms in the twelfth and final round.[113]

Years later, when asked about the fight with Conn, Tony would complain that he had to force the fight. "He fought like I was the big guy. I had to come to him. He didn't make the fight. That's no way for a fighter to be," he said with disgust.[114]

The Associated Press scored the bout ten rounds to Billy and only two to Tony. Unlike the fight against Louis, when he was the badly outweighed and was the fighter the crowd was rooting for, Billy was the one with all of the physical advantages this time around. He was booed for his failure to stop the smaller middleweight champion as he made his way to his dressing room.[115]

Whatever people thought of this bout, Billy and Tony both went into it looking for a knock-out. Tony, out of necessity, had worked his way through the quality middleweights in the Chicagoland area, so he started working out with light heavyweights.

None of them could hit or move like Billy Conn. Both men, prior to their war effort, were in need of a quality payday. This bout offered entertainment and most importantly, crowd draw. The outcome was a promoter's dream.

Billy went on to receive the much anticipated rematch with Joe Louis, but it didn't come until June 19, 1946; only one day later than the five year anniversary of their first match. Before the second fight someone suggested to Joe that Billy might outpoint him because of

---

113 *Chicago Sun*, Zale Goes The Distance, February 14, 1942.
114 *Sport Magazine*, Tough Tony Zale, March 1966.
115 O'Toole, Andrew, *Sweet William. The Life of Billy Conn*, Illinois Press, Chicago, IL 2008.

superior hand and foot speed, and Joe replied with what became a classic line, "He can run, but he can't hide."[116]

The second fight at Yankee Stadium was the first heavyweight championship ever broadcast on television. It failed to live up to expectations though, as Billy was no longer the fighter he'd been before the war, and Joe caught up with him and knocked him out in the eighth round. Billy's poor performance in the fight earned him the dubious "Flop of the Year" award from the Associated Press for 1946, as 35 writers out of 73 named him as their first pick in the year-end poll.[117]

Billy fought two more times in 1948, before hanging up his gloves for good. He was inducted into the International Boxing Hall of Fame in 1990 and passed away on May 29, 1993, at the age of 75.

Five days after Tony's fight with Conn, on February 18, it was reported that Tony planned to enlist in the armed forces after a month's vacation. He was resting at home in Gary, Indiana, and hadn't yet decided whether he would join the Army or Navy.[118] Two weeks later it was announced the Chicago naval recruiting offices had received authorization from the Great Lakes Naval Training Base, in Illinois, to accept Tony for immediate enlistment as a boxing instructor. Tony hadn't yet applied for enlistment, and the assignment was contingent upon passing a physical examination.[119]

On March 9, it was announced that 28-year-old Tony was to be married on April 11 to Adeline Richwalski, a 19-year-old piano teacher from East Chicago, Indiana. They had become frequent dance partners at PNA dances around the region after meeting on the South Shore commuter train. On one hand it seemed an odd pairing with Tony being a champion boxer and Adeline a classical musician from a wealthy family. But Adeline seemed to understand that Tony was an artist as well. Obviously not in a traditional sense, but in the way that he went about sizing up an opponent to develop a counter to their attack and a strategy to win a fistic contest. It seemed to her that what he described was like a chess match, where one built an

116 *Galveston Daily News*, Joe Louis Tells How He Won Last Fight With Conn, June 10, 1946.
117 *Freeport Journal-Standard*, Conn's Failure Is Rated "Flop Of The Year", December 19, 1946.
118 *Syracuse Herald Journal*, Tony Zale Planning To Enter Service, February 18, 1942.
119 *Wisconsin State Journal*, Navy Says Tony Zale Will Be Accepted, March 9, 1942.

offensive strategy based on anticipated response and a willingness to sacrifice a pawn or two in order to accomplish a greater objective.

She knew the demands of a classical music piece and understood how intense that could be. The practice and dedication involved in achieving perfection was all consuming and she imagined it was like that for Tony as well. Tony saw this as a positive understanding on her part of his chosen profession. He felt she would truly comprehend the sacrifice it would require of them during the early part of their marriage.[120]

When Tony had approached Adeline's father to ask for her hand in marriage, he was surprised when her father tried to talk him out of it. He warned Tony that there was something *not quite right* about her. He told Tony that her behavior could become quite erratic and irrational. But Tony was deeply in love and wouldn't believe it.[121]

It was planned that after their upcoming wedding ceremony, Tony would go to the Great Lakes Naval Base to talk with Lt. Commander J. Russell Cook, the base athletic officer, concerning his probable enlistment.[122]

In early April, it was reported that George Garrett, chairman of the local Navy Relief Chapter in Washington, D.C., planned to talk with boxing promoter Mike Jacobs concerning the possibility of staging a match between Tony and Georgie Abrams. Georgie was stationed with the U.S. Naval Air Station in Jacksonville, Florida, and had volunteered his services at no charge for a naval relief show scheduled in Washington on May 21. He requested he be matched with Tony, but if that was not possible, said he'd like to fight Steve Mamakos. At the same time, followers of a young African-American fighter name Ezzard Charles out of Cincinnati were lobbying for a fight between him and Tony. Charles defeated Billy Pryor for his 25th win in 27 fights, and many considered him a serious contender for the middleweight crown.

Tony enlisted in the Navy on April 9 and was immediately sworn in as a Specialist, First Class. A petty officer had come across the name Anthony Zaleski and noticed he'd listed his occupation as a professional fighter. When Tony arrived, this was the conversation:

"So you're a fighter?" he said. "Who'd you ever fight?"

---

120 Thad Zale interviews with Tony Zale.
121 Thad Zale interviews with Tony Zale.
122 *Capital Times*, Marines Get Barney Ross, Ring Champ, March 10, 1942.

In response, Tony reeled off an impressive list of opponents.

"But I suppose you lost to most of them," said the officer. "Say, we're getting a *real* fighter in here this afternoon, Tony Zale, the world's middleweight champ. How come you never fought him?"[123] Tony replied in one of his rare bursts of humor, "That's one bum I could always lick." One can imagine the poor petty officer's embarrassment when Tony enlightened him to the fact that he was one in the same.

He would now have just two weeks with his new bride before reporting for duty as a boxing instructor on April 27.

On April 11, 1942, two days after his enlistment in the U.S. Navy, Tony and Adeline, or Adele as the Zale family would come to refer to her, were married. The Richwalski-Zale wedding was a grand affair with over 200 guests at the church ceremony and some 500

attending the formal reception. An evening of dining and dancing provided a wonderful opportunity to watch the young couple dance the night away. Both were excellent dancers and really began their serious relationship by attending Polish National Alliance dances together around the region. Their honeymoon though, would be short-lived and spent around the Chicagoland area due to Tony's enlistment in the U.S. Navy. Being together such a short time prior to their wedding, and now with Tony leaving for the service during the war, was not a good omen.

---

123 *Wisconsin State Journal*, It's An Idea Mike Jacobs Might Try, June 11, 1942.

George Foster, coincidentally, the author's father-in-law, recalled witnessing Adeline plowing into a big oak tree as she drove recklessly around the high school in East Chicago, Indiana. The students all watched as several passengers on this joyride poured out of the car. Nobody was hurt seriously, but the car was spitting steam out of the radiator and the front end was severely damaged. The situation was made light of since the car was purportedly Champion Tony Zale's and he was away at training camp. It became a joke around the high school campus. This was another omen of unfortunate things to come.

On May 21, the Naval Relief Show in Washington, D.C., was staged, but Tony was not allowed to participate. So, Georgie Abrams and Steve Mamakos were matched, and Mike Jacobs promised the winner an opportunity to fight Tony for his title. Abrams won a decisive victory over Mamakos, and in early June, discussions were held concerning another Naval Relief show to take place in Chicago, sometime around July 10. It was hoped Tony and Abrams would meet, but those plans were scuttled when Tony was ordered to sea duty later that month.[124]

The possibility of a match between the two men was raised again on July 25 when Sheldon Clark, Chairman of the Illinois Athletic Commission, said plans for a fight were being considered. On August 3, Jacobs announced he'd signed both men for an outdoor fight in Chicago that would be staged in September. But once again the plans had to be cancelled in late August when Tony's manager, Sam Pian, advised that Tony was unable to get enough time off from his naval responsibilities to train for the fight.

On September 17, a day before Jacobs had originally planned to have Tony fight Abrams in Chicago, it was reported that Tony was in route to Norfolk, Virginia, from where he would await transfer for duty. Neither Tony nor fellow champions Joe Louis, Gus Lesnevich, or Freddie Cochrane were able to defend their crowns at the time, as the Army and Navy would not permit them to box. By late November Tony had reported to the Naval Air Station in San Juan, Puerto Rico, where he was in charge of boxing instruction. His new bride of seven months, Adeline, now pregnant, was back at their home in Gary, Indiana.[125]

---

124 *Clovis News Journal*, Sports Roundup, June 25, 1942.
125 *Chicago Daily Tribune*, Tony's a Long Way from Home, December 1, 1942.

THE WAR YEARS

In 1938, Admiral Arthur Hepburn headed a board that became known as the Hepburn Board, and was responsible for reviewing America's national defense structure as international relationships continued to deteriorate. For Puerto Rico, the board recommended the development of a 340-acre site named Isla Grande in the San Juan Harbor as a secondary air base to one in Guantanamo Bay, Cuba. The San Juan base was to contain facilities for one carrier group, two patrol-plane squadrons, complete engine overhaul capabilities, and berthing for one carrier. Congress approved the recommendations in May of 1939, and that October, a fixed-fee contract was awarded for the development of the air station in Puerto Rico.

By June of 1940, with construction already underway, orders were issued to expand the air station so it could accommodate six patrol squadrons and two carrier groups, with additional facilities for the temporary use of two more patrol squadrons.

That September, President Franklin D. Roosevelt appointed another board under the direction of Rear Admiral John W. Greenslade to survey the naval shore establishment with a view toward the maintenance of a two-ocean Navy. In January 1941, that board recommended the development of a major operating base at Puerto Rico as the keystone of the Caribbean defense, with facilities capable of supporting a large portion of the fleet under war conditions. Puerto Rico was to become the "Pearl Harbor of the Caribbean."

In November 1942, San Juan became Tony's home for the next two-and-a-half years. When he arrived, the instructors in charge of training the men quickly realized that he was in outstanding shape and they named him a platoon leader. By the end of basic training,

Tony had helped both his platoon and the entire company reach their peak physical condition. At that point, they were all sent off to Specialty School.

Gary's Tony Zale in Puerto Rico

San Juan, Puerto Rico.—Anthony Florian Zeleski, of Gary, Ind., (left above) otherwise Tony Zale, middleweight champion of the United States, has reported to the Naval Air station here to become part of Lieut. E. R. Bowman's (at right) recreation staff. Zale will have charge of boxing instruction. His rating is that of specialist, first class, and he has been in the navy since last April. His navy training was at the Great Lakes Station, near Chicago. He reported here for duty this week.

Zale got into boxing through the Golden Gloves route almost 10 years ago, and won his Golden Gloves championship in 1934. Shortly thereafter he turned professional and has been in the ring most of the time since. He is the fourth of five brothers, all of whom have done a great deal of boxing in their day, all of them but Tony as amateurs. Tony's last fight, some months ago, was with Billy Conn, light heavyweight, to whom he lost. Mrs. Anthony Florian Zaleski, a bride of seven months, remained at the Gary home. (Official U. S. Navy photograph).

As one might expect, Tony excelled in hand-to-hand combat and the drill instructors began to use him to demonstrate how to dispatch an opponent with one's fists. He began by teaching them how to throw a left jab, and of course, how to throw a right-cross over the left jab of an opponent and add a left hook for a knockout. He also taught the men how to defend themselves against those same punches. He discovered that he was a natural when it came to providing this form of instruction. He just had a knack for breaking the steps down and communicating the information in an easy-to-understand manner.

The fact that Tony was such a humble and genial individual earned him many friends among the non-commissioned men and commissioned officers alike. Those in charge quickly realized how fortunate they were to have him at their disposal, and maximized the use of his skills and temperament to boost the condition and morale of the men.

Tony's days began early and ended late. His work was usually only interrupted with a short break to catch his breath and take in a meal. He taught the men how to box and while doing so, he would analyze their abilities and try to correct any areas of vulnerability that he uncovered. He also matched the men to spar against one another based on their levels of proficiency.

Every once in a while one of the men would have a higher opinion of their boxing ability than they should have. Many would issue a challenge to the reigning middleweight champion of the world. Lucky for them, Tony knew there was a significant difference between an amateur and a seasoned professional, and wouldn't take the challenges seriously.

None, that is, except for one man. There was a light-heavyweight who wouldn't take no for an answer. He kept egging on Tony, daring him to get in the ring with him. He claimed he was the next Billy Conn, and continually urged Tony to spar with him. Tony took the ribbings from the ensign in good humor, but it wore him down, and he finally accepted the challenge.

Before their sparring match occurred, Tony warned the persistent ensign that he would not pull any punches. The ensign told him he would "take his head off," just like Billy Conn had. Tony just smiled as he inserted his mouth guard. The cocky, confident ensign practically ran across the ring when that first bell rang, and immediately began throwing several left jabs. Tony easily slipped the jabs and delivered a solid right to the body that sent the ensign to the canvas. The young man lay there gasping for breath while Tony and the other drill instructors quickly came to his aid. Needless to say, no one at the base ever challenged Tony again.

The duration of Tony's time at the base was spent training the men as well as conducting boxing shows for the entertainment of the troops. While he wasn't able to train as he would have back home, and did not engage in any other sparring himself, he did his best to stay in shape by exercising, running, and working on both the light and heavy bags.

While he and other boxing champions like Joe Louis, Gus Lesnevich and Freddie Cochrane were inactive in the ring as a result of their military service, the governing bodies froze their titles. As a result, other professionals who rose to the top of their respective divisions during the war years became known as "interim" or "duration" champions.

New Yorker Jake LaMotta was one of those men. A fierce fighting middleweight with an ability to absorb tremendous punishment, Jake became known as the "Raging Bull." In early 1943, while Tony was getting his feet wet in Puerto Rico, Jake pulled off an upset when he earned a surprising 10-round decision over previously undefeated "Sugar" Ray Robinson. The loss by Robinson brought an end to his streak of 129 consecutive amateur and professional victories. Robinson entered the ring weighing 144 ½ pounds, 15 ¾ pounds lighter than LaMotta, but Robinson had been a strong favorite.

Not everyone was convinced of Jake's greatness as a result of the victory, though. Columnist Jack Cuddy thought him a mediocre middleweight and said he was confident that Zale would "belt his brains out."[126] Still, only a month later, there was talk of an attempt to match LaMotta with Tony for the middleweight title should he continue to fight as well as he did against Robinson. This, of course, could only occur if a leave of duty could be arranged for Tony. Although it didn't seem likely, there was some thought that the Navy might go along with the idea if the bout could be staged as a military benefit.[127]

LaMotta wasn't the only man yearning for a shot at Tony's title. In late April of 1943, Georgie Abrams, himself serving as an instructor for the U.S. Navy, said he'd love another shot at Tony. Georgie suffered an eye injury in the second round of his fight with Tony in 1941, and figured he would make out better the second time around.

"Zale was just a blur to me after the second round, but I waited so long for a chance at the title that I wanted to keep going," he said. "Some of the doctors said I wouldn't be able to see again in the injured eye, but it's as good as ever now. I don't know when it will be, but I sure would like to have another crack at Zale. I've never lost in a rematch and I don't think I'd lose this one."[128]

But the U.S. Navy turned thumbs down on any leaves or any championship bouts, so Abrams and all the other title aspirants would have to wait.

In the meantime, Gary, Indiana, was booming during the war. The Gary Works Steel Mill was operating at full capacity, with women holding down many of the mill jobs vacated by men in uniform. More folks were arriving in the city than those departing, and there was a housing shortage as a result.[129]

While Tony was in Puerto Rico the first year, Adeline gave birth to the couple's first child, a daughter named Mary Alena. Tony finally had an opportunity to meet the newborn, and spend some time with his young family when he received a furlough from duty. He returned home for a short visit in November of 1943. While home, when interviewed by the local newspaper concerning his

---

126 *Brainerd Daily Dispatch*, LaMotta Climbs Scale in Upset Robinson Bout, February 6, 1943.
127 *The Daily News*, Sport Window, March 3, 1943.
128 *Ogden Standard-Examiner*, George Abrams Uses Right Hand to Work Out Sketches, April 26, 1943.
129 *Traces Magazine*, The Man of Steel With a Heart of Gold, Spring 2007.

future boxing plans, Tony said that he had no thoughts of defending his title until the war was over.[130]

While home, he and Adeline hosted Tony's brothers and sisters for card games during Thanksgiving and the pre-Christmas holidays. Tony was so proud to show off baby Mary that he couldn't wait to have them all come over to celebrate and play pinochle.

That afternoon, Adeline appreciated all the compliments concerning the baby, but she was really more interested in establishing a baby-sitting network with all of the nieces in the Zale family. She seemed to make a point to separately speak with each sister-in-law independently with the aim of enlisting enough help that would enable her to re-launch her music career. By the time she was finished, she realized she could literally get twenty-four hour babysitting coverage, regardless of what Tony was doing.

That evening, she and Tony were playing pinochle with Tony's brother Joe and his wife Frances, while their daughter Lucille cared for Mary. In the middle of the card game, Adeline stood up from the table, turned and abruptly ran out the door muttering something unintelligible. Tony, Joe and Frances immediately looked at each other in amazement and thought that they had done something to offend her. Frances thought that her taking the bid and calling for diamonds as trump may have been the reason for the sudden departure. They all got up from the dining room table and told Lucille to please stay with the baby and they would be back shortly because they needed to find Adeline before it became too dark.

The three returned some thirty minutes later without Adeline. Each of them had taken a separate direction, east, west and north, in their search, but had no luck locating her. Joe and Tony then decided to head south this time. They walked the area with each taking a different street. But once again, they returned home empty handed. Joe asked Tony what this was all about, but Tony was at a total loss for an explanation. He told Joe that the same thing had happened when their brother John and his wife Jeanette were over earlier in the week. That time, they had found Adeline hiding behind a fence at a neighboring house two or three doors south of them. She had given no reason for her departure and they were confused by her behavior. She thought it was all perfectly normal to hide from them.

---

130 *Wisconsin Rapids Daily Tribune*, Zale Won't Defend Title Until War Ends, November 12, 1943.

Tony and Joe continued to search to no avail. After a time, they decided it was best to return to the house. As they were walking, Joe, as the oldest brother, suggested that Tony "be gentle and loving" when Adeline returned. "Be as understanding as you can, because there is obviously something wrong," was his brotherly advice to Tony.

When Tony and Joe arrived home, Adeline and Frances stood at the door waiting for them. Tony greeted her with a kiss on the cheek and asked where she had gone. She said she needed some air and all of a sudden felt closed in. Tony, Joe and Frances said they understood, but asked her not to run out of the house like that again. Joe and Frances left with Lucille without completing the card game.

During that year, it did not take long for all of the sisters-in-law to begin comparing their common experiences when trying to befriend Adeline. No one in the family could understand her odd behaviors. They all agreed to continue to try to help her if they could. The confusion over her actions would even become more pronounced as reports circulated around the Zale family about the experiences many of the nieces had while babysitting for her. This was compounded over the next several years by concerns they shared with their parents about what they believed was abuse of the children.

Jeanette Zale-Stachura related one of her experiences concerning the care for young Mary and second daughter, baby Teresa. When Jeanette was dropped off by her father to babysit, Adeline was on the porch alone waiting for her. Jeanette asked where the children were, and Adeline told her they were in the basement washtubs. Jeanette immediately headed downstairs where she found the two children, in water, in the washtubs. Her first thought of them was that they could have drowned. Why would Adeline leave them alone in such a precarious situation? This was not the first time that Jeanette arrived and found the children unsupervised inside as Adeline waited on the porch for her arrival.

Lillian Kordys-Lopez related a story of a time when she was assisting Adeline with the children, and Tony came home from training camp unexpectedly early. Lillian, playing with the children, saw Tony enter the front door, set down his suitcase, and greet the children warmly with a lot of hugs and kisses. As Adeline heard the commotion, she came in from the kitchen and screamed to Tony at the top of her voice "Damn you!" She ran to Tony and actually tore the shirt off of his back saying he wasn't supposed to be home yet. Buttons flew everywhere. Everyone stood in shock. This was the last time Lillian ever babysat for her uncle. She had no desire to experience anything like that again.

Tony was back on base in San Juan by December 1, 1943. To help pass the time in his absence, Adeline continued to play her music. Her name appeared in the social section of the newspaper in East Chicago as a result of accompanying professional singers on the piano at various womens social events. By January of 1944, it was announced that she had returned to her profession of concert pianist under the name, "Adele Rich." Clearly, the talented musician had professional ambitions of her own, and Tony and the rest of the Zale clan would come to learn just how ambitious those plans really were.

In February of 1944, word reached the States that there was a talented French middleweight serving his own country, named Marcel Cerdan, who had made quite an impression in the Allied North African boxing championships who could present Tony with quite a challenge if the war ended anytime soon. It was said that he had made a big impression upon American boxers Jack Sharkey and Fidel LaBarba with his performances in the tournament.

At the time, Marcel was recognized as the middleweight champion of Europe by the International Boxing Union. The British Board of Boxing wouldn't go that far, but conceded he was the best French middleweight. The 26-year-old, who had reportedly won 101 of 103 professional bouts, was serving in the French military at the time, but wrote *The Ring* editor Nat Fleischer, expressing his intention to bring his wares over to the Americas for a go with its top middleweights, providing he wasn't too old by the time the war ended.[131] Meanwhile, Jake LaMotta continued to make a name for himself back home, and claimed the "duration" middleweight crown. Rocky Graziano was also making quite a name for himself in New York's boxing arenas. When he was asked if he could beat LaMotta, Rocky replied, "I could always beat him in reform school."

By July 1, 1944, Tony was home for another brief furlough before reporting for duty at the Norfolk Virginia Naval Station. Tony said that his boxing skills had atrophied as a result of inactivity. The reason for this was he refused to get into the ring and hurt any of the many young amateur fighters that he was training. "I couldn't

---

131 *Reno Evening Gazette*, French Sailor May be Champ, Threat to Zale, February 22, 1944.

box with the kids," he said. "I have to wade in and punch. I can't hold back. If I started pulling my punches to protect the kids, I would never get over the habit. I would have lost my punch. So I simply didn't fight. The war years took its toll on me." [132]

On August 15, it was reported that Marcel Cerdan would arrive in the United States within the next two weeks with the intention of fighting Jake LaMotta in Madison Square Garden in late September. A Montreal promoter named Armond Vincent believed American fans would love him because of his punching and his modest personality. He was confident that Marcel could defeat LaMotta. He also believed that should Marcel do so, the U.S. Navy would permit Tony to defend his title against him. [133]

That November, Tony was busy teaching boxing skills to the Navy recruits as the senior boxing instructor in Virginia. At the time, he believed that some of the nation's best boxing talent would emerge from the amphibious forces once the War ended.

"Some of the boys I get are naturals," he said, "and could become championship material with a little development." [134]

That Christmas, Tony was able to surprise his wife when he received a brief furlough and arrived home on Christmas Day to celebrate the holiday with his family. It was a joyous occasion, and there was reason to hope that the war might not last much longer. But once the holidays were over, Tony returned to Virginia where he carried out his duties into the late fall of 1945. He was soon thereafter honorably discharged.

---

132 *Traces Magazine*, The Man of Steel With a Heart of Gold, Spring 2007.
133 *Brainerd Daily Dispatch*, Sports Parade, August 15, 1944.
134 *Gazette and Bulletin*, Soose, Zale and Cochrane Toughen Tars for Big Scrap, November 11, 1944.

December 29, 1945

RETURNING TO THE RING

The summer of 1945 was one full of hope and optimism for the majority of folks in the United States. After all the sacrifices and misery associated with the war, people were anxious to move on with their lives. Sports fans eagerly anticipated the return of all the popular sporting figures from the various branches of military service. The country had enjoyed what many claimed was the greatest decade in sports history, the "roaring twenties" after World War I, when the exploits of men like Babe Ruth, Red Grange, Jack Dempsey and Bill Tilden filled the sports pages, and with the return of huge stars such as Joe Louis, Billy Conn, Joe Dimaggio, Ted Williams, Tony Zale and many, many others, it appeared as though the dawn of another spectacular era of sports had arrived.

The first thing Tony did after he was discharged from the navy was return home to Gary, Indiana, to enjoy a brief vacation with Adele, his two-year old daughter Mary, and become acquainted with his second newborn daughter Teresa, who was born in late August of 1945. As was usual with Tony, he continued the navy regimen of rising early. He continued to work out between reunions with his mother Catherine, his siblings and their families.

In the midst of his new life back in Gary, his brothers began to inform him about the many rumors that were now circulating about Adele and the resumption of her musical career. Brothers Joe and John were the most concerned about how Tony would react to what was being said about his wife. Brothers Frank and Walter decided to stay out of it, but provided information to Joe and John about things that they had heard. This was not the way Tony had hoped to resume his married life and in his humble fashion, he listened to the rumors, but refused to believe any of the negative implications. This would ultimately take a toll on him and his marriage. Now though, he just simply wanted to enjoy the time with his new baby, his two-year old daughter, and Adele. He was in a state of denial, and understandably so.

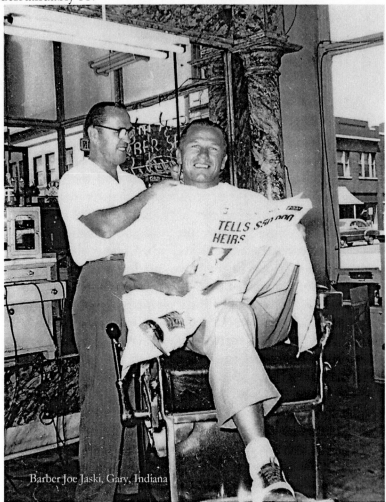

Barber Joe Jaski, Gary, Indiana

In 1988, the Champ wrote a personal letter about this puzzling time in his marriage during 1945. Here he was, just home from the service and enjoying his daughters, when Adeline got angry with him for the way he changed a diaper. She deliberately kneed him in the groin and then once the children were napping, wanted him to make love to her. This occurred two or three more times shortly after the first incident. He decided that her masochistic behavior was not in the best interest of their marriage and refused her further sexual advances. This created more internal conflict for Tony than he ever imagined. He began to think he was better off at training camp.

Tony had resumed his professional relationship with Art and Sam after his return home. In mid-October, N.B.A. President Abe Greene announced that all champions had been notified that they were going to be required to defend their titles. This order meant that they would defend against valid contenders once they had received a proper period of time in which to get themselves into condition. He said that three of the champions, including Tony, Joe Louis, and Gus Lesnevich, would receive a full period of rest because they had each just got out of the military.

Logical contenders for Tony's middleweight title included Jake LaMotta, Georgie Abrams, Holman Williams and Rocky Graziano. The latter, Graziano, was a New York middleweight who had been relatively unknown only a year earlier. He enjoyed a meteoric rise in the rankings as a result of knockout victories over Billy Arnold, Solomon Stewart, "Bummy" Davis, welterweight champion Freddie Cochrane (twice), and Harold Green during the year. Rocky was named the best new fighter of the year by *The Ring* magazine, and received honorable mention for their annual Boxer of the Year Award.

In early December, the N.B.A. notified Tony that he must sign up for a championship bout by June 1. On December 3, Freddie Sommers, a Kansas City boxing promoter, announced that Tony would make his return to the ring in that city in a ten-round overweight contest on January 9. He would fight against the winner of a December 12 fight between Deacon Logan and former welterweight champion, Fritzie Zivic. Two weeks later, however, Sommers advised that Tony's opponent would instead be an African-American club fighter out of Buffalo, New York, named Bobby Giles, and the two men would fight on January 7. It was a practical choice for Tony and his managers, given the amount of time he'd been out of the ring.

As expected, the fight didn't prove very difficult for Tony. Giles kept Tony off with a long stabbing left jab in the first two rounds, but Tony drove him to the ropes in the third round, and began to find the mark. He put Giles down twice, before landing a series of body shots that kept him down for the full count at one minute and 33 seconds of the fourth round. Afterward, his co-manager, Art Winch, said, "He had a little trouble with his timing but after another four or five fights he will attain his true fighting edge. He can still punch."

Ten days later, Tony was back in action in the City Auditorium in Norfolk, Virginia, where he knocked out another journeyman named Tony Gillo in the fifth round of a scheduled ten-round contest. Tony had dropped Gillo for a count of seven in the preceding round, and finished him off only 45 seconds into the fifth session. Tony weighed 162 ½ pounds for the fight, while Gillo came in at 165.

Oscar Boyd of Buffalo, New York, was next on the tune-up parade of opponents for Tony, and he went down by way of a third round knockout in Des Moines, Iowa, before 5,000 fans on February 7, 1946. For the first time since his return to the ring, Tony weighed in under the middleweight limit of 160 pounds, coming in at 159 pounds, compared to Boyd's 166 ½. The Champ was back.

Later that month, on February 26, Tony fought Bobby Claus in Houston, Texas, for promoter Ralph Smith. Smith was hopeful of signing Tony to defend his title in Houston in June. Tony softened Claus up during the first three rounds of their match, and then sent him down for the first time in the fourth round for a count of nine with a straight right hand blow to the chest. Claus had barely regained his feet, when Tony landed another right that sent him through the ropes. Claus climbed back into the ring, but Tony quickly delivered another right that brought an end to his night, one minute and 35 seconds into the round.

On March 1, it was reported that Johnny Buckley, the manager of New England middleweight Al "Red" Priest, had offered Tony $25,000 to defend his title sometime within the next month in Boston against Priest. Priest had only lost one bout at that point in his career, and had recently defeated former welterweight champion, Fritzie Zivic in a 10-round decision in the Boston Garden in January. In all likelihood, Tony would have handed Priest his second loss, but he wasn't the kind of tune-up Tony's team was interested in, as he continued to work his way toward a more lucrative title match that coming summer.

So Tony signed to fight in Omaha, Nebraska, on March 25, against an opponent yet to be determined. Ira Hughes was ultimately selected as the other man, but the fight had to be delayed when Tony suffered a sprained ankle. The bout was re-scheduled for April 12.

Meanwhile, Thomas Rocco Barbella, aka Rocky Graziano, continued to make a name for himself and was quickly becoming the man that everyone wanted to see fight Tony for the middleweight title that summer. Rocky had earned a unanimous decision over

Sonny Horne in Madison Square Garden on January 18, and followed that up by blasting welterweight champion Marty Servo out in the second round of a non-title fight in the same venue on March 29. Some were referring to Graziano as "Rockabye" Rocky as a result of his penchant for putting his opponents to sleep. There was a strong belief that the next time he would be seen in a ring, it would be against Tony Zale, for the middleweight championship of the world. Well-known New York promoter, James Johnston, was already picturing Rocky as the coming champion. "He oughta knock out Tony Zale," said Johnston, after witnessing Rocky's destruction of Servo.

By March 31, it was being reported that Tony had already been signed to defend his title against any one of five challengers, with Rocky's name heading the list. All that remained to make the fight a reality for what was expected to be one of the richest middleweight championship fights in history was to obtain Rocky's signature on the contract. As that match continued to take shape, it was announced that Tony would fight in Memphis, Tennessee, on May 2, against an opponent yet to be determined.

Then, on April 3, promoter Mike Jacobs confirmed that Tony would fight Rocky for the title when he issued a statement announcing that the pair had been matched to meet in Yankee Stadium on July 25 for a 15-round title bout. He anticipated the event would produce a gate of more than half-a-million dollars. It would be the first time that an undisputed world middleweight champion had defended that title since 1927.

On April 12, in the City Auditorium in Omaha, Nebraska, Tony kept his string of knockouts alive since returning from the service by stopping Ira Hughes in the second round of a scheduled ten-round non-title bout. The Champ basically toyed with his over-matched opponent in the first round, before knocking him out in the second session.

In late April, Eddie Rossi was tabbed as the man who would face Tony in Memphis, Tennessee, on May 2, in his last bout before defending the title against Graziano. Rossi was a top ranking middleweight in New England and former Golden Gloves and AAU champion from that region of the country.

The day before Tony's bout with Rossi, it was reported that his wife, Adele, had filed for divorce on April 30. Her charges against

Tony were "cruelty." She asked for $50,000 in alimony and $500 in monthly support for herself and their two young daughters.

Tony had discovered serious allegations of child abuse through his brother John, and though warned by John not to act hastily, Tony brought the concerns directly to Adele.

His marital problems undoubtedly weighing heavily on his mind, Tony climbed into the ring on May 2, to face Eddie Rossi in the Memphis Auditorium in front of 3,000 fans. He knocked out his sixth straight opponent since his discharge from the service when he stopped Rossi in the fourth round. Tony, who weighed 160 pounds, to Rossi's 165, missed often with his punches and his timing was off from long range. He depended on a vicious body attack to soften Rossi up for the knockout blow.

In late June, popular columnist Walter Winchell wrote that while Tony was going to defend his title against Rocky Graziano in Yankee Stadium the next month, he had no plans to contest his wife's divorce actions. Tony continued to try and breech the gap that had been formed by their early April confrontation, but was unsure who this person he married had become.

Before he left for the service, she was like an angel. Now, he no longer recognized who she was. In the same personal journal he'd written in 1988, Tony noted that Adeline's own mother, in a private discussion with him, had advised him not to reconcile with her. She had just divorced Adeline's father for adultery and warned Tony that "she had many of his tendencies."

ROCKY GRAZIANO

Like Tony, Rocky Graziano was tough as nails, but other than the fact that neither came from what you would call affluent families, that's really where the similarities ended between the two men. While Tony was a quiet, gentle and humble, but well-spoken young man outside the ring, Rocky was a brash, cocky youngster with a chip on his shoulder the size of a boulder. He used terms like "dem" and "dat" in place of "them" and "that." Tony was admired by the press for the way he fought, but was a man of few words, and far from what anyone would consider a colorful figure to interview and write about. Rocky, on the other hand, was the polar opposite. A juvenile delinquent from the Lower East Side of New York, Rocky was as colorful as they came. You couldn't dream up a story any more entertaining than his. In fact, it was so good that his autobiography, *Somebody Up There Likes Me,* became a best seller in 1955 and was made into a movie by the same title starring Paul Newman a year later.

Born on January 1, 1919, Thomas Rocco Barbella became a stereotypical product of his environment. Both of his parents drank, and his father, a former professional boxer known as "Fighting Nick Bob," used to get drunk with his cronies. He made three year old Rocco put on the gloves with his six year old brother Joey, and laughed and cheered as Joey knocked the stuffing out of the little guy. His father hoped that Joey would one day become a great fighter and urged him on as Rocky served as a tearful punching bag.

Rocky's father was typically out of work and the family was extremely poor. Rocky didn't seem to think school was the place to be and was a frequent truant. When he did attend school, he was constantly in trouble and stole other kids' lunches. Of course, he was in even more trouble outside of school where he and his fellow delinquents stole food, coal to heat their families' apartments, and anything else of value they could get their hands on.

When his mother suffered a nervous breakdown and his father was unable to control him, Rocky was sent to live with his grandparents. But his thieving ways continued and at age 11, he was sent to a Catholic protectory after stealing a bike. It was there that he finally learned to read and write and received his initial boxing lessons from the school's athletic instructor. A year later, he was sent back home to live with his father, Joe, and two younger sisters in a small tenement. At age 15, he was sent back to the Catholic protectory for a second term, but broke out after only five months. Rocky spent the majority of his time from the ages of 14 to 17 running his own gang of young hoodlums on the Lower East Side. He robbed stores and he robbed people. Later he would say that they only stole things beginning with an 'A': a piece of fruit, a watch, a pair of shoes, a bicycle.

At age 17, Rocky was finally sentenced to jail time after he and his friends robbed a school, and two years later he was leading the toughest gang in the New York City Reformatory, also known as "The Farms." Once he was released from the reformatory, his buddies tried to talk him into representing a local boys club in an upcoming amateur tournament in place of a kid who was sick. Rocky resisted initially, but then agreed to meet the boy's trainer, Cus D'Amato, a man who later achieved fame as the manager of champions Floyd Patterson, Jose Torres, and Mike Tyson.[135]

D'Amato had heard a lot about Rocky, but when he watched Rocky work out with one of his friends, he found it hard to believe he was the same kid who had knocked out some 40 to 50 kids on the streets. He didn't seem to know how to fight at all. While Rocky and the other kid were still fooling around in the ring, Cus pulled one of Rocky's friends aside and asked him how Rocky got into so many fights on the street.

"Oh," he answered, "every time we have a fight in the neighborhood between blocks, Rocky's the leader. We go over there and the leaders meet and start talking."

"And then what happens?" Cus asked.

---

135 Graziano, Rocky, *Somebody Up There Likes Me*, Simon and Schuster, New York, New York, 1955.

As the kid demonstrated what happened, he imitated Rocky's actions. Cus realized that just before Rocky hits the other fellow, he put his arms down, just enough to make the other fellow unsuspecting. Then with his hands on his hips, it looked as though he wasn't going to do anything to cause any trouble.

They continued to talk and Rocky had his arms down to keep the guy he's talking to from expecting anything to happen. Then, while the other guy was listening, suddenly, Boom! Like a bomb. Rocky would lay the guy out. One punch and the guy would be gone.

He was hitting guys when they weren't looking, when they didn't expect it: sneak-punching. Since he carried such a good punch, the guys he hit didn't provide any opposition, they just went down. If they got up, he knocked them down again, and it was all over. Cus believed that was the real reason that Rocky didn't want to box, because he didn't have the confidence that 40 to 50 victories in "fair" fights would have given him. Since, he wasn't a bad looking fellow he didn't want to spoil his looks. Rocky said the same thing in his autobiography, about not wanting to get his face messed up by boxing.

Cus told him that if he did as he taught him, he'd never get hurt. So Rocky agreed to let Cus train him, but he asked him not to tell anyone. So Cus told him to come in at 2 o'clock every afternoon because the others didn't come in until four, and he trained Rocky for three to four months.[136]

Rocky fought in that tournament in place of the sick boy and ended up winning the welterweight title. All of a sudden, a number of gangsters and retired fighters were all trying to convince him to become a professional fighter, and to let them manage him. This included his father too. A fellow known as Lupo the Wolf offered Rocky what he thought was the best deal. He wouldn't have to train, there would be little waiting period between matches, and anytime he fought he would receive $10 to $15. So Rocky had a number of fights under Lupo, but under the name Rocky Graziano instead of Rocco Barbella. Many people had no idea he was fighting for money, including his own parents. He was an especially crude fighter, with no style whatsoever, rarely using a jab. He just came out and tried to kill his opponent, and he always had a hard right hand punch.

---

136 D'Amato, *Making Neighborhood Heroes*, Community Documentation Workshop, New York, New York, 1982.

But then Rocky was arrested for a crime he said he didn't commit and was sent back to the New York City Reformatory for another stretch. When he got out, he went back to fighting for Lupo the Wolf. Then one day, another fellow named Eddie Coco arranged to have one of his men pick up Rocky for a fight instead of Lupo. Rocky was told that he was fighting for him now. That lasted until the mother of his sixteen year old girlfriend accused him of statutory rape and he found himself again back in the reformatory shortly after New Year's Day 1941. At the reformatory, he was accused of being one of the parties that incited a riot and was transferred to Riker's Island where he served out the rest of his time.

Shortly after Rocky was released from Rikers Island, he was inducted into the army and sent to Fort Dix in New Jersey. But Rocky and the army mixed like oil and water. While the other five young men rose early in the morning as they were instructed for breakfast and drills, Rocky simply rolled over in his bunk and went back to sleep. When a corporal came to the tent later in the morning and ordered Rocky to address him as 'Sir' and commanded him to pick up a cigarette butt on the ground outside the tent, Rocky hauled off and belted him in the head, sending him sprawling to the ground. Rocky grabbed him by the collar, pulled him to his feet, slapped him around a bit, and told him that he was the one running this tent and that if he ratted on him, he'd receive more of the same treatment.

He left the base and went to town without a pass and couldn't understand why any of the creeps from his tent wouldn't join him. The military police eventually came to his tent, and hauled him in to see the base captain. Once they arrived at the office, the captain dismissed the MPs and told them he'd call them if they were needed. The captain was seated behind his desk.

"Soldier," he said, "I see by your record you're from New York City."

"Yah," replied Rocky.

"You mean Yes, sir!" said the captain.

"Yah. Yes, sir," said Rocky.

"And I see from the way you talk you're like all the rest of those Jews and Italians from New York City. We got to teach you a lesson, and knock some of that New York out of you. There's no place in this man's army for a wise guy. Understand?"

"Listen, you bum, you may be a captain and all that, but you don't impress me so hot. If you think you're tough, come on outside and I'll fight you," Rocky replied.

"Soldier, are you crazy?" said the captain.

"Maybe I'm crazy, but at least I ain't yellow," said Rocky.

The captain rose from his chair and Rocky thought he was going to come at him right then and there. He drew back his right hand and immediately clipped the captain with a hard right to the jaw and knocked him cold. Only then did it occur to Rocky that the captain was really only reaching for the phone to call the MPs.

Rocky wasn't sure what to do. He walked back through the outside office where everyone was working and nobody paid him any attention. So Rocky just continued walking and left the base. He deserted the army and went back home. Of course, he was eventually caught and taken to military prison. Then he was released on his own recognizance and instructed to immediately report to Fort Dix. But what does Rocky do instead? That's right. He goes back home and doesn't let anybody in on his situation. Eventually he goes back to boxing, but now it's for a new manager, a man by the name of Irving Cohen.

Cohen was a soft spoken, shy, pudgy little man with blue eyes and thinning red hair. He and his wife used to run a small dry goods store that was burglarized and stripped of all inventory. Forced to start over, the couple decided to specialize in women's wear, and his wife decided he was of little use in the store and suggested he take it easy. Irving, who used to box as an amateur, decided to try and get in shape at a Jewish Community Center in Brooklyn. Pretty soon he began to give boxing lessons to some of the boys for fun. Eventually he started handling some of the boys in amateur tournaments, and when some of them turned professional, they asked him to manage them. He resisted initially, knowing little about the professional game, but he caught on quickly and built up a stable of fighters.

Irving said that one day, one of his fighters brought Rocky in to meet him. Irving had heard about him and knew that a few others including Chris Dundee had tried working with him, but quickly gave up on the undisciplined youngster. Irving decided to give him a try anyway. He was extremely crude, but Irving saw something in Rocky and was determined to stick with him.[137]

Just like before, Rocky refused to train, and basically just showed up to fight. But he couldn't hide forever, especially in such a high profile profession, and one day as he was weighing in for a fight, two MPs show up to arrest him. He was escorted to Fort Dix where he received a dishonorable discharge, and was sentenced to a year of hard labor in the Fort Leavenworth, Kansas, prison.

While serving his sentence at Fort Leavenworth, Rocky finally started to grow up a bit. He began to realize that he'd been his own worst enemy, in many cases, and made some very good friends among the officers once he made the prison's boxing team. By the time he was discharged, he was in the best shape of his life. He resumed his boxing career under Irving Cohen's management, and with the assistance of his younger sister, met the woman he would marry and actually settle down with. He realized he could make a good living as a boxer and lost all interest in the criminal activities of his past. By 1943, he went so far as to try to become reinstated in the army, but he was turned down because of his criminal record.

By the end of 1944, Rocky had a wife and a baby daughter. He became more serious about boxing as a career. It never changed the way he fought though, as soon as the bell rang. When, it was only he and his opponent within the ring, he was out to kill that other fellow. His style, while crude, was pleasing to the crowd. They were eager for action and always appreciated an aggressive fighter who carried a punch. There were some setbacks along the way. For example, the times he lost two consecutive bouts to Harold Green by decision in Madison Square Garden in late 1944. Rocky's bouts produced very good gates, and Green barely escaped a knockout at the end of their second fight, though he won by a decision.

Rocky's big break came in March of 1945, when he received an opportunity to fight Billy Arnold in Madison Square Garden. Up until that point in time, the only blemish on Arnold's record was a majority decision loss to Fritzie Zivic. Some were calling the 19 year old a second Joe Louis, and he was established as a six to one favorite entering the bout with Rocky.

Cohen and Rocky's trainer, Whitey Bimstein, weren't sure Rocky was ready to tackle a fighter like Arnold. In fact, Irving said Arnold looked too tough and he wanted no part of him. But since Rocky had lost two fights to Green, he was a little desperate. He kept stalling Madison Square Garden's matchmaker, Nat Rogers, when

Nat tried to schedule the contest. Rocky knew what was going on and said to Irving:

"Did you make the match with Arnold?"

"Why do you want to fight him?" Irving asked. "What makes you think you can beat him?"

"Because he don't run," Rocky replied.

"But, he punches," said Irving.

"I punch too," Rocky said. "Don't worry about punchers. If you want to worry, worry about runners. Anybody that can punch, you get him. Get Arnold."[138]

So Irving made the match. He and Whitey made Rocky promise that he would train properly. For the first time in Rocky's career, he went away to a training camp to prepare for the contest.[139]

On March 9, 1945, Rocky and Billy Arnold met before 14,037 fans at the Garden. Rocky weighed 152 pounds for the bout, compared to Arnold's 149 ¾. Rocky surprised the crowd, winning the first round by a wide margin as he landed several swings to Arnold's head and roughed him up. But Arnold came back strong in the second round, opening a gash over Rocky's left brow and bloodying his nose. By the end of the session, it appeared certain that he'd stop Rocky as he had so many of his other opponents.

But the roof fell in on young Arnold in the third round. It started out innocently enough, with Arnold sharpshooting at Rocky's bleeding brow from long range, but then while trying to pull away from one of Rocky's wild swings, Arnold didn't pull back quite far enough and a hard right exploded on his chin. Down went Arnold. He was dropped two more times in the round before Referee Frankie Fullam stepped in to save him from any further punishment at the 1:54 mark of the round. The crowd, that included Vice President Harry Truman, produced a gate of $49,997 for the event.[140]

The press ate up Rocky's story, calling him an underprivileged East Side kid who'd punched his way out of the gutter. Popular sports columnist proclaimed Rocky the new Stanley Ketchel. Ketchel was one of the greatest middleweight champions of all time

---

138 *Sport* magazine, I'll Take Tony Zale, March 1947.

139 Graziano, Rocky, *Somebody Up There Likes Me*, Simon and Schuster, New York, New York, 1955.

140 *Dunkirk Evening Observer*, Graziano Kayoes Billy Arnold In The Third Round, March 10, 1945.

and died in the prime of his career in 1910. Another scribe said Rocky was the deadliest killer in the ring since Jack Dempsey.[141]

Rocky was on his way. He knocked out Solomon Stewart a month later in Washington, D.C.; then he stopped Al "Bummy" Davis, welterweight Freddie Cochrane twice in two overweight matches, and avenged his defeats against Harold Green by knocking him out in the third round over the course of the rest of the year. The latter four fights were all fought in Madison Square Garden and solidified Rocky's popularity with the fans in that area.

He opened 1946 with a unanimous decision victory over Sonny Horne in the Garden on January 18, and then knocked out the new welterweight champion, Marty Servo, in another overweight match at the Garden on March 29.

And just like that, charismatic Rocky Graziano became the fighter that Mike Jacobs decided would be the ideal opponent to fight for Tony Zale's title. He was the guy that more of the fans wanted to see in action, and would help produce the largest gate. Less than a month later, Jacobs made it official, announcing that Rocky would be Tony's opponent in Yankee Stadium. The stage was set for the first of what would ultimately become one of the greatest trilogies in boxing history.

141 Graziano, Rocky, *Somebody Up There Likes Me*, Simon and Schuster, New York, New York, 1955.

ZALE vs. GRAZIANO I

The first fight for the middleweight championship of the world between Tony Zale and Rocky Graziano was scheduled to take place in Yankee Stadium on July 25, 1946. The event would mark the first defense of the undisputed middleweight world title in almost 17 years, since Mickey Walker defeated Ace Hudkins in 1929.

Tony arrived in New York on July 8, and spoke briefly with a number of sportswriters before he continued on to Pompton Lakes, New Jersey, to train for the contest. He told them that while he had never seen Rocky fight, he wasn't disturbed by talk of his punching power because he had won the title from Al Hostak, another big puncher, whom he considered a harder and straighter puncher. Rocky was already training at Greenwood Lake, New Jersey.[142]

The *Saturday Evening Post* described Rocky as "the most sensational knockout walloper, and the hottest box-office attraction in the ring business below the heavyweight class." Joe Williams of the *New York World-Telegram* predicted that the fight between Rocky and Tony would draw one of the ten largest gates in the history of boxing.[143] Both men were much better known for their offensive skills than their defense and the public was anticipating an entertaining knockdown brawl. The fighters signed formal contracts on July 17, and it was reported that Rocky would receive 25% of the gate, while the Champion would receive 35%. Rocky was immediately installed as a 12-5 favorite to defeat Tony. For the first time in recent memory, the contract didn't contain a clause guaranteeing the Champion a return match should the challenger win the title.[144]

Tony, who may have been a little irked by all the attention Rocky was receiving and the fact that the majority of folks assumed Rocky would win the fight, announced he would knock Rocky out inside of six rounds. "All I want to know is who did Graziano ever kill?" Tony said. "So he's a puncher. A puncher has to go to an opponent, and if he comes to me as I expect, I'll knock him out inside of six rounds. I hope he does. If he doesn't come to me, and tries to be cute in there, I'll go catch him and I'll have him out along about the sixth."[145] Tony's managers, Art Winch and Sam Pian, backed him up, wagering $5,000 that Tony would defeat Rocky.[146]

When Rocky was told of Tony's remarks, he said he expected to defeat Tony, and grinned when he added that body punching was Tony's most effective style of fighting, and he planned to give as much as he took.[147]

---

142 *Syracuse Herald*, Tony Zale Takes Over Pompton Lake Camp To Train for His Fight With Rocky Graziano, July 9, 1946.

143 *Berkshire Evening Eagle*, The Referee's Sporting Chat, July 13, 1946.

144 *Walla Walla Union Bulletin*, Middleweights Stand Chance For Survival, July 18, 1946.

145 *Walla Walla Union Bulletin*, Tony Zale Claims He Will Flatten Rockabye Rocky, July 19, 1946.

146 *Laredo Times*, Managers Back Tony Zale, July 19, 1946.

147 *Wisconsin State Journal*, Graziano Says He'll Beat Zale at Own Game, July 19, 1946.

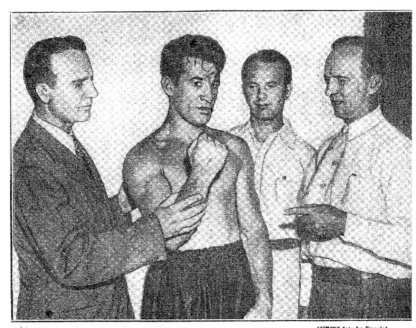

Ready to Set Zale. John, Walter and Joe Zale (l. to r) size up Rocky Graziano in Stillman's gym yesterday. They scouted Rocky for brother Tony, who meets Graziano Thursday.

(NEWS foto by Engels)

Winch said Tony had been running four miles every morning and sparring six rounds every day and claimed Tony felt strong and always wanted to box more at the end of every session. They planned to stay at the Pompton Lakes Camp right up until the morning of the fight, when they would drive into New York for the weigh-in at the commission office. Ray Arcel had been brought in to assist with Tony's training. Tony had a bad right elbow and Ray would stay up at night massaging it for him. Just a week away from the fight, the odds in Rocky's favor had dropped a bit and were being reported as anywhere from 9-5 to 7-5 as Tony continued to gain more support among the betting fraternity. It was anticipated that Tony would outweigh the challenger by approximately six pounds, 159-153, and enjoy a small advantage in height, but Rocky had the advantage in years, being over five years younger. Both men were reportedly in excellent condition, and on July 22, the ABC and NBC networks each announced their plans to televise the bout.

Fight fans everywhere were disappointed on July 23, however, when it was announced that the contest was going to be postponed because Tony had suffered an attack of inter-costal neuritis, an inflation of his ribcage caused by a virus, and the fight was going to be pushed back to a date of September 26. Tony first felt the pain following his workout on July 20. He was given hot applications at the source of the pain, but the condition worsened over the next few days. He insisted he be allowed to go forward with the fight, but he was overruled by his managers. Tony was on his way home to Gary, Indiana, a day later, on July 24, to receive treatment. Ultimately, the date of the fight was pushed back an additional day, to September 27, because the Jewish new year, Rosh Hashanah, fell on September 26.

Initially, there were some who believed the report of Tony's ailments were phony, but on July 27, it was announced that Tony was in fact suffering from low grade pneumonia and had been admitted to Mercy Hospital in Gary, Indiana. His family physician, Dr. J. L. Danieleski, took an x-ray and identified pneumonia in the lower portion of his left lung. He said Tony would be in the hospital for two weeks, and he wasn't expected to be able to resume training until September.[148]   Art Winch said that once Tony could train again, he would do so in Chicago until six days before the fight and then they'd travel to New York.

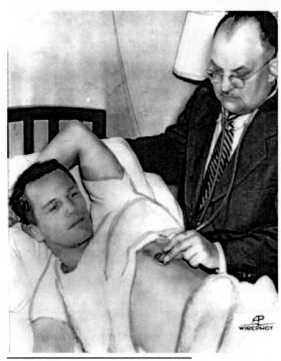

Tony was released from the hospital on August 10, and said he would begin training in early September. He also announced that he and his wife, Adeline, who had withdrawn the divorce suit, were leaving for a ten day vacation.[149]   Even though she had filed for divorce, she realized that she was more responsible for the conflict in their marriage than Tony

148 *Hammond Times*, Zale Has Pneumonia, July 27, 1946.
149 *Janesville Daily Gazette*, Boxer Tony Zale Leaves Hospital, August 10, 1946.

had been. Adele had been brought up in a severe disciplinarian environment where harsh punishment for young children was imaginable. She had been a victim of physical abuse herself and only felt it was fair to treat the children, no matter what age, in this inappropriate manner, and sometimes severely injuring them. Once Tony and Adeline returned from their vacation where issues seemed to be settled, she promised that she would never hit the kids again with a carpet tack board, nor would she ever knee him in the groin. When Tony returned home, Winch said he would have him do some light gymnasium work for a week, and then start boxing a week later.

Tony started boxing on September 3, and two weeks later he was down to 162 pounds, only two away from the middleweight limit of 160. He arrived in New York on September 17 to put the finishing touches on his training for the title defense to be held ten days later. By September 21, the odds in Rocky's favor were 9-5, but once again were expected to decrease to either 7-5 or 6-5 as a result of the impressive performances from Tony at Stillman's Gym in New York City.[150] Joe Louis, the reigning heavyweight champion of the world, offered his opinion a few days before the fight by picking Tony to retain his middleweight crown.[151]

Both men concluded their training on September 24, and three days later, awaited the weigh-in session scheduled for 12:30 p.m. on the day of the fight. The day before the fight, Gene Kessler of the *Chicago Daily Times*, came out and predicted a Zale victory. He gave three reasons for picking Tony over his younger and faster opponent. First, in his workouts, Tony convinced Kessler that he'd regained most of his old form and was very close to the durable puncher who had overpowered Al Hostak five years earlier. Secondly, he thought Graziano was overconfident. Finally, he felt it was the old story of a good, big man fighting a good, little man. He believed that regardless of their weights, Tony was bigger and stronger.[152] Very few felt the fight would go the full fifteen rounds and expected that one or the other fighter would stop their opponent well before the contest went that far.

As it turned out, the fight exceeded just about everyone's expectations. A crowd of 39,827 showed up at Yankee Stadium on

150 *Salt Lake City Tribune*, Odds Favor The Rock, September 21, 1946.
151 *Portsmouth Times*, Joe Picks Tony Zale, September 24, 1946.
152 *Chicago Daily Times*, Doping Zale – Graziano Fight, September 26, 1946

September 27, 1946, and produced the largest gate in history for a middleweight fight, a total of $342,497. It was reportedly the second largest amount ever taken in for a non-heavyweight battle. It was exceeded only by a Benny Leonard vs. Lew Tendler lightweight bout at New York's Polo Grounds in 1923 that produced over $450,000 in receipts.[153] Tony outweighed the challenger by six pounds, 160 to 154, and to the surprise of almost everyone in attendance who believed he was all but finished when the sixth round began, turned the tables on his younger opponent and knocked him out instead.

It was a brutal slugfest from start to finish, the advantage swinging back and forth between both men, and bringing the fans to their feet throughout much of the contest. Tony enjoyed the earliest success in the opening session, hooking a left to the body, followed by a short right to Rocky's head. He then landed a right to the chin, but received a left to his mug in return. Rocky forced him to the ropes with a right to the head, but Tony shocked Rocky with a left hook that floored him for a count of four. Rocky appeared more surprised than hurt, but when he regained his footing, Tony pounded him with a hook to the body, followed by another to the head and Rocky was forced to cover up. Tony concentrated his attack on the body and continually sent Rocky to the ropes. But Rocky landed a right to the ear at close quarters and three more right hand punches to Tony's head as he shook him up near the round's end while the crowd cheered wildly. It was Tony's round.

The action was just as furious in round two, both men connecting with heavy blows. Rocky landed a right to Tony's face that produced a flow of blood from his mouth. He followed up with three more right hand blows to Tony's face before Tony responded with an uppercut to Rocky's face. Rocky finally floored Tony with two hard right punches to the head and the referee reached a count of three as the bell sounded. The second round belonged to Rocky. Tony stumbled to his corner and told his handlers that his right hand hurt.

"Forget it," said Winch, "Use your left as much as possible, just go out there and punch."

"Yes sir," Tony replied.[154]

---

153 *Chicago Tribune*, Zale Knocks Out Graziano; Retains Title, September 28, 1946
154 *The Saturday Evening Post*, Hardluck Champion, July 5, 1947.

In Rocky's corner, his trainer Whitey Bimstein urged him to go for Tony's head.

"Keep going for his head and you'll finish him if you watch out for his left," Whitey said.[155]

In the third round, Rocky staggered Tony with two hard rights, then landed a hook and another right as Tony tried to jab him with his left to keep him off. Tony connected with a left hand swing, and Rocky charged in with left and rights to the head in return. Rocky landed two more rights to the head, and then staggered Tony again with a left. Midway through the round, Rocky caught Tony coming off the ropes with a smashing combination. Tony drew blood from Rocky's nose with a hard left, and they were still trading lefts at the bell.[156] In the words of one scribe, "Rocky hit his swaying, staggering opponent with everything but the American flag in this round, but Tony still came back to stagger Rocky near the end."[157] Still, it was clearly Rocky's round and Tony seemed dazed as he started for the wrong corner upon the round's conclusion, before realizing his mistake and altering his course.

The fourth round opened in a tamer fashion as the two fighters pecked away at each other with left jabs. Eventually, Tony caught

155 Graziano, Rocky, *Somebody Up There Likes Me*, Simon and Schuster, New York, New York, 1955.
156 *Chicago Daily Times*, Record Of First Zale – Graziano Fight, September 28, 1946.
157 *Syracuse Herald Journal*, Tony Zale Knocks Out Graziano Before 39,827 Fans In New York, September 28, 1946.

Rocky against the ropes and went to work with both hands to the body before landing a right to the head. Rocky threw two wild rights and then both men landed heavy right hand blows to the body. Tony then shook Rocky up with a big right to the ribs.

Rocky said later that the blow almost took his wind away, and he backed off. Tony drove Rocky to the ropes, and once again unleashed a barrage of blows to the body with both hands. Both men were bleeding from facial cuts. Tony shook Rocky up with hard rights and landed an uppercut to the chin at the bell.[158] "Every time I tried to rock back on my feet he caught me with a left to the head, a left and a right to the ribs. He was too fast, too friggin fast. I was jumping back and sideways, waiting for the bell," said Rocky.[159] Tony staggered the challenger on three separate occasions during this round in the course of earning the laurels for the session.[160]

A well-known sportswriter named Damon Runyon scribbled on his notepad at ringside to a colleague: "I'll take 10 to 1 on Zale."[161]

In his corner, Graziano told his trainer he had Tony opening up, and that once he opened up a little bit more, he then would get him in the next round. "Go get him kid!" said Whitey.[162]

The two men picked up where they left off as the fifth round opened, rushing to close quarters where they mauled one another. At one point in this round, Rocky landed two overhand rights high on Tony's forehead and straightened him with two lefts. Rocky landed a hook and two pulverizing rights that staggered Tony, who was swaying from side to side and looked as though he was about to go out. Tony's mouth was badly cut and Rocky landed two rights to the head at the bell.

It was Rocky's round in what was deemed the slowest of the fiercely contested battle. Nat Fleischer of *The Ring* magazine, who served as timekeeper for the bout, said that most of those in attendance gave Tony little chance after the beating he received in this round. In fact, according to Nat, he turned to a sportswriter

---

158 *Chicago Daily Times*, Record of First Zale – Graziano Fight, September 28, 1946.
159 Graziano, Rocky, *Somebody Up There Likes Me*, Simon and Schuster, New York, New York, 1955.
160 *Syracuse Herald Journal*, Tony Zale Knocks Out Graziano Before 39,827 Fans In New York, September 28, 1946.
161 *Sport* magazine, I'll Take Tony Zale, March 1947.
162 Graziano, Rocky, *Somebody Up There Likes Me*, Simon and Schuster, New York, New York, 1955.

sitting at his side and remarked, "Too bad, it'll be all over next round. Zale can't stand that punishment much longer." And Damon Runyon scribbled another note to his companion: "It's no bet. His (Zale's) legs are gone."[163]

But Ray Arcel, who worked Tony's corner for all three of his fights against Rocky, and Tony's other handlers, Izzy Cline and Joe Niedwick, worked him over frantically during the intermission in order to prepare him for the next round. They doused him with cold water, applied ice to his neck, massaged his legs, and slapped his face to bring him to life.[164]

"The fifth round was just a murderous round," Arcel would later say. "Graziano was winning hands down. But when Tony got back to the corner, I said to him, 'Tony, don't let this guy take your title away from you. This is the last round. Hit this guy with your best punch. Just load one up and take a chance.'"[165]

Over in the other corner, Rocky was thinking to himself that this guy was tougher and quicker than anybody he ever fought in his life. This is a fighter, this Tony Zale, he thought to himself. Anybody else I ever fought would be dead by now.[166]

A number of folks at ringside were convinced that Tony was through and urged Referee Ruby Goldstein to end the fight. Goldstein went to Tony's corner.

"How do you feel?" he asked Tony. Ruby, a former fighter, later said that he'd never known a fighter in those circumstances to say, "I feel lousy. Get me out of here." They all say they feel great, because even if they know they can't last much longer, courage and pride prevents them from admitting it. But Ruby had been officiating for a while now, and felt like he instinctively knew, no matter what the fighter said.

True to form, Tony gave Ruby a very definite assurance when he replied, "I'm all right, Ruby."

Ruby looked at Pian and Winch, whom he held great respect for, and whom he knew wouldn't let their man take any unnecessary

---

163 *Sport* magazine, I'll Take Tony Zale, March 1947.
164 *The Ring*, Rocky Meets His Master, December 1946.
165 Jarrett, John, *Champ In The Corner. The Ray Arcel Story*, Stadia, Stroud, Gloucestershire, U.K. 2007.
166 Graziano, Rocky, *Somebody Up There Likes Me*, Simon and Schuster, New York, New York, 1955.

punishment. They nodded in agreement, and Ruby decided to let the fight continue.[167]

The warning buzzer sounded and a moment later the bell rang and Rocky sprang into action. He began with a right to Tony's body as he pressed the action. Tony delivered his own right to the body and a left to the ribs. Rocky threw two wild lefts to the body and took one in return. Tony landed a hook to the face and Rocky tried to retaliate with a wild right to the ribs. They traded rights to the body.

Finally, Tony called upon all the reserves left in his tank, and floored Rocky with a right hook to the midsection followed by a left hook to the head, and the challenger was on the floor in a squatting position, with one hand on the lower rope. As Goldstein counted, Rocky struggled to regain his bearings and he reached for a higher rope. He leapt to his feet immediately after the count of 10, and Goldstein had to wrestle with him to prevent him from reaching Tony as he tried to convince him the fight was over. Later, Rocky would say, "All I heard was the 8-9-10 and that count came awfully fast."[168]

AP Wire Photo

---

167 Goldstein, Ruby, *Third Man In The Ring*, Funk & Wagnalls, New York, New York, 1959.
168 *Abilene Reporter News*, All I Heard Was 8-9-10, September 30, 1946.

But of the finishing blow to the head, Rocky added, "That jolt shot through my head to my feet. The feeling went out of my feet and I went whang on the canvas, like I didn't have any feet at all."[169] The end came one minute and 43 seconds into the sixth round.[170]

Fleischer noted that there were many seated at ringside who thought that Graziano had been the victim of a fast count by Goldstein. But Fleischer maintained that wasn't the case. "I had two watches on the fight and my time pieces showed ten and three-tenths seconds," said Nat. "Rocky lost out by a fraction of a second." Nat also expressed the belief that Tony was saved from a knockout himself at the end of the second round when the bell rang early in the referee's count. "He could scarcely get to his feet when aided by his seconds, yet he showed amazing recuperative powers when he came out for the third round and stood up under withering punishment," said Nat.[171]

Some thought Rocky had chosen to quit, rather than accept any further punishment. As he made his way through the crowd toward his dressing room, a fan accused him of just that, hollering: "Yah yella, yella bum, yah quit." Rocky angrily spun around and threw a punch at the fan, but the fan pulled his head back at the same time and managed to avoid the full impact of the blow. Nearby fans laughed in response.[172]

Tony looked more like the loser than a winner as he was led from the ring to his dressing room on trembling legs with a glazed look in the eyes behind a battered and lumpy face. As soon as he reached the room, he plopped down on a chair, exhausted, and winced as he dipped an injured right hand into a bucket of ice. As the newsmen pushed their way into the room in search of a word with the Champion, Winch urged them to give him a chance to recover. "Don't try to make him talk now," he said. Tony opened his eyes and tried to say something, then shook his head and closed his eyes again.

A reporter stood there, looking down on him. "I never saw anybody with as much guts," he said. "I told you," Pian said, "I told you all along. You wouldn't believe me when I told you he would

169 *Traces*, The Man Of Steel With A Heart Of Gold, Spring 2007.
170 *Chicago Tribune*, Zale Knocks Out Graziano; Retains Title, September 28, 1946.
171 *The Ring*, Rocky Meets His Master, December 1946.
172 Bromberg, Lester, *Boxing's Unforgetable Fights*, The Ronald Press Company, New York, New York, 1962.

win."[173]   Another reporter who visited Tony's dressing room that night said Tony's eyes had the dead, unseeing look of a man in a coma. He got the impression that Tony wouldn't have known the difference between a bucket of ice or one of boiling water at that point.[174] While Arcel was taking care of him, Tony remarked, "You know, Ray, I said many prayers and God heard me." Arcel said later, "Tony was a devout Catholic."[175]

Over in the loser's locker room, Rocky Graziano offered no alibis. He was the picture of a victor in an easy fight compared to Tony. He was unmarked, alert, and appeared carefree as he sat on a rubbing table and puffed away on a cigarette.

Over 25 years later, Rocky said of this fight with Tony, "The first fight, between me and you, I was a wise guy. I wasn't training that

173 *Sport* magazine, I'll Take Tony Zale, March 1947.
174 *Daily Capital News*, Whitney Martin Picks Zale to Repeat Win Over Graziano, July 12, 1947.
175 Jarrett, John, *Champ In The Corner. The Ray Arcel Story*, Stadia, Stroud, Gloucestershire, U.K. 2007.

well, and I figured I'll knock this guy out whenever I want. I didn't train that well for that particular fight. I thought I had a right hand and I can knock anybody out. I didn't know how tough he was, and finally he gave me a couple of good shots in the stomach and I went down. See, from the first round to the fifth the guy is banging you in the body. And finally I started weakening and I lost."[176]

176 Heller, Peter, *In This Corner, Simon and Schuster*, New York, New York, 1973.

AP Wire Photo

In the opinion of a number of observers including Jimmy Cannon and Hugh Fullerton, Jr., the fight had to be classed among the greatest fights of all-time. In Fullerton's view, it had everything and Zale, by coming back to gain a knockout victory after taking Rocky's best punches, showed he was a real champion.[177] Former heavyweight champion Gene Tunney called Tony's comeback in the fight, "the greatest exhibition of heart I'd ever seen."[178] He also said the fight was one of the best he'd witnessed in 25 years.[179] In 1955, longtime ring announcer, Don Dunphy, called the fight, "the most

---

177 *Hope Star*, Sports Roundup, September 30, 1946.
178 *Traces*, The Man of Steel With A Heart Of Gold, Spring 2007.
179 *Mansfield News Journal*, Best Fight, February 17, 1947.

thrilling sports event he ever covered."[180]   It was the first time Rocky had been knocked out in his professional career.   Two days later, Winch announced Tony had suffered a chipped bone in his right thumb in either the first or second round of the fight and would have to wear a cast for at least three weeks.   He would then undergo physical therapy for another month.   As a result, Winch said Tony would not fight again in 1946.[181]

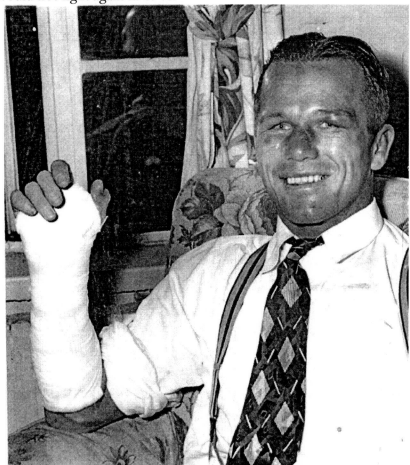

Of course, the brawl between Tony and Rocky had the fans clamoring for more.   There was immediate talk from the offices of promoter Mike Jacob's office of a rematch sometime early in 1947. It was thought that a second bout between the pair would need to be

---

180   Syracuse Herald Journal, January 26, 1955
181   *Bluefield Daily Telegraph*, Tony Zale Will Not Fight Again In 1946, September 29, 1946

held in an outdoor venue in order to accommodate the number of fans it would draw. Jacobs was reluctant to provide a breakdown on the distribution of the receipts from the first fight, and it was learned that each fighter received 30% of the gate, so it appeared that Jacobs didn't want to reveal that the challenger had been paid as much as the Champion. That meant that each man pocketed approximately $80,000 for their work.[182]

A few days after the fight a brass band and a large crowd headed by Mayor Joseph Finerty turned out at the train depot in Gary, Indiana, to welcome the Champion home. Tony's wife and daughter were among the first to greet him. Tony was presented with a wrist watch by the mayor as a token of appreciation from the city. At home things between Tony and Adeline were at an even keel.

On October 28, Mike Jacobs announced that Graziano would meet middleweight contender "Cowboy" Reuben Shank of Denver, Colorado, in a ten-round bout in Madison Square Garden on December 27. The entire promotional profit was going to be donated to Mrs. James J. Johnston, the widow of the well-known fight promoter who had passed away during the year. The contest was ultimately cancelled shortly before it could take place when Rocky complained of a back injury that made it impossible for him to go forward with the fight.

While it seemed a foregone conclusion that a rematch would take place between Tony and Rocky sometime early in 1947, the National Boxing Association (N.B.A.) responded to a protest made by the managers of middleweight contender Charley Burley of Pittsburgh, Pennsylvania. Burley's managers contended that their man was deserving of a shot at the middleweight title, but under the present setup would not receive a chance to fight for it for at least a year. The N.B.A. agreed, and its President, Abe J. Greene, suggested three elimination fights be staged to determine the opponent for the winner of a return bout between Tony and Rocky. Greene's recommendations were as follows:

(1) Georgie Abrams vs. Marcel Cerdan, the French champion
(2) Burley vs. Jake LaMotta
(3) Winner of (1) vs. winner of (2)
(4) Winner of (3) vs. Zale   Greene maintained this would be the fairest way to determine the rightful challenger for the middleweight title.[183] Unfortunately, for Charley Burley and his team, Greene's recommendations concerning a bout between Burley and LaMotta weren't followed. This great fighter never did receive an opportunity to fight for a championship.

On the other hand, it appeared as though Marcel Cerdan, who was being hailed as the greatest French fighter since Georges Carpentier, might have a chance to fight for the title one day. In early November, he was preparing for a long awaited invasion of the United States where he was scheduled to meet Georgie Abrams in New York. He was confident he could defeat Abrams and hopeful that it would be an important step toward a match for the middleweight title in the coming year. The 30-year old Frenchman made a big hit with the fans in Madison Square Garden on his way to a unanimous decision victory over Abrams on December 6. The fury of his attack and the surprising effectiveness of his body attack proved too much for Abrams to overcome and furthered Cerdan's case for a middleweight title shot.

On November 17, 1946, Tony and his family suffered a heartbreaking loss when his 72-year-old mother Catherine passed away in Gary, Indiana's Mercy Hospital as a result of complications from a recent heart attack. Tony was at her bedside when she passed away and she was buried four days later, on November 21, 1946.

---

183 *Galveston Daily News*, NBA Complains About Middleweight Monopoly, October 30, 1946.

After the death of Tony's father, Josef, in 1915, Catherine provided the spiritual foundation of the family. She became the sole provider of their family's physical and financial needs. After her death there was a tremendous void in the Zaleski clan's lives, and it was difficult for everyone to imagine life without her presence. Because of their deep rooted faith, they realized she would be missed, but was in a far better place.

The following month, on December 4, the boxing world awoke to the news that its most influential promoter, 66-year-old Mike Jacobs, had suffered a cerebral hemorrhage the previous day. He collapsed in a Manhattan building. A day later he was able to take some nourishment, but the right side of his body was paralyzed. It was expected that he would remain hospitalized for some time. There was a great degree of uncertainty concerning his future.[184]

The year ended on a more positive note when *The Ring* magazine named Tony's fight against Rocky Graziano the "Fight of the Year" for 1946 and also tabbed Tony as their "Fighter of the Year."

---

184 *Kingston Daily Freeman*, Mike Jacobs Still Is Seriously Ill, December 5, 1946.

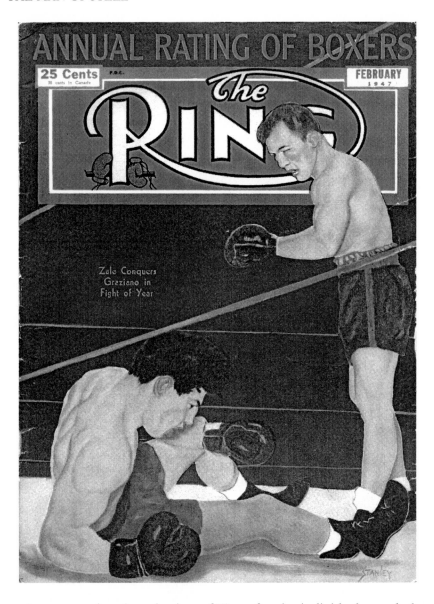

In announcing the selection of Tony for the individual award, the magazine's founder and editor, Nat Fleischer, said he was delighted with the choice and that Tony had recaptured the title because he was not only a credit to the game and himself, but could point to a four year stretch of service to the Navy.[185] "None who witnessed Zale's thrilling performance against Graziano will ever forget the fight in

---

185 *The Ring*, Tony Zale Named The Boxer Of The Year, February 1947.

which Tony picked boxing off the floor. It had been left there, in the estimation of the public, by the Louis-Conn fiasco," said Nat.

Tony was also the recipient of the New York Boxing Writers Association of the Edward J. Neil Memorial Trophy as the man who did the most for the sport of boxing in 1946. The award was named in memory of an Associated Press sports writer and war correspondent that was killed during the war in Spain in 1938. Only Joe Louis had previously won both the Neil Award and *The Ring* magazine's "Fighter of the Year" award in the same year.[186] The coming year promised to be a very interesting one for the middleweight division.

---

186 *Troy Record*, Middleweight Tony Zale Sweeps 1946 Boxing Honors As "Fighter Of Year," December 30, 1946.

REMATCH PLACED IN PERIL

On January 15, 1947, it was announced that Tony would be in New York on January 21, to receive his Edward J. Neil Memorial Trophy. He had been signed to fight a ten-round, non-title contest in Omaha, Nebraska, on February 3. His opponent hadn't been determined yet, but was expected to be selected from among a list including "Cowboy" Reuben Shank, Jackie Burke, Ramey McKnight or Nathern "Deacon" Logan. At the time, the expectation was that Tony would face Graziano in a rematch on March 21, and he would engage in two tune-up fights before that date.

A week later, "Deacon" Logan, was named as Tony's opponent for the Omaha fight. The biggest news in boxing during the month of January though was the news that Rocky Graziano was under investigation by the grand jury for his failure to report an offer to "fix" his fight against "Cowboy" Rueben Shank the previous month. The fight scheduled to take place on December 27 was ultimately cancelled on December 24 when Rocky withdrew from the bout complaining of a back ailment.

New York District Attorney, Frank Hogan, and two aides questioned Rocky for a total of 15 hours from Saturday, January 18, until 5:00 a.m., Sunday morning. They were interested in knowing the circumstances that prompted the cancellation of the fight. It was reported that a syndicate of New York gamblers bet as much as $135,000 on Shank, who was a 4-1 underdog given very little chance of winning by New York sportswriters. If that amount was correct, a win by Shank would have resulted in a payout of over half-a-million dollars for the bettors.[187]

---

187 *Council Bluff Nonpareil*, Graziano in Juror Bout, January 24, 1947.

By January 28, it was reported that Rocky had admitted to receiving an offer of $100,000 to "take a dive" against Shank, but he insisted that he thought the man was kidding. Col. Edward Eagan, the New York State Athletic Commissioner, had summoned Rocky to appear before a board hearing on January 31. The commission's rules required that a fighter who is asked to participate in a "sham or collusive contest" report it to the commission. Some believed that Rocky's failure to report the offer would result in the cancellation of his return engagement with Tony, and cost him a share in what was expected to be another very large gate. District Attorney Hogan was convinced that Rocky hadn't yet told him everything and planned to continue to press him for the name of the man who offered the bribe. News of the investigation was being kept from Mike Jacobs, who was recovering in a local hospital for fear that the promoter might suffer a serious relapse upon receiving the shocking news.[188]

Hearing of Graziano's 15-hour interview with the district attorney, New York sports columnist, Bill Corum, said, "I have tried once or twice to interview Rocky without, I must confess success." 'I never remembered to bring along somebody to draw the pictures.' He has a vocabulary that goes something like 'yeah' and 'nunh,' and when he is in a veritable lather of conversation he occasionally goes all out and says, 'Oh, yeah?' with or without the question mark."[189]

A day before appearing before the commission, Rocky maintained the position that he believed the bribe offer was a joke so there was no reason for him to report it. He reiterated that stance in his 1955 biography: "As far as bribes in fighting are concerned, payola offers for throwing a bout come your way all the time. All I ever done, all most boxers ever done, was laugh them off. You never had any idea how serious these nuts might be with their deals. If you reported each and every one, not only would the cops laugh you out the station house, but you wouldn't have no time to train."

Rocky also disputed the accusation that he faked a back injury to get out of the fight with Shank. He maintained that one afternoon, while he was preparing for the bout, he wrenched his back while doing back bends to warm up. "The pain shoots down into my right arm and I have to quit for the day. I don't tell Whitey (Bimstein)

---

188 *Lowell Sun*, Rocky Graziano Admits Being Offered $100,000 To Throw Fight, January 28, 1947.
189 *Lowell Sun*, Was Graziano-Shank Match Really Case for Probers?, January 28, 1947.

what happened. The next day my back and my side and my arm still hurt. I can't weave to the left. Whitey asks me what's the matter. Just my back, I tell him, that's all. He rubs me down. When it hurts, I take in my breath."

"Ok, kid," says Whitey, when he's through. "We're not going to fight this boy, Shank."

"Whatta ya mean, not fight him," I said. "I never dogged no fight in my life."

"You want to make 'Cowboy' Shank your last bout? He's not that important. We're not going in the ring with him."

"What bothered me was somebody might get it wrong and think I dogged it, that I was yellow. And that was only a warm-up, a tune-up, a workout. So it was called off and I forgot about it."[190]

By all accounts, it appeared that the New York State Boxing Commission would reach one of five possible decisions concerning Graziano: revoke his boxing license, suspend him, fine him, reprimand him or exonerate him. There were very few who believed the commission would let Rocky off with a reprimand that would enable him to go forward with the March 21 fight against Tony. District Attorney Hogan said that Rocky admitted that he told the man to "see him again later," and there was another meeting between the two, although the bribe was never collected. Rocky stuck to this story about not knowing the name of the individual who offered the bribe, but Hogan believed he was just afraid to reveal it.[191] Tony figured that he stood to lose as much as $135,000 in potential earnings if the fight with Rocky was cancelled.[192]

On February 3, Tony defeated "Deacon" Logan in Omaha by way of a technical knockout in the sixth round. For the first five rounds, Logan displayed some good infighting skills while evading the majority of Tony's big right hand blows, but he suffered a freak accident in the sixth round that brought a sudden end to the contest. It was in that round that Logan received a blow that spun him around and he fell heavily on his outstretched right arm, dislocating his shoulder. Referee Alex Fidler delivered a count of ten as Logan lay on the floor, and then pointed to a rip in the canvas that

190 Graziano, Rocky, *Somebody Up There Likes Me*, Simon and Schuster, New York, New York 1955.
191 *Waterloo Daily Courier*, Graziano Tells Bribe Story to Ring Commission, January 31, 1947.
192 *Kokomo Tribune*, To Lose $135,000, February 3, 1947.

contributed to Logan's fall.[193] Tony weighed in at 162 ½ pounds for the contest, while Logan was weighed at 164.

A day later, Assistant District Attorney Alfred Scotti testified before the boxing commission and said that Rocky told him he had used a "kink in his back" as an excuse to pull out of his December fight against Shank. He didn't want to take a dive against him, and was afraid "those guys" might have thought the deal was on and that he'd double crossed them if he went on with the fight and defeated Shank. Scotti said that Rocky told him the man that made the bribe offer was the same party who'd offered him a $100,000 bribe prior to his 1945 bout with Al "Bummy" Davis. Rocky knocked Davis out in the fourth round of that contest.

Scotti said that he didn't believe Rocky was telling the truth about not knowing the name of the man who offered the bribe.[194] The chances of the March title fight taking place between Rocky and Tony were rapidly dwindling.

Top middleweight contender Jake LaMotta was an interested attendee at the hearings. For a number of years, while Tony was serving in the navy, LaMotta had built up a reputation as the leading contender for the title, and it was expected he'd get the first shot at Tony's title once he was discharged from the service. But as explained in an earlier chapter, Rocky's meteoric rise and box office appeal enabled him to receive the opportunity in Jake's place. It's not hard to imagine that Jake was hoping to capitalize on Rocky's misfortune.[195]

On February 7, the New York State Athletic Commission issued its decision. Chairman Eddie Eagan read a statement announcing that they were revoking Rocky's boxing license and cancelled his return fight on March 21 with Tony in Madison Square Garden. Eagan essentially said that it was the commission's stance that they had no other choice as a result of Rocky's own admission that he had received bribe offers on three separate occasions and failed to report them as required by the commission's rule number 64. "It was not your privilege to determine whether or not you should report these

193 *Hutchinson News Herald*, Freak Knockout Gives Match To Tony Zale, February 4, 1947.
194 *Times Recorder*, DA Probing Chief Admits No Effort To Take Up Offer, February 5, 1947.
195 *Amarillo Globe*, LaMotta 13th Guest, February 6, 1947.

requests or suggestions to the commission. It was your duty to do so," said Eagan.[196]

But while it was clear that there would be no title fight between Tony and Rocky in New York, an opportunity for the two men to fight in another state wasn't yet ruled out. The N.B.A. hadn't given their stance on the matter yet, and a Chicago based promoter named Ben Zenoff wasted no time offering to stage the bout in that city. "The N.B.A. hasn't barred Rocky yet, and we can hold the fight here under the N.B.A.," Zenoff said. He informed the press that he was prepared to offer Tony and Rocky 60 percent of the gate as a purse for the match.[197]

While boxing fans were left to wonder when and where the next middleweight title fight would take place, Tony went ahead with his second non-title bout of the year, facing Canada's middleweight champion Len Wadsworth in Wichita, Kansas, on February 12, before a crowd of 3,075. He knocked Wadsworth down in the second round, and then knocked him out at the 2:13 mark of the third round. Tony weighed 162 pounds for the bout, while Wadsworth came in at 163 ½.[198]

On February 19, N.B.A. President Abe Greene announced that its members were free to proceed with making any matches involving Rocky Graziano as they saw fit. Greene said that in reaching this decision, they had acted on the basis of the recommendations received from their members. He went on to take a shot at the New York Commission's recent actions, calling into question the decision to revoke Graziano's license for failure to report a bribe. They had only suspended Sugar Ray Robinson for 30 days for his failure to report an offer of $25,000 and failing to make the required weight for a welterweight title contest. In Greene's words, the New York Commission's actions "smacked of unbalanced justice, if not of political witch-hunting."[199]

The Ring magazine editor, Nat Fleischer, thought that had Mike Jacobs been healthy, he might have been able to exert some influence upon the situation that Rocky got himself into with the New York

---

196 *San Antonio Express*, Rocky Gets Virtual Life Ban As N.Y. License Is Revoked, February 8, 1947.
197 *Berkshire Evening Eagle*, Graziano and Zale May Meet In Chicago, February 8, 1947.
198 *Walla Walla Union Bulletin*, Tony Zale Scores KO In Third Round of Bout, February 12, 1947.
199 *Beckley Post Herald*, NBA Gives Clean Slates To Boxers, February 20, 1947.

Boxing Commission. But once Rocky was banned from fighting in New York, the empire that Jacob built known as the Twentieth Century Sporting Club, began to crumble.

Jacob was born on St. Patrick's Day in 1880, grew up in a poor family in the Lower East Side of New York, just as Rocky did. He demonstrated a nose for business at an early age, selling newspapers near the Staten Island ferry-house, and then selling concessions on summer excursion boats at age 17. By age 23 he became the sole owner of the concessions on the Coney Island boats. Then he and his father went into the business of providing a chaperone service to the thousands of immigrants landing on Ellis Island who were in need of advice, housing, clothing and railroad tickets. They helped many of these folks get settled in their new country.

Then Mike moved into the ticketing business and he opened an agency at Broadway and 39th Street, across from the Metropolitan Opera House, and he began brokering tickets to popular events. Before long he became the premier ticket agent in New York. In 1910 he befriended the famous boxing promoter "Tex" Rickard, and when Rickard moved into New York in 1915, he helped him get established. By 1921 he was working as a trusted advisor to the man who went on to run Madison Square Garden.

When Rickard died unexpectedly in 1929, Mike hoped he would be selected to succeed him, but a man named Bill Curry was chosen to take Tex's place. Mike waited in the wings for his opportunity. It arrived a few years later when Mrs. William Randolph Hearst invited him to help promote fights for her pet charity, the Hearst Milk Fund. Hearst had originated the idea of holding annual boxing events to raise money to provide pasteurized milk for the poor kids of New York, and in time it became necessary to involve a promoter from the outside. Mrs. Hearst selected Jacobs for the job.

Mike helped stage a number of successful shows for the Milk Fund. Then when a heavyweight sensation named Joe Louis came along and his management group was looking to line up some important fights for him, he convinced them to sign a three year agreement with him as the sole promoter. At the same time, he was shrewd enough to include an option that allowed him to renew the agreement. In much the same way that Tex Rickard capitalized on Jack Dempsey's success and popularity, Mike Jacobs was thus able to become the biggest promoter in boxing as a result of his relationship with Joe Louis.

After Mike staged an event he called the Carnival of Champions in September of 1937, the men in charge of Madison Square Garden realized that he controlled much of the best talent in boxing and they brought him in as a partner of a group that ran the Garden known as the Twentieth Century Sporting Club. A month later he promoted his first fight in the Garden and then went on to do so for the next 12 years.

A key to Jacob's success was his ability to tie up the challengers for the boxing titles. "Never leave yourself without the champion, never take anything for granted, and never fail to protect yourself in the clinches," was his business motto. According to Nat Fleischer, when Mike promoted his first event at the Garden, he agreed to pay Pete Sarron an amount to fight Henry Armstrong for the featherweight title. That meant he wouldn't turn a profit on the event. But in return, the contract stipulated that Sarron agree to let Mike promote his fights for the next three years. He had a similar agreement with Armstrong. So regardless of who won, he would be sure of having the promotional rights of the winner for the next three years. It was the same way with Joe Louis. Mike knew that the key to Rickard's success had been his ability to sew up Jack Dempsey's services and he was determined to use the same tactics during his reign over Madison Square Garden. He was so successful, that by 1938, he became a 50/50 partner in the Garden's operations.

International News Photo

But the cerebral hemorrhage that Mike suffered in December of 1946 was the beginning of the end of his reign over boxing. He was able to carry on in a reduced role over the next two-and-a-half years, but ultimately retired on May 5, 1949.[200]

The N.B.A.'s decision concerning Graziano meant that he and Tony's management teams were free to enter into an agreement to stage a title fight in any one of the state's under the jurisdiction of that authority. However, the New York boxing commission had a rule which said that "nothing in their rules was deemed to define or restrict the powers of the commission in disciplining, penalizing or controlling any corporation or person under its jurisdiction for violation of the letter or spirit of the law and rules as it may determine by particular action in any situation that may arise." As a result, it seemed clear that any fighter licensed to fight in New York, including Tony, who chose to fight Graziano while his license was revoked, might find himself banned from appearing in New York in the future as well.[201]

But that didn't appear to concern Tony, for he came out and said that he was still anxious to give Rocky a return bout, and he was willing to leave the time and place up to the promoters.[202] Tony was well aware that a return match with Rocky presented him with the greatest financial award at the time, and at that stage in his career, was not very likely concerned with the possibility of getting banned in New York as a result. But it was clear that any return bout between Tony and Rocky was going to take place later, rather than sooner, so Tony was signed to meet Tommy Charles on March 20 in another 10-round non-title bout in Memphis, Tennessee.

While Tony prepared to face Tommy Charles, the European middleweight champion, Marcel Cerdan, arrived in New York on March 6 with an entourage including his wife and children to begin an American campaign that he hoped would result in a title match later in the year. A number of knowledgeable fight fans felt that a match between Tony and the crowd pleasing Cerdan would be a real brawl. A day later, Tony attended the Tournament of Champions in Chicago Stadium to honor the winners of the year's Golden Gloves

200 Daniels, Daniel, *The Mike Jacobs Story*, New York, New York, 1950.
201 *Walla Walla Union Bulletin*, Road Is Rocky For Graziano, February 21, 1947.
202 *Troy Record*, Zale Anxious For Return Bout With Graziano, February 22, 1947.

and presented The Zale Sportsmanship Trophy to Nick Ranieri, a C.Y.O. middleweight.

On March 20, Tony weighed in at 162 pounds while his opponent, Tommy Charles, scaled 167 pounds for their bout before 4,000 fans in Memphis. Tony wore Charles down with body punches throughout the first three rounds and then knocked him out with a big right hand blow to the head at the 1:42 mark of the fourth round.[203] Three days later the N.B.A. notified Tony that six months had passed since he'd defended his middleweight title and asked him to let them in on his plans. But it was clear that Tony and his managers were still hoping his next title defense would come against Graziano and Tony had said as much in Memphis on March 18.[204]

Still, some believed that if Cerdan defeated middleweight contender Harold Green on March 28, and the New York boxing commission remained adamant concerning its revocation of Graziano's license, that there was a good chance Tony would give Cerdan a shot at the title that summer. The Twentieth Century Club was certainly interested in staging a bout in Madison Square Garden between Tony and Marcel, especially after he ended up knocking out Green there in the second round before 18,116 fans.

Nat Fleischer attended the match between Cerdan and Green and had nothing but praise for the Frenchman. Cerdan reminded Nat of the great former middleweight champion Mickey Walker. "I think he (Cerdan) will be the next world's champion in his class. He can box and punch and he's plenty smart and I believe he would knock out both Rocky Graziano and Tony Zale, the present champion," he said.[205]

But unfortunately for Cerdan, while Tony's manager, Sam Pian, said that Marcel was unquestionably a great fighter and attraction, Tony preferred Rocky for a title bout, even if the event had to be staged outside of New York. A bout between Tony and Rocky was the one that was guaranteed to produce the largest gate and as long as there was a chance of that happening, Marcel would have to wait.

While the date and opponent for Tony's next title defense remained uncertain, his managers made sure he would stay in shape by immediately booking him for another non-title bout. Tony was

---

203 *Wisconsin State Journal,* Zale Knocks Out Charles in Fourth, March 21, 1947.
204 *Port Press Herald,* Zale To Defend, March 18, 1947.
205 *Winnipeg Free Press,* Time Out, April 22, 1947.

scheduled to fight against a lanky fighter named Al Timmons in Kansas City, Kansas, on April 1. The Cleveland based fighter didn't pose much of a threat to Tony, but the bout would help him stay sharp.

Three days before Tony's bout with Timmons, fight fans began to get a glimpse of Sam Pian's plans for Tony. Sam spent two hours listening to Sol Strauss and Nat Rogers of the Twentieth Century Sporting Club as they tried to talk him into signing Tony to fight Cerdan for the title that June in Yankee Stadium. Sam told them he'd get back to them with a counteroffer no later than April 15. While he didn't provide any details, it was believed that it would include a title defense between Tony and Graziano in Chicago in June, followed by another defense in New York in September against Cerdan.

Sam was sure that the biggest gate would be produced by the return match between Tony and Rocky, but he also knew that there was a lot of money to be made from a match between Tony and Marcel in New York, and making both fights would maximize their earnings. Sam promised to sit down with Strauss and Rogers again before he announced his decision on April 15.[206]

The likelihood of Tony facing Graziano, and then Cerdan, should he defeat Rocky, only increased on April 1, when Art Winch said that their camp considered Cerdan a threat to the middleweight crown, but that Graziano "comes first."[207] Later that day, Tony defeated Al Timmons in the fifth round of their scheduled 10-round contest in Kansas City's Memorial Hall when referee Walter Bates stopped the fight after Tony opened a deep cut over Timmons left eye with a right-hand blow. A disappointing crowd of only 2,200 was on hand for the event and produced a gate of only $4,638. Tony weighed 162 ½ pounds for the bout, while Timmons weighed in at 171.[208]

Knowing that there was more money to be made if they could fight Tony in New York, Rocky and his manager, Irving Cohen, made an appeal to the New York boxing commission on April 11 to have Rocky's boxing license re-instated, but it was denied. The next day, Pian said that the way things looked now, Tony would probably defend his title sometime in June in a rematch with Rocky in Chicago. He planned to meet with Cohen to finalize their plans and

---

206 *Portland Press Herald*, Graziano Then Cerdan Looks Like Pian's Plan, March 30, 1947.
207 *Emporia Gazette*, Middleweight Champ Into Ring Tonight, April 1, 1947.
208 *Joplin Globe*, Tony Zale Wins Over Al Timmons By T.K.O., April 2, 1947.

then file a request with the Illinois Athletic Commission to hold the fight in Chicago.[209]

On April 14, Pian announced that he and Cohen had reached an agreement for a fight between Tony and Rocky in early summer. They planned to leave for Cleveland to entertain an offer to stage the fight there, and then go to Chicago to listen to promoters' offers there. Pian said that after he and Cohen reached an agreement between themselves, they met with Sol Strauss of the Twentieth Century Sporting Club and told him that if Tony retained the title after his bout with Rocky they'd be willing to fight Cerdan in New York in September.

On April 18, the Illinois Athletic Commission met at the request of Sam Pian to rule on a proposed bout between Tony and Rocky in Chicago so that Sam could go ahead and entertain offers from Chicago based promoters. The commission approved the match on the condition that both fighters post a $10,000 appearance bond for the fight within 30 days. It was anticipated that the bout would be staged in either Wrigley Field or Comiskey Park sometime between June 25 and July 15 and would generate a gate of at least $500,000. Fight promoter Irving Schoenwald said the fighters would split 60 percent of the receipts. A few days later, the management groups agreed that Tony would receive 40 percent of the gate, and Rocky would earn 20 percent. The title fight would be the first held in Chicago since Tony defended his N.B.A. title against Al Hostak in 1941.

In late April, it looked like Wrigley Field would be the site of the event when the Illinois Athletic Commission approved the site and a date of July 16, but a potential fly in the ointment appeared when it was learned that three Illinois State Senators planned to submit a resolution to the State Senate Executive Committee directing the commission to rescind its approval of the fight. If the resolution was favorably received, the group planned to prepare a bill to bar an appearance in Illinois by any fighter under suspension or suspicion in any other state. Since he had been inactive since his first fight with Tony, Rocky planned to fit in two or three tune-up fights before the rematch.

On May 1, the Illinois Athletic Commission tabled the resolution to halt the fight. While there were some additional efforts made to

---

209 *Iowa City Press-Citizen*, Rocky To Make Chicago Trial, April 12, 1947.

stop it in the ensuing weeks, the commission's action, or inaction if you will, effectively blocked those efforts. Five days later, the estimate for the size of the gate for the title fight dropped when word leaked that the venue for the event would have to be changed from Wrigley Field to Chicago Stadium.

The change in plans was caused when it was determined that the necessary lumber and materials to convert Wrigley Field into a satisfactory arena for a fight was unavailable because of the current housing shortage and need for the materials for that cause. While Wrigley Field could have accommodated as many as 45,000 paying customers, Chicago Stadium could only hold 21,000, and even with the higher ticket prices that would be charged there, it was anticipated that this change would result in a gate of at least $100,000 less. Since the fighters' managers had already agreed to accept 60 percent of the total gate, this meant an estimated reduction in earnings of $40,000 for Tony and $20,000 for Rocky.[210]

A week later in Youngstown, Ohio, Tony fought the last of his tune-up bouts in another overweight non-title bout against Cliff Beckett of Sudbury, Ontario. Tony, who weighed 161 pounds for the fight, knocked his 164-pound opponent to the canvas six times before the referee finally stopped the contest in the sixth round of the scheduled ten-round affair. Pian and Winch were pleased with Tony's performance and declared that he was in top-notch form.[211]

On May 17, the Illinois Athletic Commission gave their final approval on the movement of the title fight from Wrigley Field to Chicago Stadium. The commission wasn't happy that word of the potential move had been leaked earlier in the month before they had a chance to rule on the matter. Once they had an opportunity to study the matter and realized it would cost $25,000 to build temporary seats in Wrigley Field and lumber might not be available, they gave their approval.

The only concession that they requested, and received in exchange for granting their approval, was that the price of the highest ringside seats be reduced from $32.50 to $30.[212] Representatives of both fighters then posted their ten thousand dollar bonds with the

---

210 *Kokomo Tribune*, Fight Transfer Cuts Zale-Graziano Take, May 6, 1947.
211 *Syracuse Herald-Journal*, Tony Zale Stops Beckett in 6th, May 9, 1947.
212 *Lowell Sun*, Graziano and Zale Title Bout July 16, May 19, 1947.

commission on May 26, guaranteeing their appearance for the event.[213]

Three days later it was announced that Tony would leave Chicago on May 31 to begin training at Lake Lac De Flambeau in Minocqua, Wisconsin, for the title fight with Rocky. He planned to spend two weeks chopping wood and running to begin to condition his body for the battle.

213 *Port Arthur News*, Zale, Graziano Put Up Bond Forfeits, May 27, 1947.

As planned, Rocky participated in a couple of tune-up fights himself, winning via technical knockouts over Eddie Finazzo in Memphis, Tennessee, on June 10, and Jerry Fiorello in Toledo, Ohio, on June 16.

Rocky was especially pleased with his performance against Fiorello. After stopping him in the fifth round of their contest, he happily told reporters that it would be a different story when he and Tony met in the ring for the second time. "I'm a guy wot never brags; but I can't help admittin' I never felt so good in the ring as I did last night. Watch my smoke at Chicago," said Rocky.[214] He arrived in Chicago on July 1 to complete his training for the fight with Tony and proclaimed himself in great shape.

A few days later, Pian wired trainer Ray Arcel, who was working with heavyweight Joe Baski in Sweden, and requested his assistance in preparing Tony for the fight with Rocky. Arcel was one of the best trainers in the game, and of course, worked the corner of Billy Soose when he defeated Tony in 1940. Arcel said he would fly to Chicago the next week to help put the finishing touches on Tony's training.

Six days away from the fight, Tony predicted he would knock Rocky out when the two met in Chicago Stadium. "I am more confident that I will win this time than I was in our previous bout last September. I broke my right hand in the second round of my first fight with Rocky, and I had to use it sparingly the rest of the way," said Tony. "I am punching better with my right than I ever did. I'll have two hands to work with in there this time."

In response, Rocky said, "I'm ready now. I wish the fight was tonight. I'm not going to fight Zale any differently than I did last time. I only know one way to fight. This business about a boxer can change his style, that's baloney. I only fight one way all my life."[215] Rocky's manager, Irving Cohen, claimed that Rocky was ruining his sparring partners and that they were running out of men for him to work with. Rocky confirmed that was the case many number of years later. "I was throwing thunderbolts all over the place in that Chicago gym. Twice I run out of sparring partners. Every time I knocked one out, three others lam it out of there, and they have to raise the ante to get any bums to stand up in the same ring with me.

---

214 *Winnipeg Free Press*, Rocky 'Het Up, June 18, 1947.
215 *Lowell Sun*, Zale Predicts Win by Kayo, July 10, 1947.

Every guy I put the gloves on with was Tony Zale to me. I killed them all just like I was going to kill Tony Zale."[216]

As the date of the fight neared, Tony and his team moved their training camp into Chicago's Ringside Gymnasium. Both men were examined by Dr. J. J. Drammis, of the Illinois Athletic Commission staff on July 11, and pronounced fit. From here on out, the fighters would taper off in their training routines in order to avoid the possibility of overtraining. Neither fighter believed their second fight would last very long, Tony predicting he would win by a knockout inside of six rounds, while Graziano insisted he would be the one delivering the knockout blow, and that he would do so within the first four rounds. "I'm in the best condition of my career right now,"

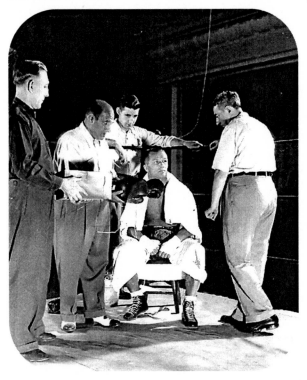

said Rocky. "Yes, much better than I was when he beat me in that last fight. I couldn't be in better shape."[217] But Tony said he was also in much better shape than the last time they fought, and reminded everyone that he suffered an illness that caused him to endure a two-week hospital stay prior to their first bout. Tony was a 7 to 5 favorite in the betting odds at the time, and former heavyweight champions Jack Dempsey and Joe Louis both predicted that Tony would be the victor. Trainer Ray Arcel arrived in Chicago from Sweden on July 13 to help wrap up

216 Graziano, Rocky, *Somebody Up There Likes Me*, Simon and Schuster, New York, New York 1955.
217 *Kokomo Tribune*, It's Unanimous, July 12, 1947.

Tony's preparation for the bout.[218]   Co-promoters Irving Schoenwald, Jack Begun, and Jack Hurley announced that $385,000 in revenues had already been collected from ticket orders.   They anticipated a total gate of anywhere from $425,000 to as much as $476,000 if the event was sold out.   Another $30,000 had already been paid for the radio broadcast rights to the fight.[219]

While it might seem a bit odd to bring Arcel in so late in Tony's training, the fact of the matter was that he was one of the best cut men in the business in addition to being a superb ring tactician.   He learned his craft under the guidance of two of the most respected and legendary trainers in the sport, Frank "Doc" Bagley and Dai Dollings. This was the kind of fight where it could come in very handy to have an outstanding cut man on hand.   In fact, Graziano had one in his corner as well in Whitey Bimstein, Arcel's former partner.

The great lightweight champion Benny Leonard respected Ray so much that he asked him to become his trainer when he was forced to make a comeback after he lost all of his money in the great stock market crash of 1929.   Winch and Pian turned to Ray for help with their future lightweight champion Barney Ross very early in his professional career in the 1930s.   As far as they were concerned, you couldn't have a better man working in your corner for such an important fight.

The day before the fight, Tony reiterated his prediction that he would knock Rocky out within six rounds and said that he'd promised his mother after the first fight with Rocky that he'd win another one like that.   After he defeated Rocky in their initial bout, his mother Catherine had told him she hoped she lived to see him win one more like it.   While she had never witnessed Tony's fight with Graziano, she listened to the broadcast by radio.   She died a few months later.

"I promised then," said Tony, "that I'd win another like that. This is it.   I'm doing it for her."

Pian said he was going to ask the boxing commission to instruct the referee to let the fighters' handlers decide whether the fight should be stopped because of an injury or bad beating.   Rocky's manager Irving Cohen agreed.   "We don't want anyone to get hurt, naturally," Sam went on, "but at the same time we don't want a

---

218 *The Times Record*, Even Bookies Now Confused On Wednesday Bout, July 14, 1947.
219 *Olean Times Herald*, Zale Favored To Repeat Earlier Win Over Rocky, July 14, 1947.

158

fighter stopped by some official who might become panicky after a knockdown. After all, the handlers know their fighter best."[220] Rocky and his manager were more concerned with the possibility of a fast count in the event of a knockdown. Even though Chicago was a city in which the official timekeeper yelled his count into a microphone so that every fan in the stadium could hear it, Rocky requested that a man from his camp be allowed to sit with a stopwatch in hand right next to the timekeeper in order to prevent a long count for Tony or a short count for himself.[221]

On the day of the fight both boxers weighed in under the middleweight limit of 160 pounds. Tony was scaling 159 to Rocky's 155 1/4 pounds.[222] Their fight at Chicago Stadium later that night was scheduled to be broadcast by the National Broadcasting Company at 10:00 p.m. A poll of twenty-five United Press writers determined that seventeen believed Tony would emerge victorious, while eight thought the hard hitting younger man would pull off the upset. Only one of the twenty-five writers thought the bout would go the full fifteen rounds.[223]

The time for talk was over. The City of Chicago was poised to host what promised to be the boxing event of the year and probably the century.

220 *Billings Gazette*, Writer Enumerates Five Factors Giving Zale Edge Over Graziano, July 15, 1947.
221 *The Daily News*, Graziano Wants Personal Check On Ref's Count, July 15, 1947.
222 *San Mateo Times*, Tony Zale Has Slight Weight Advantage, July 16, 1947.
223 *Altoona Mirror*, Tony Zale Is Favored To Again Take Victory, July 15, 1947.

ZALE vs. GRAZIANO II

July 16, 1947, was a sweltering day in Chicago. The temperature outside Chicago Stadium measured 90 degrees, but according to a thermometer that a United Press editor named Jack Cuddy thought to bring along with him, it was 105 degrees at ringside.[224] If the heat was going to have an effect on the outcome of the fight, there were many who believed that Tony, as the older of the two men, would suffer the most. The stifling heat that night must have reminded him of his days in the steel mills back home in Gary, Indiana.

Eighteen thousand, five hundred, forty-seven fans braved the heat and produced a new record of $422,918 in paid receipts for an indoor boxing show. The figure remained a record for an indoor boxing event until 1961, when the third heavyweight championship fight between Floyd Patterson and Ingemar Johansson produced a figure of approximately $485,000 in the Miami Beach Convention Hall.

People from all walks of life were in attendance. Governors from a number of states had flown in from a convention in Salt Lake City to witness the event. Stars of stage, screen and radio including the likes of Al Jolson, George Raft, Harry James and Frank Sinatra were scattered around the ring. Financiers, industrial leaders, doctors, lawyers, political leaders, matchmakers, managers and boxers, including former heavyweight champions Jack Dempsey and Gene Tunney, were all on hand to view what many believed would be the boxing event of the year.

Also in attendance was Tony's 16-year-old sister-in-law, Genevieve Richwalski. Genevieve lived with Adeline and Tony in

---

224 Bromberg, Lester, *Boxing's Unforgettable Fights*, The Ronald Press Co., New York, New York 1962.

1946 and 1947, after their mother passed away. Although their father Frank was still alive, he and his wife had divorced and he lived in Wisconsin where he operated a resort. Whereas, Adeline couldn't bear the idea of coming to one of Tony's fights and watching him receive punishment, young Genevieve thought it terribly exciting and she couldn't refuse an opportunity to attend the fight. She and a local priest were perched in the first balcony to witness the action.

An organ turned out festive jingles between rounds of the preliminary bouts and was used to belt out the song, "Back Home Again in Indiana," as the Champion appeared first and made his way toward the ring. "The Sidewalks of New York" was the tune of choice when the challenger followed and joined Tony in the ring.[225]

During the playing of "The Star Spangled Banner," Tony stood motionlessly at attention, while Rocky fidgeted and made a few remarks to a fellow just below his corner. A number of the many dignitaries in attendance were introduced to the crowd, former heavyweight champion Jack Dempsey receiving the loudest ovation. Welterweight champion Sugar Ray Robinson was on hand and decked out in a green checkered sport coat, yellow slacks and a lilac colored shirt.

As the crowd waited in eager anticipation of a battle that might match the fighter's previous encounter, Tony and Rocky were brought to the center of the ring to receive their final instructions from Referee Johnny Behr. Rocky appeared restless and nervous. He was unshaven and it made his complexion appear darker, while Tony, who was clean shaven, looked calm and confident, almost as though he was happy to be there.[226]

Those who had hoped to see a repeat of the pair's first fight were not disappointed. There was no feeling out period during the opening session. The two men seemingly prescribed to the theory that the best defense was a good offense, and they wasted no time putting that methodology to use in the first round. "Seldom do you see a championship fight where both are so scornful of taking a punch, where both are so imbued with the desire to settle the affair

225 Irving, Marsh, *Best Sports Stories 1948*, E.P. Dutton & Co., New York, New York 1948.
226 Bromberg, Lester, *Boxing's Unforgettable Fights*, The Ronald Press Co., New York, New York 1962.

with the least possible resort to defense," one reporter said afterward.[227]

Throughout the round, Rocky rushed in, swinging wildly with lefts and rights aimed at Tony's jaw, looking to land an early knockout blow. At one point, he landed three rights in succession to the chin, causing Tony's knees to buckle. Another combination sent Tony back on his heels.

But Tony refused to go down and he fought back with solid lefts and rights to the body and staggered Rocky with short rights to the jaw that sent him reeling into the ropes. As he so often did, Tony concentrated his early attack on the midsection where he believed Rocky was the weakest. A right hand blow from Tony ripped open a deep gash over Rocky's left eye and a number of left hooks prompted a swelling around his other eye.

Pounded steadily in the later stages of the round, Rocky's face was smeared with blood by the time the bell rang, and his right eye was already beginning to close.[228] Looking back on the fight in his autobiography eight years later, Rocky said, "This was no boxing match. It was a war and if there wasn't a referee, one of us would have wound up dead. I still can't look at the pictures of that fight without it hurts me and I get nightmares that I am back in the ring on the hot July night and I am looking through a red film of blood." The first round was awarded to Tony and the crowd buzzed with excitement as he strode confidently to his corner.

Of the right hand that opened the deep cut over his left eye in the first round, Rocky said, "It was like he crashed a gun butt over my eye. I couldn't see out of it no more, and the blood starts pouring out. They closed it between rounds, but in the second, Tony hit it a number of times and the blood started running again."[229]

Rocky rushed out to open the second round and tried to land a big left hook to the jaw, but in no time at all, he was on the receiving end of a succession of short rights and lefts that reopened the cut over his left eye and reproduced a flow of blood and forced the challenger to retreat. Rocky fought back, but he was wild with most

---

227 *Wisconsin State Journal*, Graziano Stops Zale in Sixth Round, July 17, 1947.
228 *New York Times*, Graziano Knocks Out Zale in Sixth Round to Take World Middleweight Title, July 17, 1947.
229 Graziano, Rocky, *Somebody Up There Likes Me*, Simon and Schuster, New York, New York 1955.

of his blows and Tony steadily rained lefts and rights upon his opponent, alternating his attack between the head and body.

As the third round opened, Tony jabbed at Rocky's eyes, the left one badly bothered by a flow of blood, and the right gradually closing. Then, early in the round, Tony sent Rocky crashing to the floor with a right to the chin as the crowd roared in surprise. More embarrassed than hurt, a sheepish Rocky jumped up before the referee could begin a count and smiled behind his blood smeared mask. Tony pounded Rocky all over the ring in this session, landing powerful blows with both hands to the body that caused him to double over, and then forcing him to retreat with punches to the head. Rocky tried to fight back, but more often than not, his desperate blows missed their mark. Rocky looked shaky and seemed headed toward certain defeat when the round ended.[230]

Of that round, Rocky later said, "The third was the worst round I ever lived through in the ring. Before I could put a glove on Zale, he belts me a right on my jaw and the arena is spinning and when it stops I am sitting on the frigging canvas looking up with one good eye blinking through the blood. I jump to my feet before there is even a count. But before I can square off he is all over me again, whamming me in the middle, trying to cut off my wind like he done in Yankee Stadium. He caught me an awful whack like a policeman's bat socked me across the belly and it doubled me over. Then he quick goes for my head. I can't see nothing for the rest of the round, only this red blur that comes at me, fades away, comes at me. My head is knocked to the left, to the right, like it is going to come right off my neck. I hold up my hands, but he smashes them back into my face. I lunge out at the blur, but there is only air. My arms and legs feel like they are made out of lead and I almost topple over. When the bell rung I ached from my head to my feet."

When Rocky returned to his corner, Whitey Bimstein rushed to work on his eyes. His right eye was so swollen Whitey had to lance it, and another assistant, Frank Percoco, pressed a quarter against it to bring down the swelling so Rocky could see out of it again. Then, Whitey went to work on the cut over the left eye.[231] The first thing Rocky saw when he looked up was the referee looking him over and

230 *New York Times*, Graziano Knocks Out Zale in Sixth Round to Take World Middleweight Title, July 17, 1947.
231 Fried, Ronald, *Corner Men*, Four Walls Eight Windows, New York, New York 1991.

shaking his head. "Looks pretty bad, don't it," Whitey said. Cohen said later that Rocky was in such sorry condition at this point that he was hoping the fight would be stopped.[232] Rocky knew what they were thinking, they were wondering if they should stop the fight. Rocky shook his head and banged his fists together. Whitey asked Behr to give Rocky one more round.

Behr made a face and said, "If this wasn't a championship fight, I would never let him last out the third round. One more and if he don't come out of it, I got to stop it. They give you the chair for murder in this state."[233]

Sportswriter Bill Stern, who was seated ringside, said later, "The man who patched Rocky up after that round deserves all the credit in the world for helping him win the title." Stern said the ringside physician was seated right next to him and that he had to be careful what he said aloud for fear that the doctor might stop the fight at any moment. "Graziano was that bad off," said Stern.[234]

Knowing the fight was in danger of being stopped if he didn't reverse the tide, Rocky sprang from his corner in the fourth round with a renewed passion. It was in this round that the first sign of the impact of the heat began to tell on Tony. Rather than follow-up on the advantage he'd gained in the third session, Tony appeared to be content to box Rocky in this round and he looked tired during what wound up being the slowest round of the fight. Rocky was leery at the beginning of the round, possibly wondering if Tony wasn't playing possum. But when he landed a glancing blow that produced a light counter punch by Tony that hit nothing but air and caused him to sprawl forward on his hands and knees, there seemed little doubt but that the Champion was badly tiring.[235]

While the life seemed to drain from Tony's body during the fourth round, the challenger got a second wind during the intermission between the fourth and fifth sessions. When the bell rang in the fifth stanza, Rocky bolted across the ring and shook the Champion up with three rights to the head and a left hook to the jaw. Encouraged by Tony's weakened condition, Rocky tore after the

---

232 *Abilene Reporter News*, Zale-Graziano Scrap Won't Go The Distance, June 5, 1948.
233 Graziano, Rocky, *Somebody Up There Likes Me*, Simon and Schuster, New York, New York 1955.
234 *Portland Press Herald*, Bill Stern Vacations In Maine, August 3, 1947.
235 *New York Times*, Graziano Knocks Out Zale in Sixth Round to Take World Middleweight Title, July 17, 1947.

Champion with a furious exchange of lefts and rights that brought the crowd to its feet. Tony was being hit with punches that he'd stepped away from earlier in the fight.

He managed to evade some of the blows and pull away from others to lessen their effect, but Rocky would not be denied and continued to rain in a succession of lefts and right hooks and uppercuts, and many of the blows began to find their mark.[236] It was in this round that Rocky said the turning point in the fight occurred. "I hit him with a right to the ribs that made him moan," Rocky said. "The next time Zale threw a punch, he had no steam left. I knew that was it, because it didn't hurt."[237] Rocky's blows staggered Tony a number of times during the round and had him bleeding from the lower lip upon the rounds' conclusion.[238]

Thirty seconds into the sixth round, Rocky landed a hard right to the head that caused Tony's knees to buckle and then followed with a swinging left to the head as Tony staggered back. The crowd roared as Rocky tore in for the kill. Tony tried to fight back, but he was too weak and Rocky shook off the punches and drove him into a corner, where he surely would have gone down if not held up by the ropes. Tony managed to escape the corner, and clumsily weaved around the ring with Rocky on his heels, delivering a succession of blows to the head that sent Tony spinning into the ropes which he laid draped over with his head down, while Rocky pounded

UPI Photo

---

236 *New York Times*, Graziano Knocks Out Zale in Sixth Round to Take World Middleweigh Title, July 17, 1947.

237 *Iowa City Press-Citizen*, Turning Point, July 25, 1947.

238 *Syracuse Herald-Journal*, New Yorker Stops Champ in 6th After Absorbing Bad Lacing, July 17, 1947.

away at his sides.[239]

It might have been better if Tony had gone down and taken a count of nine in order to recuperate at some point during the onslaught, but he was fighting on instinct in this round and that was against the nature of his fighting heart. Covering the fight for the *New York Post*, Jimmy Cannon counted a total of thirty-six unanswered punches in a row that Rocky landed on Tony, before Referee Behr stepped in and waved him off, bringing an end to the fight two minutes and 10 seconds into the sixth round.[240] Many thought Rocky had fouled Tony as he continued to pound him on the back of the head as Tony was draped over the ropes. When Referee Behr stopped the fight, even Rocky's managers were afraid that the fight had not been called in Rocky's favor.

239 *Syracuse Herald-Journal*, New Yorker Stops Champ in 6th After Absorbing Bad Lacing, July 17, 1947.
240 *New York Post*, Graziano Proves His Courage, July 17, 1947.

UPI Photo

As Tony's handlers rushed to his aid, it took a few moments for it to sink in for Rocky. At first he struggled to get away from his own seconds as they swarmed him in celebration of his victory, as if he didn't realize the fight was over. But then it sunk in, and he strode across the ring to shake Tony's hand, posed for pictures and stepped to the microphone for a radio interview. After answering some questions, Rocky conveyed a message to his mother back home in New York when he bellowed into the microphone, "Hello Ma, the bad boy done it," and he had. Rocky Graziano was the new Middleweight Champion of the World.

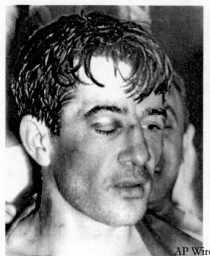

AP Wire Photos

Tony and his managers complained bitterly that Referee Behr had stopped the fight too soon. "Tony wasn't hurt," Winch shouted. "Tony's been in worse fixes than that. He could've come through," added Ray Arcel. Someone questioned Behr about the timing of the stoppage, and Behr snapped in reply, "What do they want up there, murder? Somebody asked if I saw the first fight in New York or if I was thinking about what happened to Jimmy Doyle in Cleveland (Doyle had died after suffering a knockout against Sugar Ray Robinson three weeks earlier in a welterweight championship bout). No! I was just thinking about what was happening up there in that ring."[241]

"I should have stopped the bout when Zale was slumped in the corner in the sixth round because his eyes had ceased to focus. But, because he was champion, I let him continue until he was a completely helpless target – with absolutely no hope of recuperating," added Behr.[242]

But Tony was adamant in his belief that the fight should have gone on. "I knew what was going on," he protested. "I had 50 seconds left until the bell, and I think I could have lasted it out, although my legs started to tie up a bit in the fifth round."[243] He

241 *The Daily Journal-Gazette*, Behr's Decision Added to Fistic World Legends, July 17, 1947.
242 *Syracuse Herald-Journal*, New Yorker Stops Champ in 6th After Absorbing Bad Lacing, July 17, 1947.
243 *Freeport Journal-Standard*, Spectators Faint; Zale and Graziano Go Under Own Power, July 17, 1947.

asked Jimmy Cannon of *The New York Post* if he thought the fight should have been stopped when it was. "Yes," Jimmy replied, "You might have been killed."

"I got a right to get killed for my own championship," Tony responded.[244]

But many of those who witnessed the ending were convinced that Behr had made the correct decision, including Joe Williams of *The New York World Telegram* who wrote, "There never was a more real knockout than the one Graziano planted on Zale. It was technical only to the extent that it wasn't murder."[245]

The loser's locker room was quiet. A *Chicago News* cameraman was on hand talking with Sam Pian as Arcel soaked towels in ice water and draped them over a leather table. Arcel looked at Winch and said, "It was the heat that got him, not Graziano. He just couldn't breathe."

"When did he first complain of the heat?" asked the cameraman.

"Never," said Arcel. "He never complains about anything. But you could see after the third round that he wasn't coming back from those shots to the head. And he wasn't punching the way he had been. The heat was sucking the strength from his body."

"Do you think age had anything to do with it?" the cameraman asked.

"It could be," said Arcel. "Age goes a long way in this business. I mean it goes a long way to beat you."[246]

Many years later, Arcel recalled that Tony was bothered again with arthritis in his right elbow prior to this fight. "I'd stay up all night putting heat on it toward the end of training camp," Arcel said. "I kept a lamp focused on the elbow to keep it hot. So I had to watch the lamp so he didn't get burned or that it didn't catch fire."[247] This was the same elbow he later had operated on in 1949, to have five bone chips taken out. The doctor who performed the surgery, with Tony's doctor, Dr. Danielski assisting, said the elbow may have sustained permanent damage if they had not removed the bone chips.

Tony admitted the heat got to him. Slumped on a table in his dressing room with his head down he said, "The heat got me in the

244 *New York Post*, These Honest Pugilists Are All Blood and Guts, July 17, 1947.
245 Bromberg, Lester, *Boxing's Unforgettable Fights*, The Ronald Press Co., New York, New York 1962.
246 Jarrett, John '*Champ In The Corner*, Stadia, Stroud, Gloucestershire, U.K. 2007.
247 Jarrett, John, *Champ In The Corner*, Stadia, Stroud, Gloucestershire, U.K. 2007.

fifth and I couldn't do any good after that." Make no mistake, the heat that evening was brutal. No less than 10 spectators fainted because of the heat and were treated in a first aid room before being released to go home. One writer, Henry McCormick, who covered the bout from the third row for the *Wisconsin State Journal*, said it was hotter than you know what where he was sitting, and that one could imagine how much worse it was up in the ring directly under 36 burning floodlights.[248]

But as far as Tony was concerned, it was a combination of the heat and a poor decision of the referee to stop the fight when he did that cost him his title. "I was hit harder and was in worse shape in the second and fifth rounds of our New York fight than I was in this one," he said.[249] He firmly believed that he would have come back and defeated Rocky if he'd been allowed to continue. To the day he died, he contended that this fight should not have been stopped. "I would have come back and beat him just like I did in the first fight," Tony said.

His sister-in-law, Genevieve, also believed the fight was stopped too soon. "The blood on Tony was all Rocky's," she said. "They just wanted a third fight between the two and they got it."[250]

Sam Pian blamed the Illinois Athletic Commission for events that he felt contributed to Tony's loss. He said that Sheldon Clark and his subordinates did everything in their power to hinder Tony's chances of winning. In his view, it started with the long, tiring weighing-in ceremony during which Clark kept Tony and Rocky sitting in the ring in intense heat for more than an hour while he issued instructions in the middle of the day when a fighter should be relaxing prior to a grueling fight.

"That harmed a boxer of Zale's age tremendously," said Pian, "but it was only the start."

"I pleaded with Clark to open the doors during the fight to keep the building as cool as possible. I also requested that the main bout go on before the usual intermission, or before the big crowd filled the building with tobacco smoke. And I asked that the fighters be allowed to put on the gloves downstairs in the dressing room before

---

248 *Wisconsin State Journal*, Playing The Game, July 18, 1947.
249 *Nevada State Journal*, Rocky Scores in Comeback, July 17, 1947.
250 July 2011 interview with Genevieve Bancroft.

coming up, so they wouldn't have to sit under those scorching lights any longer than possible. Every request I made was refused."

What infuriated Pian most, was that the main point of Clark's instructions while he kept the fighters sitting in a hot ring for more than an hour earlier in the day, was ignored during the fight. That was the agreement that the referee wouldn't stop the fight if one man seemed to be in trouble without consulting his handlers.[251] Pian wouldn't forget these "slights" when it came time to agree on a site for a future title bout.

Tony was asked what his wife thought about the fight. "She's never seen me fight, but she wanted me to get this one. I think she wanted it because she knows I want it more than anything," he said.[252] It was a bitter defeat for Tony, but he believed he would receive a chance to regain his title. For the time being, he would have to try his best to enjoy some well-earned time off with his family, and content himself with the knowledge that his end of the purse was a whopping $140,682. After the contracted split, Tony's $70,341 was hit with the cost of the usual training expenses, and federal income taxes. In the end, he took home approximately $20,000 to put in the bank.

The winner's dressing room was an absolute mob scene. Rocky blew kisses at the cameras and the newspapermen in a dressing room so hot that one of the photographers passed out.[253] "After the fourth, I knew I had him and I told Irving (Cohen) I was going to get Zale in the same round he said would get me. And I did," said Rocky.[254] He was asked how it felt to win the title when he was still under suspension back in New York. "Tell th' people of New York th' black sheep becom' the champ," he replied.[255] Deliriously happy over his win, Rocky was a sight to behold, his right eye almost closed and a deep cut over his swollen left eye. Truth be told, it was a repeat of the first fight between the two, where the winner wore the features of a badly beaten man afterward. Anyone who hadn't seen the finish and looked in on the two afterward would have guessed the winner must have lost.

---

251 *Chicago Sun-Times*, Zale Won't Fight Here, June 10, 1948.
252 Jarrett, John, *Champ In The Corner*, Stadia, Stroud, Gloucestershire, U.K. 2007.
253 *Nevada State Journal*, Rocky Scores in Comeback, July 17, 1947.
254 *Nevada State Journal*, Rocky Scores in Comeback, July 17, 1947.
255 Bromberg, Lester, *Boxing's Unforgettable Fights*, The Ronald Press Co., New York, New York 1962.

It was learned that there was an agreement between the fighters and their management that a return bout would be staged within ninety days if the title changed hands as a result of their second contest. Since that occurred, it appeared as though a third title bout between the two was imminent. When Tony found his way to Rocky's dressing room to offer his congratulations, he was assured by Rocky that he'd get a chance to win his title back. "You're the guy I want to fight," he told Tony.[256] "Tony gave me a shot at the title," Rocky said, "and I got to give him a chance at it too."[257]

Some believed it was the end of the line for Tony and at 34, that he'd reached an age where his reflexes had declined. "Zale beat Father Time last September," when he defeated Rocky in their first title contest wrote one scribe, "but the old guy with the long beard and scythe caught up with him this time."[258] Jack Dempsey, who believed that winning the championship would improve Rocky at least 25 percent, was among those who now believed Rocky would defeat Tony in a third match between the pair, saying Rocky should whip Tony "thoroughly and finally" when they met again.[259]

Many were calling the first two fights between Tony and Rocky the greatest slug fests of all time. Rocky had evened the score, and boxing fans were already eagerly anticipating the rubber match.

---

256 *New York Times*, Graziano Knocks Out Zale in Sixth Round to Take World Middleweight Title, July 17, 1947.
257 *Nevada State Journal*, Bruised But Happy Rocky To Head Brooklyn Parade, July 18, 1947.
258 *Wisconsin State Journal*, Graziano Stops Zale in Sixth Round, July 17, 1947.
259 *Kingsport Times*, Manassa Mauler Favors Graziano, September 15, 1947.

TITLE LOSS BLUES

Rocky Graziano's win over Tony put the New York State Athletic Commission in the unenviable position of having a man now recognized as the undisputed middleweight champion of the world, who was under suspension in his home state. Commissioner Eddie Eagan was asked if Rocky's victory would prompt a lifting of the suspension of his boxing license in the state. He said he had no desire to talk about the issue at the time, but added that any change in Rocky's status would require a decision on the part of the entire commission.[260]

Joe Williams, of *The New York World Telegram*, expressed his belief that Rocky would be reinstated in New York in time for his first title defense. "One of Eagan's responsibilities is to encourage and stimulate boxing in New York State," wrote Williams. It was clear in his mind that an ongoing suspension of Rocky's license wouldn't serve that need, and as far as Joe was concerned, it would be ludicrous for the state to continue to force a gate attraction as large as Rocky to perform out of state.[261]

Regardless of his suspension, Rocky returned to Brooklyn, New York, as a conquering hero. He rode home from the Grand Central train station in an open automobile to signs of welcome and congratulations on storefronts in his neighborhood. A corner bar had a table set up filled with sandwiches that had been contributed by local merchants. There was a large cake, sent from a nearby baker, with a miniature boxing ring and picture of Rocky.

Sidney Moses, an assistant commissioner of Borough Works, gave a short speech and said that the Second Avenue Businessmen's

---

260 *Oakland Tribune*, New York Ring Body Silent On Rock's Victory, July 18, 1947.
261 *El Paso Herald Post*, NY Likely to Lift Rocky's Suspension, July 18, 1947.

Association planned to circulate petitions in an effort to obtain 50,000 signatures asking the athletic commission to reinstate Rocky's license in the state. In the meantime, Rocky planned to rest at home for a few days and then take a family vacation for two to three weeks in Ellenville, New York. A coast to coast exhibition tour that would begin in mid-August was also being arranged.[262] There were no plans for Rocky to fight for the balance of the year.

The only real unfavorable aspect of Rocky's return to Brooklyn was that his home was burglarized while he was in Chicago. The crooks jimmied open a window, and took all of Rocky's suits, sports jackets and sweaters, cuff links and jewelry. The Graziano's lived in the lower half of a two-story home, and their upstairs neighbor returned home on July 8 and noticed that Rocky's front door was open. Upon investigation, she discovered the home had been robbed. Rocky's manager, Irving Cohen, was advised about the burglary while they were with Rocky in Chicago, but decided to keep the news from him until after the fight.[263] Of course, today there's no way that something like this would have been kept out of the news.

While Tony returned home and spent some time with his family, his managers began to receive offers for a third fight between Rocky and him. On July 26, 1947, it was reported that Sam Pian had accepted a guaranteed offer of $75,000 from promoter Harry Voiler, a Miami Beach, Florida, hotel operator, for a title fight with Rocky to be held in Miami Beach sometime in February. Rocky was offered a guarantee of $150,000. Pian said that Voiler had agreed to pay Tony $25,000 upon signing the agreement, and would pay him the remaining $50,000 when they were 48 hours away from the contest.

Three days later, Chicago promoter Harry Hannin announced that he was working toward staging a return match between Tony and Rocky in Chicago in the spring of 1948. Hannin said he'd wired an offer to Cohen that guaranteed a total gate of $500,000. He asked Cohen to specify the percentage of that figure that the Champion would require in order to sign for the fight. According to Hannin, he had the backing of a group of Chicago sportsmen, and the bout would be staged in an outdoor stadium.

---

262 *Wisconsin State Journal*, Coast to Coast Exhibition Tour Planned by Graziano, July 19, 1947.
263 *The Charleston Gazette*, Burglars Raid Graziano Home, July 20, 1947.

Pian hadn't ruled out the possibility that Rocky's suspension in New York would be lifted, and the fight would take place there. But he was confident the fight would happen one way or another regardless of whether it was in New York, Miami or Chicago because Rocky and Cohen had told them that Tony would be Rocky's opponent in his first title defense. The location of the fight was all up to Cohen as the Champion's manager.

On August 18, *The Ironwood Daily Globe* reported that Tony and his wife had visited Ironwood, Michigan, while they were vacationing in the Minocqua, Wisconsin, area. The couple posed for a photograph for an Ironwood cameraman during their brief visit that ran in the paper two days later and they appeared happy and relaxed.[264] On this trip the couple had also visited Adele's father at his Wisconsin resort.

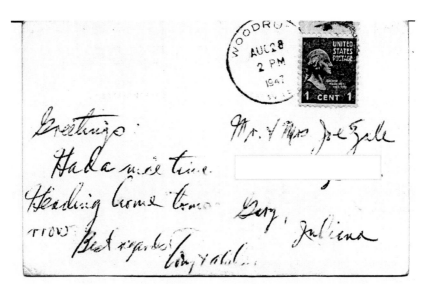

In late August, Abe Greene, President of the National Boxing Association, expressed the organization's disappointment over the length of time that important titles were being tied up as a result of contracts calling for return bouts and/or rubber matches between two fighters. He suggested that it was a practice that had become all too common and was very unfair to other top title contenders. Greene promised that the association would make a ruling requiring

---

264 *Ironwood Daily Globe,* Zale Visits In Ironwood, August 18, 1947.

that title fight winners of all divisions be required to defend their title against another "logical contender" before staging a return bout with an opponent from their last title fight. And should the "logical contender" win, they would be required to then defend the title against the original champion.[265]

The original title fight between Tony and Rocky had been scheduled for July of 1946, before it was moved to that September. Since neither man defended his title, nor was going to defend it against any other opponent until they had met for a third time, that ultimately meant that nobody else ended up fighting for that title over almost two full years. This obviously resulted in a great amount of frustration on the part of other great fighters and their managers.

On September 23, 1947, it was announced that Tony would officiate several bouts at a boxing show in Dixon, Illinois, on October 13. The proceeds from the show featuring boxers from the Peoria, Illinois, and Gary, Indiana, amateur boxing clubs were going to be used to help purchase a two-way radio system for the local police. Tony's nephew, Joe Zale Jr., was going to participate in a 135-pound match. According to Joe, before his fight, Tony instructed him to make good use of his left hook. Since Joe's father had taught it to him, Tony knew that it was a knockout punch. Using his uncle's advice, Joe succeeded in knocking out his opponent in the second round.

A week later word came out of Chicago that Rocky Graziano would be banned from competing again in the state of Illinois. Already under suspension in New York, Rocky learned that he could no longer fight in Illinois either because that state's athletic commission issued a ruling barring dishonorably discharged servicemen from boxing in the state. They expressed their regret that the war department hadn't shared Rocky's service record prior to the fight the previous July. They indicated they would not have allowed the fight to go forward if they had known Rocky's service record.

While Rocky couldn't be reached for comment, Cohen issued a statement in response that read, "I can only say now that when Rocky entered the army he was a wild kid up from the city streets, a kid who never had the privileges of most youngsters as he grew up. He had to learn the hard way that the army wasn't fooling when it

---

265 *Wisconsin State Journal*, NBA Has Modern Ruling Planned to Boost Boxing, August 27, 1947.

gave him a new pattern to live by. The Graziano of today is as different from the Rocky who entered the army as day and night."[266]

The prospect of Tony fighting Rocky a third time didn't get any better when N.B.A. President Abe Greene said their association might bar Rocky from any further fighting if the war department's report was confirmed. He promised a thorough investigation into the circumstances of the dishonorable discharge. If the N.B.A. barred Rocky, it meant that he would be barred from fighting in every state except for Massachusetts and New York, and he was already under suspension in the latter. Greene left the door ajar, however, when he said that if Rocky's dishonorable discharge was suspended by the army, as Cohen claimed, they might not bar him. Greene said the burden of proof rested with Rocky, but he'd have every opportunity to prove his innocence.[267]

This didn't prevent Miami Beach promoter Harry Voiler from working to bring the title fight to Florida. On October 12, word was leaked that he and Rocky's manager Irving Cohen had reached a financial agreement that would not only allow the pair to fight there on February 12, 1948, but give Voiler exclusive rights to the promotion of Graziano's bouts for a ten-year period.[268] The real kicker, though, was that it was reported that the entire proceeds from the fight would be donated to charity with 50% of the profits going to the Damon Runyon Cancer Fund, and the balance divided among local charities.[269]

On October 13, 1947, Tony officiated three of the six bouts held in Dixon, Illinois, and was greeted with a loud ovation. After, he gave a short speech to the crowd. Tony's nephew Joe whipped his Peoria opponent, Garnet Meichner, as the Gary boys captured five of the six contests. Asked about a third match with Rocky, Tony said, "I really want to meet Graziano again in the worst way. I know I can lick him this time. I just hope nothing goes wrong to upset the Miami plans. I want the fight more than anything." When informed that

---

266 *Waterloo Daily Courier*, Says Illinois Rule Barring Dishonorably Discharged Vets Refers to Graziano, September 30, 1947.
267 *Titusville Herald*, Thorough Check of Circumstances Promised by NBA, October 1, 1947.
268 *Wisconsin State Journal*, Report Graziano, Zale to Meet In Orange Bowl Feb. 12, October 12, 1947.
269 *Salt Lake City Tribune*, Graziano, Zale Fight Feb. 1 At Miami, Cohen Reveals, October 13, 1947.

Florida's governor was objecting to Rocky fighting in the state, Tony said he had no knowledge of that. He complied with the many autograph requests between posing for photographs for cameramen.[270]

Three days later, it was reported that a wave of opposition to the fight was sweeping through the city of Miami. Veteran groups, and at least one boxing commissioner, had gone on record as opposing the fight because of Rocky's dishonorable discharge from the service.[271] Then, without waiting to be asked, the Miami Boxing Commission announced that they were going to bar a match in the city between Rocky and Tony for the middleweight title.[272] Voiler immediately turned to his lawyers in the hopes of finding some way to stage the fight without the blessing of the commission. He was still working to make the fight happen at the end of October after receiving assurance from the Miami Beach Chamber of Commerce that they hadn't gone on record against the contest.

On November 19, Tony appeared in Rockford, Illinois, to officiate at a Swedish gym's amateur boxing show in the Shrine Temple.

At year-end, *The Ring* magazine editor Nat Fleischer named the second Zale-Graziano fight as the "1947 Fight of the Year." So, for the second consecutive year, the magazine selected that middleweight title bout as the highlight of the boxing year.[273] In their end of the year rankings, the N.B.A. placed the Frenchman Marcel Cerdan ahead of Tony among the top middleweight contenders. It was apparent that many believed that Tony had slowed up, and Cerdan now represented a greater threat for the middleweight crown.

As the year came to a close, it remained to be determined if Tony and Rocky would get a chance to fight in the rubber match that so many fans were hoping to see. Although Tony lost his title in 1947, he could console himself to some degree with the knowledge that only heavyweight champion Joe Louis earned more than he did inside the ring during the year.

Back in Gary, talks were deteriorating between the troubled couple as Tony was still confused and having difficulty understanding

---

270 *Dixon Evening Telegram*, Zale Pines for Bout With His Conqueror, October 14, 1947.
271 *Lima News*, Miami Doesn't Want Zale-Graziano Bout, October 16, 1947.
272 *Wisconsin State Journal*, Bar Graziano Bout, October 19, 1947.
273 *Winnipeg Free Press*, Lesnevich Is Named Fighter Of The Year, December 29, 1947.

Adele's continuing mood swings. One minute she was as saintly and as attractive a person you could ever expect to meet. Then the next moment, it was as if the devil had taken over her personality. For Tony, life's journey was always simple. You work hard and concentrate on family while achieving your goals. For Adele, her life was becoming more and more about herself and her music, while family was secondary. It was obvious that what she wanted to do was to further the career of Adele Rich, the musician. She also began delivering blows to Tony's groin area again and then demanding sexual relations. More upheaval awaited around the corner.

ZALE vs. GRAZIANO III COMES TOGETHER

As fans awaited news of a third fight between Tony and Rocky, Tony's managers made sure he would remain sharp by scheduling him to fight in a main event bout in Grand Rapids, Michigan, on January 23, 1948. Ultimately, Al Turner of Buffalo, New York, was named his opponent. While Tony prepared for the contest with Turner, Rocky resumed training as well. Rocky was reportedly eighteen pounds overweight as a result of his enforced layoff.[274]

Turner provided Tony with little more than a good workout before 2,000 fans at the Armory in Grand Rapids on January 23, where he suffered a fifth round knockout. The opening round was uneventful, but Tony opened up thereafter and began to land punches at will against the rangy black man over the next two rounds. He knocked Turner to the canvas two times in the fourth round, Turner taking a count of nine on each occasion, and then knocked him through the ropes in the fifth round. Turner, who suffered cuts over both eyes, was counted out while attempting to climb back into the ring. He weighed 159 pounds to Tony's 161.[275]

On January 28, boxing promoter Al Weill, who would later go on to manage heavyweight champion Rocky Marciano in the 1950s, announced that he had offered Rocky Graziano $120,000 to defend his title against Tony at the Atlantic City, New Jersey Convention Hall in May. Tony was offered $60,000. Weill extended the offer on behalf of a small group of New York businessmen who billed themselves, "Tournament of Champions, Inc." A few days later, Weill severed his relationship with the group, saying that they couldn't come to an agreement on compensation for his services. The group was clearly still interested in staging the bout. A couple of weeks later, Pian confirmed that plans to hold a match between the two men in Atlantic City in May were being discussed.[276]

The state of Indiana also threw its hat in the ring when promoter W.C. Nunnally of Michigan City announced that he had offered Sam Pian a guarantee of $60,000 against 20 percent of the gate. He planned to offer Irving Cohen and Rocky a $120,000 guarantee against 40 percent of the gate. However, Nunnally hadn't consulted with the Indiana Athletic Commission prior to making his

---

274 *Chronicle Telegram*, Today's Sports Parade, January 17, 1948.
275 *Marshall Evening Chronicle*, Tony Zale Knocks Out Turner At Grand Rapids, January 24, 1948.
276 *Frederick Post*, Graziano-Zale Go Headed For Atlantic City In May, February 17, 1948.

announcement and that organization's secretary, Walter Ringer, said it would take a lot of study to determine whether or not the middleweight championship bout between the two men could be staged there.

So, with nothing settled concerning another match with Rocky, Tony agreed to fight 24-year-old Bobby Claus in Little Rock, Arkansas, on March 8. No doubt fearful of Rocky being rusty, Cohen made arrangements for their own fighter to fight in Washington, D.C., on April 5, against George "Sonny" Horne. In order to grease the skids and ensure that bout wouldn't be opposed, it was agreed that Rocky would only receive one dollar for the fight, with the balance of his purse being donated to a polio fund.

On March 8, Tony appeared in Little Rock and dominated Bobby Claus on the way to a four round technical knockout victory over the younger man. Tony was the aggressor all the way and dropped Claus twice with left hand punches to the body during the one-sided affair. Claus, who was on the floor upon the conclusion of the fourth round, wasn't allowed to come out for the fifth because of a cut upper lip. Tony weighed 160 pounds to 157 for Claus.[277] Three days later, it was announced that Tony would face an opponent named Lou Woods of Detroit, Michigan, in Toledo, Ohio, on March 19.

Woods suffered a deep cut over his left eye in the first round of his bout with Tony, but he came out and made a fight of it in the second session, basically fighting Tony on even terms over the course of that round. But gameness only goes so far, and Tony drove him across the ring with a two-fisted attack before using a left hook to the jaw to knock Woods out one minute and twenty seconds into the third round.[278] A paying crowd of 5,500 was on hand to witness the action. Tony weighed 160 pounds for the contest and Woods 162.[279]

Three days later, Irving Cohen revealed that plans were once again in the making for a title fight between Rocky and Tony. The outfit known as the Tournament of Champions had a new man, Andy Niederreiter, directing negotiations. They had their sights set on a June date. Sam Pian was scheduled to join the discussions and Cohen was optimistic the fight would be made this time.[280] On

277 *Wisconsin Rapids Daily Tribune*, Zale Knocks Out Claus In Fourth, March 9, 1948.
278 *Evening Independent*, Tony Zale Wins Bout With Woods, March 20, 1948.
279 *European Stars and Stripes*, Zale Scores Kayo Over Woods in 3rd, March 21, 1948.
280 *Cumberland Evening News*, Zale, Graziano May Soon Meet In Title Bout, March 22, 1948.

March 25, New Jersey's *Bayonne Times* quoted Rocky as saying that he had signed a contract to defend the title against Tony at Roosevelt Stadium in Jersey City on June 9. Jersey City was selected over Atlantic City because it was closer to New York fight followers.[281] (Later, the site was changed to Ruppert Stadium.) The Tournament of Champions posted a $10,000 bond for the use of the stadium.

Rocky defeated "Sonny" Horne in his own tune-up bout on April 5, but appeared rusty in winning a ten round decision. His timing was off and he missed repeatedly, sometimes by as much as six inches. Rocky summed up his feelings concerning the bout afterward, when he said, "I needed this one. If they don't ban me out of the ring, they'll rust me out." Many of those in attendance were dissatisfied with the performance and booed when the decision was announced.[282] Sonny Horne later died of ALS at the age of 35.

In his biography, Rocky admits it wasn't one of his better fights, but he claims he had Horne in a helpless condition in the sixth round and that when they came together in a clinch, Horne begged him not to knock him out. "Horne is a nice, clean-cut guy, and I liked him since the first time we fought. So I let him hang on for the distance," said Rocky.[283]

Tony and Rocky met in New York on April 8 and officially signed for the fight in the presence of Niederreiter, N.B.A. President, Abe Greene, and head of the Tournament of Champions, Ben Bodine. "I think I'll do better this time," Tony said. "And it won't go as long as it did before." At his own table, Rocky said, "Sure, they said I looked bad against Horne the other night. But, how can you keep your mind on a fight when all this other stuff is bothering you?"[284]

Tony still maintained that their second fight was stopped too soon. "Rocky was terrific out in Chicago. But I wish that fight had been held down here (New York). I think they stopped it too quick. I was clear at the count of three and had my hands up when they stopped it. This fight will be shorter than the last two. I've learned things about Rocky in those fights. I think I can beat him. If I lose it

---

281 *Lowell Sun*, Graziano and Zale Reported Signed June 9, March 25, 1948.
282 *Mason City Globe-Gazette*, Champion Shows Effect of Layoff, April 7, 1948.
283 Graziano, Rocky, *Somebody Up There Likes Me*, Simon and Schuster, New York, New York 1955.
284 *Racine Journal-Times*, Not So Cocky Rocky Ponders The Effects of His Suspension, April 9, 1948.

badly, I'll think about retiring."[285] Pian and Winch felt the same way and said that if Tony lost and showed any signs that he no longer had it, they would insist on him retiring from boxing. Tony was thrilled that this fight would be held outdoors and he wouldn't have to worry about experiencing the kind of suffocating heat that he felt led to his defeat against Rocky in Chicago.

In mid-April, Tony departed for Hot Springs, Arkansas, to rough it and perform his road work in the Ozark Mountains. Over the next three weeks, he and Winch would set up training quarters at Klein Shore on Lake Hamilton and his days would be filled with ditch digging, wood chopping, running, long mountain climbs and jogs to strengthen his legs. He also planned to make some time to swim or fish in the cool lake waters. Meanwhile, Rocky Graziano was preparing to depart for Ellenville, New York, where he would undergo light workouts for the next three weeks.

While a number of folks believed that Tony's age would be a determining factor in the fight, he would be 35 when he and Rocky fought again, Tony maintained that ring-wise veterans like himself knew how to keep themselves in condition and spread out their training periods to realize maximum benefits. "Rather than rushing through a training period to get into shape, a fighter should remain in top condition all the time," Tony said.[286] It was the main piece of advice that another great middleweight Marvin Hagler said that Tony passed along to him when the pair met each other many years later.

On May 8, it was announced that right-hand punch-happy Rocky was startling onlookers in his training camp with a sharp left hook. One reporter indicated that Rocky's punches lacked the speed and sharpness to defeat a tough customer like Tony at this point and was surprised to see him spending so much time working on his left, instead of his mighty right-hand wallop.

Rocky's camp was set up at a year-round resort called the Nevel Country Club, where the guests were comprised primarily of honeymooners. Rocky was reportedly doing fourteen miles of roadwork each morning and working in the gym in the afternoons. Asked about the focus on improving his left hand, Rocky said, "I'm

---

285 *European Stars and Stripes*, Zale Considers Retirement In Event of Defeat by Rocky, April 13, 1948.
286 *Portland Press-Herald*, Tony Zale, Approaching 34, Figures Age An Advantage, April 26, 1948.

getting better with the left. It'll hurt someone. But no use kidding, I'll have to do the business with my right when I get in there with Zale again."[287]

By May 20, Rocky had returned to New York City and was training within the more familiar confines of Stillman's Gym. Much more at home in the city than he was in the country, Rocky said that he was going to try to get Tony out as quickly as he could when he was asked how he thought he would do against him when they met for the third time. Tony's own training had shifted to Chicago by this time, and was operating in high gear in preparation for the June 9 contest. He was commuting to Chicago from his home in Gary, Indiana, for his daily workouts. Just as confident as Rocky, Tony said he expected to get Rocky quick this time, maybe in three rounds. He was looking very sharp in his workouts, and Winch said their main job was to slow Tony up from here on out to prevent him from overtraining and going stale. "He's been working out with almost fanatical zeal. This boy has only one thought in mind, to win back that title," Winch said.[288]

While the two fighters were busily preparing themselves for their match, the number one middleweight contender, Marcel Cerdan, was upset by 22-year-old Cyrille Delannoit on May 23 in Brussels, Belgium. The loss was the first of Cerdan's career other than two previous losses suffered as a result of fouls. It occurred shortly before negotiations were completed for him to face the winner of the title fight between Tony and Rocky and placed his chances of fighting for the title in jeopardy.

On May 27, Tony arrived in New York to complete his final two weeks of training. The local media found him in good shape and confident of regaining his crown. "I like to fight. You know I even like to train, so why shouldn't I be in good shape," he told them. Listening in on the conversation, his trainer, Ray Arcel, added, "More fighters should be like Tony. But they let that hero worship go to their heads. First thing you know when they should be training they're off somewhere with a blonde and a bottle." Tony's bottle of preference was Coca Cola.

In fact, according to an ex-sailor who visited one of his training sessions at the CYO gym in Chicago, Tony was called "The Coca-

---

287 *Gastonia Gazette*, Graziano Ready For Title Bout With Tony Zale, May 13, 1948.
288 *Wisconsin Rapids Daily Tribune*, Tony Zale In Fine Shape, May 22, 1948.

Cola kid." "That's all he would drink. No parties. No booze. In bed by 9 o'clock every night, I'm telling you, the swellest man I ever worked for in the Navy," the former sailor said.[289] Tony, who was set to turn 35 years old on May 29, said he felt great, but told the press he would quit as soon as he felt that he didn't have it anymore.[290] Tony's primary concern was that the referee would stop the fight too soon. The last thing he wanted was a repeat of what happened in Chicago, where the fight was stopped without anyone counting ten over him.

But while Tony was confident of victory, the majority of the press favored the younger man. The nation's sports editors were polled and asked for their thoughts of the outcome and 221 of the 262 ballots received selected Rocky. Out of those, 113 picked Rocky to do it via a knockout by no later than the middle rounds.[291] Some felt that Rocky would knock Tony out even quicker this time around.

Long-time fight manager, Dumb Dan Morgan, was one of those who felt otherwise, and predicted a Zale victory. Morgan, who managed the likes of "Battling" Levinsky, K.O. Brown, and Jack Britton, among many others during a long career, didn't believe that Rocky knew the first thing about defensive boxing and that Tony was beaten by the heat in their match in Chicago. "Zale is 34 (actually 35), and as you get older you can't stand the heat so well," Morgan said. "When I had Jack Britton, when he was 38 or 40 years old, I used to lay him off during August because the heat would get him and fellows he would toy with when the weather was cool would push him around."

Commenting further concerning Rocky's defense, or lack thereof, Morgan said, "He doesn't know a thing about boxing. All he knows how to do is throw his right hand. Zale is smart and always in condition. He'll figure out what he did wrong in the last fight and correct it. He's a fighter of class. And Graziano won't take the beating he did in the first three rounds at Chicago and come back for more."[292] On June 2, both fighters were examined by New Jersey State Boxing Commission doctor Max Stern and neurologist David Flicker for two hours and were both pronounced fit. Dr. Flicker

289 *Chicago Sun-Times*, Louis Contempt for Jersey, June 1948.
290 *Altoona Mirror*, Tony Zale is Type of Fighter That Boxing Business Needs, May 28, 1948.
291 *Daily Capital News*, Rocky Graziano Is Favorite to Chill Tony Zale Again, May 28, 1948.
292 *Florence Morning News*, Sports Trail, May 29, 1948.

performed an encephalogram test to identify any head injuries. The commission decided that eight-ounce gloves would be used instead of the usual six-ounce gloves. It was decided to waive a compulsory eight-count knockdown rule for the fight. The N.B.A. had a rule that required that any fighter who was floored stay down for a count of eight. The state of New Jersey had not yet adopted the rule, and Rocky's camp objected to the use of the rule. Pian and Winch agreed to the rule, but once they learned that Rocky and his team had a problem with it, they had no problem with the dismissal of the rule. It was also agreed that there would be no judges for the fight. The referee would be the sole arbitrator.[293]

Five days away from the fight, Tony was listed as a 12 to 5 underdog but remained confident. He'd done everything he could to prepare for the fight, training as hard as ever. When someone commented on how hard he'd trained, he said simply, "The only way to do a thing is to do it right. If I can't be on top, I don't want to be in this business. I don't know yet what I might do if I lose. But I don't expect to lose. I think I learned enough about him in our two fights. One time I boxed him, and the other I slugged with him. Now I think I know what to do," Tony said.

Asked about their strategy for the fight, Pian and Winch were reluctant to share too much information. "We have ideas, sure," said Winch, "that's the way we always have worked since Tony came to us. First he will try out what we tell him. If that doesn't work, he'll try his own. You know, he's a pretty good thinker in that ring." Winch believed there would be less pressure on Tony in this fight since he wasn't defending the title and would be playing the role of the underdog. Rocky's handlers anticipated that Tony would come out fast and try for an early knockout. Rocky was being prepared to meet an aggressive early attack with one of his own.[294] He promised that he would be the one to set the pace in the fight.

At least one writer expressed the opinion that Tony would be the more likely of the two to win if the fight ended within four rounds, but it would be to Rocky's advantage if the fight were go beyond that point. If the third meeting was anything like the first two, the big

293 *Morning Herald*, Zale, Graziano Pronounced In Top Shape for Return Battle Next Week, June 3, 1948.
294 *Racine Journal Times*, Tony Zale a 12 to 5 Underdog For Third bout With Graziano, June 4, 1948.

question was which of the two fighters would prevail in the face of another beating and enforce his will upon the other man.

Four days away from the fight, a total of $225,000 had already been collected in revenues and "the seven millionaires" financing the show believed the gate would reach a figure of at least $400,000. They figured they needed to reach that amount in order to realize a figure of $300,000 after taxes and make a profit on their investment.

Workmen completed work on the ringside layout at Ruppert Stadium on June 8, and promoter Andy Niederreiter announced that the revenues taken in had already assured that the fight's investors would do no worse than break even on the event. Despite threatening skies, warm, fair weather was in the forecast for the day of the fight.

United Press sportswriter Oscar Fraley decided to pay a visit to a local psychic named Madame Pandora to get her read on the upcoming fight. After asking for and receiving their birth dates and a description of each man's complexions from Fraley, the psychic announced that both were under the sign of Gemini.

"It's a tough fight," Pandora said. "Jupiter opposes them and they'll have to work like hell. But according to the cards, and I've proved it three times, the blonde one (Zale), will win!"[295]

In actual fact, Fraley provided the psychic with an incorrect birth date for Rocky, telling her he was born on June 7, 1922, a common misconception among many people at the time. As a result, many newsmen reported him as being three years younger than he really was at the time. Rocky was born on January 1, 1919, and was 29 years old, and therefore five and a half years younger than Tony.

Chicago Sun-Times columnist Gene Kessler visited Tony on his last day of training and found an extremely confident fighter. 'I feel stronger than I did in Chicago and stronger than I did for the first Graziano fight here in forty-six. This is one fight I've got to win," Tony told him.

Kessler said he hoped he was wrong, but he believed that despite Tony's confident demeanor and appearance, he was burned out inside and only a shallow shell of the once durable fighter of the past. He visited Graziano afterward for one last visit with the champion and found a man whom he thought looked surprisingly good at boxing as opposed to his usual practice of brawling.

---

295 *Record Eagle*, Sports Parade, June 8, 1948.

After the workout, Kessler asked him about the increased use of his left hand. "Sure I'm using the left more now," said Rocky. "A champeen has to be smart in there. Got a title to protect now. That guy (Tony) hurts in the belly. He paralyzed me here in the first fight. Maybe Rock'll surprise him with a few body thumps this time," Rocky said. Kessler thought that Rocky would be the one who was surprised. He thought Rocky would end up being surprised at how much Tony had deteriorated over the past year.[296]

The official weigh-in for the bout was held at 11:00 a.m. at the Newark City Hall on the morning of the fight. Approximately 150 people, the majority of which were photographers, jammed their way into the city council chamber on the second floor to witness the event. Rocky, wearing black trunks with a red stripe down each side, was first on the scale. N.B.A. President Abe Greene mistakenly announced Rocky's weight as 185 ½ pounds before embarrassingly catching his mistake and correcting the figure to 158 ½ while a number of folks snickered. Tony, in purple trunks, then stepped on the scale and weighed in at 158 ¾ pounds.

Rocky's weight was the heaviest he'd ever weighed for a fight to that point in his career. He was 155 ¼ when he defeated Tony in Chicago. Dr. Max Stern examined both men and pronounced them in fine condition. Rocky's blood pressure was revealed as 124 over 74, while Tony's was reported as 122 over 72. Stern said that Tony struck him as a conservative individual, totally unaffected by what took place around him. Rocky, on the other hand, he found to be more emotional. Tony noted that Rocky spent much of the time at the weigh-in laughing, but told Greene afterward that he thought Rocky was as nervous as a cat.

Weight wasn't the only thing the two fighters had in common. They were nearly identical in terms of their physical characteristics. Both men stood 5'8 ½" and there was almost nothing to separate them in terms of the size of their chests, waists, biceps, necks and so on. Tony enjoyed a miniscule ½ inch advantage in reach.

Once the fighters had completed their weigh-ins, they were asked to square off and pose against one another. Scores of flash bulbs went off as photographers called out instructions. Rain pounded at the windows and the crack of thunder could be heard over the din inside the chamber. Nobody on hand believed the fight would take

---

296 *Chicago Sun-Times*, Tony, Rocky Both Confident, June 9, 1948.

place that night. Both fighters were staying in Newark until the fight took place. Rocky indicated that he and his party were staying at the Robert Treat Hotel. Tony declined to reveal where they were staying because he wanted to make sure they weren't bothered.

Former heavyweight fighter Paul Cavalier was selected as the referee for the contest and it was scheduled to begin at 9:00 PM. Mel Allen and Russ Hodges were assigned to deliver the blow by blow report and color commentary over radio station WCLO. For only the second time in the state's boxing history, a knockdown timekeeper was engaged. Nat Fleischer of *The Ring* magazine was assigned to serve in this capacity.

Ultimately, a steady rain throughout the day forced the bout to be postponed for a day and fight fans were left to wonder which, if either fighter might benefit from the delay. Some thought that it might adversely impact Rocky, he being the nervous type and an individual that couldn't really sit still or relax as the time for a fight approached.

Others thought Tony might benefit from the fact that the two fighters wouldn't have to weigh-in again the next day by adding a few pounds. But Tony maintained he was still a natural 160-pounder. It was more important for him to be quick in his fight with Rocky. He said that a little thing like stepping inside a punch and hooking to the body can win or lose a fight and it can happen in the hundredth of a second and be the most important part of the fight.

While the two men waited an extra day for the fight, it was revealed that Rocky would sign with the same promotional group, the Tournament of Champions, Inc., for the defense of his title again in the fall if he defeated Tony. His opponent would be Marcel Cerdan, provided the Frenchman regained his European crown in a rematch against Cyrille Delannoit later in the month. Otherwise, he would be matched against welterweight champion Sugar Ray Robinson, who was anxious to move up in weight and challenge for the middleweight title. Most fans anticipated a victory for Rocky, but Tony said this was one fight he was definitely going to win. When informed of Tony's comment, Rocky said, "I'm sorry bud, but Tony is mistooken. I'll knock him out early this time."[297]

Rocky maintained that if ambition, courage and skill counted for anything, he'd still be champion when it was all over.

---

297 *Chicago Sun Times*, Tony Banks On Early Kayo, June 10, 1948.

ZALE vs. GRAZIANO III

A noisy crowd of 21,497 showed up at Newark's Ruppert Stadium on the night of June 10, 1948, to witness the third and final act of the Zale-Graziano wars.   The ticket sales revenues of $335,646, combined with broadcast and motion picture rights of $70,000, generated a total gross gate of $405,646.   Once taxes, the fighter's purses and other expenses were deducted, promoter Andy Niederreitter estimated that the investors cleared approximately $50,000 on the venture.[298]

Rocky was the first of the two fighters to enter the ring. Tony, who came into the ring wearing long pants under his robe, followed shortly thereafter. "Too hot in Chicago, too cold here, huh Tony?" one fan yelled. As the two fighters stood in the ring before the fight and received the referee's instructions, Art Winch asked, "What about the roughing…and wrestling?" nodding toward Rocky. "I'll be

---

298 *Chicago Sun-Times, Zale Through With Rocky,* June 11, 1948.

the judge of that," replied the referee, Paul Cavalier.[299] Tony's four brothers were on hand to watch him attempt to regain the title.

Once the ring was cleared and introductions were out of the way, the battle commenced. The fighters boxed cautiously in the opening seconds, circling each other while looking for an opening. Midway through the round, Tony leapt in and caught Rocky with a left hook to the jaw as he was backing away, and the Champion was deposited on his hind quarters. He quickly bounced back to his feet before the referee could begin a count.

Photo Courtesy of AP Wire Photo

When they resumed action, Rocky threw a left hook, followed by a weak right hand swing, and received a hard right to the body in return. Rocky's timing looked off and he was wild with his punches. Tony looked sharp and punished him to the body. Rocky tried to establish his left hand throughout the round, and was driven to the ropes where he was hit with a vicious right to the body followed by another right to the jaw and a left hook to the head. He was taking further punishment to the body as the round came to a conclusion. The opening round was all Tony.

---

299 *Chicago Daily News,* The Barber Shop, June 11, 1948.

Photo Courtesy of AP Wire Photo

Rocky said later that when he returned to his corner after the first round, his trainer, Whitey Bimstein, encouraged him to keep throwing left hooks, and that they had Tony off balance because he wasn't expecting them.[300] If true, it's hard to imagine what Bimstein was looking at, because Tony appeared far from confused in that opening round.

The second round started out in a manner much like the opening session, both fighters circling one another and Graziano looking for an opportunity to launch an attack behind a pawing left jab. Rocky tried to land a left hook to the head but Tony easily evaded the blow.

---

300 Graziano, Rocky 'Somebody Up There Likes Me, Simon and Schuster, New York, New York 1955.

Tony dropped down and landed an uppercut to the body followed by a right to the head. Rocky continued to try and land his left while Tony delivered a hard right to the body. Rocky threw a right hand lead and received a left hook to the head in return. Tony assumed the role of the matador in the latter part of the round as Rocky tried to find his way in.

Tony hurt Rocky to the body and the Champion threw wild punches in response. Then as the round neared an end, Rocky became more aggressive and he began to batter Tony about the ring, landing a hard right to the head. But, while Rocky was throwing a lot of leather, most of his punches were landing on Tony's arms or missing altogether. Still, some of the punches were connecting and he landed a chopping right to the head as Tony backed away. Tony landed some hard shots to the body, but it was a much better round for Rocky and belonged to him on the strength of his offensive attack over the second half of the round.

At the sound of the bell to open the third session, Tony quickly stood up and advanced to the center of the ring where Rocky missed badly with two wild swings. As they circled one another, Rocky tried to land a big overhand right, but Tony blocked it with his left arm and quickly countered with a right to the body followed by a left hook to the head.

UPI Photo

Then, as Rocky leaned forward as if to search for an opening, Tony leapt in and threw a sweeping left hook that landed flush on Rocky's jaw and sent him stumbling backward into the ropes. Tony sprang forward and quickly tried to land a right to the body followed by another left to the jaw. The punches didn't land solidly, but another left to the jaw did; and as Rocky turned to his left and tried to evade further punishment, he was forced to grab the middle rope to keep from going down. As he regained his footing, Tony was all over him, sharpshooting with right and left hand blows to the body and head. Rocky looked dazed and his legs were wobbly. Tony backed away slightly and Rocky advanced and missed with a wild overhand right that left him exposed for a textbook combination from Tony: a brutal right to the body immediately followed by a left hook to the point of the jaw.

UPI Photo

Rocky spilled over onto his stomach and grasped the lower rope with his left hand as he struggled to his knees and then shakily got back on to his feet at a count of seven. He tried to steady himself by holding onto the top rope while he fell backward, the ropes holding him up. Cavalier stepped forward and grabbed both forearms and pumped them as he looked him over, an action that at least one reporter later suggested may have actually helped Rocky stay on his feet at the time. But, after a quick shake of Rocky's arms and look into his eyes, Cavalier backed away and allowed the action to continue.

Tony delivered a series of blows to the body while Rocky was pinned against the ropes but was knocked away by a left hook from Rocky. Rocky stumbled backward toward the center of the ring as he circled away from the ropes, and Tony quickly advanced. The moment he was back in range, Rocky tried to ward him off with a left jab, but Tony slipped it with a deft tilt of his head to the left and delivered another right to the body followed by a booming left hook that landed on the point of the chin. Rocky collapsed in sections, his tailbone hitting the deck, then his back and finally his head thudding against the canvas in a whiplash-like fashion.

UPI Photo

There was no doubt about it this time, and Referee Cavalier quickly bent down and removed the guard from Rocky's mouth as he called out a count of ten over the fallen figure below him. Tony calmly wheeled around and headed for his corner where his jubilant handlers awaited him. Remarkably, 35-year-old Tony Zale had become the first man to regain the middleweight title after losing it since Stanley Ketchel performed the feat forty years earlier against Billy Papke in 1908.

UPI Photo

In his autobiography, Rocky said of the left hook that knocked him out, "What I didn't realize was that with that left hook in the third round, the last of Rocco Barbella had been knocked out of me. The wild kid was gone forever, the street fighter, the animal and trouble maker."[301]   Tony had that kind of effect on the men who faced him in the ring, and like Al Hostak before him, Rocky had entered the lion's den for a third time.

Journal-American Photo by Frank Rine and George Miller

---

301 Graziano, Rocky, *Somebody Up There Likes Me*, Simon and Schuster, New York, New York 1955.

Dr. Max Stern entered the ring to examine Rocky and once he knew it was alright to move him, helped his handlers escort him back to his corner where he sat quietly while Tony posed for pictures and bathed himself in the fans applause.

International News Photo

Once Tony reached his dressing room, a mob of reporters jostled for position in an attempt to obtain a quote from the modest Champion. Tony spoke in a calm, measured tone that gave no hint of the surprising victory he had just achieved. It seemed as though everyone wanted to shake his hand and congratulate him.

Tony grimaced when someone asked him if Rocky had hurt him in the second round.

"Of course not," he said. "I wasn't alert that's all. But don't get the idea he hurt me – ever."

And, then, with a quick smile he added, "I guess, I'm getting younger, going the wrong way, instead of getting older."[302]

"How did you do it?" someone hollered.

Tony smiled and said, "I knew I had him in the first round when he went down after that left hook. It was just a question of time, then."[303] He told the reporters that he wanted to keep on fighting, "a couple more years anyway." But, he made it clear that he was through with Rocky, saying, "I'll not fight Rocky again. I gave him three cracks at my chin, what more could he ask?"[304]

Down the hall, in Rocky's dressing room, the scene was much more subdued. Rocky lay on a table while Dr. Vincent Nardiello of the New York State Commission examined him.

"How are you, Rocky?" the doctor asked.

Rocky rolled his head in the direction of the doctor. There was a deep cut on his nose and a lump on his forehead. He looked a little confused.

"I'm Dr. Nardiello," the doctor said.

"Oh, yeah, I know, now," Rocky replied.

"What happened, Rock," somebody asked.

"I couldn't get off, I couldn't get off," Rocky said.

"You mean you couldn't get off the floor?" a reporter asked.

Rocky looked at the man through glassy eyes, and replied, "No, I mean I couldn't get started. I never had my full strength."

"When did he hurt you most?" he was asked.

"I guess it was that left hook in the first round," Rocky answered.

"Were his body punches pretty hard?" another asked.

"I imagine they were," mumbled Rocky in reply.

Dr. Nardiello looked puzzled as he left the dressing room. "I don't think he recognized me," he said. "He may have a brain concussion. We'll have to look him over."[305]

Rocky said that he never got over the first punch, a left that Tony landed to his temple. "I never even remembered the last round," he

302 *Nevada State Journal*, Rocky—Bad Boy of Boxing—Back in Doghouse Today, June 12, 1948.
303 *Chicago Sun-Times*, Tony Knew he had Title After First Round, June 11, 1948.
304 *Chicago Sun-Times*, Zale Through With Rocky, June 11, 1948.
305 *Chicago Sun-Times*, Tony Knew he Had Title After First Round, June 11, 1948.

added.[306]   He told reporters that he'd like to fight Tony again. Nonetheless, the pair never fought again. Many years later, when Rocky reflected on their trilogy, he said of Tony, "Tough guy, Tony Zale. He was a tough-fighting Polish boy. No, the truth is, he was the toughest man I ever fought. He was quiet outside the ring, but not quiet in it."[307]

Rocky's trainer, Whitey Bimstein, found his fighter's performance hard to believe. "I can't understand what got into him. He seemed petrified when he got into the ring."[308]

Sportswriter, Hugh Fullerton, Jr., speculated that Rocky's big mistake may have been his decision to try and employ the use of the left hook he'd been working on so hard. "He tried it three or four times in the first round, then Zale demonstrated the same blow and clouted Rocky right on the chops," Fullerton wrote. "It all seems to prove the Rock knew what he was talking about one day up in the Catskills when he explained seriously: "Every time I try to think, I take a hell of a licking."[309]

306 *Ogden Standard-Examiner*, Tony Zale Flattens Rocky Graziano to Regain World Middleweight Title, June 11, 1948.
307 *The Ring*, The Dynamite Kid, March/April 1988.
308 Fried, Ronald '*Corner Men. Great Boxing Trainers*, Four Walls Windows, New York, New York 1991.
309 *Arizona Daily Sun*, Sports Roundup, June 11, 1948.

Shortly after the bout ended, Art Winch rushed to a telephone to place a call into the *Chicago Sun-Times* to take a jab at their columnist, Gene Kessler, for his pre-fight description of Tony as a "shell of his former self."

Kessler, genuinely fond of Tony, admitted he was wrong. "He knew his own strength when I doubted it. I never enjoyed being so wrong on a prediction," he wrote. "Tony made good in every way. He outsmarted Rocky by making him lead with a long right, then stepping inside with a counter left hook, which proved the pay off."[310]

Tony's wife, Adeline, listened to the fight on the radio with many friends and relatives from their home in Gary, Indiana. Described by one reporter as "an excited, wonderfully bewildered woman who has never seen her husband fight," Adeline said she was happy that Tony had regained the title, but hopeful that he would decide to retire from the ring.

"I hope he quits, really I do. Of course, it's up to him, but that's what seems best to me. We've talked about him going into business,

---

310 *Chicago Sun-Times*, Zale Moves Into Immortality, June 10, 1948.

but everyone seems to want him to go into the tavern business and that's too hard on a person. I think it would be a terrible grind for him. What he's spoken of and, I think, really wants to do is coach boxing. Maybe he can retire undefeated and then teach the sport at some university. And you know Tony would be good at it," she said.[311]

Asked what went through her mind when the fight was delayed a day due to the weather, Adeline replied, "I didn't worry too much about the one day postponement. Tony thought he'd win, I believe him and the people here have been grand. I guess I'm just excited about the whole thing."[312]

Rocky was examined by his personal physician the day after the fight, and while the doctor found him depressed over the loss of his title, he pronounced the fighter fit and said he found no evidence of a concussion.

Tony's managers said the only definite plans for their fighter at the time were that he would return home to Gary, Indiana, where some ceremonies had been arranged to take place on Sunday morning. Winch said Tony's first title defense would be for the Tournament of Champions, and that it would probably take place in September. It was believed that either Marcel Cerdan or Sugar Ray Robinson would be his opponent.

When Tony arrived in Gary, Indiana, on June 13, he found a large crowd of excited admirers on hand at the train station to welcome their Champion home. He'd been welcomed home in a similar fashion in 1941 after defeating Georgie Abrams to become

311 *Miami News*, Hopes He Quits, June 10, 1948.
312 *Chicago Sun-Times*, Mrs. Zale Hoping Tony Will Retire, June 11, 1948.

the Undisputed Middleweight Champion, and again in 1946, after defending the title against Graziano, but the size of this celebration dwarfed the first two. Mayor Eugene Swartz was on hand to lead the welcoming committee, and while he couldn't provide an official count, he said there were more than 20,000 there to greet the Champion.

As the train pulled into the station, a band began playing "Hail, Hail, the Gang's All Here," and hundreds pushed forward to be among the first to catch a glimpse of Tony. Among the first to greet Tony as he got off the train was his wife Adeline, with a big hug and kisses, and his young daughters, Mary and Teresa. After many photographs were taken, two members of the Silver Bell Club, a lodge affiliated with the Polish National Alliance (PNA), lifted Tony to their shoulders and carried him to his new car for a parade.[313]

A large crowd lined the streets and applauded Tony and his family as the car made its way through Gary to the Kosciusko American Legion post. Once the guest of honor arrived at his destination, Tony gave a short speech, and then Mayor Swartz said a

313 *Chicago Tribune*, Gary Turns Out 20,000 Strong To Greet Zale, June 14, 1948.

few words and presented Tony with the key to the city. Tony said a few weeks' rest was his first order of business. But when his wife mentioned the idea of giving up boxing, he replied, "I can't quit now." What Adeline was really hoping for with the possibility of Tony's retirement was not just an end to the long separations. Maybe this would give them a chance to have a more normal life together. Her early years at her own childhood home were spent with her mother and father continually arguing. She used her music ability to hide in her own little world. She could perfect her music, rather than exist in the unhealthy reality of her home. Besides, Tony would be around more, and he would discipline the children, because she knew she often got carried away.

Tony was very much in demand, and he spent the next month making celebrity appearances all over the region. He was truly thankful to the Lord for his good fortune and he thanked all those who continued to believe in him. Whenever possible, he made sure to include his family, to make them a part of the fun. But maintaining his level of fitness was always a top priority. No matter where he was, he continued to do his road work, calisthenics and get in some shadow boxing. Much to Adeline's chagrin, his managers were already at work lining up his next opponent.

So, while it was clear that his wife wished he would retire, Tony wasn't ready to do so. A title defense before year-end was in his future, and the decision to continue fighting put a greater strain on their marriage.

Adeline had come to resent all the time that she was left alone at home with the children while her famous husband was out in public being showered with so much adulation. After all, she was an artiste herself, an accomplished musician who could flawlessly perform the classical pieces of the greatest musicians in history. Tony couldn't do that, and she felt as though he didn't appreciate her talent. In her mind, all he could do was lace up a pair of gloves and batter the likes of Graziano into unconsciousness.

Now, he was going to go off to another training camp and leave her alone again. She knew what she needed to do. As she had on the other occasions when he had left her alone, she would find a friend to spend time with, providing she could get Tony's relatives to watch after the girls.[314]

Whether Tony liked it or not, maybe she could find a part-time job playing the organ at a local nightclub as she had done in Calumet City, Illinois. All she needed was someone to watch the kids. She'd show him, if he didn't recognize her talents, and appreciate her, she'd find others who did.[315]

---

314 Thad Zale interview with Jeanette Zale.
315 Thad Zale interviews with Tony Zale.

BATTLES ON MULTIPLE FRONTS

While Tony quietly celebrated his victory and enjoyed some well-earned time off with his family, Andy Niederreiter and the Tournament of Champions organization were working to find his next opponent. By all accounts, Tony was expected to defend his title in September of 1948.

On July 1, it was reported that Niederreiter and some of the others in his group were flying to Belgium to watch Marcel Cerdan in a rematch with Cyrille Delannoit on July 10. Delannoit had captured Cerdan's European middleweight title in a stunning upset in May, and any chance that Marcel had of fighting for Tony's world championship belt hinged on the outcome of his attempt to recapture the European championship. If he was successful, he would be Tony's next opponent. If he failed, it would be either Delannoit or world welterweight champion Sugar Ray Robinson, who would give up his title and challenge Tony for the middleweight crown.

Robinson had a lot of difficulty making the 147-pound welterweight limit in his last fight against Bernard Docusen, whom he defeated by decision. He would run out of serious opposition in that lower weight class. Given that Ray would have an advantage in both height and reach, and was a lot younger than Tony, it was believed that he would be favored over Tony if they were matched to fight. On the other hand, most seemed to believe that while Cerdan was a worthy opponent, he lacked a big punch, and wouldn't be able to stand up against Tony's body blows. Still, not everyone shared that view. Some who had seen Marcel's victories over the likes of Holman Williams, Georgie Abrams and Harold Green, weren't so sure that he wasn't the man to defeat Tony. Marcel had never been stopped in over 100 career fights.

On July 10, Marcel effectively sealed the deal when he won a grueling 15-round decision in front of 15,000 irate fans in Brussels over Cyrille Delannoit. It was a very close decision, and Marcel had to be protected by ten members of Brussels police force on the way back to his dressing room. The Associated Press scored the fight dead even, giving six rounds to each man and the other three even, but the Spanish referee, Senor Cabailero and two judges, were unanimous in awarding the fight to Cerdan.[316] Marcel knocked down Delannoit in the fourth round with a right hand blow to the chin. He opened a deep cut over Delannoit's right eye in the seventh round during the action-packed bout.[317]

Niederreiter wasted no time in signing Cerdan to fight Tony for the middleweight championship. By July 12, it was announced that the Tournament of Champions had secured Marcel's signature to meet Tony that September in a location to be determined. This would most likely be at Ebbets Field in Brooklyn, New York. While it was Tony's right to reject Cerdan as an opponent, Sam Pian said that Cerdan was alright with them.[318]

A week later, Sam and Art Winch were in New York and signed for Tony to defend his title against Cerdan. They spoke with reporters for some time about their fighter. Winch admitted to being worried about Tony's age (35). "You don't know when he might crack up," Art said. "He can't go on forever."

"He's giving it a good try," noted one of the reporters in attendance.

"I guess that's because he works so hard and stays in good condition," replied Art. "The first day he worked I had to urge him to get out of the ring. The city gave him a new car after the Graziano fight, but does he use it? No. He still takes the suburban (South Shore train line) 60 miles a day to train in Chicago," he added.[319]

Tony's routine was predetermined by his managers. Their plan called for him to begin building up his physical stamina in the month of July, and then spend a short time relaxing back home in early August. After that, Tony would engage in a rigorous schedule of ring work until they traveled to New York, where Tony would then

316 *Bridgeport Telegram*, Cerdan Regains Title By Unpopular Verdict, July 11, 1948.
317 *Syracuse Herald Journal*, Cerdan Defeats Belgian, July 11, 1948.
318 *Oelwein Daily Register*, Cerdan, Zale Meet In September Bout, July 12, 1948.
319 *Alton Evening Telegraph*, How Long Can Tony Zale Keep Rolling Along?, July 19, 1948.

participate in some light workouts designed to help him maintain his edge for the September date with Marcel Cerdan.

By the later part of July, Tony was back along the shores of Lake Hamilton in Hot Springs, Arkansas, with Art Winch to begin preliminary training. His daily routine consisted of jogging, hiking, swimming, boating and other physical drills. They planned to return to Chicago on August 9. Tony's last fight against Rocky convinced him that he had reached his pre-war level of performance, and despite his age, he believed he was at his peak. While he wasn't ready to retire quite yet, he knew the day was coming. It was erroneously reported that Tony had recently used some of his earnings to purchase a bowling alley back in Gary. The truth was, his brothers John, Frank and Walter actually bought *Zales Bowling Emporium*, and they used Tony's name to promote the business with Tony's permission.

Zale Bowling Alleys
125 W. 5TH AVE.
Phone 2-5359   Gary, Ind.

On July 30, Niederreiter announced the Tournament of Champion's September fight card would include a second championship fight, and that light-heavyweight champion Freddie Mills of England would defend his title against Gus Lesnevich. He said they planned to arrange for seating of 55,000 for the doubleheader. The Tournament of Champions was clearly pulling out all the stops in their ongoing battle with Mike Jacobs' group, The Twentieth Century Sporting Club, and seemed intent on becoming the preeminent boxing promoters in New York.

Unfortunately, for the Tournament of Champions, Freddie Mills withdrew from the event a week later complaining of ill-health. Mills had been suffering from severe headaches since winning the title against Lesnevich on July 26, and hadn't been able to train as a result.[320]

Some in the media thought the cancellation of the light-heavyweight title bout may have been a blessing in disguise for the promoters. They thought the two fighters would have cost the group $150,000, and probably wouldn't have added that much value to a card already featuring the Zale vs. Cerdan fight.

Adding intrigue to the battle between the two promotional outfits was the announcement that the Twentieth Century Sporting Club planned to stage their own lightweight championship fight between Ike Williams and Jess Flores at Yankee Stadium on September 22, the day before the Zale vs. Cerdan fight. The media viewed the Zale vs. Cerdan bout as the better of the two.

Tony returned home to Gary, Indiana, in early August for a brief rest. His return was a week earlier than scheduled, but he was anxious to spend a few days with the girls and go out with Adeline to discuss an argument they'd had about her going back to work. He figured he would head to church at St. Hedwig that coming Sunday morning, and then go on to camp in Wisconsin for a month of serious training.

But things didn't go as Tony had envisioned. On his way home, as he had done many times before, he was dropped off at the home of one of his best friends, Mel Beckham, for a short visit and a ride home.

It was around 9:30 p.m. and Mel and his wife were just arriving home themselves. Mel was visibly upset and Tony didn't know why. But Mel met Tony's eyes and told him Adeline was stepping out on him. Tony gritted his teeth and clenched his fists as Mel began to tell the story.

Mel and his wife had gone to Calumet City for an evening of dinner and dancing. To their surprise, they saw Adeline playing the organ at the club. She didn't see them and they observed her leaving after her last set with one of the patrons. They were about to leave themselves, so Mel talked his wife into following the pair as they drove to a local public park.

---

320 *Lethbridge Herald*, Mills Pulls Out Of Proposed Bout, August 7, 1948.

Tony couldn't believe what he was hearing. So, Mel drove him to the nearby park and there was the car with its windows all fogged up. Tony asked Mel to stop. He got out and walked over to the vehicle and knocked on the passenger window. Adeline rolled it partway down and said, "Tony, this isn't what it looks like." Tony didn't say a word. He just turned around, walked back to Mel's car, and requested that he take him home.

How could he have been such a fool? He looked and felt like a beaten puppy. He had put all of his faith in Adeline and believed she would always do the right thing for their family. Now, there she was sitting parked in a remote area with another man.

When Mel dropped Tony off at home, he asked him if he wanted him to stay. Tony didn't think that was necessary. He was so bewildered that he didn't know what he was going to say to her. Mel suggested he avoid conversation with Adeline that night.

Tony was obviously in shock. The rumors his brothers had warned him about were true. Both Adeline's parents had also warned Tony not to reconcile with her after the 1946 divorce filing, but he was still in love with her and didn't heed their advice. Now, he faced what they had warned him about.

When they walked in the front door, Tony was greeted with shouts of joy from his two young daughters. Tony's niece Jeanette was there watching them and in the process of preparing them for bed. She greeted her uncle with surprise since his arrival was a week earlier than planned. Adeline had hired her to babysit every Friday night until mid-August because she had a job playing the organ in Calumet City. Normally, Adeline was home by midnight after the kids were fast asleep. Jeanette would stay overnight and be picked up by her father John the next morning. But since Tony was back, she wondered if Mel could take her home now. Tony and Mel agreed, as the newly enlightened husband needed some time alone to think. Tony would put the kids to bed. This was the end of his marriage.[321]

After Mel and Jeanette left, Tony sat down with the children and told them how happy he was to be home with them again. They were the most important thing in the world to him and he loved them dearly. He told them he was afraid that he might not be able to live with them anymore and only visit. The oldest daughter Mary, a

---

321 Thad Zale interview with Tony Zale.

five-year-old, said, "You mean just like when Uncle Jake and sometimes Uncle Mike visit?" Mary looked up at her father and added, "They come to visit. We wake them up in the morning because they sleep on the couch. They are fun and nice to me and Tere."[322]

Tony's heart sank. How could Adeline do this to him and their daughters? How could he have been so blind? How could this happen to a champion of the world? Was he that bad? Hadn't he lived up to what he'd been taught, obeying the Ten Commandments, living a clean life, always trying to do the right thing? Wasn't that what the Good Lord asked of him? What was he to do now?

Nothing made any sense to Tony. But the kids needed to be put to bed, so that's what he did. There was nothing else to do now but wait and see how things would play out.

Adeline walked in the door an hour or so later and locked it behind her. When she turned around, she found Tony sitting on the stairs with his head in hand. As he stood up, she approached him, saying she hadn't been doing anything but talking. But Tony cut her off, grabbed her hair and shoved her up the stairs toward their room. His young daughters had sneaked out of bed when they heard the front door open and close. They watched in surprise through their partially opened bedroom door. They wondered why Daddy had pulled Mommy's hair like that.[323]

Morning came quickly for Tony. He slept downstairs on the couch just like the "uncles" had. When the sun rose, so did he. He phoned Mel to come and pick him up. Nothing more needed to be said, but he wanted to sneak upstairs and kiss his girls before he left as he did not know when he would see them again.

When Mel arrived, Tony was waiting on the porch. It was early, and Tony didn't look like he'd slept a wink. Mel asked his friend if there was anything he could do to help. "Yes, take me to St. Hedwig," Tony replied. He needed a moment alone to pray.[324]

When Tony arrived at the church, he prayed to the Father above. His first real confrontation with Adeline had occurred back in April of 1946, sometime before his scheduled first bout with Rocky Graziano. It was after he found out from family members that she

---

322 Thad Zale interview with Mary Medeiros.
323 Thad Zale interview with Mary Medeiros.
324 Thad Zale interview with Tony Zale.

had spanked their daughters with a carpet tack board. That was too much for Tony to imagine, much less ignore.

A physical confrontation initiated by Adele occurred. Tony's brother John had told Tony that his daughter Jeanette was babysitting for his two children one evening when Adele had one of her engagements to perform in Calumet City. Jeanette was instructed by Adele to bathe both children before bedtime. She was going to help the girls undress for their bath, when Mary, as young as she was, insisted she could do it herself.

While preparing Teresa for her bath and giving Mary a little privacy by standing just outside the bathroom door, Jeanette discovered bloody stains on Teresa's diaper. When she turned to approach the tub which Mary had gotten into by herself, she gasped in horror at the reddish colored water.

Realizing that both of the girls had been physically injured, Jeanette asked Mary what happened. Mary said that they were punished for misbehaving and that their mommy used the tack board on their bottoms. She told Jeanette that "she got more spankings than Teresa because she is older."

Jeanette bathed them and afterward placed whatever antiseptic she could find on the neat row of tiny puncture wounds. Little Teresa, who had just started walking on her own, had a few punctures, but none like Mary's. How could these young children ever deserve this kind of punishment?

When Tony heard this horrifying news, he came to the realization that his young children were being physically abused by their mother. How could Adeline inflict such injuries on those darling little girls she claimed to love?

Tony was bewildered by his brother John's description of what had happened. Sure, he left Adeline alone often while he was in training for fights or in the military. The burden of caring for their children fell solely upon her, but how could she punish them so severely? Tony could not justify such a horrible form of punishment.

He purposely confronted Adeline about the incident while her younger sister Genevieve was present. Tony did that, not expecting Adeline would physically attack him in front of her own sister. Instead, she threw a right cross at him as she had on another occasion. Tony stepped to the left and instinctively countered with a left hook over her outstretched arm. It had occurred in a flash and she went down hard on her rear end, bleeding from the mouth. Tony thought, "What in the world have I done?"

He was stunned and so was she. Tony had never imagined in his wildest dreams such a thing would occur and that he actually would have to defend himself against her. He was so proud of his ability to maintain control in and out of the ring in all situations. Maybe this combative behavior she displayed was how she reacted in anger when the children misbehaved. He found himself wondering if she often lost control of herself with them in a similar manner when he wasn't around. Adeline's abuse of the children was difficult for him to comprehend. Now, so was his reaction to her physical attack on him.

Because of the confrontation that afternoon in 1946, he took Adeline to the hospital. Then the next day they went to see Tony's cousin, the family's dentist. He assessed the situation with her tooth. All his praying did not seem to ease the mental anguish he suffered over what had transpired. Saying he was sorry just didn't seem enough, but he was still perplexed about her behavior with the children. Soon after, Adele filed for divorce based on "cruelty." Although Tony's immediate family knew of the tirades that Adele would have behind the scenes, this wasn't known to the public.

Now, though, his prayers are about this latest incident. Yes, he'd grabbed her by the hair. Yes, he'd shoved her up the stairs. But now, Tony realized that he and Adeline did not and could not *ever* have a true marriage. Tony had made it to the Champion of the World status, but little did outsiders know his own world was falling apart.

As Tony knelt in prayer and reflected on his marriage, he realized he had a train to catch for a scheduled meeting with his managers. In spite of everything that had occurred with Adeline the night before, he still had the fight with Cerdan to prepare for. The timing could not have been worse. This fight was what he had to concentrate on now. That was difficult of course because his heart was broken and the recent events would weigh heavily on him in the weeks ahead.[325]

On August 9, the Twentieth Century Sporting Club won an important victory when the New York State Athletic Commission approved their plan to stage their fight in Yankee Stadium on September 22. The Tournament of Champions applied for a license for their fight as well, but was told to come back four days later to

---

325 Thad Zale interviews with Tony Zale.

receive the commission's decision. Ultimately, after an hour long meeting with New York State Athletic Commissioner, Eddie Eagen, The Tournament of Champions withdrew their application to hold the fight in New York. On August 13, they announced their middleweight title fight would be staged at Roosevelt Stadium in Jersey City on September 21, one day before the Twentieth Century Sporting Club's title fight.[326]

It turned out that during their meeting with Eagen, the commissioner had suggested the Tournament of Champions hold their fight in New York on an October date. But Niederreiter and his group said the September date was the only one that would work for them in Brooklyn. When Eagan spoke with Sol Strauss of the Twentieth Century Sporting Club about changing the date of their fight at Yankee Stadium, the promoter said their plans were already set. So, Niederreiter and his group decided to move their fight to New Jersey, and undoubtedly chose the September 21 date to spite their competitors.[327]

While the battle between the two promotional outfits raged, Marcel Cerdan remained at his home in Casablanca, Morocco. He had just purchased a large farm 10 miles outside the city as part of his plan to earn a living as a farmer once his boxing career was over. Asked to comment on his upcoming fight with Zale, he replied, "Tony Zale is a dangerous man. I've never seen him fight, but I know he's dangerous." He planned to go to Paris to receive some treatment for an injured right hand, and to begin training. He also indicated he would leave for New York at the end of August.[328]

On August 16, the Tournament of Champions announced that they had secured the services of Joe Walcott to face Gus Lesnevich on the same card with the Zale vs. Cerdan fight for $50,000 each. They appeared to be doing everything they could to make sure that their tournament would be the more attractive of the two rival September promotions.

Marcel Cerdan was scheduled to arrive in the States on August 23, but had to turn back on his first attempt to depart Paris due to the harsh weather conditions. He didn't leave Paris as scheduled on the second try either, but ultimately arrived in New York on August 25.

---

326 *Oakland Tribune,* Zale, Cerdan Bout Location Switched, August 13, 1948.
327 *Manitowoc Herald Times,* Big Boxing War Hits New York, August 14, 1948.
328 *Bluefield Daily Telegraph,* Marcel Cerdan Will Continue Use of Hands, August 11, 1948.

He planned to train at Lock Sheldrake, New York. That same day, the Twentieth Century Sporting Club announced they had moved their show at Yankee Stadium from September 22 to September 23 to lessen the chances that rain might force the possibility of two events to be staged on the same evening.

Once Marcel arrived, he proceeded to a midtown New York restaurant where he and Tony officially signed for the fight. While Tony awaited Marcel's arrival, he predicted confidently that he would knock the Frenchman out in the fifth round.

Zale and Cerdan sign for bout in New Jersey restaurant. Seated, left to right: Zale, Commissioner Abe Greene, Andy Nied-erreiter. Standing: Jersey Joe Walcott, promoter Frank Paula, former light heavyweight champion Gus Lesnevich.

AP Wire Photo

Asked to comment further, Tony said, "I've never seen the Frenchman fight, but I know he's good. He's a great combination puncher – throws four or five hooks in a series from different angles. He's fast on his feet and a good blocker. I figure he's fast enough to give me a lot of trouble for about three rounds and keep away from me while he's doing it. But then I'll begin coming to close quarters and tearing him down with shots to the body. And I'll put him away in the fifth. It won't take long after I get to him."

Asked how he compared Cerdan to Graziano, Tony said that Cerdan was a better all-around fighter than Rocky, but that the Rock probably punched harder.[329]

By August 31, Niederreiter reported that the first four days of ticket sales for the fight had exceeded $100,000, far surpassing the first four days ticket sales for the previous Zale vs. Graziano bout. He optimistically forecast the show would draw a gate of more than $500,000.

Tony planned to increase the intensity of his workouts on September 2 by boxing six rounds daily. Meanwhile, Cerdan was settling into his own routine under the watchful eye of his manager, Lucien Roupp. Marcel and his trainer focused on his speed on September 3 as he shadow boxed for three rounds, worked on the heavy bag for two rounds, spent two on instruction during which Roupp put on the gloves, and then concluded with one round of calisthenics. A crowd of 200 was on hand to witness the European champion go through his paces.[330] The man referred to as the "Tiger of France" looked strong. His first batch of sparring partners arrived on September 5.

Tony continued to express his confidence in a victory from his training quarters in Chicago. Speaking with the press on September 5, he said, "I don't know how I know it, but I just feel that I'm going to win. And I know the fight isn't going the full 15 rounds. Both of us can hit. I don't think there's another middleweight that can hit any harder than I can, and they tell me Cerdan can too. So, I can't see how the fight can go the distance."

Tony said he didn't plan to make any changes in the way he fought when he faced Cerdan. "I've never seen him fight, but they tell me he bores in and hits to the body and the head. That's just what I like."

Tony said that regardless of the outcome, he had no plans to retire. He didn't plan on any further fights for the rest of the year, but he said he felt like a man much younger than his actual age. He planned to leave for New York with Pian and Winch on September 8

---

329 *Racine Journal Times*, Tony Zale to Receive $8,000 A Minute for the Cerdan Bout, August 25, 1948.
330 *Morning Avalanche*, Cerdan Stresses Speed In Eight Rounds Of Training, September 4, 1948.

and conclude his training with a series of lighter workouts at the C.Y.O. gym.[331]

Former lightweight champion, Barney Ross, predicted that Tony would knock Cerdan out if the fight didn't go more than five rounds, but thought Cerdan would knock Tony out if the fight went beyond that point. Either way, Ross was convinced the fight wouldn't go the full 15 rounds.[332]

Like Tony, Marcel had no plans to alter the way he typically fought, at least according to his manager, Lucien Roupp. When asked how Marcel would fight Tony, Roupp replied, "Just as he fought everyone else. You can tell a fighter to fight just so. He will follow orders for a few seconds, and then he will start to fight just as he always fought. You cannot change them."

Cerdan was working late, but taking care not to exert himself too much. "In France," said Roupp, "Cerdan works after 7 o'clock at night because his body is used to fighting at that hour or later and it lessens the strain on his nervous system. Here we work late in the day, starting at 3:30 or 4 o'clock.

"I do not understand how many American fighters can go through four or five weeks of vigorous training. They do so much work, it is a wonder they don't wear out their batteries. I think many of them leave their fights in training camps." Unfortunately, for Tony, the Frenchman was correct. Tony would leave some of his strength in training camp, and the emotional baggage that he carried from his marital problems would wear him down as well.

Cerdan's roadwork began with a brisk walk. Then he sprinted 100 yards or so. He compared that to early mixing with an opponent, to see what he has. Then it's back to a fast walk, which he compared to the tactic of circling around one's opponent. Then he broke into dashes from 100 to 200 yards, which he considered the equivalent of furious exchanges with his opponent. He believed in alternating his roadwork in that manner each day to accustom his body to sudden changes in his fighting technique.[333]

"Cerdan's philosophy concerning roadwork was somewhat similar to that of Tony's," said his manager Art Winch. When Tony was training for his third fight with Rocky, he looked very bad in

---

331 *Syracuse Herald Journal*, Zale Predicts Victory, September 5, 1948.
332 *New Castle News*, Barney Ross Sees Zale By Knockout, September 7, 1948.
333 *Portsmouth Times*, Cerdan Will Fight Zale As He Fought The Others, September 9, 1948.

training a week before the bout. Art discontinued his boxing briefly and went out on the road with him. He discovered that Tony was running the entire five to six miles. He covered it all at top speed. Right away, Art determined that Tony had run himself stale. He made him revise the way he was doing his roadwork, so that he would walk briskly for a block, then run a block. He snapped out of his stale routine. Art was convinced that Tony didn't fully recover from his "overtraining" until the day of the fight with Rocky, and that the one delay due to weather, had benefited him immensely in that regard.

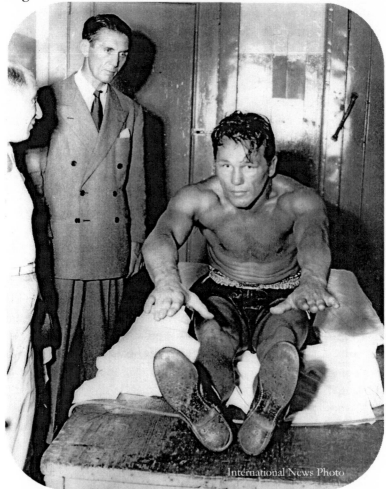

On September 13, the *Gary Post-Tribune* published an article in which Cerdan expressed his own confidence of victory. Concerning the upcoming match, Marcel said, "I do not worry about this fight.

Let Monsieur Zale do the worrying. He says he will knock me out in five rounds. Well, in 110 fights, nobody has knocked me out yet. I do not intend to start now." Listening in on the conversation with his fighter, Roupp said, "Marcel, he is too modest. He is the greatest fighter pound for pound in the world today, and he will prove it against Tony Zale. He is like an assassin at in-fighting. He gives his opponents terrible body beating. Zale will have to have great courage to stand up against such blows."

Marcel piped in again, "I do not underestimate Tony Zale. I have heard he hits very hard. I hit hard too. I have heard that he has courage. If I lack courage, I have yet to find out. But, I have also heard that Monsieur Zale is easy to hit. That I like. Give me the target and I will find it often. That is what I train for, for speed and accuracy. I will hit him perhaps more often than he will hit me and may the better man win."[334] Marcel had once had a contract to fight Henry Armstrong for his welterweight championship in Paris in 1939, but the war interfered. The opportunity to finally fight for a world championship was one that he did not take lightly.

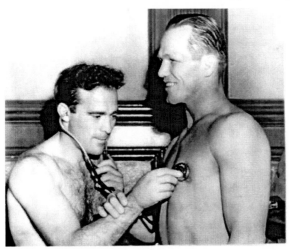

Although Roupp didn't allow his fighter to view the film of the third Zale-Graziano fight, because he thought Rocky looked so bad, and Tony so good, he viewed them himself and claimed he saw a few things that might be useful in terms of their strategy for the upcoming bout.[335]

Former heavyweight champion, James J. Braddock, watched the European champion in training and was one of those who believed he might just have what it took to take Tony's crown. "If anybody is to beat Tony Zale it will be Marcel Cerdan," Braddock said. "Here's

334 *The Gary Post-Tribune*, Monsieur Zale, Cerdan No Worry, September 13, 1948.
335 *Beatrice Daily Sun*, Marcel Cerdan Confident About Fighting Zale, September 16, 1948.

a fighter who knows his way around a ring. He's in top condition and he can hit. This camp was my lucky charm, and it may be Cerdan's."[336]

On September 16, the fighters on the events card were all gathered together for a discussion concerning the rules and their physical examinations. Dr. Harry Cohen examined the fighters and pronounced them all in excellent condition and fit to box in their scheduled fights. New York's Broadway bookies had established Tony as a 6½ - 5 favorite to retain his title against the Frenchman at that point.

Chicago sports columnist Gene Kessler picked Tony to win by a knockout inside of nine rounds. Although he had a healthy respect for Cerdan's boxing ability, Kessler didn't believe the Frenchman would be able to withstand Tony's attack to the body. Kessler thought the battle might be similar to one Tony had against Al Hostak, where Hostak out-boxed him in the early rounds, but was ultimately worn down by Tony's body attack. However, Kessler said that one of the few fight managers whose judgment was really respected by New York writers was Al Weill, and Weill had informed them he was betting his money on Cerdan.

"This Frenchman has the speed and boxing ability to stay away from Zale for five or six rounds. After that, he has the fast, straight punches to beat Tony on the draw and take the play from the champion. I wouldn't be surprised if he knocked out Zale in the later rounds. Remember, Tony hasn't gone 15 rounds since the war. He has to win early and Cerdan is too clever to get hit by knockout punches early," said Weill.[337]

Three days before the event, The Tournament of Champions announced that their doubleheader would have to be reduced to a single feature. The Lesnevich-Walcott bout was called off because of a freak accident that occurred to Lesnevich. The former light-heavyweight champion slipped and fell while descending the steps of a post office in Cliffside, New Jersey, on September 16, and broke the little toe on his right foot. Efforts to find a replacement proved

---

336 *European Stars & Stripes*, Cerdan Capable of Defeating Zale, Braddock Claims, September 14, 1948.
337 *Chicago Sun Times*, Zale to Knock Out Cerdan, September 16, 1948.

unsuccessful, and the price of ringside tickets were reduced from $40 to $30 as a result.[338]

Niederreiter still believed the show would attract a crowd of at least 30,000 and more than $250,000 in revenues. Tony proclaimed himself in better shape than he had been in any time since before the war. "I feel even better than I did before my two wins over Rocky Graziano," he said.[339]

The day before the fight, Cerdan once again expressed the belief that he would fulfill his ambition to win the middleweight crown. "For the first time in America, I feel good before a fight. I am in good shape," he said.[340]

Cerdan claimed that he'd been sick to his stomach when he fought Anton Raadik in Chicago in October of 1947, and he complained of a cold when he defeated Georgie Abrams in December of 1946. Even when he defeated men like Harold Green and Lavern Roach in the States, he said something was the matter with him. But not this time. Now he had nothing to complain about in terms of his health.

It was revealed that should Cerdan capture the title, Tony was guaranteed a return title match with the Frenchman within six months. Marcel requested that Paris be considered as a possible site for a return match, but the Tournament of Champions Organization said it would have to take place in New York, Jersey City or Chicago. If Tony won, as expected, it was believed that he might meet Sugar Ray Robinson next in a Chicago ring.

Tony spent the last day before the fight doing a little road work and resting. Cerdan also took things easy in Jersey City. Both men were scheduled to weigh-in for the bout at noon on September 21 for that evening's contest. The radio broadcast of the fight was going to be heard on station WFHR beginning at 8 o'clock with Mel Allen and Russ Hodges calling the action.

The day before the fight wasn't as relaxing for Cerdan's manager. Roupp had to meet with Niederreiter for some last minute re-negotiation concerning Marcel's compensation for the fight. Niederreiter was trying to get Cerdan's team to accept 17½ percent of the net proceeds instead of the $50,000 figure that was previously

338 *Altoona Mirror*, Gus Lesnevich, Walcott Bout Is Cancelled, September 18, 1948.
339 *Altoona Mirror*, Zale in Best Shape for Go With Cerdan, September 18, 1948.
340 *Chicago Sun-Times*, Cerdan, Zale Both Confident, September 20, 1948.

guaranteed.[341] Neiderreiter didn't expect the crowd to exceed 25,000, and while he hoped for a gate of $300,000, many doubted it would reach $250,000. If the figure fell below $230,000, the promoters would lose money on the show. Cerdan's guarantee was ultimately reduced to $40,000 and the agreement stipulated that if he won, the whole amount would be held in escrow by the National Boxing Association until Cerdan granted Tony a return title match.[342]

But once again the training period was over and the time for another important middleweight championship bout was at hand. Most believed the title would remain in America's possession, but there were some Frenchmen who had other ideas about that.

---

341 *Lowell Sun*, Cerdan – T. of C. In Term Tussle, September 20, 1948.
342 *Tucson Daily Citizen*, Cerdan Makes Foreign Bid For Boxing Crown, September 21, 1948.

SHOWDOWN WITH THE FRENCHMAN

AGE	32	34
HEIGHT	5 FT. 8 IN.	5 FT. 8½ IN.
WEIGHT	160 LBS.	159 LBS.
NECK	16 IN.	16 IN.
REACH	69 IN.	69 IN.
CHEST NORMAL	40½ IN.	38½ IN.
CHEST EXPANDED	44¼ IN.	40½ IN.
FOREARM	11¾ IN.	11¾ IN.
FIST	12 IN.	9 IN.
WAIST	32¼ IN.	31½ IN.
BICEPS	12 IN.	13 IN.
THIGH	23 IN.	24¼ IN.
CALF	14¾ IN.	14½ IN.
ANKLE	9¼ IN.	9 IN.

CERDAN

ZALE

On Tuesday evening, September 21, Marcel Cerdan and his handlers drove to Roosevelt Stadium. On the way, Marcel asked that they stop at a small church where he lit a candle in memory of his deceased mother. She had passed away 13 years earlier on his 19th birthday, and he'd made a habit of leaving flowers on her grave prior to each of his fights. He then lit a second candle and asked the Virgin Mary to watch over his fight, another personal tradition.

They reached their destination at 8:30. Roosevelt Stadium was built by the edge of the sea, and had three tiers of covered terraces. The ring had been set up so that it was surrounded on all four sides by seven rows of bleachers. It was a humid night. Once Marcel reached his dressing room, a uniformed policeman stood outside to prevent any unauthorized visits.

Marcel put on the blue shorts with white stripes that his mother had made for him. He decided he would wear them under the white trunks that the organizers had provided him to wear. Marcel had a medallion of the baby Jesus given to him by his mother sewn into the black belt of the lucky shorts. He covered himself with a lavender blue colored robe. He was reading through various letters and telegrams of encouragement when Sam Pian arrived and entered the dressing room to check on the bandages on his hands. Billy West, one of Marcel's handlers went off to do the same with Tony's bandages.[343]

When Tony was being driven to the stadium, he told his brothers Joe and John he "didn't have it tonight." Joe asked him what he meant, and Tony replied, "Yesterday I had it, today it's gone." Johnny told Tony not to worry about things back home, but just to concentrate on the fight. Tony replied, "I just don't feel it tonight, but I must go on anyway. I'll pray silently once I'm at the stadium, and hopefully that will clear my mind."

It was obvious that he was worried about something, and not just the fight.[344]

Finally, the preliminaries were over and it was time for the main event. Tonight's fight would be the first international fight of title magnitude in ten years, or since Joe Louis knocked out Nazi Germany's pride and joy, Max Schmeling, in 1938.

---

343 Grimault, Dominique, *A Hymn To Love, Piaf and Cerdan*, W.H. Allen, London, England 1984.
344 Thad Zale interview with Joseph Zale, Jr.

The attendance fell far short of the number that Niederreiter had hoped for, as a total of 19,272 made their way through the turnstiles that evening. The fight generated a total gate of $242,840 which ensured a small profit for the promoters. A light breeze blew in from the sea and the evening began to cool a bit as Marcel entered the ring. The Master of Ceremonies introduced former champions to the crowd, including Gene Tunney, Billy Conn, Georgie Abrams, and a numbers of others.

Then the crowd cheered and rose to their feet as the Champion appeared and made his way to the ring. Tony was wearing a white robe and had a towel draped over his head. Once both men were in the ring, their gloves were placed on their hands and laced up. The French and American national anthems were played and the fighters met in the middle of the ring to receive instructions from referee Paul Cavailier. The instructions were translated to Marcel who could not speak English. The Champion weighed 159 pounds for the bout, while the challenger scaled one pound less at 158.

The main event finally began at 10:15. From the outset, it didn't appear as though Tony had his heart in the fight. He just didn't appear to have the killer instinct and the level of determination that he had in his prior fight against Graziano. Against a fighter of Cerdan's stature, that was a recipe for disaster. It was clear from the start that Cerdan was a very strong fighter, and the combinations he threw were fast and furious. Both men landed a number of hard blows during the opening round, but more often than not, it was Marcel backing Tony up rather than the other way around.

It was more of the same in the second round, with both men throwing heavy punches and coming together in clinches. Tony opened a cut on Marcel's forehead during the round, but from that point on in the round it was Marcel who was doing the faster punching. He was the more aggressive of the two.

In the third round, Tony landed a hard right to the stomach and then crowded Marcel to the ropes. He led with a right and hurt Marcel with another right to the jaw. Both men landed a number of telling blows in the round, but it was one of Tony's better sessions in the fight.

The fourth round was the best of the fight for Tony. They exchanged left hand blows and Marcel missed with a left hook. Tony landed lefts and rights to the body and outscored Marcel during the next exchange of punches between the two. Tony landed a hard right to Marcel's jaw that buckled his legs and forced him to hold on while he gathered his senses.

On another occasion in this round, Tony wrenched himself free of a clinch and delivered a terrific right just below the heart that caused Marcel to wince in pain. The Frenchman missed with a combination at the sound of the bell.

Rounds five through ten followed a similar pattern, both men throwing blows and then clinching, but it was Marcel that was

landing more frequently and who was forcing the fight and dictating the pace for the most part. As the fight went on, it was clear that the Frenchman was gaining the upper hand and that his punches carried the greater amount of steam behind them. He spun Tony around with two left hooks to the face in the ninth session.

By the tenth round, Tony had a lump under his left eye and Marcel backed him into ropes where he landed a number of left hooks to the head. Despite the number of hard blows that were landed, neither fighter ever appeared close to suffering a knockdown during the first ten rounds.

UPI Photo

It was in the eleventh session that the stocky 5'8" Frenchman really stepped up and asserted his dominance. Tony looked like a very tired fighter. Marcel moved in and pounded Tony with lefts and rights to the body. Always moving forward, Marcel hooked some more to the jaw and Tony was backed into a neutral corner by another left hand blow. Marcel landed another left to the jaw. Tony fought back and landed a right to the side of Marcel's head, but it had little effect, and Marcel sent Tony back on his heels with another hard left to the jaw. He pounded Tony against the ropes and the Champion appeared dazed. Marcel landed a big right to the head, followed by another hard left hook just as the bell rang.

The Champion swayed momentarily on unsteady legs, arms dangling at his sides with glassy eyes pointing downward and then he pitched forward to his knees. Referee Cavalier reached down and steadied the fallen fighter with his hands under his armpits while Art Winch and Ray Arcel rushed out and dragged their exhausted fighter to his corner.[345]

---

345 *Chicago Sun-Times*, Blow by Blow Description of Marcel Cerdan's Victory, September 22, 1948.

Once in his corner, Tony was doused with sponges of ice water but it failed to revive him completely. Before the twelfth round could begin, Pian and Winch told the referee that their man was unable to continue. Cavalier waved to Cerdan's corner to indicate that the bout was finished.

Roupp leapt into the ring and flung his arms around his fighter. Marcel broke into a grin and returned the embrace. The Master of Ceremonies entered the ring and grabbed the microphone and declared that the Frenchman was the new Middleweight Champion of the World. Before Cerdan left the ring, Tony offered him his heartfelt congratulations on his victory.

The world middleweight title, an exclusive American property since Robert Fitzsimmons gave it up, now belonged to a foreign land. It was 4 o'clock in the morning when the news of Cerdan's victory was flashed on the screen of a Paris theater, but a huge crowd began a riotous celebration and broke out in song. Several morning newspapers rushed out special editions to announce the victory.[346]

Referee Cavalier later disclosed that he counted Tony out while he sat in his corner. Tony's managers declared that they had asked the fight to be stopped, and that it should be ruled a technical knockout instead of a knockout. Pian maintained that in New Jersey the referee could count a fighter out in his corner after the bell sounded to start the action in a round, but not during the minute's rest between sessions. Ultimately, it went into the record books as a 12-round technical knockout since Tony had finished the eleventh round.[347]

Although Tony put up a game fight, it was a pretty one-sided affair. Referee Cavalier had scored the bout eight rounds for Cerdan and three for Tony at the time the bout ended. Some felt that was a charitable score.[348]

It took Cerdan a full ten minutes to reach his dressing room and once he arrived, he was greeted by a swarm of reporters and photographers. Marcel sat on a wooden table as he tried to comply with the multiple requests for photos and field the many questions that were fired his way. As the writers crowded their way around the

346 *Edwardsville Intelligencer*, Frenchman Celebrate Cerdan's Ring Victory, September 22, 1948

347 Goldman, Herbert G., *The Ring 1986-1987 Record Book and Boxing Encyclopedia*, Ring Publishing Corporation, New York, New York 1987

348 *Chicago Herald-American*, Frenchman KO's Weary Zale in 12ᵗʰ, September 22, 1948

new Champion, Marcel jokingly protested, "Mon Dieu, I now take more punishment that I did from Zale."

"Yes, he would fight Zale again," he said through his translator.

Asked if Tony had hurt him at any time, Marcel winced a bit and said, "Yes" as he pointed toward a spot high on his head. Tony's body punching had hurt him as well, especially in the fourth round he told the group of reporters. He also said that Tony punched harder than anybody he ever fought, but told the group that he knew he had him in the seventh round because from then on he could feel him growing weaker in the clinches and his punches began to weaken.

By the tenth round, Marcel began to believe that he would knock out Tony. But Marcel said Tony was a great fighter, very game and a good sportsman.

Over in his own dressing room, Tony told another group of reporters that he "just didn't have it tonight. Usually when an opponent comes to me with punches, I fight my best. This time I just didn't have it."[349]

On the night of the fight, Tony had told his brothers that he wasn't feeling good. "The night before the bout, he was in wonderful mental shape. If he had fought Cerdan that night, he could have beaten him. The next night everything he did was wrong. Something happened between the day before and the night of the actual fight that changed his mental state. Maybe it was the call that he received from Adeline a few short hours before the fight. His brothers knew he should not take it."[350]

Ray Arcel chimed in and told Tony that he was not really knocked out by any one punch, but had dropped from exhaustion from the cumulative effect of the action and blows. New Jersey State Athletic Commission physician, Dr. Cohen, verified the exhaustive condition of the former champion.

Tony couldn't remember having landed a clean shot at the Frenchman until a reporter reminded him of a solid punch he'd landed on Cerdan's jaw in the fourth round. "Yeah, yeah," Tony replied, as the recollection of the punch came back to him.

"He hits pretty fair," Tony told the group. But when asked to compare Marcel's punching power with that of Rocky's, he added, "No, he doesn't hit as hard as Graziano."

---

349 *Chicago Sun-Times*, Cerdan Will Return; Zale is Undecided, September 22, 1948.
350 Thad Zale interview with Joseph Zale, Jr.

Tony told his questioners that he didn't intend to quit boxing and said he'd be willing to fight Cerdan again. Arcel, filling in the conversation, said he knew by the fifth or sixth round that Tony just didn't have it. He explained Tony's tiring as the fight went on by reminding the reporters that Tony hadn't gone 15 rounds in seven years. Except for a swollen right eye and a bruised lip, Tony showed little outward effects of the fight. But he was clearly a very tired fighter.[351]

Although he didn't mention it right after the fight, many years later Tony said that his right elbow had played a role in the defeat. "Before the Graziano fights, my right elbow had gone bad. It was its worst in my final bout with Rocky. Ray Arcel, my trainer, constantly worked and rubbed that elbow down during and after training. He had to limber it up enough to allow me to use my right to the body

effectively. After a blow to Cerdan in the third round, I was never able to use the arm again because of the pain. When I needed it most, it went out. But, you see it was time. God was telling me," he said.[352] When Tony retired, he had five bone chips removed from around his elbow that had caused all the pain. Tony's method of throwing that right to the body without turning his arm and wrist over to spread the shock of the impact had literally caused the right elbow to shatter. He lived with the pain for many years, and simply considered it an inconvenience until the pain became unbearable.

351 *Chicago Daily News*, Length of Bout, Age Too Much, September 22, 1948.
352 *The Ring*, The Dynamite Kid, March/April 1988.

Contacted at home by phone immediately after the fight, Adeline said she knew "it would have to all end sometime." When asked if she thought Tony would take advantage of the option for a rematch, she replied, "I hope not. I am going to try and persuade Tony not to fight again. After all, he can't keep going through all that and expect his health to stand up. He has two children to think about. I haven't seen him since he left for New York about three weeks ago, but from his letters and a phone call, he was very confident."[353]

Adeline said that neither money nor glory was worth it to her. She hoped that Tony would set an example for young people by getting into some youth activity, teaching boxing and trying to inspire them. "I'd be much happier that way," she added, "and Tony's always talked about doing that after his ring days."

Tony's brother Walter had other ideas. "This fight was just a warm-up. Tony'll beat him the next time," he said.

After getting a full night sleep and having more time to reflect on the matter, Tony wasn't as sure about fighting again. "I'll decide later whether I'll try a comeback," he said the next day.[354]

Tony arrived home late morning within the next week and was welcomed by a delegation headed by Mayor Eugene Swartz and other city and civic leaders.

On December 29, unofficial announcements hinted that 35-year-old Tony might soon announce his retirement from the ring. The Most Reverend Bernard Sheil, Director General of the Catholic Youth Organization in Chicago, said Tony had been appointed a member of the C.Y.O. staff as a boxing instructor.[355]

In the same month, *The Ring* magazine selected Tony's fight against Marcel Cerdan as their "Fight of the Year." It marked the third consecutive year that one of Tony's fights was chosen for the honor.

By year-end, it remained to be seen whether or not Tony would actually retire from the ring. Regardless of his decision, it was pretty obvious that Tony had done as much or more than any other fighter for the sport since the war had ended and his title bouts during that period of time were the most exciting of that period.

---

353 *Chicago Sun-Times*, Knew It Would End Sometime, September 22, 1948.
354 *Chicago Sun-Times*, Cerdan Will Return; Zale is Undecided, September 22, 1948.
355 *Kingston Daily Freeman*, Hint Tony Zale Ready to Retire, December 30, 1948.

RETIREMENT

Although his wife and managers urged Tony to retire, in early 1949, he was determined to try and regain his title for a second time. "I don't know what Art wants to do, but I know what I want to do. I want to fight Cerdan again," he said. He was confident that he could defeat Marcel if they met again.[356]

While Art and Sam continued their efforts to convince Tony to retire, the Tournament of Champions began to formulate their plans for a return match between Tony and Marcel. Lew Burston, Marcel's American representative, advised that the Champion was ready to fulfill his contract with that organization, and more than willing to fight Tony again.

By mid-February, the Tournament of Champions had in their possession a letter from Tony's attorney ending speculation of Tony's retirement from the ring. A spokesman for the group said negotiations for an outdoor return bout sometime in the summer would begin immediately. In early March, Art said that Tony would begin training for the title fight, but that he would need several tune-up bouts before tackling Marcel again in June.

Despite Art's announcement, there was quite a bit of speculation during the month of March as to whether or not Tony would really ever fight again. Many believed that he not only would, but should, retire from boxing. Consequently, the Tournament of Champions also began making plans for a potentially more lucrative match between Marcel and the reigning welterweight champion Sugar Ray Robinson, in the event Tony suddenly decided against a comeback. Some believed that a return match between Tony and Marcel would

---

356 *Amarillo Globe*, Zale Planning on Fight Cerdan Again, January 11, 1949.

produce a gate of only $200,000, while a title contest between Marcel and Sugar Ray might produce one as high as $500,000. Although Ray was planning to defend his welterweight title in June, he'd already indicated his desire to give up his title and challenge Marcel for the middleweight crown if the opportunity presented itself.[357]

While the boxing world waited to learn what Tony would do, Notre Dame University awarded him with their first annual *Bengal Bout Recognition Award* as the man in boxing who had contributed the most to youth of America by his example and competitive spirit. The university's yearly boxing championships, or 'Bengal Bouts', received their name from the fact that the proceeds are funneled to the Bengal missions in India." They praised Tony and he felt truly honored as their first recipient. This tournament began in late March and Tony was scheduled to act as the honorary referee for the finals.[358]

---

357 *Salt Lake City Tribune*, Cerdan Bout Looms for Welter King, April 1, 1949.
358 *Wisconsin State Journal*, Tony Zale Receives Notre Dame Award, March 29, 1949.

Meanwhile, in Cerdan's first fight since capturing the middleweight title from Tony, he knocked Britain's Dick Turpin out in the seventh round of a scheduled ten-round non-title affair on March 29. Marcel ended Turpin's night with a hard right to the body followed by a short left hook to the jaw before 7,000 Londoners at Earls Court Empress Hall in Kensington, London. Burston said he planned to take Marcel to the United States soon for a couple more tune-up bouts before defending his crown.[359] Ultimately, Marcel had only one more non-title bout, against Lucien Crawczwk in Morocco on May 8, before defending his championship. He knocked Crawczwk out in the fourth round.

Joe Longman, a boxing promoter in Paris, France, was managing Cerdan by this time. He asked the Tournament of Champions to co-promote a rematch between Marcel and Tony in Paris that coming June, but the New Yorker's rejected the proposition. While the organization was still privately hoping that they would be able to stage a match between Cerdan and Robinson at New York's Polo Grounds, it still appeared that they might be stuck with a rematch between Marcel and Tony while their rivals, Mike Jacobs and the Twentieth Century Club, ended up staging a welterweight title match between Robinson and Kid Gavilan.[360]

However, there was also a chance that the Tournament of Champions might be able to find a way to stage both title fights on the same card. Robinson had an existing contract with Jacobs' organization, but Ray's publicist Pete Vaccare claimed that contracts of that nature never held up in court and was convinced Ray could make a deal with the Tournament of Champions, if he chose to do so. Still, it seemed unlikely that the promoters would be able to figure out a way to generate enough revenues to cover the cost of paying the fighters for both title fights along with the Polo Grounds rental fee.

On April 10, Tony still sounded very much like a man who was dead set on a return to the ring. He was convinced he could defeat Marcel if given a second opportunity. "I reached my peak one day too soon when we first met. I am very anxious to meet him again and I will not be satisfied until I do," he said.[361]

359 *Hutchinson News Herald*, Cerdan Wins Another Fight, March 30, 1949.
360 *Lima News*, Rival Groups Wage War for Control of New York Boxing, April 7, 1949.
361 *European Stars & Stripes*, Zale Predicts Cerdan Defeat, April 11, 1949.

On April 13, it was announced that Tony would fight Jimmy Hayden in the feature bout on a May 4 boxing card in Clarksburg, West Virginia, as a tune-up for a rematch with Cerdan. The event was originally scheduled for April 27, but Tony requested a postponement so he would have more time to train for it.

Tony's wife and co-managers were not alone in their desire to see Tony retire. On the same day the match with Hayden was announced, Pennsylvania Athletic Commission Chairman, Leon Rains, came out and voiced his opinion that Tony should not be allowed to fight Marcel again.

"It would be a tragic mistake to allow Zale to fight again and endanger his life," Rains said. "When he was stopped by Rocky Graziano in Chicago two years ago and by Cerdan last fall, Zale took two of the worst beatings a top-notch fighter ever had to suffer. Any ordinary fighter would have retired. But Zale, because of his long and honorable record in the ring, was entitled and allowed to make that decision for himself. He hasn't done so. Tony has all the money he needs and should be thankful he is still sound in body and mind, instead of risking everything once more."[362]

But the idea of walking away from the game without trying to win his title back from Cerdan was a tough pill for Tony to swallow. He had no fear of another match with the Champion. Sportswriter Jimmy Cannon contended that Tony had more guts than any other fighter, living or dead. He spoke of Tony's loss to Graziano in Chicago, where in his words it looked as though Tony's bones had melted when he was draped over the ropes. The fight was stopped, and he admired the fact that Tony protested the stoppage because he felt the only way to lose one's title should be on one's back. Cannon ended his praise of Tony with the following quote from Graziano: "There's only one way you can lick Tony Zale. You got to kill him."[363]

When he was informed of Rain's comments, Tony replied, "Who took the worst beating in Chicago? Graziano or me? I was wilted from the heat, but Graziano was battered and bleeding. I understand Graziano is being reinstated, even though he was through a long time ago. Joe Walcott is permitted to fight, despite his age and the beating he took from Joe Louis. So why pick on me?"

---

362 *Wisconsin State Journal*, Boxing Official Would Force Zale to Retire, April 13, 1949.
363 *Berkshire Evening Eagle*, The Referee's Sporting Chat, April 14, 1949.

"I'm getting ready for the bout that Cerdan has to give me and I won't make the same mistakes I did the last time we fought," Tony added.[364]

On April 22, it was reported that Tony had been replaced as an opponent for Jimmy Hayden on May 4. Tony had requested a second delay in order to properly prepare for the contest. Jimmy Columbo, the event's matchmaker, decided instead to replace him on the card.

Just four days later, and just a little more than two weeks shy of his 36th birthday, Tony officially announced his retirement from boxing. Reading from a prepared statement, Tony said, "After a lot of deliberation and argument within myself, and with my managers too, I have decided to call it quits as far as boxing is concerned, and retire. It is not an easy thing to do, but I guess that's all."

At that point, Sam Pian stepped forward and said, "Three things entered into this. It was his pride, his determination to regain the championship, and third, money. But he overlooked two things, and we made him see it, his health and his family. His health may be impaired if he continues." Tony nodded in agreement.[365]

"I looked bad against Cerdan," Tony said. "I realize I've passed my peak. It was to satisfy my pride that I wanted to meet Cerdan again. But now I'm satisfied to rest on my past. At first, I couldn't believe that the fault probably was due to my long campaign. After working out for a proposed tune-up in Clarksburg, West Virginia, May 4, I finally came to the realization. My coordination was slipping."

"What about Cerdan, Tony?" someone asked.

"I thought I beat him the last time," Tony said.

"That's the way to go out," said Art Winch. "Go thinking you licked him."

"Well, I thought I did," Tony said, though clearly everyone who witnessed the fight thought it was a one-sided affair in Cerdan's favor.

"I wanted to fight him again, but my managers told me no," Tony added.

---

364 *The Daily Republic*, Title Bout is All Tony Zale is Asking, April 14, 1949.
365 *Wisconsin State Journal*, Tony Zale Decides to End Ring Career, April 27, 1949.

"Yes," Winch said. "There was only one thing we wanted. Not money, not glory. We just wanted to know the kid would never step through the ropes again."

Upon reaching the decision, Tony gave up a $60,000 guarantee for the return match with Cerdan.[366]

With Tony out of the picture, Cerdan had his choice of four opponents for his June title defense. They were Ray Robinson, Steve Belloise, Jake LaMotta or Rocky Graziano. Ultimately, LaMotta was selected and the pair we're matched to fight in Briggs Stadium in Detroit, Michigan, on June 16, 1949. LaMotta had waited a long time for the opportunity. As far as he was concerned, he should have received a shot at the title in 1946. "Any way you look at it, I was the top contender, and when Tony Zale came out of the service, I should have been given the first shot at him," he said.[367] But who had the greater draw, LaMotta or Graziano? The promoters opted for the greatest paycheck when they signed Graziano to fight Tony Zale and they created one of the greatest trilogies in boxing history.

When Jake and Marcel fought for the title, Cerdan suffered a tear of the supraspinatus muscle of the left shoulder in the first round, and was essentially a one-armed fighter for the rest of the contest, dominated by LaMotta. The fight was stopped during the intermission between the ninth and tenth rounds after Cerdan was examined by the ring doctor.[368]

Tragically, Cerdan lost his life on October 28, 1949, while traveling to New York for a return match with LaMotta. The Air France plane he was flying in crashed in the Azores Islands in the North Atlantic Ocean and there were no survivors among the 48 onboard. The fight had originally been scheduled for September 28, but was delayed four days before the bout because of a training injury suffered by LaMotta. As fate would have it, the fight's delay led to Cerdan's premature death. The outstanding fighter, who suffered only four losses in a professional career of over 100 fights, was greatly admired for his fighting skills and many had expected him to regain the title against LaMotta. Longtime fight manager, Dumb Dan Morgan, considered him one of the greatest combination punchers

---

366 *Janesville Daily Gazette*, Tony Zale Ends Boxing Career, April 27, 1949.
367 *Record Eagle*, Fight is Set for June 15, May 24, 1949.
368 *The Times Recorder*, LaMotta Wins Title With KO, June 17, 1949.

he ever saw and thought he was one of the three greatest all-round fighters of the decade 1940 to 1950.[369]

After announcing his retirement from the ring, Tony quickly settled into his routine as a boxing instructor for the CYO. By mid-May, he had also been named as one of two sports editors of the new FM radio station WFJL, where he was put in charge of sportscasts and interviews.

Photo Credit Davis B. Lannes

Through all of the talk of retirement, Tony dealt with the stress produced by the thoughts of his impending and well-publicized divorce. On more than one occasion, Tony had actually asked his brother John if *he* would approach Adeline, and ask her for the divorce. John refused.[370] Tony, who was no longer living at home, was working at the CYO gym in Chicago and had begun counseling with Bishop Sheil. He knew his marriage was over, but he didn't have the courage to approach this with Adeline. He was still afraid of her quick temper.

He was lost in confusion over his retirement from the ring and thoughts of what he would do for the rest of his life after the loss of his family. He had no formal training for sports broadcasting, but figured he knew enough from the hundreds of interviews he'd participated in to give it a go.

Contrary to prevailing thought, Tony was not in decent shape financially. He knew that once the divorce proceedings began and everything was sorted out, what funds were left would be quickly depleted. Like most, he had a mortgage to meet on a home that was going to require funds to maintain. He wondered how he was going

---

369 *Syracuse Herald Journal,* Morgan Has Praise for Boxer Cerdan, November 6, 1949.
370 Thad Zale interview with Jeanette Zale.

to be able to work with the kids at the CYO, meet the requirements of the job at the radio station, see his own children during the week, and meet all of the maintenance requirements on their home.

Meeting all of his obligations was a major concern and weighed heavily on his mind. He was concerned he had split himself in too many directions. He feared being unable to do any of them well. The one thing he did know how to do better than anything else was box. Now, having been a boxer since the age of 15, that part of his life was over, or so he thought at the time.

But as it turned out, Tony was an excellent coach when it came to working with the kids at the CYO gym. His low baritone voice struck a friendly chord with all the kids he worked with, and to so many, there was an immediate connection. These young, aspiring boxers couldn't help but have a lot of respect for the former world champion. They knew he was more than *just* an instructor. Tony cared about them and he wasn't bashful when it came to sharing life's lessons that he had learned through pugilism.

UPI Photo

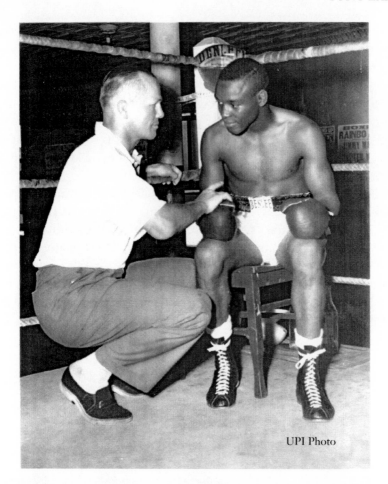

UPI Photo

Most of the kids whom Tony worked with came from poor or lower class families, and many of them had received little in the way of positive direction up to that point in their lives. Tony instilled them with pride in themselves and was a positive role model for them to look up to.

On the other hand, Tony was a bust when it came to the radio announcing job. He just didn't excel as a speaker in that arena. As a columnist for the *Chicago Tribune*, his quotes were better than his prose. It was clear he wasn't cut out for either of these roles. He was sure that if he continued to put his faith in God, he would succeed. The lucrative wages from any better-paying career would not materialize. Tony grew up without money, and other than the fact that he needed it to live and to support his family, money was not of key importance to him. Tony prayed morning, noon and night that God would take hold of his life and use him as He saw fit.

Many reporters and news people believed that Tony was well off financially with plenty of cash in reserve. What they did not know, was that everyone in his corner had received a piece of the pie. Adeline too soon discovered that there was nowhere near as much money in Tony's personal savings account as she had thought.

As stated earlier, Bishop Sheil was responsible for appointing Tony to the CYO Boxing Program that he had developed for the Diocese of Chicago. The Bishop had been a fan of Tony's career and had even witnessed him in action in his 1947 fight in Chicago against Graziano. He realized what a skillful ring technician Tony was when he laced up those gloves. He was a positive role model both in and out of the ring. The humble, contrite and caring characteristics that Tony demonstrated were exactly what the CYO needed from an individual to head their boxing program. His mild manner, boxing skills and knowledge, along with his life experiences, would help instill the kind of discipline and dedication that this generation of youngsters needed. Tony's philosophy from the beginning was "keep the kids off the street and in the gyms."

Tony was a natural in this role. He was honest, hard-working, and a man of great integrity. Every young boxer quickly recognized Tony for his sincere character. Yes, his word was his bond and the boys immediately knew he was a friend and mentor they could count on. Tony was the perfect choice for this job.

Tony also began to referee a number of amateur and professional boxing contests around the country to supplement his income from the CYO job. He didn't quit refereeing until the mid 1970s. He even refereed one of Thad Zale's fights, his own nephew, when he fought for the Gary, Indiana, CYO in July of 1967.

As Tony explained in late May of 1949 to a Canadian reporter while he was in Winnipeg to referee a bout, he was far from being financially independent. As an example, he told the writer that his top purse was the $140,000 figure he received for one of his three fights with Rocky Graziano. Half of that figure went to his managers, a smaller portion to his brother John who continued to receive a 10% managerial cut for the length of Tony's career, and a big piece of what was left was taken for federal income tax. Besides that, Tony covered all training expenses which included costs of sparring partners and trainers; all of the equipment needed for training purposes; the rental of the training facility itself; and the cost of food for everyone. In this article, Tony did not reveal his final net of the $140,000 purse, but hinted that it was not much more than $20,000.[371]

UPI Photo

---

371 *The Lethbridge Herald*, Tony Zale Not Financially Independent, May 31, 1949.

THE REAL STRUGGLE BEGINS

Tony's financial situation suffered from a risky investment in the Tucker automobile in the late 1940s. The Tucker 48 was the brainchild of the charismatic Preston Thomas Tucker. He represented one of the last attempts by an independent car maker to break into the high-volume car business dominated by the big three Detroit automakers.

During World War II, automobile company operations were dedicated to the war effort. There were no new car models produced over a four-year period. Once the war ended, the public was anxious for new designs and Tucker decided it was the perfect time for him to launch his dream car.

Preston was a man of big dreams. He wasted little time in purchasing the old Dodge plant in Cicero, Illinois. Comprised of 475 acres, the plant was used to build B-29 bomber engines during the war. The main building covered 93 acres, which made it the largest building in the world at the time. The prototype of the Tucker 48 quickly garnered a lot of attention with its sleek design and innovative features.

That "dream car of the future" contained: disc brakes; a rear-mounted engine with hydraulic valves instead of a cam shaft; self-sealing tubeless tires; a built-in roll bar; direct drive torque convertors for each wheel instead of a transmission; fuel injection; padded dashboard; independent spring suspension; sidebar chassis protection; a laminated windshield; and, of it's three front lights, the large middle one moved in the direction the driver turned the steering wheel. These are just a few examples of Preston's numerous innovations and patents.

Preston needed to raise a lot of capital in a hurry if he was going to be able to successfully get his operation off the ground. He decided to raise the needed funds by selling dealership rights before the car was available, and through a large stock offering. At the urging of one of his sister in-law Frances Zale's relatives, Bill Price, chief machinist for Tucker and co-designer of its 589 cubic inch engine, Tony was one of those who invested in the stock. This investment consisted of all of what was left of his boxing earnings.

Shortly after Tony's investment, The U.S. Security and Exchange Commission launched an investigation into the company that resulted in over 30 charges of conspiracy, securities and mail fraud. Ultimately over time, Tucker and his associates were cleared of any wrong doing, but during the ensuing legal battle, franchise sales fell. Stock issues were delayed and Tucker's reputation, along with public interest in the automobile, were severely damaged. Consequently, the Tucker Company folded on March 3, 1949. Tony and many others lost every penny of the monies they had invested. Tucker's story, albeit somewhat dramatized in typical Hollywood fashion, was told in a 1988 movie starring the actor Jeff Bridges titled, *Tucker: The Man and His Dream*. A total of 51 cars were built before the company officially folded.

Even though Tony had finally complied with Adeline's wishes to retire from the ring, it failed to help save their marriage. From the views of both sides of the family, their marital relationship had been very tumultuous and sometimes violent, ever since Tony's discharge from the Navy in 1945. There had never been a great deal of time for them to actually get acquainted beyond being frequent partners at P.N.A. dances around the area. Tony had entered the U.S. Navy immediately after their marriage. His departure so soon after left little time for them to settle into a husband and wife relationship. Adeline's younger sister, Genevieve, as previously mentioned, lived with the couple for a time during a few of her high school years. When she was asked to comment on their relationship during the writing of this book, she said, "My sister was very intelligent and a good musician. She was very proud and independent. She made good money as a musician and always said she never worked for scale. He (Tony) didn't seem to appreciate her musical background. You guys (men) are always trying to run things."[372]

The couple's youngest daughter, Teresa, said her mother had a very high IQ and was a child prodigy who played in the Chicago World's fair in 1934 with a string band. In addition to the piano, Teresa said Adeline could play many other instruments including the organ, accordion, violin, mandolin, guitar, flute and clarinet. "At one time," Teresa said, her mother "was one of the top ten performers in Chicago and even had her own breakfast radio show." She also said that her mother always had a wonderful dry sense of humor.

---

372 Interview with Genevieve Bancroft, dated July 8, 2011.

Genevieve loved her sister and Tony, but called them a "mismatch from the beginning." She remembered seeing them argue at times and referred to both as "volatile people." But she and Tony's youngest daughter seem to be the only two parties the authors came across that ever said anything about Tony being volatile in any fashion outside of the ring. It is possible that Adeline may have been the only party capable of provoking that type of behavior out of him. Teresa, and her sister Mary's daughter, Sophia Wells, both believe that Adeline's excessive mood swings were likely the result of an undiagnosed bipolar disorder. Mary herself had described her mother's mood swings as transitional, and compared them to a "swinging kitchen door."

Mary was as talented musically as her mother, but her mother could not tolerate a single note being misplayed. If she made an error on a musical piece, she knew what her mother's response would be. She would be choked, shaken, slapped and literally picked up off the piano bench that she had been sitting on. There were times when her mother choked her so hard that she thought she might have passed out.

After one of these incidents, Mary woke up to discover that there were bruises on her neck. When she told her father about the bruises, he warned Adeline that she better never hurt the kids again physically. She also believed her mother had three distinct personalities. One was abusive, vindictive and wildly detached. The second was the total musician and cabaret performer. Finally, the third was a good natured, loving and fun personality that was not seen often enough behind closed doors. Adeline inter-changed between the three personalities with a blink of an eye. Mary sadly explained, "That's when Mommy changed her tactics."

As the children grew into their teens, Adeline began to abuse the girls mentally and emotionally because she knew she should not physically hurt them anymore. She heeded Tony's warning, albeit late in their formative years. As Thad's interview with Mary continued, it became abundantly clear how hurt Mary felt and how abandoned and lonely she was as a child without her father being present. Two weeks of visitation with her father were just not enough to repair the emotional damage that had been caused by Adeline. She finished the conversation by saying, "If Daddy could have only won in court, our lives would have been so different."

Mary also stated that Teresa did not receive the same level of physical punishment that she did because she was too young, and because Teresa did not possess the same musical talent. Teresa suffered from several maladies, including Crohn's Disease and Multiple Sclerosis, at an early age. Her mother would have been aware that subjecting her to physical abuse might worsen her condition.

In another phone interview that took place after her father's death with Thad, Mary was inquisitive and wanted to know more about her family, her dad's life, and his funeral. She knew that he had worked at the Chicago CYO and for the Chicago Parks Department, but she had no idea how many young people he had helped throughout his 36 years of coaching, and how many came to the funeral to pay their respects. She said she was almost jealous of all those admirers who had a chance to look up to him as a father figure. She felt that they had been cheated by her mother for taking them away from him after their divorce.

Mary remembered their yearly summer visits with her dad and how difficult it was to return to her mother's care. She felt that her own adult life had been negatively affected by her up-bringing with an individual, her mother, who really never resembled what a child would want a mother to be. One moment, Adeline was loving but could flip her personality. In spite of Teresa's ill health, Mary said Adeline would slap her for innocent mistakes of any kind.

In this phone interview with Thad, Mary mentioned Adeline's second husband Johnny, but could not recall his last name at that time, but did later. He and Adeline had married secretly in 1955, but the kids just thought Johnny was living with them. The marriage lasted for just over a year when Johnny, a naval aviator, died in an air crash during a training mission. Mary believed he had deliberately crashed his plane when he realized what and who he had married. There is no proof to support her theory, though. Mary said Tony and Johnny got along very well and liked each other and that Tony was saddened by his death.

Asked about her grandparent's relationship, Mary's daughter Sophia said, "Call it a love/hate relationship. There are always two sides of a story, but I believe what my mother (Mary) told me about the relationship between Adele and Tony. She physically abused him and that is why they split. You'd think it would be the other way around, but knowing Adele, I believe she did hit him. She also physically abused Mary and Teresa as children, and then as adults, she was mentally abusive. My mom and aunt dealt with it because they knew she was mentally sick. My grandfather was a very gentle man. He was sweet-hearted, kind and happy."[373]

Sophia added, "Even though Adele is my grandmother, it doesn't mean I have to like her. In fact, there were many times when I wanted to kill her or strangle her. She made me so mad at times that it created that kind of rage that could push me over the edge.

---

[373] Personal email to author from Sophia Wells, granddaughter of Tony and Adeline Zale, dated July 21, 2011.

Luckily, I was too scared to do such a thing. But, yeah, I don't like Adele, and our relationship ended badly the week of my mom's passing."[374]

Teresa, the youngest daughter, said Adeline was abused as a child, and as a result, that was what her mother knew, so she treated her daughters in kind, beating them with a belt, a board or a paddle. She also abused them both emotionally and verbally. Teresa said Adeline provoked Tony and did everything she could to hurt him. On the other hand, she said that her father never laid a hand on *either* of them.[375]

The troubled relationship between Tony and Adeline reached a head in the summer of 1949 when Adeline filed for divorce, for the second time, on August 31. In her complaint, she claimed that she had been treated in a cruel and inhumane manner over a period of many months, resulting in impaired health. Further, it concluded, that married life between the parties was impossible as a result of their irreconcilable differences. She asked for custody of the children and $350 in monthly maintenance until alimony payments could be set after an accounting of Tony's ring earnings and property.[376] Her suit claimed that Tony had large amounts of cash and holdings in addition to a new car which was given to him by the City of Gary (actually the Silver Bell Club) and a bowling alley in Gary, Indiana, worth $300,000.[377] In truth, the bowling alley belonged to Tony's brothers, John, Frank and Walter. John used the 10% share he derived from Tony's ring earnings for managerial related duties, to purchase his share of the business. Tony had no financial interest in the venture.

Adeline felt that John shouldn't have continued to receive a share of Tony's earnings once Sam Pian and Art Winch took over the primary managerial responsibilities for his career. On the other hand, Tony felt that his brother John had dedicated a good part of himself to Tony's early career and deserved to receive a continued portion of his ring earnings.

Early in 1949, Tony had moved out of their marital home. Since his brother John had been his coach and manager all these years in

---

374 Personal email from Sophia Wells, Tony's granddaughter, July 17, 2013.
375 Interview with Teresa Zale, dated July 9, 2011.
376 *Racine Journal Times*, Wife of Tony Zale Files for Divorce, September 2, 1949.
377 *Vidette-Messenger*, Zale's Wife Asks Court For Divorce, September 3, 1949.

boxing, Tony knew there was always a room for him at Johnny's. He also knew that any of his brothers and sisters would always have an open door for him. But Tony would never take advantage of their generosity unless he absolutely had to. When he started working for the CYO in Chicago, his friend E. John, President of Second Federal Savings and Loan, mentioned they owned a vacant tenement house that Tony could stay at free of charge if he would act as the superintendent-night watchman. The problems that Tony would face in this capacity were numerous, including no running water or heat. As the super, Tony would simply occupy a room with a bed at the main entrance. His primary responsibility was to keep out the vagrants who would often try to find their way inside to steal anything that was available and of value. Tony acquired a blank starting pistol that he would often fire into the air to scare off any unwanted visitors.

As directed by the court, Adeline was to receive a sum from Tony of $250 per month for the support of her and the children. He was also instructed to pay any family expenses and attorney fees accrued up until the date of August 31, when she filed for divorce. In reply to Adeline's complaint, Tony ultimately filed a cross-complaint in which he claimed that Adeline had been guilty of cruel and inhumane treatment and had committed adultery with various parties during their marriage. He also claimed that she was an unfit mother, and asked the court to award him sole custody of their two children.

Walter (Sonny) Zale, Tony's nephew, came into possession of hundreds of pages of court documents pertaining to Tony and Adeline's divorce which was part of his father's collection. As he read through the details, he came across a file folder titled, "Detective Reports." Within that file folder were listed subject after subject who admitted to having a relationship with Adeline. Since her father owned a coal and lumber yard in East Chicago, Indiana, Adeline retained keys to the gates and administrative offices. Often, after an evening of performing professionally in the Calumet City nightclubs under the name of Adele Rich, she would adjourn with her suitors to this location before returning home. Unfortunately, after Tony's death, rather than keeping all of the divorce files, Sonny decided to destroy them.

As is often the case in divorce proceedings, the next few months were filled with accusations and hostility. It had been stipulated that Tony would be allowed to visit the children on a scheduled basis, but a November 9 court petition stated that his visits had become "progressively disagreeable" as a result of Adeline's behavior toward Tony. On several occasions, Adeline had prohibited him from seeing his children. Tony also claimed that after his failed investment in the Tucker 48, he was unable to afford the $250 per month support payment.

That same month, the court ruled that the amount of the monthly support payment was to be reduced to $200 per month effective December 1. Adeline was directed to make the children available to Tony at the home for three days per week and both parties, if Adeline was present, were instructed to refrain from quarreling with each other during the visits. Additionally, both parties were ordered to cooperate with the other party's attorneys to determine the exact amount of personal property that each had in his or her possession.

Of course, just because the court orders two parties to behave in a specific manner during divorce proceedings, that doesn't mean things will go smoothly from that point forward. In April of 1950, Adeline charged that Tony was three months behind in his support payments and he was ordered to appear before the court to show why he should not be held in contempt. Tony countered by asking his lawyer to request that Adeline be held in contempt of court for not making his children available for his visits as ordered.

Judge Felix Kaul ordered them both to appear before him on April 14. After listening to each party, the judge ordered them and their attorneys to get together on the visits and support payment issues, or he would require them to return to court and he would "help."

"You are both wrong in thinking you are both right," he told the couple.[378]

Tony continued to accept opportunities to referee some fights to supplement his income in various parts of the country such as Omaha, Nebraska, Waterloo, Iowa, etc. He also made an appearance, playing as himself, in a movie about the Golden Gloves that premiered that May starring James Dunn titled *The Golden Gloves Story*.

The movie was 76 minutes long, and featured a love triangle involving two middleweight amateur boxers who kept colliding in the

---

378 *Wisconsin State Journal*, Zale, Wife Ordered to Settle Dispute, April 15, 1950.

ring in their efforts to woo the 21-year-old daughter of a referee. The movie was filmed in Chicago and Tony had one short line in the film. While it didn't receive rave reviews, it did receive some acclaim for its promotion of the Golden Gloves.[379]

When he was officiating in Waterloo, Iowa, that July, Tony took the time to sit down with a local sports columnist and offer his assessment on the current state of the game of boxing. Tony believed that there was a general lack of good boxers in the country because boys didn't have to work hard enough. "It's too easy to make a dollar," he said. "Kids don't have to be tough to earn a buck. That's the reason boxing is falling off." He was worried about the current state of boxing but believed he was helping the sport with his work in the CYO program.[380] His work with the boys in that program and the various officiating gigs around the Midwest offered him an opportunity to think of something else besides his financial difficulties and the impending loss of his family over the next year.

He and Adeline continued to battle with one another in the court room into early 1951. That February, Adeline's lawyer filed a petition to cite Tony for contempt of court on the grounds that he was $1,400 behind in his support payments. Tony paid $500 before the month was over, but still owed a balance of $900 by March 16.

That November, Adeline's lawyer requested a change in venue on the basis that his client could not receive a fair and impartial trial in a county where the defendant, Tony, was so popular. But a month later, on December 15, 1951, the divorce was granted and Adeline was awarded custody of the children. Tony was ordered to pay $108 per month in support of his former wife and children and it was agreed that their property would be equally divided.[381] (Author's note: Adeline passed away on May 7, 2014.)

Tony was satisfied with the final divorce decree in all aspects, but one. His heart and mind would not allow him to feel satisfied with the loss of his children. Numerous times he would scrimp and save every penny he could until he had enough money to once again hire an attorney for another bout in court. He knew Adeline was an unfit mother, but, as the courts demanded, he would have to have more witnesses and testimony to prove his case.

---

379 *Cedar Rapids Gazette*, Golden Gloves Needs More than James Dunn, June 3, 1950.
380 *Waterloo Daily Courier*, Ney's Column The Sports Alley, July 20, 1950.
381 *Post-Herald*, Wife Wins Decision, December 19, 1951.

In April of 1952, Tony's former adversary, Rocky Graziano, received a shot at the world middleweight title that was in Sugar Ray Robinson's possession by that time. Two months beforehand, Tony expressed an opinion that there was not a middleweight in sight who stood much of a chance to take Robinson's title from him. "Rocky might stop Sugar if he got his best punch in," he said, "but Sugar can box rings around him any night."[382]

Tony made time to visit Rocky during one of his workouts prior to the bout with Robinson. He was ringside when the two men met on April 16, 1952, in Chicago Stadium. In fact, he was introduced to the crowd beforehand, as he climbed into the ring to shake hands with both men to wish them luck. He had a large smile on his face when he walked over and whispered a few words to Rocky and one sportswriter imagined that he most likely encouraged Rocky to give Ray some of what he had given him in their first two epic contests.

Rocky gave it his best shot, flooring the champion at one point in the third round, but Robinson climbed back to his feet and delivered a lightning fast combination which dropped him for a

---

382 *Cedar Rapids Gazette*, Red Peppers, February 27, 1952.

count of ten to retain the title. Rocky climbed through the ropes one more time, five months later against a fighter from Michigan named Chuck Davey. For this Graziano vs. Davey contest, Tony was contacted, and asked if he would help prepare Davey for the upcoming fight with Rocky. Tony agreed, and headed for Michigan State University in East Lansing, Michigan, where Chuck Davey was training. He accepted a small stipend for his effort. Rocky called it a career when Chuck Davey won this bout by a unanimous decision.

In May of 1952, Tony became ill with pneumonia and entered St. Catherine's Hospital in East Chicago, Indiana. He remained there for a total of 16 days before being released on May 28, one day before celebrating his 39th birthday.

In September, Tony filed a petition with the court in another attempt to gain custody of his children. He charged Adeline with neglect and said that she wasn't giving them proper moral training and was an unfit mother. Adeline was threatening to move with the children to Chicago where she was anxious to resume her musical career. He asked that the court deny any request to move the children outside of its jurisdiction. But ultimately on September 9, 1952, Adeline was granted the right to move the children outside of the court's jurisdiction on the condition that she remained subject to their further orders. They also reserved the right to require the children be returned into their jurisdiction at a future date. Tony's visitation rights were amended to have custody of the children for the first two weeks of July of every year.

On September 12, Tony refereed a contest in Jersey City, New Jersey, between a Cuban heavyweight boxing champion named Omelio Agramonte and the world junior heavyweight wrestling champion,

Marvin "Atomic" Mercer. This was a contest *staged* to attempt to answer the age old question of whether a wrestler can beat a boxer. Events of this nature have usually proven to be a bit of a farce, and this contest was no exception. Tony was described in his role by one newspaper as "alternately bewildered and embarrassed" during the performance.[383] The event was attended by no more than 600-700 people, and Tony named Mercer the victor upon its conclusion after five un-entertaining rounds.

In mid-December, Tony was one of many nationally known sports figures who were featured at the 17th annual Good Fellers dinner in Racine, Wisconsin. He entertained the crowd with stories of some of his outstanding bouts as he often did at various events after his retirement from the ring.

At this point in his life, Tony was committed to working with young boxers to help them develop their skills in and out of the ring. He was a strong supporter of the Golden Gloves. "If it wasn't for the Golden Gloves, professional boxing would be dead today," Tony said. "Without the tremendous and closely knit organization of Golden Gloves, interest in amateur boxing would die."

Tony was very concerned about the future of boxing and was a willing participant whenever he was asked to contribute to the advancement of the sport. Like many others, he lamented the decline in the number of boxing clubs throughout the country. "The Golden Gloves alone aren't enough to produce and keep going such a big business as boxing has grown into today. There must be other clubs functioning as well," he said.[384]

As the year 1952 came to end, the results of a poll of the nation's sportswriters to name the greatest fight of the century were announced. The Jack Dempsey-Luis Firpo heavyweight title bout of 1923 was chosen, followed by the famous Gene Tunney-Jack Dempsey long-count fight, and then the middleweight bouts between Tony Zale and Rocky Graziano. If the writers had been asked to name the greatest fighting trilogy of the century, the three Zale-Graziano contests would undoubtedly have been chosen.

Then, as we have all experienced, life has a way of throwing curve balls at you. Chicago's version of "This Is Your Life" Tony Zale was held on November 27, 1952. It was called "The Sports Scrapbook."

---

383 *El Paso Herald-Post*, Big Three Had Big Chance for Giants, September 15, 1952.
384 *The Lowell Sun*, The Lookout, December 27, 1952.

Tony was featured with all of his brothers and sisters, his two managers Sam and Art, Earl Mastro, a featherweight contender from Chicago, Barney Ross, former world lightweight and welterweight champion, and two military officers.

During the show, Colonel Holloway Watts, Training Officer for the 88th Military Police, re-enacted Tony's induction into the U.S. Army Reserves for a period of approximately eight years. Also on hand, was Commander Kermit Motts, representing the 9th Naval district. He said upon being asked how he felt about Tony "going into the Army and deserting the ranks of the Navy" Commander Motts replied, "Tony was such a great champion that they would have to share him with the rest of the services, I guess."

This program was a show that brought all of Tony's family together, but left him with one nagging thought. This would have been the type of event he would have loved to have shared with his children, but they were nowhere to be found. It was as if they had disappeared from the face of the earth. No one in the family knew where they were. It was later discovered that they were purposefully being hidden from him to hurt him, which it did.

Soon after this program, Tony was contacted by comedian Jerry Lewis who was in Chicago for an engagement. Jerry asked Tony if he would be willing to fight one more time against Sugar Ray Robinson. Tony was offered the sum of $500,000 if he would climb into the ring once again. Tony thought, that's more than I made in all my fights combined and it would allow me to find my children and get them back.

Immediately after Jerry Lewis's phone call, Tony met with his brothers at Joe's home on W. Ridge Road in Gary, Indiana. Joe, John, Frank, Walter and nephews Joe, Ray, Danny and young Thad, listened as Tony explained how Lewis had contacted him about "one more fight." Even at four years old, the author vividly remembers the excitement that surrounded this conversation.

His opponent would be Sugar Ray Robinson. Sam and Art agreed to do one more fight for Tony if they could get him in shape. Since he had been training in Chicago with several very good middleweights, he figured it would be easy to return to good fighting form. The conditioning that Sam and Art would put him through in the months prior to this fight assured Tony that he would get back in shape. He would also engage in several tune-up bouts so they could determine his readiness and capacity to perform once again.

Tony told his brothers that even after expenses, taxes, and splits with management, he could end up with enough money to set himself up for the remainder of his life. Joe, the eldest spoke first.

"Tony, you were a great champion and no one can ever take that away from you. You have your health and you are providing great service to the youth of our country through the CYO. So, why would you want to risk all that for one more fight?"

John and Walter immediately agreed to disagree with Joe. They felt that one more shot at the title was worth the risk. They did not believe that Sugar Ray could beat Tony. Tony simply hit too hard to the body and though Ray was a great champion, they believed in the end, Tony would put him down for the count.

"Look," said John. "He hasn't stopped training since he lost the title to Cerdan. He's had his elbow repaired and now can deliver that right to the body without hesitation. The arm doesn't hinder him anymore."

Frank sided with Joe and said, "Tony, you're nearly forty. Why risk it?"

Tony appreciated their candor, but he was determined to proceed with a title shot if Lewis could arrange it. He was sure he had one more great fight left in him. But the fight was never made and he didn't get the chance, even though five years later there was once again talk of a possible match against Robinson.

In February of 1953, he received the Everlast Company's first award for "Sportsmanship and Citizenship In and Out of the Ring." Over the next three years, Tony devoted most of his time working with kids in the Chicago CYO program, refereeing various contests, making public appearances and of course, maintaining his commitment to the military.

He became a popular speaker for local events, and those venues would typically include a viewing of his title bout with Graziano, followed by a question and answer period. He always provided his fans an opportunity to receive an autograph and good conversation with the former Champ.

Tony would inevitably use these speaking engagements as a platform to give advice to the youths in attendance. "If you want to be a good athlete in any sport, live right, train right, go to church, listen to your mother and dad and treat others as you would like to be treated," he would tell them. For those with aspirations to become a fighter, he would tell them that you have to like to fight to become a fighter. "But don't fight in the streets. Go to the gymnasium where you can learn what the score is," he would urge them.[385] Tony influenced the lives of many boxers during this period of time, and he would do so for many years to follow.

---

385 *The Vidette-Messenger*, 13 May 1953.

UPI Photo

In summary, as 1952 ended and his divorce concluded, Tony was down to his last pennies. He knew he could stay with family but he wanted to make it on his own. He had the clothes on his back, his friendships from over 24 years of boxing and the Good Lord as his guide. All might be lost for some, but for this man of steel, as long as he had the Spirit to guide him and his faith to lean on, life would not tear him down. Better times were around the corner but not on his time table.

FINDING HIS WAY

The Champ had four part-time jobs through the fifties to help him live and support his children. The CYO coaching job was always considered his primary employment, but his United States Army and Navy Reserve pay and refereeing helped supplement that income. He gave his permanent address as his brother John's home back in Gary. But, as stated earlier, he actually lived in that near south side tenement house without heat or running water in exchange for managing the property until it was sold. He used a sleeping bag and a small, cheap electrical heater to keep warm during the cold, Chicago winters. Tony would take care of the building and the Savings and Loan would not charge him rent in lieu of his policing the facility. This would be his temporary home base and would allow him to save and provide for his family. Though it was a good distance run from the tenement to the CYO gym, running was nothing new for the Champ and it helped him stay in top physical condition.

By 1956, Tony had been working as the head boxing coach of the Chicago Catholic Youth Organization for seven years. That service and his part-time jobs enabled him to solve several of his financial concerns and provided him with enough money to acquire a small efficiency apartment with heat and running water on Chicago's near north side.

It was a welcome relief for Tony and meant that he no longer had to make the long, morning run from the tenement to the CYO gym on Jackson Boulevard to shower and shave. For the first time in seven years, he didn't need his sleeping bag, but he kept it, nonetheless, in the bottom of his closet as a reminder of the hard times he had endured. In the years ahead he often reminded family and friends that we take too much for granted. He believed that folks should be thankful for the blessings they receive and felt we all have an obligation to give back to the community in some manner.[386]

Tony's service in the U.S. Army Reserves, 88th Military Police, provided him with an additional opportunity to teach boxing and life skills to many of his fellow servicemen. In lieu of summer camp in 1955 and 1956, he was ordered to participate in entertaining the troops through two USO shows. The first rounds were in France and Germany and the second in South Korea and Japan. The troops enjoyed Tony's stories about boxing and the show concluded with his film of the last Graziano battle with Tony's narration. He learned how to play the harmonica too, thanks to the touring Harmonicats.

Tony would often hitchhike home from whichever training center he was required to attend in the early days to save bus fare, but ultimately his financial situation improved. (Tony was in the Naval Reserve at the same time as the Army.) Later he was comfortable enough to afford a bus ticket. He no longer had to offer an excuse.

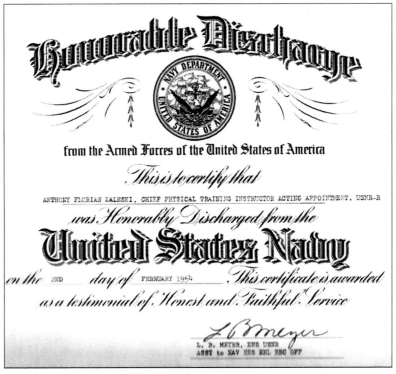

February 2, 1954

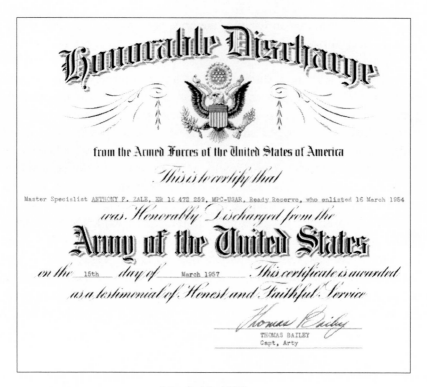

Honorable Discharge

from the Armed Forces of the United States of America

This is to certify that

Master Specialist ANTHONY F. ZALE, ER 16 472 259, MPC-USAR, Ready Reserve, who enlisted 16 March 1954

was Honorably Discharged from the

Army of the United States

on the 15th day of March 1957. This certificate is awarded as a testimonial of Honest and Faithful Service

Thomas Bailey
THOMAS BAILEY
Capt, Arty

March 15, 1957

It wasn't that he was too proud, but he was a little embarrassed to admit that a former world champion couldn't afford bus fare.

Although life had presented many early post-ring career challenges, he slowly recovered with a dogged level of determination and a steady dose of prayer. He had clawed his way back. Along the way, he had been appointed as a board member of the Second Federal Savings and Loan of Chicago. As a result, this appointment enabled him to receive free meals at their cafeteria. Finally, he no longer needed to accept offers such as that. He could once more pay his own way.

The bank president and other board members enthusiastically greeted Tony at every quarterly board meeting. Tony studied the savings and loan quarterly reports and balance sheets to make sure he was familiar with how they operated so he could knowledgeably vote as a board member. He earned a quarterly stipend for his board membership. The support of friends and fans helped him realize his own worth and regain the former swagger he once had as a champion.

Bishop Sheil's counseling benefitted him too, as he finally came to grips with his own faults and the loss of his children. He became an advocate for women as well. "Never, never, never hit a woman" became part of the instructions to his boxing students for the rest of his life. Defending yourself would forever mean parrying away and blocking an attack by anyone. He eventually learned to reconcile his faults in his own mind's eye. His faith gave him the strength and resolve he needed to carry out his daily duties and persevere in spite of the everyday challenges of life.

Tony and the rest of the Zale family had to call upon that strength and resolve on March 19, 1957, when his oldest brother Joseph suffered a cerebral hemorrhage while driving home from work. Joseph stopped his car, got out and placed his hands on the hood, and leaned his head against the vehicle. A passerby, knowing him as Gary's Fire Chief, helped him to a doctor's office across the street. He was then rushed to Gary Methodist Hospital but expired shortly after when doctors were unable to relieve the pressure on his brain.

It was an unexpected and difficult blow for Tony and the close-knit Zale family to overcome. For years after the death of their mother, Joe had been the glue that held the family together. When their mother passed away in 1946, it was Joseph to whom Tony and his siblings went to for personal advice. Brother John was Tony's mentor for most matters related to boxing, but it was Joe to whom he turned to on all other personal matters.

Thad Zale, who was only eight at the time of his father's death, remembers his Uncle Tony hugging him with tears in his eyes and promising his mother Frances that he would help the family in any way he could.

But of course it was an impossible task to fill the void left by Joe's untimely death. Joe's funeral procession was huge, stopping city traffic for many miles. Since Joe was the current Fire Chief of Gary at the time, his remains were honored by being carried on the back of a fire engine pumper throughout the city.

Thad remembers the procession going past each Gary fire station one by one. At every station, all the engines and ladder trucks had been placed outdoors with firemen standing at attention in their dress blues and saluting as their fallen Chief passed by.

Bishop Carl Mengeling, a retired Catholic Bishop for the Diocese of Lansing, Michigan, was at that time, an associate pastor at the Joe Zale family's home church of St. Mark's. Years later, he recalled the funeral as the largest he had ever witnessed. (The author believes that honor still stands today.) The Zale family leaned upon one another and their faith to carry them through another very difficult period of time.

From that time forth, Tony was always there for his family. No matter the event, a holiday, christening, wedding, funeral, reunion or family gathering of any kind, Tony was there. Family events were always a top priority for him. He was there to share in the joy or sorrow with his genuine warmth and smile. Tony made it a point to stress to the younger members of the family that one could succeed at anything they set their mind to and that it was all a matter of focus and trust in God. He continually assured the various members of the family that if they would believe in something, they could achieve it.

In 1958, some of the bank board members approached Tony with a proposal to open a restaurant and bar on the near north side of Chicago to be located at 744 North Rush Street. They offered to front the necessary cash if Tony would agree to be manager and host for the establishment and lend his name. Tony agreed with some hesitation and pointed out that his afternoons and early evenings belonged to the CYO. The paperwork was prepared with that stipulation and "Tony Zale's" opened to good reviews for food and sports talk. It opened its doors that September and was one of the city's first sports bars.

That month Tony was asked how he thought he would have fared in his prime, against the champions Sugar Ray Robinson and Carmen Basilio.

"Carmen Basilio is too small. He couldn't have caused me trouble," Tony replied. "Basilio takes too many punches. His strong point is stamina. That was mine, too. I was always getting off the floor. I think I really would have battered Basilio."

As for Robinson, Tony said, "At his best, Robinson could hit hard and was fast. His height always gave him an edge over other welterweights and middleweights, but I would have folded him up with blows to the body."[387]

Tony's restaurant and bar was an immediate success. Unfortunately, the more popular the place became, the more difficult it was to maintain its reputation as a sports club. Over the year, Tony discovered that a number of *ladies of the evening* began dropping in for a "drink." He sent them away, but soon found them returning with men issuing ultimatums. When Tony refused to allow them to ply their trade out of his establishment, he soon discovered that garbage

---

387 *Lima News*, September 18, 1958.

pickup service became sporadic. Towel and cleaning supplies came late, or not at all.

When Tony complained to local officials, they suggested he become "more cooperative." When he spoke to law enforcement officials, they suggested he might look the other way. Tony wasn't about to do that and if this was the only way he could successfully manage the club in Chicago, he would close it down. That's exactly what he did as he was not about to compromise his principles. He met with his backers and informed them of the situation and they closed the doors with little fanfare and sometime later, they filed for bankruptcy. Tony couldn't compromise in the ring and he would not compromise in his life outside of it.

The loss in revenue from his work with the restaurant prompted Tony to consider going back to the ring for one more shot at the title. He was still in fine form in his mid-forties as a result of his daily workouts at the CYO. Whenever he'd shovel snow out front of the restaurant during Chicago's notorious winters, he'd do it so vigorously and with such enthusiasm that many of the patrons who witnessed this encouraged him to give the title another shot.

Tony gave the idea serious consideration going so far as to apply for an Illinois boxing license again. Jerry Lewis and others had tried to set up a fight in the early fifties, but they could not accomplish it. Ultimately, Tony decided against a comeback, knowing his best days were well past and refusing to do it for money alone. He would only lace up the gloves solely for the purpose of teaching others how to defend themselves and to help them develop their self-confidence as a life skill.

In the summer of 1958, the National Boxing Hall of Fame notified Tony of their plans to induct him into the hall of fame. He was being recognized for his performance in and out of the ring. He had proven his mettle in 1948, and became the second man to ever regain the middleweight championship. It was the first of many ceremonies Tony would go on to attend in the years ahead for his work in promoting the sport he loved. The recognition helped him realize how truly blessed he had been in spite of the many challenges he had to overcome.

As 1958 drew to a close, Tony began attending dance marathon weekends at the Martinique Night Club in south Chicago. He would tag along with one of his best friends, Gus Latsis and his wife Josephine. There he would dance the night away doing the two-step, the polka and the waltz. There were many celebrities who enjoyed this nightclub. Stars such as Karl Malden, Martha Raye, Eli Wallach, Jimmy Durante, Pat O'Brien, Jerry Lewis, Dean Martin, Walter Pigeon and Frank Sinatra, to name a few, were regular visitors when in town.

Tony was recognized as a celebrity himself among the stars. The more he was recognized, the more he was invited to their private parties held outside the club. Gus recalled that on one occasion during that period of time, a fight fan recognized Tony and came up to him and said, "Aren't you Tony Zale?" Tony's reply, being the humble man he was, would be, "No, I just look like him. He's a lot tougher than me."

Through 1959 and into the early 1960s, Tony was often seen in these celebrity circles on weekends when he wasn't traveling with the CYO boxing team. He had a standing invitation to the Martinique and any other venue around town. He was invited to audition for Chicago theater and films, and won a few supporting roles. One was in a 1965 play called *The Happiest Millionaire* starring Walter Pigeon. Tony played the role of an ex-fighter and buddy of a turn-of-the-century fight fan named Anthony J. Biddle. Tony also had three other acting credits in 1970 to 1975 while acting in *The Godfather and the Lady*, *Cauliflower Cupids* and *The Men from Poland*. Asked to compare acting to fighting, Tony said that, "acting was more nerve wracking, but it didn't hurt as much."[388] Folks loved to listen to his fight stories and he had developed a new nickname around town, the "Dance Man."

He took his thespian endeavors very seriously and even landed a role in a movie playing himself in *Somebody Up There Likes Me, the Rocky Graziano Story* in 1956. It was a role that Rocky helped him secure, and all his expenses would be paid while earning a stout paycheck of $10,000 (about $100,000.00 today). The producers decided he fit the bill perfectly, especially since he wouldn't have any lines in the movie. While filming, Tony was provided with first class accommodations, as well as a chauffeured limousine.

Unfortunately, Tony was not able to fulfill the obligation. He was removed from this role when he got "too rough" with the film's star, Paul Newman. During the first rehearsals for the choreography of the first fight between Tony and Rocky, Tony was instructed to let Newman get in punches. Paul was instructed to pull [pretend] the head punches, but not the body punches. Nobody believed that Newman would be able to hurt Tony with any blows to the body.

Repeating his own version of what happened next, Rocky Graziano said that once the cameras started rolling and the two men started throwing punches, Newman suddenly grabbed his side and doubled over, and yelled, "Whoa man! You trying to kill me?"

Rocky jumped up in the ring and confronted Tony. "Ey! What the heck ya doin?"

"I din mean it, Rock," Tony apologized with his mouth piece half out.

But Rocky knew how much it hurt to receive a blow to the body from Tony. He had once said of his historic bouts with Tony, "When he went to work on my body it felt like he was pouring concrete blocks at my stomach. After every fight with him I had to go to the hospital to stop internal bleeding."[389]

Rocky could see that Paul was afraid at that point. Now he realized that Newman could get his mouth busted up and his teeth knocked out. "When Zale's in there swinging, all he's gotta do is

---

388 *Tucson Daily Citizen*, January 9, 1965.
389 *The Danville Bee*, April 23, 1952.

hear a bell an he don't know no more that it ain't for real," said Rocky, "to him the gong means go, just like the green signal light on the corner."

Next thing they knew, everybody was up on the ring apron, having a big conversation about how Tony needs to pull his punches or their star could be badly hurt. Tony nodded as this was explained to him.

So, Paul looked nervous as the bell rang and they resumed action. After a few minutes had gone by, Rocky said he looked at Tony's face and could see that he was slipping into his "for real" stance again.

Tony shook Paul up with a couple of light hooks to the head and then came in with a right to the stomach that sent the latter to the canvas gasping for air. Five minutes went by before he regained his breath and once he did, he exclaimed:

"That's it! Take off these damn gloves," said Newman.

It happened as fast as Tony's punch that he was out of a job. They paid him for the work he'd put in so far and then went out and found a less dangerous, professional actor, named Court Sheppard for their man to work against.[390] Court played the part perfectly and they used a lot of good old fashioned makeup to help him resemble Tony.

During the first two practice rounds, Tony had repeatedly warned Paul not to hit him full steam. Unfortunately, for both parties, the young actor was either unable, or chose not to follow that advice. After a few more practice rounds, Tony finally had enough. Years later, Tony would say that he thought Newman caused the problem trying to deliver too many hard blows.

"He was trying to knock my block off," Tony recalled. "I don't mind waltzing a little bit, but you gotta show who the boss is," he said concluding his own explanation of the incident.[391]

---

390 Rocky Graziano, *Somebody Down Here Likes Me Too*, Stein & Day, New York, 1981.
391 *European Stars & Stripes*, September 19, 1982.

Paul Newman, for his part, stated on the Mike Douglas show several years later that he stopped doing his own movie stunts as a result of getting into the ring with Tony Zale. Still, this "acting" experience left Tony with enough money, some $3000, to finally open a savings account.

As the 1950s came to a close, Tony shared his concern over what he referred to as "soft living" on the fight game.

"Soft times have spoiled the parents; they have more than they ever did before. So they pass it on to the kids." They say, 'Here, take this and have a good time.' So the kids are spoiled too. In the fight game, it shows up the most.

"You know why? Because a fighter has always got to be tough and to listen."[392]

But, like so many others, Tony figured that television and the opportunity it was providing for so many fans to watch the matches for free in the comfort of their own homes was hurting the game as well. It played a major role in the death of the small time boxing clubs.

"In the old days, each club provided the livelihoods for as many as 30 to 40 full time fighters. They were the bush leagues, the testing grounds and the farm clubs of future champions."[393] Sadly, the dying off of many of these old fight clubs has seriously crippled boxing and nothing is being done to reverse that trend.

In February of 1959, Tony held a press conference and announced that two parties were once again willing to put up a $500,000 guarantee on his behalf for a match against the current middleweight champion, Sugar Ray Robinson.[394] It seemed pretty far-fetched for the 45-year-old to seriously consider a comeback against Robinson. He had kept himself in very good shape since his retirement, but he hadn't fought in over 10 years.

Nevertheless, Tony was serious and insisted he would go through with it if a fight could be made with Robinson. One more match, just one more time, since Tony was being approached about it for now a third time.

"I know one thing," he said, "What I give to the body, Sugar can't take. I'm sure I'd get to him. Robinson is a good boxer and a good puncher, but he likes to pick his opponents too. I hear he wants out of that Basilio fight.[395]

One of Tony's former opponents, Billy Soose, vouched for the effects of Tony's bodywork almost two years later when he was quoted as saying that when the pair fought in 1940, Tony belted him in the liver "so hard I was gasping for air for the next three rounds."[396]

---

392 *Grand Prarie Daily News-Texan*, January 21, 1959.
393 *Ogden Standard Examiner*, January 12, 1959.
394 *Montana Standard*, February 26, 1959.
395 *Galveston Daily News*, April 29, 1959.
396 *Simpson's Leader Times*, February 24, 1961.

Although Robinson was six years younger, Tony believed that he might be younger physically. He only weighed 164 pounds and felt he'd have no trouble making the middleweight limit. A month later, on May 29, Tony celebrated his 46th birthday. When the restaurant that bore his name filed a petition for bankruptcy the following month, many believed financial difficulties were the primary reason for his comeback talk. That being said, the truth was that Tony had no financial interest in the business that bore his name other than a salary from his work with them.

This fight with Robinson failed to materialize too, and it's probably just as well. Tony undoubtedly believed he could return to the ring one more time and defeat Robinson. But it's hard to believe he would have been able to overcome a decade long absence from the game, especially at the age of 46. Ring time is what every fighter needs and Tony simply had not had any serious work in the ring in some 10 years. Remembering his brother Joe's advice back when all of the brothers last met together brought him back to reality.

Tony continued to search for a new career and in September of 1959, the First United Life Insurance Company announced that Tony had joined their firm to try his hand as an agent and would be working out of their Chicago office. He was also writing his own column for *Boxing Illustrated* at this time, titled 'Zale's Corner,' and was discussing a position as host at another restaurant known as The Tangiers Club in the Chicago loop to help make ends meet.

THE POLITICS OF LIFE

The decade of the 1960s included a large investment of Tony's time in the political arena. He became an avid campaign supporter of John F. Kennedy and volunteered many hours of time to his candidacy in the Chicago and Gary areas. His participation in numerous rallies, door-to-door politicking and the Polish National Alliance (PNA) "Poles for Kennedy," were a daily occurrence for a time. If he wasn't working with the kids at the CYO, he was at one of the campaign headquarters.

The future of the community and nation at large was at stake, and Tony felt an obligation to lend his support to the Kennedy campaign. Tony always admired winners because he understood the sacrifice it took to achieve a victory. He celebrated Kennedy's win, but as usual, with no alcohol just a Coke in a muted, humble fashion amongst cheers and speeches. Even though others might imbibe, he didn't participate in the practice himself. He never relished a lack of control or the woozy feeling it gave him. He just didn't need it and a good cup of coffee or soft drink suited him fine. For extra energy, he often mixed a concoction containing parsley and spinach, first boiled and then cooled, which he drank like iced tea. He thought it helped his iron deficiency, though its aroma alone could knock one out. Coca Cola was another choice he relished in, and his friends often kidded him about being the "Coca Cola Kid." He really enjoyed a refreshing bottle when he was in the U.S. Navy and for many years afterward.

The 1960s ushered in a new era with its first Catholic president, and was full of hope. But there was cause for concern as well. The Cuban Missile Crisis was a prime example. At the time, Tony was very concerned that we were on the brink of nuclear war, and as we know today, we were. But he used his political contacts to stay abreast of the situation and assured all that the level heads in Washington and Soviet Premier Khrushchev, at the Kremlin, would find a way to avoid a cataclysmic event. Tony was convinced that faith, prayer, trust and the love of God would prevail over the evil on earth, and it did.

Tony was greatly saddened by the tragic political events of the mid-1960s. The assassination of John F. Kennedy in 1963 affected him deeply, as did the senseless murder of Dr. Martin Luther King, almost five years later.

When Robert Kennedy announced his own presidential candidacy, Tony took heart in another of the Kennedy's rising to the challenge. He campaigned tirelessly for JFK's younger brother. It renewed his hope for the future, and he became an active member of Robert's entourage as he wound his way through Indiana and Illinois.

When Robert spoke in Indianapolis on April 4, 1968, he spoke of the threat of disillusionment and divisiveness as a result of King's death.   He reminded the audience of King's efforts to replace violence with understanding, love and compassion. He empathized with the crowd by recalling his own feelings after the death of his brother, but urged that thoughts of violence and lawlessness be replaced with love, wisdom and compassion toward all races.   He urged prayer for our country and its people.

Just over two months later, Robert Kennedy was himself assassinated and Tony was even more distraught when his new friend was gone. It was an incomprehensible and senseless act of violence, and in Tony's mind, it only served to solidify the fact that evil was still a force to be reckoned with on this earth.

Despite those tragedies, Tony never lost his resolve, and he continued to devote his time and energies in the years ahead to the many worthy charitable causes and activities to shape the youth of this nation.   Whenever an organization like the Veteran Boxers

Association, Cauliflower Ear Club, or any other number of clubs along those lines asked for his help and support, Tony was there front and center to lend a hand in any way that he could. If his money was short, he'd donate his time and sign autographs for free, covering his own expenses.

To stay in shape, Tony continued to train himself on the speed and heavy bags while he worked with the kids at the CYO. He could make that old jump rope sing and religiously did his road work. One hour a day, five days a week, he'd go for his runs and it always made him feel good. Staying in shape kept him feeling young.

The Champ remained a popular speaker and guest throughout the decade. He continued his work with the CYO boxing program and refereeing various amateur and professional bouts throughout the region.

One such refereeing opportunity occurred in April of 1964 when Tony refereed the U.S. Atlantic Fleet Tournament at Norfolk, Virginia. Tony of course, couldn't resist the opportunity to get in the ring and teach the sailors some of the fundamentals of the pro circuit versus. what they had learned as amateurs. It brought a smile to his face whenever he thought about the Navy, this particular base, and Puerto Rico, because he was stationed at those bases during the war.

Official Photo U.S. Navy

Many of the young military fighters were exceptionally talented and Tony thought for sure that a new champion was amongst them.

Tony also provided refereeing services to several aircraft carrier tournaments during that decade. He always enjoyed revisiting that part of his life and savoring the camaraderie of those in the military.

Official Photo U.S. Navy

Tony rushes in to make heavyweight Willie Jenkins take mandatory eight count after knockdown by Dave Zyglewicz.

Official Photo U.S. Navy

Tony meets boxers competing in the Atlantic Fleet Boxing Tournament shortly after arriving in Norfolk.

In May of 1965, Tony lamented the current state of boxing during an interview. He said, "It was the eleventh hour for boxing.

Look at the sport today," he said. "Youngsters with 20 and 30 fights behind them are controlling entire divisions. The main problem is a lack of talent which breeds a lack of interest by the public. I had over 200 amateur bouts before I turned pro and 70 for money before getting a crack at the title. Today, kids with a dozen YMCA wins are ranked."

"I fought because I liked it and I had to live. In the depression, I got $6 a match and glad of it. Now times are good; things are easy; kids are spoiled."

"We have greedy promoters, greedy managers and greedy participants."

Still, Tony admitted that maybe all the pros needed was some stiffer competition. With a grin, he added that even at his age (52), he thought he could teach a thing or two to some of the kids.[397]

In 1973, Rocky Graziano phoned Tony and requested that he come to New York to help promote the grand opening of Willie Pep's new restaurant along with Sandy Sadler. Tony quickly rearranged his schedule of duties with the Chicago Park District boxing program so he could comply with the request, and he and Rocky took the city by storm that spring. They made numerous appearances for charitable fundraisers together and they had fun.

---

397 *Pacific Stars and Stripes*, May 20, 1965.

In November of 1966, a heavyweight title fight between Cassius Clay and Cleveland Williams held in the Houston Astrodome finally eclipsed the 19-year-old record gate figure for an indoor event when it produced a gate of $461,290. This beat the $422,918 total generated from Tony's second title fight with Rocky Graziano in Chicago in 1947.

In March of 1968, a newspaperman spoke to Tony and wrote that the former Champion was living a lonely life. Since his divorce from his wife Adeline, whom he told the reporter was living somewhere in Minneapolis, he never saw or heard from his girls. He believed his oldest daughter Mary may have been married and living somewhere on the west coast. Tony hoped to save enough money and travel to California to make contact with her and also find out where Teresa has relocated. He admitted to not having much money and said he spent the bulk of his time working with kids and teaching them boxing.

"That's all I know. It's where I belong. I've had other jobs but they didn't work out," he said.[398] It was an all too familiar response and one he didn't like to be reminded of, but it was true. He was lonely.

A couple of days later, Tony was in New York's Madison Square Garden with a host of former champions to witness a contest between Emile Griffith and Nino Benvenuti. One by one, ring announcer Johnny Addie introduced the former ring giants and invited them to come up onto the apron.

Rocky Graziano was already in the ring when Tony was introduced and stepped through the ropes. This would not be the last time that they would meet in the ring. On several occasions from 1968 through the 1980's, they would engage in three one-minute round exhibitions to raise needed funds for charities throughout the eastern United States and Canada.

---

398 *The Daily Times*, March 10, 1968.

Tony looked as fit as he did when he retired 20 years earlier. When he spied Rocky, he playfully feinted a hook to the liver, and Rocky doubling over in mock pain, cocking his right hand. The pair laughed and gave one another a warm embrace.[399] Later that month, the two former antagonists would pair up for a playful exhibition bout in New York City for the benefit of the Damon Runyon Cancer Research Fund.[400]

399 *Winnipeg Free Press*, March 12, 1968.
400 *Chronicle Telegram*, March 28, 1968.

Damon Runyon was a journalist who wrote short stories, some of which were eventually turned into a Broadway production known as *Guys and Dolls*. He passed away in late 1946, but was at ringside for the first Zale vs. Graziano bout. His death from cancer shortly after that first epic battle prompted columnists, journalists, and friend Walter Winchell to begin the cancer research fund that bears his name. The mission of the fund is to provide assistance to young, bright scientists for the purpose of discovering a cure for cancer and is still active today. Walter Winchell was able to enlist the support of many celebrities including Bob Hope, Marilyn Monroe, Milton Berle and Joe DiMaggio to name a few.

When Tony was short of funds in 1968, he phoned Rocky and asked him if could help him obtain a job in New York. Rocky offered him a loan of $2,500, but Tony refused. Immediately, Rocky went to Bobby Bennett, who ran a sports bar named Gallagher's near Madison Square Garden. Bobby offered Tony $200 per week to serve as a host at his restaurant. Tony accepted the position and regaled the patrons with his boxing stories and became a popular attraction for the restaurant.[401]

That job and the funds he received from refereeing and numerous public appearances really kept him afloat as he received very little pay for his work with the CYO boxing program back in

Chicago. It was a Spartan-like existence for the "Man of Steel." The year 1970, and an introduction to an attractive woman he would come to lovingly refer to as "Mighty Mouth," would liven things up and bring about a big improvement in his financial situation in the years ahead.

---

401 *Logansport Pharos-Tribune*, May 6, 1969.

MIGHTY MOUTH ENTERS THE RING

After the assassinations of the 1960s, Tony joined Rocky during the spring of 1968. Thanks to Rocky, Tony had been invited back to

New York City to work at Gallaghers Restaurant. These champions looked great, worked well together and were representative of the toughest division in boxing during the 1940s. They became an instant hit again when they were running the New York City streets as well as working out in the city gyms and were regularly making personal appearances at Madison Square Garden for all boxing events. Reliving the past became an inspiring experience for both the fighters and those that witnessed this reunion. They raised a considerable amount of money for charities throughout the city and the greater New England area. Tony loved working with the kids and for the charities and so did Rocky.

This was a time in Tony's life where he finally had begun to see an end to his personal poverty. Now, knowing the whereabouts of his married children, he could resume sending money to them. The cost of living in New York was approximately the same as in Chicago, and Gallaghers hosting position was providing him with room and board in Manhattan. The heart-breaking losses of John Kennedy, Martin Luther King and Robert Kennedy gave Tony pause to reflect on his own mortality. Now that he was in New York, he felt he could help train kids at the CYO gyms there, just as he had in Chicago. He could have the best of both worlds, and still maintain his commitment to the Good Lord to teach life skills to the young.

Before coming out to New York, Tony had lost most of his hearing in his left ear due to an episode at one of the CYO gyms. Tony did not know if one of his former coaches, whom he previously had a problem with, had set him up or not. One late afternoon, somebody attacked him with a baseball bat after he exited the shower. He was working out and after his work-out, when the gym was empty, he went in to shower. When he came out, he got clobbered and knocked unconscious. All he remembered was a swinging baseball bat. He was found unconscious by other CYO staff with blood flowing out of his left ear. They had him immediately transported to a Chicago hospital after the incident and discovered that he had suffered a severely damaged eardrum which resulted in about 90% hearing loss. He was lucky to be alive, and now happy to be moving on to a new career.

Thinking back, Tony felt the attack at the CYO gym on Jackson Boulevard was as a result of him redressing one of his CYO boxing coaches about a month earlier. As Tony travelled to the three CYO city gyms, he always made sure the care of the kids was paramount in the minds of his coaches. When he walked into this particular gym that afternoon he was shocked by what he heard. One of his chosen coaches from Gary, Indiana, (let's call him Chuck) was cussing up a storm with four-letter epitaphs flowing like water. Chuck was really on one of the young boxers, tearing the young man down and spitting him out.

Immediately alarmed, Tony interrupted the scene and asked to talk to Chuck in the office. In private, Tony told Chuck to never treat the kids like that – no matter what they did wrong. Chuck looked at Tony and said, "**** you Tony Zale," and began to swing a right hand at the Champ. Tony's training and instinct kicked in and before Chuck's right connected, Tony slipped it and popped a quick left hook over it, flooring Chuck. Nothing more was said, and Chuck picked himself up off the floor and left the gym with a cut lip and bruised ego.

A month or so later, Tony was attacked from behind by an unknown assailant. While Tony had no proof, he always personally felt the incident had something to do with Chuck. Whatever the case, it was time to move on with life.

Now fitted with a hearing aid, he could entertain the guests at Gallaghers with good humor and fight stories.

Fight fans became regulars at Gallaghers and everyone wanted to know first-hand from Tony about the first Zale vs. Graziano fight in Yankee Stadium. They all seemed to know who he was and what he had done. It was exciting for them to re-live those moments in sports history once again. First round, he has Graziano on the floor with a left hook. Graziano is up before the count even begins. The second round, Graziano has Tony on the floor with a looping right hand. Tony tells them that he wasn't used to the way Rocky threw that overhand right that seemed to come out of nowhere. He describes how he broke his right thumb in the second round when Rocky dropped his left elbow as Tony came in to the body with a straight right to the heart. Those were the days. These two fighters rocked the fight world back then. Tony settled into his new role at Gallaghers as host with the same vigor that he used to approach everything in his life.

Tony thoroughly enjoyed his visit to the Big Apple. He was always surprised by the recognition that he received since he had come to this city. Those he met really appreciated him, made him feel wanted, and some shared with him how much money they had made putting wagers on his fights. He only had one negative experience in the city caused by someone he befriended who took advantage of his generosity by stealing his wallet and watch. But that could have happened anywhere. What surprised Tony the most was how many of the New Yorkers recognized him. They respected him and treated him to the best that their city had to offer by showing him their town.

Tony remembered an occasion that caused him a great deal of personal stress when he had been in the city preparing for the Georgie Abrams fight. After he had unified the middleweight crown by winning a 15-round unanimous decision over Abrams, his managers decided after the fight to enjoy a little bit of New York's ambiance. They took Tony out to a restaurant where he ordered a late meal and was sitting comfortably in one of the corner booths in the back. As news spread through the restaurant that Tony Zale was there, several well-wishers arrived at his table congratulating him. Two happened to be beautiful young women who sat down on either side of Tony very close and made him feel very uncomfortable. These ladies placed their hands on his thighs which added to his discomfort. You might say, he had a minor panic attack and decided he wasn't hungry anymore and had to get back to his hotel room to get some rest. Before his meal was served, he left abruptly, with the young women still sitting at the table amused by how uncomfortable they had made him feel.

Tony grew to love New York, but was lonesome for home. His hosting employment enabled him to share his monthly earnings and build his savings. After almost two years of covering the same stories

over and over though, Tony was ready for another change. He did not mind talking about those three dramatic bouts with Graziano, but his family was a thousand miles away. He knew he was missing special occasions back home. Prayer was what he always turned to whenever a major decision had to be made, and maybe it was prayer that he needed now. Tony continued to work benefit luncheons throughout the city including those with athletes from other sports.

In late 1969, The Chicago Parks Department had voted to expand their recreational program to now include boxing. While the board was discussing ways to involve the youth in order to keep them off the streets, they thought that a disciplined boxing program would be the solution especially for the high crime areas. Ed Kelly, Park Superintendent, suggested they try to get a well-known retired boxer, someone who would be respected throughout Chicagoland.

A member of the parks department board, Dennis O'Keefe, recommended they consider hiring Tony Zale. Someone informed them that Tony was now in New York City. Surprised, Ed Kelly said, "What's Tony doing in New York? Let's bring him home!" Several other board members replied that nobody young would remember Tony Zale. Ed countered with, "No, the youth may not remember Tony Zale, but when they go home to tell their fathers who they met, there will be instant recognition."

Ed Kelly

Wes Pavalon
Owner & Founder of Milwaukee Bucks

had followed Tony Zale during his fighting days when he trained in downtown Chicago and was present at his 1947 fight with Graziano. He also knew Tony as the head of the Chicago CYO boxing program, and felt deep down that Tony was the only choice to now head up the parks department boxing program. The board finally agreed, and Ed called Tony in New York to offer him the job and a way to get back home. Tony's prayers had been answered.

Tony came back to Chicago in the summer of 1969 to temporarily room at his brother John's home. He would continue through the holidays living there until he could locate an efficiency apartment in Chicago. In the windy city on the morning of August 30, Tony met with longtime friend and former world heavyweight champion Rocky Marciano. Tony had worked out with Marciano in Holland, Michigan, back in the mid-fifties in Rocky's preparation for his upcoming fight with Joe Louis. It was during this time that Tony taught Rocky where and how to place his trademark combination, right to the body, left hook to the head. They remained close friends as a result.

WORLD'S HEAVYWEIGHT CHAMPION
AL WEILL, Manager
HOLLAND FURNACE COMPANY
TRAINING CAMP
HOLLAND, MICHIGAN

Rocky Marciano

At their meeting on August 30, Rocky asked Tony if he had any interest in opening a training camp with him down in Florida the following summer. Tony answered in the affirmative. Rocky, in his true gentlemen's agreement fashion, shook hands with Tony to affirm their business partnership to begin the summer of 1970. Tony told Rocky about being employed to organize and start the Chicago

Parks Boxing Program. He believed that it probably wouldn't be a long-term position because the Chicago Parks District had no equipment for its future boxing students.

A couple of days later, Tony heard the horrible news reporting the overnight plane crash in Newton, Iowa, killing his new partner Rocky Marciano. Tony looked up to the heavens and said, "Lord, you really do have a plan for me, don't you?"

As scheduled, Tony began working in January of 1970 back in Chicago. He was absolutely thrilled by the fact that he was back home again. To introduce Tony to the 26 gymnasiums located throughout Chicago, Ed Kelly began driving Tony to each location. When they visited one south side gym in particular, there were several gang members with cigarettes hanging out of their mouths, wearing their gang colors and hats indoors. Tony called them on it immediately. Jackets, smokes and hats disappeared quickly, as Tony's request for discipline filled the air. Needless to say, Ed was pleasantly surprised and knew that he had made the right choice. He never thought these gang members would respond to anyone's request. Thanks to Tony Zale, there was a complete change of attitude that began to surface quickly in all of the gyms throughout the city.

Tony felt good about being home, but he would never forget the red carpet treatment that the New Yorkers had rolled out and welcomed him with back in 1968 and 1969. Now, the distance to his former hometown and relatives was not 1000 miles, but just 28 miles to the northwest Indiana region by train. Tony soon met with the Board of Parks and Recreation in their Chicago Parks Department headquarters to get acquainted with the board's objectives and have them explain the purpose of getting the kids into the gyms and under Tony's tutelage.

Just like the CYO, Tony would rotate through all 26 gyms regularly. But first, each gym, if they were to establish a boxing program, needed equipment. Unfortunately, the expense would be prohibitive to equip all gyms at one time. So, they decided to equip one or two gyms at a time. This was going to be the only way they could afford to make this program work. Ed Kelly suggested to the board that he might make a call to his friend, Muhammad Ali, and ask him for help, which he in fact did. To Ed and everyone's surprise, ten days or so later a moving van full of equipment pulled up in front of the parks headquarters.

Muhammad Ali had answered the call without any fanfare and requested none. Everything that was needed for the boxing students' workout regimen was provided by the moving van of equipment donated by Ali. As word spread, the city leaders were astounded by all of the Everlast boxing equipment worth hundreds of thousands of dollars that suddenly appeared at their doorsteps. It would be put to good use, and Tony could now begin his daily teaching routines at the gyms once the equipment was in place. Muhammad Ali would appear with Tony at the first Grand Opening of a Chicago Parks gym boxing training area, and some 800 kids with their parents would attend.

Tony started every morning with a prayer for one more day to have a positive impact on someone's life. He never hesitated to include the repetitive saying of the "Rosary" for special intentions. (The Rosary is a series of prayers recited by Roman Catholics as a private devotion to Mary, the mother of Jesus.) For the first time since the 40s, he actually felt comfortable. He had lost everything, and now 20 years later, his life was finally coming back together. He could even invest in a mutual fund or two for growth of capital. Sometimes he thought to himself that it seemed as though one has to lose everything to appreciate the little things in life. Tony simply did not take one thing for granted anymore. Life is too precious and so were these young boxing students under his care.

When he began his position as head boxing coach for the Chicago Park District, his game plan was the same as it was at the CYO in 1949. He would start them out as a group with basic military calisthenics to warm them up, and then to the jump ropes for endurance. Two minutes on and one minute of rest for three rounds was his formula. Then, they would work on the heavy bag, that is, after he taught them how to properly wrap their hands to prevent injury. Speed bag training ended the warm-up set as Tony would demonstrate the proper technique. Until they were all in fighting shape, there would be no ring time. Gym by gym, Tony traveled to all 26 locations and instilled this simple discipline.

When they reached the physical level that allowed them to begin two-minute rounds of ring time, Tony was there to make sure his assistant coaches were providing the proper instruction. After these young students learned to put together combinations of punches on the heavy bags, they were then taught how to counter those combinations in the ring.

The instruction was simple, positive and direct. Tony's influence was substantial. The more proficient the kids became, the more the kids brought their friends to learn as well. The more friends that they brought with them, the more street violence diminished. The system was not perfect, but it worked. Soon, every one of the 26 gyms had the staffing expertise to teach the skills, and Tony could rotate through each gym more often. Parks Superintendent Ed Kelly hired part-time ex Chicago champions to help expand and implement Tony's formula. Davey Day, Barney Ross, Leroy Murphy and Richard Guerro, to name a few, were added to the roster of other paid coaches to assist Tony.

In Tony's travels from gym to gym, he would always stop and provide some personal instruction to any eager student. He would start out with the following question: "Would you like to be world champion?" The answer he received was always an enthusiastic "Yes." "Well," Tony would say, "I have been there and I know how to get you to that level if you would do three things for me."

Waxing with enthusiasm, each would-be champion affirmed their desire. Tony would say, "Okay, here's what you do. First: You must attend church every Sunday, or Saturday, depending on your religious belief. Everything good comes from God above, and you must attend services to thank Him for His help. Second: Obey your parents. Honor them even if you do not believe they are always correct. Finally, and this is the most difficult one, give up girls. They make your legs weak."

If Tony noticed even the slightest hesitation in his would-be champion's attitude, he knew where to go with this fatherly advice. He would continue; "Where are you in your education? How are your grades and what is your commitment to school?" He would listen, and then explain to them the opportunity for a university scholarship that he passed up at the end of his amateur career. He helped them understand not to make the same mistake and how important the paths we choose can be in our lives.

Tony knew from his experience that he really could have used those education credentials to fall back on, but he did not possess them. Now, he had to scrimp and save from month to month to do the things that were important to him. He had tried his hand at sports reporting, writing boxing reviews, selling insurance, and radio talk shows, none of which were successful careers for him. He tried managing a restaurant, but his experience proved he could not give up his morals and principles for success. He tried his hand at radio sports casting, but his deep baritone voice was too soft and low for the airwaves to catch on.

If only he could turn back the hands of time, he would have taken the opportunity to advance his studies in college. Instead, he turned professional with aspirations of making a considerable income. The young people he spoke with understood Tony's message, and began to change their own lives as Tony spoke to them from his heart. He continued to give them the tools for success in life, not just success in the ring.

UPI Photo

By sharing his own experiences and mistakes, he was hoping that these young men would avoid some of the same pitfalls. They began to clearly see the mistakes of their short lives and sought Tony's advice on how to correct their errors before it was too late. Not only was Tony their coach, he was also their mentor. Tony would help them make better choices for the future than he had. Through the participation with the parks department as a boxing coach, he was able to give them direction and discipline they would need to be successful in their own lives in and out of the ring. Tony became a complete role model for them to emulate.

Tony was immediately comfortable with his mission, and the

support staff was eager to work with him as part of the parks department. "Let's get those kids off the streets and into the gyms, and provide them with discipline, and make them useful future citizens" was his mantra.

In June of 1970, Tony began spending an inordinate amount of time at one gym in particular on the near north side of the city. The staff began to wonder what the attraction of that gym could be. Tony's normal, weekly rotation through the gym system previously never gave extra attention to this location before. Sure enough, all soon found out that it was a lively, Italian women's coach, Philomena Gianfrancisco, who had quickly captured Tony's attention.

Philomena had been a member of the All-American Women's Professional Baseball League. She played for the Grand Rapids Chicks from 1945-47, and was traded to the Racine Belles in 1948. As an outfielder, she threw right handed, but batted lefty. She was always clean-up in the batting order. She is in the record books as having the honor of becoming the first woman to ever hit a home run out of Comiskey Park, center field. In 1988, she, with the other living players, became immortalized in the "Women in Baseball" permanent display at the Baseball Hall of Fame in Cooperstown, New York. Philomena and Tony enjoyed this prestigious induction with her family and thoroughly enjoyed themselves amongst baseball's greats. The women's league was active during WWII when baseball, boxing and most professional sports were suspended due to the war. It was the inspiration for the 1992 movie, *A League of Their Own*.

PHILOMENA (GIANFRANCISCO) ZALE

Nickname: Frisco
Hometown: Chicago, Illinois
Born: 04/20/1923 Died: 01/18/1992
Throw Hand: Right   Bat Handed: Left
Affiliation: Player   Positions: Outfield
History: Grand Rapids Chicks (1945, 1946, 1947)
Racine Belles (1948)

Affectionately, Tony introduced Philomena, or Phil as she became known to the family, to all of his friends and park staff as "Mighty Mouth." She was not only fun and cute, but she was always jabbering and had an unending repertoire of clean, funny jokes. Not only did she make him laugh, she lived up to her nickname, and almost relished in it. It became a fast and furious romance for these two athletes, and they flew out to Las Vegas, Nevada, where they were married on September 19, 1970.

Philomena was a "take charge" instructor for the parks department and now had become a "take charge" person of Tony's career. Upon their return to Chicago, she was determined that Tony would no longer have friends from his past. She alienated all old friendships by simply telling them that Tony was not available anymore. When friends would call like his lifelong friend Gus Latsis, she would tell them that he's not home. "She" was his friend now, and manager, and time would only be spent with her and his job at the parks department. No more "freebies" became her motto.

Throughout Tony's career, he never turned anyone away or charged for an appearance. Now, unless it was for his job, Tony did nothing for free. All expenses related to an appearance and an appropriate stipend for his time became the norm, and now they would have to pay for *her* expenses as well. She could not believe people had used her husband, the former middleweight champion of the world, without paying for his appearances.

Life had now changed and the Zale family was no exception to her new rule. Having a chip on her shoulder, Philomena redressed each family member one by one for not having been involved in Tony's post-fight career. "Why weren't you involved?" and "How dare you allow this man to be used?" became her verbal attack.

Just about all family members were appalled by her accusations. By this time, most of Tony's immediate family was deceased. Her displeasure challenged the second Zale generation, which included Tony's nieces and nephews. Most of them weren't even born or old enough to help when Tony was Champ and as children, could not have assisted in any way. They only knew that he was their famous uncle whom they loved and respected for what he accomplished. They all thought that he was doing fine in his post career. They knew much about Tony's whereabouts because they would read about him in the newspapers. They knew he worked and lived in Chicago and

New York City, and received many honorariums across the country, but they only saw him in person at family gatherings.

No one really knew how difficult Tony's life had been in the 50s as he was such a private man. Many were just too young to have had any positive impact on Tony's life in the 1960s. So these verbal assaults by Philomena were unfounded and as a result alienated her from many family members.

Tony never complained about his "down and out" lifestyle after the ring. He felt that we all have our own crosses to bear, while some think all things should be given to them. He had worked for all his accolades during his boxing career and nothing was given to him. He experienced the loss of everything that was important to him but his own self-discipline did not allow him to complain. He knew where to go for both peace of mind and peace of soul. He knew he would receive the precious Grace to succeed and was willing to work his way out of his negative lifestyle. His motto continued to be, "If you believe it, you will see it." When everything seemed stacked against him, he would help others and eventually that would help him. He learned that from his life experiences and always practiced what he preached to others.

On the other hand, Philomena only saw a "Champ" working hard to be seen. She never realized that he never felt the *need* to be recognized. She became immediately obsessed with changing his role in life, and did so by eliminating any friendships and any free appearances. In her eyes, nobody was going to take advantage of her husband anymore. She continued to chastise Tony's family until she wore out her welcome. She purposefully sought to punish someone, anyone, for not taking charge of Tony's post-fight career.

After their marriage in Vegas in September, Tony and Philomena received friends and relatives at a cocktail party on Sunday, December 13, at the Oak Lawn Elks Lodge #22 to celebrate their wedding. It was here that Philomena, to her surprise, saw many expressions of honest and sincere love for Tony from his family that softened some of her anger. She still remained leery of family, but became more accepting of Tony's relatives as a result of that reception.

Mr. and Mrs. Anthony GianFrancisco
Mr. and Mrs. Dominic GianFrancisco
wish to share the joyful news
of the marriage of their sister
Philomena
to
Anthony Florian Zale
the ceremony was celebrated in
Las Vegas, Nevada
on Saturday, the nineteenth of September
nineteen hundred and seventy

Anthony and Philomena
will receive friends at a
Cocktail Party
on Sunday, the thirteenth of December
from three to seven o'clock
Oak Lawn Elks Lodge No. 22
10720 South Central Avenue
Chicago Ridge, Illinois

R.S.V.P. before November 30, 1970
Residence: 10842 South Avenue C

BACK ON THE MAP

Philomena had an idea of how Tony should be branded and handled as a commodity. She immediately set out to eliminate all contact with his friends of the fifties and sixties, as she referred to them as the "hangers on." She also set about changing his entire wardrobe and would not allow him to look anything but top shelf. Unbeknownst to Tony, she gave all of his old, comfortable clothes to either Goodwill or to her own nephews. She dressed and presented him now in another image. Though he didn't mind the new clothing, he was *very* unhappy with her when he would see her nephews in his old comfortable sweaters, suits and shirts.

Her next effort began in 1971 through 1973, in which she brought together non-partisan support for Tony to be appointed to the President's Council on Physical Fitness under President Richard Nixon. Through family and friends, she began circulating petitions which requested that Tony receive an appointment based not just on his work in Chicago, but his national boxing achievements. Petitions circulated in Indiana, Illinois and Michigan, and were carried forth by family and friends.

When completed, thousands of signatures were forwarded to President Nixon through a local congressman's office. Word of the impending review which would lead to an appointment came back to Philomena, but nothing official ever occurred. Tony and Philomena received a pleasant letter from an aid to President Nixon thanking them for their interest and stating that this information would be kept on file for the future. Then, President Nixon resigned from his office of the President of the United States on August 8, 1974.

During 1974, Philomena sought sponsorship from a travel agency and airline. After months of working with Tony to sharpen his baritone voice, she had him singing in perfect pitch the following show tunes: "Back Home Again in Indiana," as well as several other familiar pieces such as "Gary, Indiana" from *The Music Man*, "Harbor Lights" and "The Little Dutch Boy." Becoming the host and hostess for a non-stop flight and tour to Tokyo, Japan, their routine would include her spoon playing and joke telling along with his singing. Though it was well publicized in the print media, the trip and tour were cancelled due to a lack of pre-registration.

It became obvious to family members, that Philomena had a two-fold purpose in the way she managed Tony. First, and not always foremost, was to have Tony recognized once again for his accomplishments in and out of the ring. Second, she sought some credit for herself and the All American Women's Baseball League. It seemed like a natural combination for her efforts.

Her controlling, aggressive nature craved attention and throughout the 1970s and 1980s she would seek out occasions where Tony would be recognized and she as well. Her drive to have Tony become part of the President's Council on Physical Fitness may have been thwarted by Nixon's untimely departure as President, but she had made many influential friends in spite of the disappointment.

She continued to seek ways to enhance Tony's post-fight career by managing his appearances as well as his compensation. Tony became particularly concerned about where the monies were going from these appearances, so he had a sit down discussion with Philomena about "yours, mine and ours." They agreed to keep separate accounts. Tony had become used to covering most expenses from his fighting days, so covering both of their costs from his account was not a problem. He would, however, not give up his separate checking and savings accounts. There was no argument from her, and they agreed that was the way things would be handled. Tony was determined not to lose everything again. He had been unlucky in love once and was not going to repeat history.

Also in 1974, Tony and Hank Stram were approached by The Silver Bell Club, Lodge #2365 of Northwest Indiana. This club was formed in 1925 and affiliated with the Polish National Alliance. The purpose for this contact was to establish a Hank Stram-Tony Zale Sports Award Banquet for qualified, outstanding high school athletes of Polish-Slavik descent in Lake and Porter counties in Indiana. Tony and Hank were willing to lend their names to assist fund-raising for the support of this program. Over the years, the annual awards banquet grew to one of the largest events held in that area and eventually attracted large audiences with up to nine hundred attendees.

Polish National Alliance Silver Bell Club. 1985

HANK STRAM and TONY ZALE

Awarding the Most Outstanding Lake & Porter County
High School Athletes of Polish-Slavic Descent

· May 14, 1991 ·

HELLENIC CENTER
8000 Madison Street · Merrillville, Indiana

The awards presented to the recipients were in the names of Tony Zale and Hank Stram. Every year, for over thirty years, both Tony and Hank proudly participated in this scholarship program. Hank, as a sports, radio and TV announcer, actively pursued numerous collegiate and professional sports figures as guest speakers. Over the years, these included Jim Harbaugh, Mike Ditka, Lou Holtz, Bobby Knight, Terry Bradshaw, Joe Garagiola, Stan Musial, Joe Theismann, Chuck Knox, Ray Nitschke and Mike Krzezewski, to name just a few. There was always a current celebrity attraction to enhance the banquet's attendance.

Mike Ditka - 1987

Bobby Knight - 1988

The event became a major Calumet Region hallmark. Over the years, these banquets had a number of guest emcees. They included Tom Dreesen, best known for his numerous television appearances on the Tonight Show with Johnny Carson, Mike Ditka, Head Coach of the Chicago Bears, and Hank Stram himself. Tony, of course, was very pleased to be a part of this scholarship program and spoke from his heart directly to the young college hopefuls. He also was very happy to be renewing a friendship and developing a working relationship with Hank. Growing up in Gary, Tony had spent a great deal of time as part of the Stram household in the early years. Tony needed a father figure in his life.

The older Stram, aka Henry Wilczek, was a professional wrestler and provided Tony with fatherly advice. He was a good sounding board for him. Seeing the sports celebrity list each year, it didn't take long for Philomena to realize the importance of Tony's association with this club. Unfortunately, once both Tony and Hank passed on, there was no longer a means of securing high profile sports figures like Hank had done for so many years. The Silver Bell Club's scholarship program ended a wonderful and worthwhile run after thirty-one years.

Though the Zale family may have resented Philomena's accusations and feisty confrontations during the 1970s, most agreed that it was good to have someone dedicated to caring for Tony.

Philomena was genuinely interested in his well-being. She tried and accomplished many notable achievements including development of his resume; photographs for fans with his fight record enclosed; an organized annual schedule of events including Zale family gatherings; improvement in both his speech and singing; development and perfection of a stage show featuring Tony singing show tunes; and, her playing the spoons and telling clean jokes. She catalogued all of his boxing awards and memorabilia that he had collected and established a list of annual appearances and fund-raising activities for specific charities of her interest. This was all accomplished while they continued their full-time employment with the parks department including city wide boxing tournaments and shows.

These charities included ones that provided good visibility such as Boys Clubs of America; Boy Scouts of America; The Special Olympics; Cerebral Palsy Telethon; Cook County Jail Athletic Program fundraiser; Mayor Daley's Youth Center Fundraiser; and support for area veteran's organizations including Tony's visits to veterans hospitals. She also made an effort to annually attend dinners and smokers for the following: Rotary Clubs; Lions Clubs; Elks Clubs; the Eagles; the Optimists International; the Shriners and the Holy Name Society in order to get Tony's name out in the public view. To say the least, they became an extremely busy couple and she continued to be his mouthpiece wherever they journeyed.

In the spring of 1976, Tony and Philomena were contacted by the producers of *The Way It Was* with Curt Gowdy and Don Dunphy. They were informed of their intention to produce a program based on the Zale vs. Graziano fights for the Public Broadcasting System (PBS) television through WCET in Los Angeles. They would pay Tony and Rocky for their appearance and participation on the show. They would cover all their expenses including Philomena's as well. The show would catalog and discuss their three epic dramas in the square circle. With them both narrating these battles from their perspectives, *The Way It Was* would visually show and discuss their third fight first hand.

During the taping of the show, Philomena became extremely upset with Rocky because he kept interrupting Tony's commentary. She even told Rocky after the taping, "If I were a man, I would have been the second Zale to knock you out." Graziano responded with surprise, "Yeah, you probably could!" She also stated that during the taping she stood behind the cameras shaking her fist at Graziano whenever he interrupted her husband. While protecting her husband's accomplishments, she would never let anyone take more credit than they deserved. Not even a fellow Italian.[402]

Near the end of the taping, Don Dunphy asked Rocky, "You fought Zale and you fought Ray Robinson. What would've happened with Zale at his best against Robinson at his best?" Rocky answered, "I don't know why he didn't fight Ray Robinson because this here guy coulda licked Robinson. He's a good body puncher, tough guy, in my opinion it woulda been a great fight. I fought Ray Robinson and I fought Tony Zale and in my opinion, he woulda lick 'em."

Tony chimed in and said, "Back in 1952, the movie star Jerry Lewis was in town and called me and asked if I would be willing to fight Robinson. Since I was in great shape working with the boys at the CYO and training them and myself, I answered yes I would gladly. I always wanted to fight him." Jerry later called Tony back and told him he offered Ray $300,000, and Robinson turned it down.

Later on that year in Omaha, Nebraska, Tony had one of the fighters he trained on Robinson's boxing card. As Ray Robinson and his outfit passed by Tony and his fighter, Ray saw Tony and shouted

to him, "Hey Tony, they all wanted me to fight you, they offered me a lot of money. I wanted no part of you. I knew better." Tony's end of the fight, if it could have been made, would have been $500,000 – about $4.6 million in today's receipts. The heavens had other plans for this Champion of the World.

On February 16, 1975, Don Dunphy,

---

402 Thad Zale interview with Philomena Zale, September, 1977.

was asked on WGN Chicago Sports Talk radio by Bob Elson, what was the most thrilling fight he had ever witnessed. He said that he had seen and announced Ali vs. Frazier, Robinson vs. Basilio, Louis vs. Conn and many others, but nothing compared to the first two Zale vs. Graziano battles. The first was held on September 27, 1946, in Yankee Stadium, and the second was held some 10 months later on July 17, 1947, in Chicago Stadium. Dunphy stated that what made these two stand out for him above all the rest was *not just* their ferocity alone. The way each fight turned from round to round for each of the participants is what made them so spectacular. After each of these six round affairs, the victor looked the part of the loser. Tony won the first by a knock-out but was totally out on his feet and in a daze at the end of the fight. In the second battle, Rocky won the bout but both of his eyes were swollen shut and his face was completely black and blue. Tony though, looked as if he had not even been in the ring, let alone been touched by a glove. That's what made these battles so unique in Don Dunphy's eyes as well as the eyes of the thousands of fight fans that either attended in person or listened to them on the radio. Each of the winners was a mere second away from a loss.

Once, when they were visiting Tony's children in California, Philomena made arrangements for tickets to the Tonight Show with Johnny Carson. During the pre-taping, Johnny came out to warm up the audience and thank them for their participation. She quickly stood up and asked Johnny to recognize her husband the former Two Time World Middleweight Champion Tony Zale during the show. Johnny, somewhat in shock, told her thank you and proceeded to depart the audience and go back behind the stage curtains. She was hoping that maybe he would make some recognition during the show, but he never did. She told family that she was afraid that she might have pushed it just a touch too far in her abrasive way. But she never once hesitated to introduce and tell the story of her mild mannered, shy husband.

On November 23, 1979, The Downtown Athletic Club, the same organization that provides the Heisman Trophy, presented the 4th Annual Rocky Marciano Award to Tony Zale. At 66 years of age, he was selected as "A Champion in the ring and a Champ in life." Philomena had a hand in getting Tony's name in front of the right people in hopes of him becoming a recipient of this prestigious award and it worked.

In March of 1980, Tony received a telephone call from an old CYO boxing student thanking him for his inspiration and direction. His name was Jack Sandner, Chairman of the Board of the Chicago Mercantile Exchange. Jack credited Tony with being his inspiration to graduate and continue his education eventually leading to a degree from Notre Dame Law School. When Philomena discovered who Jack was, she immediately asked Tony for the telephone. She made sure that she had all the contact information for Jack, in case there was a need for it in the future. It seemed only right to her if Tony had been an inspiration and coach that maybe with his status and down the road, Jack could help them achieve a goal or two. She had in mind an appointment for Tony to the President's Council on Physical Fitness since so much of an effort had been made in the early seventies. Thousands of signatures had been forwarded to the White House when Nixon was president, but nothing ever came of it.

In February of 1981, Tony and Philomena were contacted and invited by the President of the World Boxing Hall of Fame (WBHOF), located in Riverside, California, to attend Tony's induction into this memorial shrine as one of the greatest boxers in history. He would be joining his elite peers in perpetuity on August 21, 1981. Philomena planned the trip to also include a visit with Tony's daughters. This way, she would not have to arrange a separate trip at their expense. It was another example of how mentally organized she was and how she would literally make sure they always filled every trip with more than one purpose and spread the news that Tony Zale was back.

Once in 1979, and again in early May of 1983, Tony and Philomena made their way to Washington, D.C. Their travels were to provide support and speak to congressional representatives regarding federal legislation that would establish the Federal Boxing Protection Act of 1983. A hearing before the sub-committee on Education and Labor, House of Representatives, 98th Congress, First Session, provided Tony and other well-known champions such as Willie Pep, Carmen Basilio, Floyd Patterson and Chuck Davey an opportunity to show support at the boxer's level.

This legislation would have established an "American Boxing Corporation to regulate the sport and promote safety measures. Of particular note, was the corporation's ability to create model state standards." This legislation did indeed pass the House of

Representatives, but it died in the Senate and never came out of committee. There simply was not enough political pressure for safety in boxing at that time.

In late May of 1983 in Lansing, Michigan, Thad and Deborah Zale, with family assistance, managed to pull off a surprise 70th birthday party for the Champ. Upon Tony's arrival at their residence, waiting family members and guests were there to greet him. Also attending to celebrate with the Champ were members representing federal, state and city governments.

Tony and Philomena had arrived in East Lansing by train from Chicago. They had taken the short drive past the campus of Michigan State University and the downtown Lansing area past the Capitol to the west side of town to Thad and Deborah's residence. When Tony stepped out of the car, a loud rendition of "Happy Birthday" was sung. Tony was not only surprised, but appreciative. Then, came the honorariums.

Tony was presented a key to the City of Lansing by Suzanne Moore, a representative of Mayor Terry McKane's office.

He was given a proclamation by the State of Michigan House of Representatives, and another from the Department of State Police for his many years of community service. The Michigan Athletic Commission proclaimed May 29, 1983, "Tony Zale Day." Congressman Howard Wolpe from Michigan, presented a congressional commendation from himself as well as from Congressman Adam Benjamin, First District of Indiana.

President Ronald Reagan had also been sent a personal invitation to this birthday party. A few weeks prior to the party, a representative from the White House called and sent his regrets and graciously declined the invitation since the President would be attending an economic summit at that time. It was asked by the White House representative if the President could send his well wishes to the Champ. A few days before the party, a heartfelt personal letter from President Ronald Reagan arrived.

Governor Blanchard of Michigan also sent a congratulatory letter referencing Tony's 20 years of serving the youth of our country. He also commended Tony for his championship achievements.

During the course of the day, personal calls were received from his boxing peers. Al Hostak, Billy Soose, Rocky Graziano and Billy Conn each wished the Champ well and reminisced about their experiences with Tony's famous "right to the body, left hook to the chin." They each spent at least twenty minutes conversing with Tony, with Thad lucky enough to be listening on the extension line. It was an especially rewarding experience for both Thad and Tony. It was quite humbling to hear these men describe their memories and their experiences in the ring with the "Man of Steel."

Local news coverage at that time included Ron Savage of WLNS-TV, the local CBS affiliate, and the Lansing State Journal reporter Deb Pozega-Pierce. A large portable free-standing sign in front of Thad's home announced to the public that it was Tony Zale's 70th birthday. Because of this sign and the statewide news coverage prior to this event, several boxing fans dropped in to congratulate Tony and collect an autographed photo from this boxing legend. After all, he was the people's champion.

   The party was an all-day affair. Later in the evening, Tony and Philomena entertained the entire family with her spoon playing and jokes, and Tony's pitch perfect rendition of "Back Home Again in Indiana." They were really good entertainers, and the family was impressed with their theatrical performance.

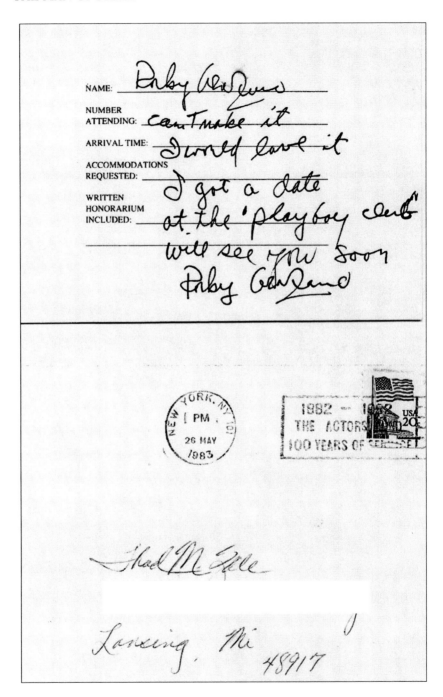

NAME: _Baby Carleaus_

NUMBER
ATTENDING: _can't make it_

ARRIVAL TIME: _I would love it_

ACCOMMODATIONS
REQUESTED: _I got a date_

WRITTEN
HONORARIUM
INCLUDED: _at the 'playboy club'_

will see you soon

Baby Carleaus

NEW YORK, N.Y.
1 PM
26 MAY
1983

1882 — 1982 USA
THE ACTORS
100 YEARS OF SERVICE
20¢

Thad M. Gale

Lansing, Mi 48917

One of the amusements of the day for the children had been a piñata attached to the home's eavestrough in the backyard. The children were each eager for their turns and were blindfolded before swinging at the colorful, dangling donkey. But none of them were able to connect. Then former professional baseball player, Philomena, aka "Frisco" during her professional playing days, took things into her own hands and stepped up to bat. Once she got a hold of that bat though, there was no more blindfolding the kids to try and hit it. She promptly took the situation into her own hands and before you knew it, candy was flying all over the yard.

It was Memorial Day weekend of 1983, and one celebration family and friends would never forget. Tony and Philomena spent a few more days in Lansing with Thad and his family sharing stories from the past and making memories for the future. It was the first of many future trips to Lansing that Tony would make over the next 10 or so years.

As time does tell, Jack Sandner would end up taking the forefront and helping Tony receive the recognition he rightfully deserved. But it was not in the same venue that Philomena had planned. Instead, Jack provided the impetus to have Tony recognized by both Presidents Reagan and Bush for his contributions to the youth of America.

On October 16, 1990, during a ceremony at the College of DuPage in Illinois, President George H. W. Bush personally awarded

Tony the Presidential Citizens Medal for his 36 years of exemplary service to our country.

Official White House Photo

To: Tony Zale — A True Champ!
Congratulations on the Well-deserved Honor —
Gz Bush

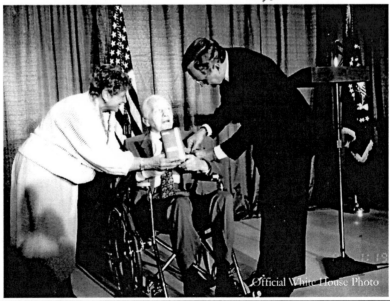

Official White House Photo

To Tony, it was another pinnacle of his life. He had not been forgotten and neither had his good citizenship. As former Congressmen Hyde, Michel, and Rostenkowski stated to President Ronald Reagan in October of 1988, boxing's "Man of Steel" was a champion of the under-privileged, urban youth throughout his life and was worthy of recognition. Clayton Yeutter, then Secretary of Agriculture, Samuel K. Skinner, then Secretary of Transportation and James R. Thompson, then Governor of Illinois, are a few others who added their support for recognition of the Champ. Jack Sandner was the "mover and shaker" behind the scenes. He did this as a special thank you for the devotion Tony gave to thousands over his lifetime.

THE WHITE HOUSE

WASHINGTON

May 6, 1988

Dear Tony:

Some time back, my good friend, Congressman Henry Hyde, passed along an article about you, and I want to take this opportunity to express my appreciation and that of every American for all you've meant to our country through the years.

Throughout life, you've quietly kept on living the sterling qualities you displayed during a boxing career that saw you become middle-weight champion of the world -- the enduring qualities of faith, discipline, and determination that every champion must have.

Youngsters need those qualities too, and it is to your credit and to our country's lasting gain that you spent decades in imparting them to young people in the Catholic Youth Organization and in city programs. Whether in boxing, in the Navy during World War II, or in youth work, you've reminded America's youngsters -- and the rest of us as well -- that the meaning of true strength and courage is found in faith, character, integrity, and sacrifice. Because of this, America knows that you're still a champ, and that you always will be.

Nancy joins me in sending very best wishes to you and Mrs. Zale. God bless you.

Sincerely,

Ronald Reagan

Mr. Tony Zale
Apartment 809
3001 South King Drive
Chicago, Illinois 60616

In 1981, Philomena's aggressive personality helped them become the only boxing couple to be invited to the Riviera Hall of Fame Golf Classic. It was an all-expenses paid trip to a pro-am golf tournament

in Las Vegas, Nevada.

While there, Tony was able to get re-acquainted and spend quality time with his old friend and boxing compatriot, Joe Louis. They compared notes about boxing in the eighties, their careers, and they enjoyed renewing a friendship that spanned four decades. Tony discussed with Joe his golf game as one which suffered from his youthful days playing baseball. He always swung a golf club as if he were going for the fence and often whiffed. He did enjoy putting though, since he could always hit the ball in a straight line.

Also, in the summer of 1981, Tony Zale was reported as deceased by the wire services which carried a story out of Yuma, Arizona. The report said that the ex-middleweight champ "had died of a heart attack in a local trailer park." Newspapers across the country reported the story of Tony's death until he cornered a reporter in Chicago. Tony told the reporter, "that this report was exaggerated all the way." As it turned out, the corpse from Yuma was an alcoholic who pretended to be Tony Zale for the latter part of his life. He told some great stories about *his* fights and had a lot of believers at the local bars in Yuma. This got him a lot of complementary "beverages." The episode gave Tony quite a chuckle and he said, "A lot of people presumed me dead before my time." [403]

At all of the benefits over the years where Tony was a guest, Philomena was never at a loss for words. She was dynamic, sometimes abrasive, and either you liked her or you did not. She played her favorites and she never hesitated to confront you if it was in her interest or Tony's to do so. She was tough and direct and she made no excuses. If you thought you could do a better job than she could, she would invite you to come up and take over the task.

Tony, easy going and soft spoken, loved his Mighty Mouth. She was the antithesis of Tony. If you didn't love her, that was alright, because he did. The Zale family, confused by her previous actions toward them individually, still felt that she was the best person to come into Tony's life. He no longer had to lead a solitary existence. He seemed genuinely happy and content to follow her lead and she never hesitated one moment in taking it. In the end, the family all grew to love her and appreciate her for who she was, in spite of her starting off on the wrong foot with virtually all of them.

403 *Eagle Magazine* August/September 1981

My Dear Husband

Back in early September, I bought you a Seiko watch, for our '14teen anner versary. I was unable to give it to you then because it was sent out for inscribing on the back of it. Then when it was ready, I was home sick in bed — and later taken to the hospital where it was discovered I had to have an operation, which brings it to you now receiving it so late.

When the Dr Furey first told me I had a cancerous tumor I thought about the inscription on the back of the watch, and thought that it was a sign from God, that I would die but, as we both know I'm alive and I love you enjoy the watch

your wife
Philomena

P.S. Look at back of the watch

BEWILDERMENT

In the fall of 1989, Thad Zale received a call from Philomena concerning Tony. He had taken off on a run after confusing her with his ex-spouse Adeline. He had called her "the devil," and left their apartment on Martin Luther King Drive on the near south side of Chicago. She was concerned that he had first confused her with Adeline, but secondly, that he might get lost because it was getting dark. Philomena's concern was that Tony had been gone for a couple of hours and it never took him that long to return. She had called the Chicago Police Department and asked them to be on the lookout for him. She also called Thad for counsel. She had been sending Tony up to Thad's home in Lansing, Michigan, for their many interviews and was curious if he had noticed anything unusual in his uncle's behavior.

After talking with Thad for fifteen minutes about the episode, there was a knock on their apartment door. She excused herself and set the phone down. The Chicago Police Department had found Tony jogging along the thoroughfare about a mile away. When she returned to the phone, she indicated that he was on his was back toward their apartment when police found him. They said he was somewhat confused as to why they stopped him, but he knew who he was and where he was going.

Thad asked to speak with Tony and they discussed the fact that he was married to Philomena and this was not Adeline that he was living with. Tony provided assurance that he knew who he was living with and joked that "sometimes Mighty Mouth overreacts." Tony then handed the phone back to Philomena and she asked if she could send Tony back up to Lansing on the Amtrak the following weekend. That was agreed upon, and she asked that we take particular note of his behaviors.

Tony arrived the following weekend in East Lansing, where he was greeted by Thad and his family. The purpose of the visit was three-fold. First, it provided Philomena with a short break. Second, it provided another opportunity for Thad to observe Tony's behavior. Last, but not least, it allowed Thad to continue the interview process for Tony's life story, and for the Champ to attend a local professional fight at the Lansing Civic Center.

Tony enjoyed the weekend relaxing with his crossword puzzles, entertaining the children, reading several newspapers front to back, and reviewing Thad's writings. While he was there, he was also treated to a local spa for a massage just like his old boxing days. No one in Thad's family seemed to notice or determine any confusion on Tony's part.

When Tony returned to Chicago, Philomena called Thad a few days later and insisted that something was happening to Tony. A month later, she sent Tony back to Michigan to Thad's home for more interviews and quiet observation.

There were more occasions in 1990 when she called Thad to request assistance in determining Tony's mental state. She continued to stress that he was becoming more introspective and less responsive to her instructions. She mentioned specifically that enroute to the train station for one of his visits to Michigan, she and Tony had been involved in an accident on the outer drive in Chicago. When she asked Tony to get information from the driver that hit her, he cooperated, but when he came back to the car, he had a bloody mouth. The other driver had hit him and she couldn't understand why he didn't retaliate. A police officer arrived and ticketed the other individual for having caused the accident. The police officer also made the two young men in the other car apologize to Tony for their behavior and for the driver hitting him.

Even though Philomena was disappointed in the fact that Tony didn't respond to being hit by the driver with his fist, Tony himself realized that even though this young man had hit him, that he could *not* retaliate. A professional boxer's hands are considered lethal weapons and there could have been many personal repercussions for Tony and Philomena if he had responded to that assault with his fists. Tony would not press charges even though he could have.

When Tony arrived at his nephew's home, he seemed cooperative, insightful and ready for crossword puzzles and more interviews. He also possessed a great appetite, so he was well fed on these trips. Tony agreed that on his next planned trip back to Lansing he would be the guest speaker at his great-nephew and namesake's D.A.R.E. graduation at St. Gerard School.

Tony kept his word. The program was organized by Sgt. Joseph Hanley, the D.A.R.E. officer from Michigan State Police. A young Michigan State football player named Tony Briningstool was another guest speaker for the program.

Tony was interviewed by the local CBS affiliate news station WLNS and provided good television copy. During the weekend, there was still no indication to Thad and his family of Philomena's assessment of Tony's deteriorating mental health.

That evening, Tony actually disregarded his speech for the sixth graders that had been prepared for him and ad-libbed a speech in his own words. He always felt a simple short story from experience was worth more than a thousand flashy words.

Grant Malecke   Tony Zale   Matt Cusick

On July 19, 1990, a celebration was held in Chicago commemorating Tony's fiftieth anniversary of winning the title from Al Hostak. Ed Kelly, Chicago Parks Superintendent, organized this affair in Tony's honor. Gathering hundreds of fans, Ed toasted Tony for not only his boxing skills but also his generous gift of self to the youth of the city. This was another occasion where Tony and Philomena were the toasts of the town one more time. This event would not be forgotten by either of them and they were thankful to Ed for organizing it. As time continued to slip by, the Champ appreciated once again the recognition of his life and worthy ambition, assisting the youth of Chicagoland.

Ed Kelly's 15ᵗʰ Annual Boxing Smoker

Honoring Tony Zale's
50ᵗʰ Anniversary on Winning the World's Middleweight Title

Thursday - July 19ᵗʰ, 1990

at the
EXCALIBUR - 632 N. Dearborn St.
Food & Drink will be served from 6:00 to 7:30 P.M.
Boxing Program will begin at 7:30 P.M.

Tony Zale 50th ANNIVERSARY OF WINNING MIDDLEWEIGHT CHAMPIONSHIP
July 19, 1990
Excalibur – 632 N. Dearborn, Chicago, IL

D	Pat O'Malley	Park President
	Stormy Bidwell	Cardinals' Football Owner
D	Ben Bentley	Boxing Ring Announcer
	Tom Carey	Hawthorn Racetrack Owner; Notre Dame QB
	John Lattner	Heisman Trophy Winner; Notre Dame All American
	Bob Kelly	Notre Dame Football Star
	Jackie Schaller	Schaller's Pub – 31st & Halsted
	Neil Hartigan	Lt. Governor; Attorney General
	Bill Daley	Mayor Daley's Brother
D	Judge Abraham Marovitz	
	Senator Bill Marovitz	State Senator
D	Gene Sullivan	Loyola University Coach; DePaul Athletic Director
	Dick Devine	States Attorney; Former Park President
	Mike Sheehan	Cook County Sheriff
D	Cecil Partee	City Treasurer; Former States Attorney
D	Ed McCaskey	Chicago Bears
	Bill Bartholomay	Atlanta Braves Owner
	Fred Hoffman	Owner of the Excalibur
D	Steve Neal	Chicago Sun Times Writer
	Joe Perillo	Pontiac/BMW Car Dealer
	Joe Ahern	Channel 2 President
D	Ray Coffey	Chicago Sun Times Writer
	Jack McHugh	Park President; McHugh Construction
	Jimmy Walker	Realtor

Judge Abraham Marovitz

Stormy Bidwell. Owner
Cardinals football team
and race track owner.

THE BIG FIGHTS INC.

9 East 40th Street, New York, NY 10016; 212-532-1711; Fax: 212-869-1745

July 11, 1990

Mr. Ed Kelly
The Ed Kelly Sports Program, Inc.
1951 West Lawrence Avenue
Chicago, Illinois 60640

Dear Ed,

I was pleased to authorize Steve Lott to process the fights of Tony Zale vs. Melio Bettina and Tony Zale vs. Billy Soose, for first time ever showing at your 16th Annual Smoker honoring Tony Zale.

Personally, I have always had the highest regard for Tony Zale as a fighter, and as a person, and am delighted to be able to cooperate with you.

The invoice enclosed covers just processing costs. We are pleased to oblige. With my best wishes for the success of your Smoker, and my warmest regards.

Cordially yours,
THE BIG FIGHTS, INC.

William D. Cayton, President

In the beginning of 1991, Philomena began talking about the possibility of placing Tony in a nursing home. Though the Zale family did not notice any evidence or difficulty in Tony's self care or inability to follow instruction, they were not his full time caregivers. What Thad and his family did notice though, was his graceful aging process. He was no longer capable of going on jogs of a mile or two that he so loved and he was less conversational and now needed some help tying his shoes, but he could still dress himself and take care of his own personal hygiene.

So, what they were noticing wasn't anything that would not be expected of a gracefully aging gentleman. It seemed a bit early to Thad for any consideration of placing Tony in a nursing facility. He told Philomena that he thought this was premature. She replied that lately Tony was not cooperating with her. When Thad asked her for an explanation of exactly how he was not cooperating, she said that when she tells him to get ready he is so slow and that she often gets angry with him. She said it takes him two hours to do the same tasks he used to do in an hour.

Thad could sense Philomena becoming more and more impatient with her husband, but again, he was not his uncle's full-time caregiver. Thad spoke to and polled other family members. Basically, they all agreed to accept whatever decision Philomena would make in Tony's behalf. Also, Thad asked Philomena that whenever she did decide to no longer continue home care for Tony, that she could please be sure to let the family know so they could visit.

In June of 1991, another highlight of Tony's career became his induction into the International Boxing Hall of Fame (IBHOF), in Canastota, New York. This village located close to Syracuse was the home of fellow Middleweight Champion, as well as Welterweight Champion, Carmen Basilio. In the mid-eighties, Carmen and several members of the community had decided to establish a hall of fame where boxers from all around the world could be remembered and enshrined. The early efforts to establish and build this hall of fame fell upon the shoulders of Edward Brophy.

Ed grew up on boxing and was seven or eight years old when he had "a kind of vision of boxing gloves flashing through his mind – he knew that the sport was going to play a big part in his life."[404] The area produced two World Champions, Billy Backus and Carmen Basilio, as well as a number of great boxing writers and sport participants.

By the time Ed was a teenager he "had even started training some amateurs and learned much about how to run a gym. He was interested in the concept of inspiring troubled youth to direct their energies into learning how to box instead of getting in trouble." By 1984, with the hall of fame only an idea, Brophy enlisted all of his friends and relatives over a five or six year period. The land was finally granted by the state of New York as the future home of the International Boxing Hall of Fame.[405]

Some of those inducted with Tony included Ray Arcel, Tony's corner man for his three fights with Graziano and the one with

---

404 Roberts, James B., *The Boxing Register. International Boxing Hall of Fame Official Record Book,* McBooks Press, Ithaca, New York 2002.
405 Roberts, James B., *The Boxing Register. International Boxing Hall of Fame Official Record Book,* *McBooks Press,* Ithaca, New York 2002.

Cerdan, Carlos Ortiz, Ruben Olivares, Beau Jack, Rocky Graziano and Marcel Cerdan (both posthumously). Tony would never forget the weekend, nor would his Mighty Mouth, as she accompanied him up to the podium and spoke with him and on his behalf as he received his hall of fame ring and certificate. In her speech, Philomena affirmed Brophy's dream of having a central location for honoring and keeping alive all of the greats of boxing. They spent the last part of the week-end at Carmen Basilio's relative's home. They entertained and serenaded the guests and other boxing greats with Tony's rendition of "Back Home Again In Indiana" and Philomena's rapid-fire repertoire of jokes and spoon playing.

Boxing Hall of Fame

Welcome to the International Boxing Hall of Fame Museum

Our mission is to honor and preserve boxing's rich heritage, chronicle the achievements of those who excelled, provide an educational experience for our many visitors, and operate our facility in a manner than enhances the image of the sport.

Annual Induction - June 9, 1991

Photo Courtesy of Pat Orr

Photo Courtesy of Pat Orr

After Tony's induction into the IBHOF, Tony and Philomena headed to California, to visit his daughters once again. It was not a good trip. Philomena seemed to belittle him for his forgetfulness and his breathing through his mouth.[406] She did not like Tony's daughters and their families; therefore, she was not happy with Tony either. She had been forthright with Tony's nephew, Thad, simply saying,

---

406 Thad Zale interview with Teresa Zale.

she did not care for them and she only endured these trips for Tony's sake.

About the same time, the Joe Zale family annual picnic was being planned for Labor Day, and Tony and Philomena had attended for the past several years.

Several unsuccessful attempts to contact Philomena to arrange transportation for them from Chicago to this family event in Indiana were made. Messages were left on their answering machine at least a half dozen times with no response. When no one was able to reach them, it was assumed that Tony and Philomena had stayed longer in California. With many attempts to contact them being unsuccessful, they never made it to that year's picnic.

Throughout the fall of 1991, continued attempts were made by the family to learn the whereabouts of Tony and Philomena. Contact was finally made in December by Jeanette Zale-Stachura with one of Philomena's sisters. The sister informed Jeanette that Philomena was seriously ill with cancer, which explained why there was no communication with them for the past several months. Surprised by this news, she then asked the sister where Tony was. She was told that he had been placed first in the Veterans Home and then transferred to the Warren Barr Pavilion, a nursing facility on the near north side of Chicago.

By the time the news traveled through the Zale family circle, it was January of 1992. Philomena's cancer had spread quickly and the Zale family was even more shocked to discover that she passed away on January 18, 1992. The day Philomena died, Jeanette was contacted by her sister who provided information concerning the funeral arrangements.

Thad traveled from his Michigan home to Chicago to take Tony to the funeral of his wife. When he arrived, he discovered that Tony had not been informed of her death yet or did not understand what had happened. Therefore, he had the unpleasant task of telling Tony about Philomena's illness which consequently led to her death. Tony told Thad that he was in the nursing facility for a checkup and this was going to be a temporary lodging for him. He had lived at Warren Barr for over two months, unbeknownst to the Zale family. Of course after her death, the Zale family concern was what was now going to happen to Uncle Tony. It seemed natural that the Zale and Gianfrancisco families would gather weeks after Philomena's funeral and determine the best course for the Champ.

Tony would forget that Philomena had passed away and would need reminders whenever we visited. He would frequently ask where Mighty Mouth was. Eventually, he understood.

In February of 1992, Raymond Zale agreed to host the gathering at his home in Crown Point, Indiana. He contacted Tony's daughters to invite them to attend this joint family meeting regarding the care of their father. Mary was the only daughter able to travel and attend, and Raymond made arrangements for her to come back to Indiana. The rest of the interested parties from the Zale family were contacted and a date was selected with the Gianfrancisco family concurrence. About twenty-five members of both Tony and Philomena's families attended. The guest of honor, Tony Zale, arrived first with Thad and his son Anthony.

> *PHILOMENA DIED OF LUNG CANCER! WE WENT TO HER FUNERAL AND SAID GOODBYE. SHE IS IN HEAVEN WITH YOUR BROTHERS, MOM, + DAD.*

> *THAT WAS IN JANUARY, 18th, 1992. THIS IS APRIL 5, 1992 JUST BEFORE EASTER 1992*
> *JUNE 13, SATURDAY AT 4:30pm*

The mood for this important meeting was very cordial between the two families. Tony, himself, commented about how happy he was to see the two families gathered together. He had been told by Thad that this meeting was to make a decision on how best to now care for him. Before the meeting, on the drive from Chicago to Crown Point, Thad asked Tony if he would like to come to Lansing, Michigan, to live. Tony said yes he would – he would like to live with family. With that being said by Tony, Thad opened the meeting with this suggestion. Everyone was in agreement that this was now the plan. No one argued against it. Further, the financial aspect of caring for Tony's well-being could be met through the creation of a trust for his benefit. This too, was applauded by all present.

One of the Gianfrancisco relatives was an attorney in Chicago. He agreed this would be the best way to provide safety for Tony's remaining assets. Thad, as a financial advisor, agreed to set up the trust at no cost to Tony's estate. The meeting lasted approximately an hour and everyone agreed to the new plan for Tony. Drafts of the trust would be done and submitted to the Gianfrancisco's for comment before being filed. All were concerned about Tony's future care. After the formal meeting, everyone sat and visited with Tony and enjoyed each other's company.

Approximately ten days later, everyone who had been present at that meeting received notice of a hearing in a circuit court of Cook County, Illinois, Probate Division. The Gianfrancisco family, after agreeing on one course of action at the family meeting, now wanted to have Tony declared as a "disabled person." The notice stated that "Mr. Zale was suffering from dementia and totally incapable of making personal and financial decisions on his own behalf," and the courts recommended the appointment of a guardian.

This came as quite a shock to the Zale family. The Gianfrancisco's wanted Patrick T. Murphy, at the time, the public guardian of Cook County, to be appointed as the guardian of Tony Zale. They wanted Tony to be made a ward of state. The Zale family would not allow this to happen. If anyone was going to oversee the care of their uncle, it would be them. After three months of wrangling in Cook County Probate Court, by petition to the court, Richard Kordys, an Illinois resident and Tony's great nephew, was appointed guardian of the estate of Anthony Zale. Upon review of the documents, Richard discovered that Tony's personal accounts net worth included checking and savings accounts of just under $15,000, and his remaining memorabilia was valued at approximately $2,200.

Philomena's trust, of which Tony was final beneficiary, amounted to only about $23,000, after all distributions to her family. Several of the Gianfrancisco's refused their distribution of her estate saying that it belonged to Tony. Further, Tony's first championship belt, won as a result of the Hostak win in 1940, was unaccounted for along with his wedding ring and his championship ring presented by the International Boxing Hall of Fame at his induction in 1991. To this day, no one in the Zale family knows of their whereabouts.

Several years later, one of the Zale family members, Greg Calendar, was listening to a local radio sports talk show back in Gary, Indiana. He called another family member, Paul Zale, and said that someone called in to that sports talk show inquiring about the value of the first Zale championship belt. The radio talk show host then asked the caller, "Why would you want to know what the value is of this piece of sports memorabilia?" The caller immediately hung up. Upon hearing this, Greg quickly called the radio station asking if they had any information on the caller, but unfortunately they had none.

Raymond Zale was appointed guardian of his person. Letters of guardianship were issued by order of the court. The Gianfrancisco's would no longer be a consideration in Tony's care. The probate court also threw out the Thad Zale request to move Tony to Michigan or have Thad joint custodian of the person with his brother. Thad instead, with Ray's permission, travelled to Chicago monthly to bring Tony up to his home in Michigan for monthly visits and interviews.

In the early fall of 1992, Tony was taken to Lakeside Hospital after supposedly trying to "escape" from Warren Barr Pavilion. According to staff and official reports, Tony had fallen inside the elevator and received several cuts and bruises. When visited by family members, they reported that the bruises around Tony's face, his swollen cheek and black eye and upper torso appeared more "fist-like" in appearance. It seemed obvious to family that someone had deliberately hit the Champ more than once. It then became a matter of petitioning the probate court to have Tony removed from the Warren Barr facility. When it was discovered that a Zale cousin worked at the Fountainview Rehabilitation Center in Portage, Indiana, the question was answered of where their uncle could spend his remaining years in comfort and family care.

As they had been all his life, Tony's prayers were answered. Family provided regular visitation and physical care for the Champ for the rest of his years. Although Tony used a walker by that time, it was easier to get him around with use of a wheelchair. The family members would check him out for summer drives, dinners, doctor appointments and family gatherings until he was no longer able to leave the grounds.

During Tony's short stay at Lakeside Hospital after the injuries he sustained at Warren Barr, his niece and her husband, Lillian and Armand Lopez, went to visit him. As they sat and spoke to him, he could not identify who had struck him. He told Armand that he felt his life and career had been a failure. He had lost his family, lost his wife, and now lost his last fight with his attacker.

About that time, an elderly gentleman knocked on his hospital door and asked if this was the room of Tony Zale the prizefighter. Armand affirmed that it was, and the man approached them and asked Tony if he could simply shake his hand. Tony offered his "right duke" and the man grabbed it gently, cupping it with both of his hands. He told Tony what an inspiration he had been to him and how wonderful it was to finally meet him in person. He thanked him for rising above the rest in boxing and for being morally principled. "Thank God for you, Tony Zale," was the last thing the gentleman said before leaving.

Lillian and Armand looked at Uncle and smiled. A few minutes went by as they chatted and there was another light knock on the door. This time, a young man in his twenties entered and asked if this was Tony Zale's room. Once again, Armand affirmed it was, and the young man approached the bed and asked Tony if he could impose upon him for an autograph. His parents had told him what a great champion Tony had been, and he just wanted an autograph to pass to his children one day with his story about "a man of steel." Tony obliged and the young man received his autograph and thanked him for all he had completed in his career.

After he left, Armand and Lillian looked once again at uncle and said, "So you think you were a failure? The world doesn't." Uncle Tony just smiled and nodded. The Good Lord does answer our prayers, Tony.

THE FINAL ROUND

It's unfortunate that so many people today are not aware of Tony Zale's boxing legacy. Most fans know nothing of his story outside of the ring. As time has slipped by, and the majority of those who had the privilege of watching him fight have gone on to greater rewards, it seems as though the only lasting memory of his pugilistic career is the three savage fights he engaged in with Rocky Graziano in the late 1940s. Still, "in the drama of boxing, Zale vs. Graziano stands as a major document, never to be glossed over in dealing with the affairs of that game."[407]

Even some of those memories have faded. *The Ring* magazine named two of the three bouts with Rocky as their "Fight of the Year," and the rivalry is still heralded as one of the greatest trilogies in boxing history. Also, *The Ring* magazine's "Fight of The Year" in 1948 was the Zale vs. Cerdan fight, and though Tony lost that bout on a technical knock-out, his last fight again demonstrated his courage and unfortunately, showed some of the rust of his boxing skills due to age.

In the first Graziano fight, "Graziano had knocked him out but his body still obeyed the instructions of his mind, and he had refused to fall down. He had punched because that is what a fighter is supposed to do. That is what they pay him to do. It did not occur to Zale that this was unusual. You're sent in there to fight, and that is what you do as long as you can, no matter what happens to you. You don't decide whether you fall down. You don't depend on flight if you are a puncher. You do exactly what Zale did, but there aren't many of them who figure it that way. It is part of the job, the licking, just as the big pay is."[408] Zale accepted both.

Three years in a row, 1946, 47 and 48, one of Tony's fights was chosen as the best overall contest in the ring. Inevitably, most have heard of Rocky Graziano because of his post-ring flamboyant personality and "wise guy" antics. But Tony not only won two of the three title fights that took place between the two men, he was the far greater skilled and admired fighter amongst the boxing fraternity. He also wore the mantle of World Champion from 1940 – 1947 and again in 1948.

---

407 *Washington Post*, Zale Was No Ordinary Boxer by Shirley Povich, March 30, 1997.
408 Cannon, Jimmy, *Nobody Asked Me, but: The World of Jimmy Cannon*, Holt, Rinehart and Winston, 1978.

What does it take to become a Champion? Many hope and wish for it like they would a lottery jackpot, but very few realize the ambition needed. It requires a single-minded degree of dedication and commitment that leads a man or woman to focus all his or her efforts toward that cause. The drive, concentration, courage and strength of will come from deep within a person.

A World Champion fighter must also have an insatiable desire to mold oneself into a machine-like system that can parry and block the punishing efforts of an opponent. This must be accomplished while countering with an effective offense of his or her own. It's not unlike a grand chess game where one must anticipate one's opponent's next move, assess his or her weaknesses, and determine how to best counter the attack. It all takes place during three minute periods of controlled violent action over the course of a fight.

Boxing requires as complete a physical sacrifice of self as any form of athletic endeavor on the planet. You either have it within yourself to make it - or you don't. It's easy to quit after that first punch in the nose is received or when the going gets tough, but the Champion of these pages *never* knew what it meant to quit.

Tony not only possessed all of the above qualities, but he was one of the most vicious body punchers the game has ever seen. Al Hostak, Georgie Abrams, Billy Soose, Billy Conn and Rocky Graziano were just a few of the men who were left with a lasting impression of his "bodywork." Soose compared a sock in the stomach from Tony to a feeling as though someone stuck a hot poker in you and left it in there.[409] But Tony was much more than just a vicious body puncher. He was a skilled technician who could deliver a combination of punches with pinpoint accuracy. Perhaps there is no better example of his ability in that regard than the combination he delivered to knock Graziano out in their third and final match to regain the middleweight championship of the world.

Boxing historian Herb Goldman ranked Tony as the tenth greatest middleweight of all-time while *The Ring* Magazine listed him as seventh. While many others might not rate him as high, it would be wise to take into consideration the fact that he lost four years of what should have been his prime to military service during World War II. During that time, he never participated in ring competition

409 Jarrett, John, '*Champ in the Corner. The Ray Arcel Story.*' Stadia, Gloucestershire, U.K. 2007

because he truly felt that he would seriously hurt the young men he was training. When comparing him to other great middleweights, make no mistake about it, Tony was a tremendous fighter. But what truly separated him from many of his contemporaries was his fighting heart. Tony Zale had as much guts as any fighter who ever entered the ring, and a number of his opponents said as much.

As proud as Tony was of his accomplishments in the ring, he was more concerned with the example he set in his daily life. Tony was a man of deep faith, who never drank, cursed, or smoked. Two days after Tony's funeral, *Post-Tribune* writer, Richard Grey recalled Tony's good friend Hank Stram's eulogy at his funeral. Grey eloquently pointed out that Tony was a great man because of who he was, not what he did.[410]

From the time that Anthony Florian Zaleski, aka Tony Zale, was beaten up by members of the "Dawg Town Gang" on his way home from St. Hedwig Grade School, to the day he passed on to the next life, he served as a shining example of how to live. His initial goal was to raise to the level of a World Champion, God willing. His second goal was to fulfill the promise he had made to the Father to help others succeed in life where he had failed.[411]

Tony lived for more than eighty-three years. He was a shy, reserved gentleman who carried the unwarranted burden and guilt of his father's death, and still rose to the level of World Champion. In the words of Jacquin Sanders, "There probably has never been a fighter with such capacity to reach inside of himself for the last unexpected reserve of strength and courage, never a fighter who could look so good immediately after looking so bad." "He could be knocked down," said ex-middleweight champ Al Hostak, "and he'd get right back up. I knocked him down every time I fought him, but, how in the hell could you keep him down?" Years later, Rocky Graziano said, "I coulda kept him down with a sledgehammer, but they'd never let me bring one in the ring. Gawdallmighty, I can still feel dem belly punches."[412]

Tony accomplished those first two goals in his life through professional boxing and he never hesitated to give of himself. When those boxing days were done, what Tony sought was to further serve

---

410 *Chicago Post-Tribune*, Friends Remember Great Boxer, More, March 23, 199.
411 Thad Zale interview with Tony Zale.
412 *Boxing Illustrated*, Tony Zale: "The Man of Steel" October 1993 by Jacquin Sanders.

God, his country and family. If he received along the way three championship belts, the Rocky Marciano Award, the Edward J. Neil Memorial Award for the man who did the most for boxing, the Presidential Citizens Medal as well as many, many other accolades, it proved to him that clean living, loving God and following His Commandments was the answer to life's puzzling challenges.

During Tony's lifetime, he went from being poor to fame and fortune, and back to having nothing but the clothes on his back as well as the love of his family. But he didn't despair or feel sorry for himself after he'd lost it all. No, instead he picked up his cross and carried on. He never quit.

No one has ever said life was going to be easy. Tony fought back through poverty in the same way he climbed the pugilistic ladder to success. He did it with sheer determination and a strength of will that would never allow him to quit. After winning back the title in 1948 and then losing it again, he struggled with what to do next. As he was always inclined to do, he prayed and found an answer through his commitment to God. His primary motivation became to help others and spread the Word to as many ears as would listen. While doing so, he became a positive role model and mentor for thousands of young men and women over the remainder of his life outside of the ring.

Tony experienced some regrets in his life. There were none bigger than the loss of custody of his children in the divorce. It truly hurt him deeply that he wasn't granted the right to raise them after several attempts in the courts. He had a hard time coming to grips with the failure of his marriage to Adeline as well. Thanks to the counseling he received from Bishop Sheil though, he was able to find some peace of mind concerning those issues. In time, he would again lead a productive life and, ultimately, find true love.

Tony regretted that he didn't receive a higher education as well. He made the decision to turn down an offer for a full-ride scholarship in favor of a professional boxing career. As a result, he always directed his young protégés to get their education first. Then, they could pursue a boxing career if it fit into their life's plan.

When it was all said and done, Tony indeed had a lot to be proud of. He was inducted into boxing halls of fame on both coasts and everywhere in between. He was the first American inducted into the Canadian Boxing Hall of Fame. He was the second man in boxing history to regain the middleweight championship of the world just as his fellow Pole, Stanley Ketchel had done some 40 years before. Finally, for his most important work, he was awarded the Presidential Citizens Medal by President George H.W. Bush in 1990 for mentoring the youth of America. This medal, along with other personal items, have been housed since 1998 at The International Boxing Hall of Fame Museum in Canastota, New York.

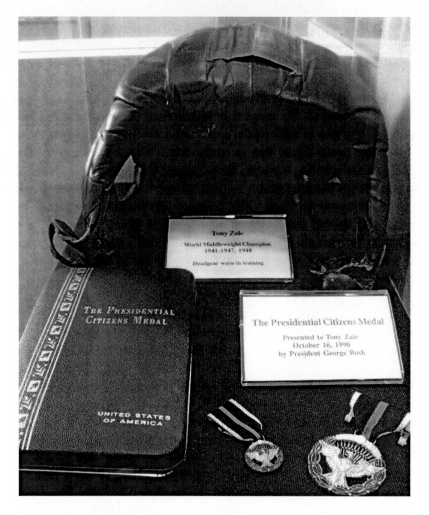

"With his dignified, quiet personality, Tony Zale remains one of the most admired fighters in boxing history – high minded and successful in upholding principles and revered by fight fans everywhere. His status in boxing as one of the sport's greatest super stars is firmly fixed."[413]

As we walk through life, there are so few who can really inspire us and lead us down the correct path. Tony Zale was one of those very special people and by the end of his own life, he was content with the knowledge that he had always given his best and had such a positive impact on so many lives, including those he had never met. "There have been champions who had more ability than Zale, but there was never one who had more dignity."[414]

Tony Zale *truly* was the finest piece of steel Gary, Indiana, has ever produced.

WELL DONE, GOOD AND FAITHFUL SERVANT

413 DeCristofaro, S. De., 'Boxing's Greatest Middleweights,' S. De. DiCristofaro, Rochester, New York, 1982.
414 Cannon, Jimmy, Nobody Asked Me, but: The World of Jimmy Cannon, Holt, Rinehart and Winston, 1978.

IN CONCLUSION

Tony and Gus Latsis were travelling to a local gym in the fall of 1958 after Tony had returned from his induction into the N.B.A Hall of Fame in California. As they drove along, Gus began talking about the Graziano book, *Somebody Up There Likes Me,* and its success. Gus suggested that Tony write his own life story and they discussed who would do it. Tony knew several reporters who had written wonderful articles about him in the past. He decided to make contact with them to find out if anyone was willing to take on such a task. Finally, Tony received the name of a local editor who was willing to discuss the possibility. About a week later, Gus and Tony met at his office. They related all of Tony's experiences during his fighting career from beginning to end. The editor listened intently for some two hours while taking notes and occasionally getting clarification on various discussions and time frames. When the two friends finally summed up his fighting career, they ended with Tony being the second fighter in history to win back the middleweight title. The editor looked at the two of them, thought for a minute, and simply said, "There's no story here. There is no sex, no dirt, no arranged dives and no pay-offs. The story you have told is too squeaky clean. It will never sell." Both Tony and Gus smiled and thanked him for his time and left. As they walked down the hallway to leave the building, Tony was disappointed but realistic. "Someday Mack, *somebody* will want to tell my story."

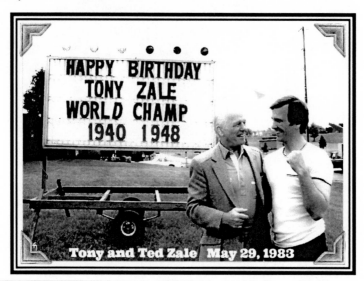

ACKNOWLEDGEMENTS

When an author takes an extended period of time to compile and finally finish a work, it is not unusual to gather a significant list of folks to thank. This particular on-and-off work has spanned many years and many lives, and I am grateful to every relative and person who contributed to this effort. It would not have been accomplished without the wonderful words expressed by my aunts and uncles, cousins, and of course, Uncle Tony himself.

I start by thanking him for first setting the bar high, but reachable, for all of us. Uncle Tony, we can all only hope and pray to contribute a handful of what you did in your eighty-three-year life-span.

Next, my thanks go to my mother, Frances Zaleski, Joseph's wife, for her words of wisdom and guidance in this book and in my life. To my older brothers, Joseph, Raymond, Eugene and Bernard and my sister Lucille Izak for their insight and shining examples they have set through their lives. After Dad's death, they were tough on me, and thank God they were.

Thank you for their insights to: Aunt Stephanie Krecik (Tony's sister); Jeanette Zale (John's wife); Delores Zale (Walter's wife); Anthony Kordys, a great amateur fighter trained by Uncle Tony and Aunt Mary Kordys' son. (Aunt Mary was Tony's oldest sister.) To Walter (Sonny) Zale, for the box full of articles saved by his father. Walter (Tony's youngest brother) for his many memories shared. Also, to Jeanette (Zale) Stachura (Uncle John's daughter) and her older brother Danny Zale for their interviews and insight of Tony's first wife Adeline.

To my loving cousins Lillian and Armand Lopez, Richard Kordys and Helen Kordys for their care of Uncle Tony and the recollections they shared.

To the members of the Zale, Kordys and Krecik families, too many to name here individually, thank you for providing such loving care and active visitation for Uncle Tony in his last few years of life.

Further, to the following friends, opponents and fans who gave interviews: Gus Latsis; Billy Soose; Al Hostak; Rocky Graziano; Hank Stram; John Sulewski, Tony's sparring partner during their teens; John Drummond, CBS News (Chicago); Ed Kelly, Retired

Chicago Parks Department Superintendent; writer James B. Lane; George Foster, my father-in-law; Bishop Emeritus Carl Mengeling of the Lansing, Michigan, Diocese and my childhood priest at St. Mark's Parish in Gary, Indiana; Bruce Keilty; Boxing Historian and DVD contributor, Grand Rapids, Michigan; Rinze Van Der Meer and Albert Stol of Arnheim, the Netherlands, for tracking the Zaleski family and providing wonderful photos.

To Philomena (Gianfrancisco) Zale, "Mighty Mouth," for her love and care for Uncle Tony from their marriage in 1970 until her death in 1992; to Tony's daughters, Mary (Zale) Medeiros and Teresa Zale, for sharing their loving memories of their father and their lives without him; to Sophia Marie Wells, granddaughter, for her detailed recollections and personal photographs; and to Genevieve Richwalski, Tony's ex sister-in-law, for her thoughts and viewpoints. To my cousin Tony Kordys, my last interviewee. When I asked him to describe what Uncle meant to him personally, Tony looked at me and started to cry. He said, "Uncle Tony was the best man I ever knew."

To my co-author, Clay Moyle, for being an accomplished writer and the main reason I finally completed this labor of love after all these years. Thank you, Clay, for your patience of Job and for your wonderful interpretations of every moment in the ring of the Champ. To my niece and god-daughter, Casey (Zale) Bergen, thank you for the introduction to Clay Moyle.

To Delores Schnarr, for her impeccable editing skills and candid comments. We're happy to have made her a fan of Tony Zale. To Angela Detwiler, typist #1, and to Jeanne Larvick from the "original cast" for her editing and advice. To Shelly Harper for her audio cassette tape transcriptions. To Cheryl Perconti-Zale, my brother Eugene's wife, who added suggestions and comments during the review process. To Joseph Tardif for his views, comments, and vital suggestions. Thank you to Jeff Hank, for his legal counsel pertaining to this wonderful endeavor. Thank you to Karlene Zale and Emily Kieliszewski for sharing their document editing knowledge with Deb. To Frank Stallone for his assistance in identifying some boxing folks in Tony's personal photo collection.

To Tony's many, many fight fans whom we have randomly met throughout our travels over the years who were anxious to read this book, we dedicate *Tony Zale The Man of Steel* to you. To those who are no longer with us and knew this book was a work in progress, we hope you have met up with Uncle in Heaven and are listening to his fight stories first hand.

To my children Anthony, Haley and Patrick, thank you for your enthusiastic support, love and encouragement.

Last, but far from least, to my wife Deb who helped me *finally* realize our long-awaited dream – to get it done. Without her inspiration, words of wisdom, creativity, typing skills, and a bit of loving nagging, I would still be struggling to complete this story. I thank her, my mother and father thank her, but most of all, Uncle Tony thanks her.

THAD (TED) ZALE, AUTHOR

In April of 2010, I contacted Casey Bergen of the Zale family through the Facebook website. I was interested in writing a biography about Tony Zale and was hoping to find someone who would be willing to provide more details concerning Tony's personal life. Within a few short hours, I was in contact with Tony's nephew, Thad (Ted.)

Having already written biographies about Sam Langford and Billy Miske, I was confident that I could gather most of the material I would need to address Tony's professional career from various sources. But it's always much more challenging to dig up the details concerning an individual's personal life.

As a result of that effort, I met Ted and learned of the promise he'd made to write the story of his uncle's life. After some discussion, Ted suggested that we team up and write the story together. I was a little leery at first, and wondered how well we'd be able to work as a team and blend our respective writing styles. But, upon a little reflection, I also realized that Ted had access to information about Tony's personal life that I would never be able to uncover. As a result, I thought there was the chance that we could produce something special if we were able to effectively work together.

I would like to thank Casey Bergen for leading me to the Zales when I contacted her about my thoughts of writing a book on Tony Zale. Once I accepted Thad's proposal of a collaboration, it didn't take long for me to realize the quality of individuals with whom I was working. Ted and his wife Deb are a class act and a first-rate team themselves. It's been a real pleasure to get to know them and some of their family as we completed this journey together. So, thank you for the opportunity to work together on this book, Ted.

I would also like to thank Dan Cuoco, John Ochs, Henry Hascup and Bill Schutte for their assistance with photo subjects identification. But, first and foremost, I wish to thank my wife Margaret for all her support and the sacrifices that she makes, and for picking up the slack whenever I became too absorbed with this project.

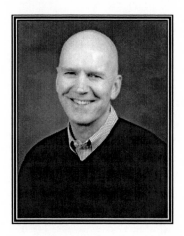

CLAY MOYLE, AUTHOR

EULOGY

ANTHONY FLORIAN ZALESKI
aka Tony Zale
March 24, 1997

"Blessed are the Caregivers"
… especially Lillian, Helen and Jeanette who gave
special care and attention to Uncle Tony.
The workers of Hospice and Fountainview who
made his transition comfortable.

Laid to rest at Calvary Cemetery in Portage, Indiana.

On March 20, 1997, the world lost a true champion. His name is Tony Zale, and he was the last of a bygone era of the likes of Joe Louis, Rocky Graziano and Billy Conn – men who entered the ring and went to work.

Tony's accolades are too many to mention. They do include Boxing Halls of Fame from around the world. Besides his three championship belts, the one award in his life that meant the most to him was the Presidential Citizens Medal he received on October 16,

1990, from President George H. W. Bush. What this prestigious award meant most to Tony was the confirmation that all of his efforts for a clean life, physical fitness and devotion to the "youth" of America was worthy of recognition.

We've had our *Rocky* movies. They were inspirational and entertaining. We had our *Raging Bull*, a true, but sad story. We also had our *Somebody Up there Likes Me*, a story about a young, tough kid from New York who came from the wrong side of the tracks. But what about that other guy who boxed in that movie? The guy who "lost" that second fight? Where was he? Where was the guy that, without him, that movie would have never been made?

Tony Zale was one of the reasons that Rocky wrote his story. Tony Zale is the reason that actors like Paul Newman chose not to perform their own stunts anymore. He got into the boxing ring with that "old man" from Chicago. Tony Zale is also the guy that Sugar Ray Robinson respected too much to get into the ring with. Tony Zale was the guy who, along with Rocky Graziano, gave us the three most memorable fights in the history of boxing.

Tony always believed that the possibilities for achieving one's goals are endless. With faith in God, a commitment to stay clear of negative influences, following the Ten Commandments, and a simple dedication to genuine, hard work, anyone can become a "Champ." He was a "Man of Steel" from Gary, Indiana.

Tony Zale's name would be listed in the dictionary under "c" for "champ." Then again a few words away under "children." A more dedicated person you'd have a hard time finding when it came to keeping kids off the streets and in the gym. He brought dignity to the sport of boxing. Ask anyone at the Chicago Park District or the CYO (Catholic Youth Organization) and they will attest to that fact. They miss Tony, but those memories will live on forever. The little tidbits of knowledge passed on are permanently etched in their minds as they sit at desks and perform their everyday duties in their own jobs and careers. They had their special, personal moments with a real champ, Tony Zale.

Tony grew up in Gary with the help of his older brothers and sisters and learned to vent his anger in the proper way, in a boxing ring. Tony turned anger into a useful tool. Not just a good tool, but it became an unbelievable, inspirational story for all those kids out there who have dreams of their own. Tony went on in his life working with boys who may have had some of the same self esteem problems that Tony did as a child growing up. Their same feelings of inadequacy were changed to real desires and determination, and he showed them how to make something of themselves and their lives.

What most people don't know about Tony Zale is that he was a genuinely humble, prayerful and gentle man. Those soft, smooth and manicured hands gripping a rosary seemed out of place for a Champ that made his livelihood with his fists, with those hands hidden under boxing gloves. Private prayers were always consistent with his everyday life. Tony had a special "aura" about him, not just because he was a "Champ," but because he was a man of God.

Tony would have been 84 years old on May 29, 1997. He's back home now with his brothers, sisters, father, and the biggest fan of all, his mother. He has closed another chapter of his life. I can just see him -- recalling and reliving all those special moments he created for his family along with thousands of fans who have joined him in that other dimension.

We WILL miss him, and we will always remember the lessons he has taught us.

The Man of Steel is not Superman, but a super man was "The Man of Steel."

Uncle, we love you and miss you. Your legend will live on in the story that will follow.

Written with love by Ted and Deb Zale.
March 24th, 1997

TONY ZALE PROFESSIONAL RECORD

Won 67 (KO 45)   Lost 18 (KO 5) Drawn 2

1934

Jun 11	Eddie Allen	Chicago, IL	W PTS 4	CT
Jun 15	Johnny Simpson	Chicago, IL	W PTS 4	CT
Jun 21	Bobby Millsap	Chicago, IL	W KO 1	CT
Jun 25	Johnny Liston	Chicago, IL	W KO 3	CT
Jul 2	Ossie Jefferson	Chicago, IL	W KO 3	CT
Jul 9	Lou Bartell	Chicago, IL	W PTS 4	CT
Jul 16	Einar Hedquist	Chicago, IL	W TKO 4	CT
Jul 30	Bobby Millsap	Chicago, IL	W PTS 4	CT
Aug 7	Bruce Wade	Peoria, IL	W KO 3	SSJ
Aug 13	Billy Hood	Chicago, IL	L PTS 6	CT
Aug 15	George Black	Milwaukee, WI	L PTS 6	MJ
Aug 27	Wilbur Stokes	Chicago, IL	W PTS 8	CT
Sep 3	Mickey Misko	Chicago, IL	L PTS 8	LT
Sep 17	Mickey Misko	Chicago, IL	W KO 4	CT
Oct 8	Yng. Jack Blackburn	Chicago, IL	W PTS 8	EI
Oct 22	Frankie Misko	Chicago, IL	W KO 6	CT
Oct 29	Jack Schwartz	Milwaukee, WI	W TKO 4	IDG
Nov 5	Jack Charvez	Chicago, IL	W PTS 8	MDN
Nov 26	Kid Leonard	Peoria, IL	L PTS 10	MHT
Dec 17	Jack Gibbons	Chicago, IL	L PTS 10	CT
Dec 28	Joey Bazzone	Chicago, IL	L PTS 6	SLT

1935

Feb 25	Yng Jack Blackburn	Chicago, IL	W PTS 6	IDG
Mar 11	Max Elling	Chicago, IL	W PTS 8	CT
Mar 27	Roughhouse Glover	Cincinnati, OH	L KO 9	CT
May 6	Johnny Phagan	Chicago, IL	L KO 6	CT
Jul 2	Dave Clark	Chicago, IL	L PTS 5	CT

1936

Apr 13	Jack Moran	Chicago, IL	D PTS 5	CT

1937

Jul 26	Elby Johnson	Chicago, IL	W PTS 4	HT
Aug 16	Manuel Davila	Chicago, IL	L PTS 4	LPT
Sep 17	Elby Johnson	Chicago, IL	W TKO 3	CT
Oct 11	Billy Brown	Chicago, IL	W KO 1	CT
Oct 18	Bobby Gerry	Chicago, IL	W KO 2	LPT
Nov 1	Nate Bolden	Chicago, IL	L PTS 5	IDG
Nov 10	Leon Jackson	Gary, IN	W PTS 6	CT
Nov 22	Nate Bolden	Chicago, IL	W PTS 5	CT

1938

Jan 3	Nate Bolden	Chicago, IL	W PTS 8	EI
Jan 24	Henry Schaft	Chicago, IL	W PTS 8	BT
Feb 21	Jimmy Clark	Chicago, IL	L KO 1	CT
Mar 28	King Wyatt	Chicago, IL	W PTS 8	CT
May 16	Bobby LaMonte	Chicago, IL	W TKO 5	CT
Jun 13	Jimmy Clark	Chicago, IL	W TKO8MHT	
Jul 18	Billy Celebron	Chicago, IL	D PTS 10	CT
Aug 22	Billy Celebron	Chicago, IL	L PTS 10	SFNM
Oct 10	Tony Cisco	Chicago, IL	W PTS 10	CT
Oct 31	Jimmy Clark	Chicago, IL	W KO 2	ODN
Nov 18	Enzo Iannozzi	New York, NY	W PTS 6	HI

1939

Jan 2	Nate Bolden	Chicago, IL	L PTS 10	WRD
May 1	Johnny Shaw	Chicago, IL	W KO 5	BDG
May 23	Babe Orgovan	New York, NY	W PTS 6	AIR
Aug 14	Milton Shivers	Chicago, IL	W KO 3	REG
Oct 6	Sherman Edwards	Chicago, IL	W TKO 3	LPT
Oct 31	Al Wardlow	Youngstown, OH	W KO 3	RJT
Nov 13	Eddie Meleski	Chicago, IL	W TKO 1	CT
Dec 8	Babe Orgovan	Chicago, IL	W KO 3	LPT

1940

Jan 29	Al Hostak	Chicago, IL	WPTS 10	CHA
Feb 29	Enzo Iannozzi	Youngstown, OH	WKO 4	PT
Mar 29	Ben Brown	Chicago, IL	W KO 3	CDN
Jun 12	Baby Kid Chocolate	Youngstown,OH	WKO 4	SHS
Jul 19	Al Hostak	Seattle, WA	W TKO 13	CDN
Aug 21	Billy Soose	Chicago, IL	L PTS 10	ICPC
Nov 19	Fred Apostoli	Seattle, WA	W PTS 10	SAL

1941

Jan 1	Tony Martin Cianciola	Milwaukee, WI	W TKO7 CDN	
Jan 10	Steve Mamakos	Chicago, IL	W PTS 10	CDT
Feb 21	Steve Mamakos	Chicago, IL	W KO 14	CDN
May 28	Al Hostak	Chicago, IL	W KO 2	CT
Jul 23	Ossie Harris	Chicago, IL	W KO 1	CT
Aug 16	Billy Pryor	Milwaukee, WI	W KO 9	CHA
Nov 28	Georgie Abrams	New York, NY	W PTS15	SHJ

1942

Feb 13	Billy Conn	New York, NY	L PTS 12	CT

1946

Jan 7	Bobby Giles	Kansas City, MO	W KO 4	WSJ
Jan 17	Tony Gillo	Norfolk, VA	W KO 5	ET
Feb 7	Oscar Boyd	Des Moines, IA	W KO 3	HT
Feb 26	Bobby Claus	Houston, TX	W KO 4	PAN

Apr 12	Ira Hughes	Omaha, NE	W KO 2 CBN
May 2	Eddie Rossi	Memphis, TN	W KO 4 WSJ
Sep 27	Rocky Graziano	Bronx, NY	W KO 6 CDN

1947

Feb 3	Deacon Logan	Omaha, NE	W TKO 6CDT
Feb 12	Len Wadsworth	Wichita, KS	W KO 3 EG
Mar 20	Tommy Charles	Memphis, TN	W KO 4 WSJ
Apr 1	Al Timmons	Kansas City, KS	W TKO 5JG
May 8	Cliff Beckett	Youngstown, OH	W TKO6NCN
July 16	Rocky Graziano	Chicago, IL	L TKO 6 CDT

1948

Jan 23	Al Turner	Grand Rapids, MI	W KO 5IDG
Mar 8	Bobby Claus	Little Rock, AR	W TKO 4 HS
Mar 19	Lou Woods	Toledo, OH	W KO 3 EI
Jun 10	Rocky Graziano	Newark, NJ	W KO 3 NYJ
Sep 21	Marcel Cerdan	Jersey City, NJ	L TKO 12 CDN

SOURCES ABBREVIATIONS

AIR	Arizona Independent Republic
BDG	Berkely Daily Gazette
BT	Bismark Tribune
CBN	Council Bluffs Nonpareil
CDN	Chicago Daily News
CDT	Chicago Daily Times
CHA	Chicago Herald-American
CT	Chicago Tribune
EG	Emporia Gazette
EI	Evening Independent
ET	Evening Tribune
HI	Helena Independent
HS	Hope Star
HT	Hammond Times
IDG	Ironwood Daily Globe
JG	Joplin Globe
LPT	Logansport Pharos-Tribune
LT	La Crosse Tribune
MDN	Moorhead Daily News
MHT	Manitowoc Herald-Times
MJ	Milwaukee Journal
NCN	New Castle News
NYJA	New York Journal-American
ODN	Oshkosh Daily News
PAN	Port Arthur News
PT	Portsmouth Times
REG	Reno Evening Gazette
RJT	Racine Journal Times
SAL	San Antonio Light
SFNM	Santa Fe New Mexican
SHJ	Syracuse Herald Journal
SHS	Steubenville Herald Star
SLT	Salt Lake Tribune
SSJ	Sandusky Star Journal
WRD	Wisconsin Rapids Daily
WSJ	Wisconsin State Journal

BIBLIOGRAPHY

- Bromberg, Lester, *Boxing's Unforgettable Fights*, The Ronald Press Company, New York, New York, 1962.
- Cannon, Jimmy, *Nobody Asked Me, but: The World of Jimmy Cannon*, Holt, Rinehart and Winston, 1978.
- Daniels, Daniel, *The Mike Jacobs Story*, New York, New York, 1950.
- DeCristofaro, S. De., '*Boxing's Greatest Middleweights*,' S. De. DiCristofaro, Rochester, New York, 1982.
- Fried, Ronald, *Corner Men*, Four Walls Eight Windows, New York, New York 1991.
- Goldman, Herbert G., *The Ring 1986-1987 Record Book and Boxing Encyclopedia*, Ring Publishing Corporation, New York, New York, 1987.
- Goldstein, Ruby, *Third Man In The Ring*, Funk & Wagnalls, New York, New York, 1959.
- Graziano, Rocky, *Somebody Up There Likes Me*, Simon and Schuster, New York, New York, 1955.
- Grimault, Dominique, *A Hymn To Love, Piaf and Cerdan*, W.H. Allen, London, England 1984.
- Heller, Peter, *In This Corner, Simon and Schuster*, New York, New York, 1973
- Jarrett, John, *Champ in the Corner. The Ray Arcel Story*. Gloucestershire, England, 2007.
- Kennedy, Paul, *Billy Conn – The Pittsburgh Kid*, Author House, Bloomington, IN, 2007.
- Louis, Joe, '*My Life Story*, Duel, Sloan and Pearce, New York, New York, 1947.
- Irving, Marsh, *Best Sports Stories 1948*, E.P. Dutton & Co., New York, New York 1948.
- *McConnell, J. Knox*, The Boxer and the Banker, Vantage Press, New York, New York, 1984.
- O'Toole, Andrew, *Sweet William. The Life of Billy Conn*, Illinois Press, Chicago, IL 2008.
- Roberts, James B., *The Boxing Register. International Boxing Hall of Fame Official Record Book*, McBooks Press, Ithaca, New York 2002.

PHOTOGRAPHS

Sometimes we don't know the date, people, event or location. But what we *do* know for sure is that Tony Zale "The Man of Steel" was, and still is, very highly respected for his craft, admired for his compassion, and loved by many for living a clean, honest and faith-filled life.

The pages of photos that follow are taken mostly from the Zale Family's collections. Photos are given credit and listed at the conclusion of these pages. We hope you enjoy a closer glimpse into the Champion's personal life.

The house where Anthony Florian Zaleski was born in 1913. Located at 1932 Delaware, Gary, Indiana. (As of this printing, his childhood home is still standing at this location.)

Front View - 1932 Delaware, Gary, Indiana

South Side View - Garage (aka slaughterhouse) in rear.

Roster of Tony's
St. Hedwig School Graduation Class of 1927.
(Page 32)

Top Row. L. to R.

1 — HENRY FRONCZAK
2 — JOE CWIKLINSKI
3 — EDWARD WAZNIEWSKI
4 — JASKULSKI
5 — DANOWSKI
6 — FRANK ZALENSKI — ZALE
7 — TED SOBIERAJSKI
8 — JOHN RZEPKA
9 — SELC
10 — BENNY PAWLICKI
11 — JOHN ROSZKOWSKI

SECOND ROW FROM TOP.

1 — IGNACE SNIEGOWSKI
2 — KLUCZYNSKI
3 — TED KOLODZINSKI
4 — ~~illegible~~
5 — ADAM OLSZEWSKI
6 — FRANK KOMENDERA
7 — LEO MIYAK
8 — WALTER KWIATKOWSKI
9 — HENTNIK
10 — ALEX CHMIEL
11 — KACZEROWSKI

THIRD ROW FROM TOP. L. TO R.

1 — ALLOIZY KOLODZIEJ
2 — DOMBROWSKI
3 — JOE ROSINSKI
4 — TONY ZALENSKI — ZALE
5 — DYMANOWSKA
6 — FLORENCE KOLODZINSKI
7 — MARIE SANOK
8 — MARY CZULKOWSKA
9 —
10 — EDWARD KRIGER
11 —
12 — JOE MANIAK

BOTTOM ROW. L. TO R.

1 —
2 —
3 — SOPHIE HENTNIK
4 — AGATHA JUZKIEWICZ
5 — KAHELEK
6 — RATAJCZAK
7 — OGIEGO
8 — HATS
9 — IRZYK ~~illegible~~
10 — JADWIGA ROSZKOWSKI

TAKEN IN MIAMI, 1930

Jack Dempsey and Babe Ruth. 1930
From Tony's personal photo collection.

AMATEUR BOXING

MILL'S STADIUM
4660 WEST LAKE STREET
Every Wednesday Night

In Case of Rain Bouts Will Be Held Following Nite

Admission 55c Inc. Gov. Tax   Ladies Free with escort, others 35c   Reserved 85c Inc. Gov. Tax

SANCTIONED BY CENTRAL ASSOCIATION AMATEUR ATHLETIC UNION

Conducted by WEST END ATHLETIC ASSOCIATION

WM. G. HARLEY—HARRY BERZ—EDW. A. MAHLKE

Call AUSTIN 7330-1-2 For Reservations

GOLDEN GLOVE CHAMPS ROCKFORD, ILLINOIS	JUNE 22nd CARD *vs.*	BELLE PLAINE A. C. CHICAGO
Sammy Fischer	118 lbs.	George Goodman
Joe Romano	126 lbs.	Anthony Muscarello
Pete Simaitis	130 lbs.	Philip Pernice
Bruno Kalveroni	135 lbs.	Al Garcia
William Celebron	147 lbs.	Anthony Zale
Isiah Gaynor	160 lbs.	Knute Kristensen
Emil Pappas	175 lbs.	Steve Selgrat
Adam Smith	Heavy Weights	Duffy Dvonch

Smith or Dvonch Will be a Member of U. S. Team Who Will Box Germany

Bring this card with you and hand to usher
FREE DRAWINGS FOR VALUABLE PRIZES EACH NITE

Mill's Stadium was *the* place for boxing in Chicago in 1932.

1933

		Red & Black Trunks		POINTS BY ROUNDS					
				1	2	3	4	Total	WINNER
1	Barry Gillette—Waukesha vs. Jackie Davis—Milwaukee	Red & Black Trunks 114 Lbs. Black & Red Trunks							
2	Mel Sneid—Milwaukee vs. Redge Marson—Madison	Green Trunks 155 Lbs. Blue & White Trunks							
3	Jack King—Milwaukee vs. Jack Sylvester — Milwaukee	Green & White Trunks 160 Lbs. Black & Red Trunks							
4	Ralph Hoppe—Milwaukee vs. Clem Kopydlowski — Milw.	Red & Black Trunks 126 Lbs. Purple & Gray Trunks							

Next Amateur Show Friday, Dec. 15th

5	Donnie Lemanski—Milw. vs. Henry Kurkiewicz—Milwaukee	Blue & Red Trunks 145 Lbs. Purple Trunks							
6	Tony Zale—Gary, Ind. vs. Luke Ebel — Two Rivers	Red Trunks 160 Lbs. Black & Red Trunks							
7	Irving Olsen—Chicago vs. Sam Clanciola — Milwaukee	Black & Red Trunks 170 Lbs. Black Trunks							
8	George Nelson — Chicago vs. Fred Chynewith—Manitowoc	Gold Trunks 137 Lbs. Blue & Black Trunks							

Amateur Fights Program from 1933.

SEVENTH ANNUAL GOLDEN GLOVES TOURNAMENT

OF

CHAMPIONS

SPONSORED BY THE

Chicago Tribune

THE WORLD'S GREATEST NEWSPAPER

at

CHICAGO STADIUM

February 26, 27 and 28, 1934
Finals March 9

Sanctioned by

THE CENTRAL A. A. U.

April 24th, 1934

TO-NITE

AMATEUR
BOXING AND WRESTLING

SANCTIONED BY C A. A. U.

FEATURING
2- FIVE ROUND BOUTS -2

April 24 1934

Paul Frazier
(SAVOY CHAMP)
vs
Tony Zale
(GARY G.G. CHAMP)

Won By K.O. 4th Round

Wm. Pillow
(SAVOY CHAMP)
vs
Tony Musto
(STOCK YARDS)

RALPH COLLIER vs HAROLD TAYLOR
(SAVOY CHAMP) [JOLIET CHAMP]
5-OTHER BOXING BOUTS-5

2-THRILLING WRESTLING MATCHES-2
JOE MARGETIC vs SUNE RASMUSSEN
[STREET CAR CHAMP] (CHASE PARK CHAMP)
WES BROWN vs JOHN SMIK
[N. W. U. BIG 10 STAR] [POLISH CHAMP]

SAVOY
SOUTH PARKWAY AT 47TH STREET

Admission LADIES 35c GENTS 44c Tax Incl.

For Ringside Reservations Call KENwood 3673

IDENTIFICATION CARD

STATE ATHLETIC COMMISSION OF ILLINOIS

3970-B

LICENSE No.   HAS BEEN ISSUED TO

Athony Zale

OF Gary, Ind.   AS A   Boxer

UNDER THE PROVISIONS OF AN ACT IN RELATION TO ATHLETIC EX-
HIBITIONS, ETC., FILED JULY 1, 1925, AND ANY AMENDMENTS THERE-
TO, AND ENTITLES THE HOLDER TO THE PRIVILEGES THEREOF.

STATE ATHLETIC COMMISSION OF ILLINOIS

EXPIRES   6-11-35   193

NOT TRANSFERABLE

CHAIRMAN

FORM 7
2873-18879   170   (OVER)   SECRETARY

Tony Zale's Illinois Boxing ID. 1935

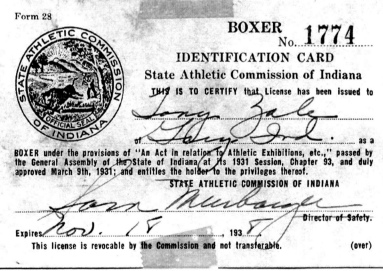

Form 28

BOXER No. 1774

IDENTIFICATION CARD

State Athletic Commission of Indiana

THIS IS TO CERTIFY that License has been issued to

of _____ . as a

BOXER under the provisions of "An Act in relation to Athletic Exhibitions, etc.," passed by
the General Assembly of the State of Indiana at its 1931 Session, Chapter 93, and duly
approved March 9th, 1931; and entitles the holder to the privileges thereof.

STATE ATHLETIC COMMISSION OF INDIANA

Director of Safety.

Expires Nov. 15 , 193

This license is revocable by the Commission and not transferable.   (over)

Tony Zale's Indiana Boxing ID. 1938

Tony Zale

It was all ahead of him.

TONY ZALE

Tony Zale, the middleweight boxing champion of the world, is a fighter who has come up the hard way. He first attracted attention around these parts as a member of the Gary, Indiana Golden Gloves team.

He has won his last thirteen fights and in his climb to the title beat Al Hostak, the famed Seattle battler in a non title bout here in Chicago and then to prove his superiority knocked him out in Seattle last month in the match that carried the title with it.

Zale is one of the real stout hearted men of the ring, in his day he has absorbed plenty of punishment and almost always come back to hand out better than he received in that department. He's the hardest hitter the middleweight ranks have seen since the illustrious Mickey Walker, and promises to bring as much fame and credit to the sport as the Toy Bulldog did at the height of his career.

BILLY SOOSE

Billy Soose, Tony Zale's opponent in tonight's important boxing contest has had a remarkable career in the boxing business. He has been actively engaged in the sport since he fought as a youngster around the YMCA at Farrell, Pa. and from triumphs in the amateur ranks he went on to the Intercollegiate championship as a representative of Penn State College. It was there that he first came to the attention of Paul Moss, Farrell boy who had made good in the motion picture colony of Hollywood as a writer. Moss, back in Farrell on a vacation, was attracted to Soose and his ring ability and took him back to the coast with him where he turned professional. There Dick Powell became interested in the boy and backed him. Since that time, he has fought 28 fights, he has won 25 of them, thirteen by knockouts. His latest victory in Scranton, Pa. where he beat Ken Overlin, New York champion, earned him his shot at Zale tonight.

Soose is 23 years old, 5 feet, 11 inches tall and weighs 161 pounds.

Mill's Stadium Zale vs. Soose Fight Program. 1940

yours truly,
Tony Zale

Tony Zale
World's middleweight Champion

Under Direction
Sam Pian & Art Winch - 180 W.Randolph St. Chicago, Ill.

N.B.A. Champion after Tony beat Al Hostak. 1941

FREE ADMISSION

Saturday Night --- August 16 --- 8:15 p. m.
Juneau Park, Milwaukee

TONY ZALE
Middleweight Champion of the World

10 ROUNDS

TONY ZALE
World's Middleweight Champion

vs.

Billy Pryor
The Colorado Bulldog

JACK DEMPSEY --Guest Referee

Plus 4 Other All-star Bouts

JACK DEMPSEY
Former World Heavyweight Champion

Tune In
WTMJ

The feature bout will be broadcast over Station WTMJ for those who are unable to attend. See your radio page for time of broadcast.

WELCOME, EAGLES
WELCOME, MILWAUKEE

The Pabst Brewing Company Invites You

ONE AND ALL!

In honor of the Eagles' National Convention, the Pabst Brewing Company invites Milwaukee to see the World's Middleweight Champion, Tony Zale, fight Billy Pryor on Saturday, Aug. 16 at Juneau Park. Admission free. Come early and bring your friends. Make this a Blue Ribbon night for Milwaukee!

Pabst Blue Ribbon Night

"The Fight That Made Milwaukee Famous"
holds the record for largest attendance at a boxing match.
This was a free outdoor venue.
Over 135,000 attended. August 16, 1941

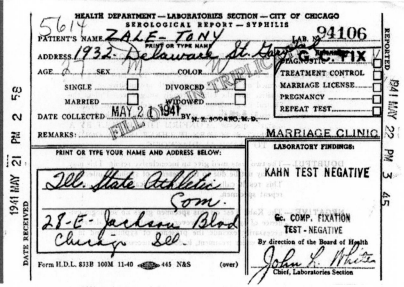

Illinois Health Dept. Serological Report.
May 1941

Joe Niedwick and Tony

GARY'S HAPPIEST FAMILY

The Zale family—left to right—Back Row—Walter, Frank, John and Joe. Front row—Mrs. Zale, Tony, the world middleweight king and his sister, Mrs. John Kirdys.

THUMBNAIL SKETCHES OF B(

By HARR'

JOHNNY COLAN is rated by boxing men as one of the most promising light-heavyweights in the country . . . Only 21 years old he is still putting on weight and may be a heavyweight before long . . . His right name is Colainno and he was born on New York's West Side . . . Garden fans saw him trounce Jimmy Casa about eight months ago . . . He has done considerable boxing in Chicago and is an ace attraction in the Windy City . . . Colan never boxed as an amateur, starting right off among the pros . . . His ring affairs are handled by Paul Damski.

WICKEY HARKINS has been boxing professionally since 1937, mostly in Pennsylvania cities, where he is a good attraction . . . During the past year he has been seen frequently in New York rings where he has made many good fights . . . He is a 24-year-old lad from Philadelphia and is managed by Charlie Bennett . . . Among those he has beaten are Mayon Padlo, Vic Dellicurti, Irwin Kay Kaplan, Paulie Walker, Andre Jessurun, Jimmy Leto, Ernest Robinson, and others.

JOHNNY CREGAN comes from Pittsburgh, is a stablemate of Billy Conn, and is managed by Johnny Ray . . . He is regarded as an excellent prospect . . . His full name is John McGrath Cregan . . . He is 20 years old and is a welterweight . . . Cregan abandoned the amateur ranks about eighteen months ago and since then has won all but two of his fights . . . He was a Pittsburgh Diamond Belt winner two years ago.

BILLY MURRAY established something of a record in 1941, engaging in 43 contests during the year . . . He won 41 . . . He fought in Miami, Palm Beach, Los Angeles, San Francisco, Hollywood, Cleveland, and a lot of other places . . . Murray, a 140-pounder, hails from Bellaire, Ohio . . . He'll be 20 years old on Feb. 26 . . . He's been boxing as a pro less than two years after a successful amateur career . . . Jimmy Grippo is his manager.

HERBERT MARSHALL comes from the British West Indies where he was born twenty years ago, but his family moved to this country when he was about 10 . . . They settled in Brooklyn . . . Herbert attended Boys High for a while and then worked as a grocery clerk, quitting to take up boxing . . . He won from Hardy Greene and Willie Addison in two Garden starts . . . He stands six feet and weighs about 170.

Tickets for Garden boxing shows may be purchased at Twentieth Century Sporting Club offices, 1619 Broadway, Room 606; or at the Garden.

BILLY CONN comes back to a New York ring tonight for the first time since his unsuccessful but thrilling attempt to lift Joe Louis's heavyweight crown at the Polo Grounds last June . . . He did no boxing after that until about a month ago when he engaged in bouts at Toledo and St. Louis, winning both . . . Tonight's fight is particularly important to Conn since a defeat at the hands of Tony Zale would prove a most damaging blow to his prestige . . . Conn is a former world light-heavyweight champion . . . He won the title from Melio Bettina in the summer of 1939 and held it until just before the Louis bout, when he relinquished it . . . Conn was born in Pittsburgh, Oct. 8, 1917 . . . He is the oldest of five children . . . As a youngster Billy used to hang around a gymnasium operated by Johnny Ray, one-time lightweight, and it was there he first put on the gloves . . . He began his ring career as a lightweight but gradually put on weight, achieved considerable success as a middleweight and then moved on to take the 175-pound division crown . . . Many boxing men rate Conn as the keenest student of scientific boxing in action today . . . He is under the management of Johnny Ray . . . Conn was married shortly after the Louis fight, to Mary Louise Smith of Pittsburgh . . . Billy recently purchased a home in the Squirrel Hill section of Pittsburgh.

Original boxing program from Madison Square Garden.
Autographed by Mike Jacobs   February 13, 1942

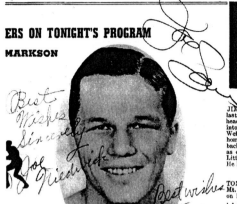

JIMMY WEBB knocked out Tommy Tucker in nine rounds in his last Garden appearance just a year ago . . . He seemed to be headed right for the top in the light-heavy class but then he ran into a slump and suffered several setbacks . . . Chris Dundee, Webb's manager, decided the fighter needed a rest and sent him home to Houston, Texas, for several months . . . But now he's back in action and showing the same form that established him as one of the best of the 175-pounders . . . Webb was born in Little Rock, Ark., Aug. 1, 1917 but was reared in St. Louis . . . He has been living in Texas for the past five years.

TONY FERRARA is one of 13 children . . . His family lives in Mt. Vernon . . . Tony was born Aug. 20, 1919 . . . He first put on boxing gloves when he was nine years old, in a boys' club . . . He competed successfully in the Golden Gloves, turning pro four years ago . . . Ferrara has now had about 50 fights in pro ranks . . . In his last Garden start he defeated Jimmy McDaniels . . . He has beaten many other good welterweights . . . Chris Dundee is his manager.

GEORGE KOCHAN has had six fights in the New York area in recent months, has won four and drawn in two . . . He comes from Akron, Ohio, and was a seaman in the merchant marine for six years, starting when he was only 14 . . . It was there he started to box . . . He has been twice around the world . . . A few months ago he drifted into Stillman's gymnasium and asked Joe Gould to become his manager . . . Gould obliged.

PETE KENNEDY is a welterweight prospect from Elmsford, just outside White Plains . . . He was born March 13, 1923 . . . After two years in the amateurs he turned pro a year ago and since then has won six and drawn once in seven fights . . . He was a good basketball and football player at Alexander High in Elmsford . . . His right name is Harry Patrick Kennedy though he's been called Pete since he was a baby . . . Kennedy now weighs about 142 . . . His fistic affairs are handled by Jack Barrett.

TONY ZALE cleaned up the confusion that had long existed in the middleweight division . . . He trounced Georgie Abrams at the Garden a few months ago to win universal recognition as world middleweight champion . . . Tonight's fight marks Zale's first appearance here since his highly impressive triumph over Abrams . . . Zale was born Anthony Florian Zaleski in Gary, Ind., May 29, 1914 . . . His father and mother came from Poland in 1911 and settled in Gary where the father obtained employment in the steel mills . . . But when Tony, one of six children, was two years old, his father was killed in an auto crash . . . Tony was ten when he donned the gloves for the first time, serving as "sparmate" for his older brothers who were amateur boxers . . . Zale also started his career as an amateur and fought in the Golden Gloves . . . In July, 1934, he turned pro but did not do well and so he quit the ring to take a job in the steel mills . . . But in 1937 he returned to action under Sam Pian and Art Winch and developed sensationally . . . He knocked out Al Hostak to become the National Boxing Assn. champion and after defending that title a couple of times went on to win world-wide recognition . . . Zale, known as "The Man of Steel," has had 61 professional fights and almost half of these ended in knockout victories . . . His title is not at stake in tonight's contest.

LORENZO STRICKLAND has been living in Brooklyn since he was six years old, though he was born in South Carolina 22 years ago . . . As an amateur he boxed under the name of Jesse Washington . . . He was a Golden Gloves winner in 1940, turned pro about a year ago, and has had twelve fights, meeting such good opponents as Johnny Colan, Mutt Womer, Bill Weinberg . . . His manager is Paul Marino.

Autographs of Joe Niedwick, Joe Louis and Tony Zale.

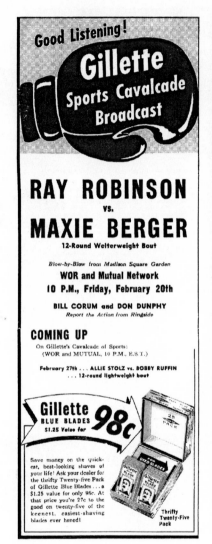

Back Cover of boxing program from 1942.

Lee Campione from Owosso, Michigan.
Light Heavyweight

Tony being examined by the New York State Boxing
Commission's Dr. William Walker. His first fight
with Rocky in Yankee Stadium had to be postponed
due to Tony falling ill with pneumonia.

'TONY ZALE NAMED
the BOXER *of the* YEAR

*Middleweight King's Six Round Knockout of Rocky Graziano Called
Battle of 1946—Made Up for Louis-Conn Flop*

By NAT FLEISCHER

Tony Zale Named Boxer of the Year. 1946

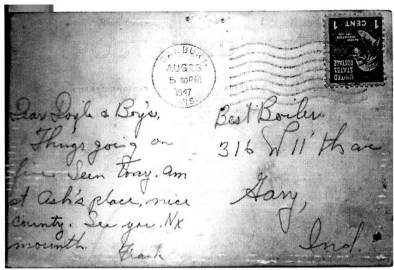

Postcard from Frank Zale. 1947

Four boxers on next Tuesday night's Tournament of Champions card at Jersey City, N. J., posed yesterday before undergoing preliminary physical checkups. Left to right are Marcel Cerdan, middleweight challenger; Tony Zale, middleweight champion; Gus Lesnevich, former light heavyweight title holder, and Joe Walcott, heavyweight. Zale will meet Cerdan and Lesnevich will take on Walcott. (AP Wirephoto)

September 17, 1948

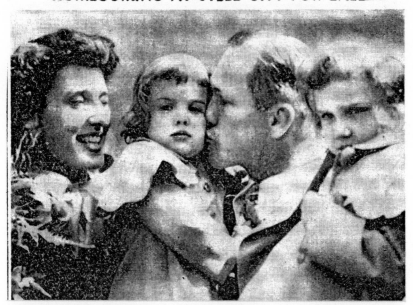

HOMECOMING AT STEEL CITY FOR ZALE

Tony and Jack Dempsey

Gus and Tony at The Martinique – Chicago

Tony and his best friend Gus celebrating another new year.

JOSEPH ZALE
Tony's oldest brother (and the Author's father)
who taught him the double left hook.
Joe was Fire Chief in Gary, Indiana, in 1957,
when one day he suddenly fell ill, and died. Joe's funeral
procession has been described by many to have been by
far the largest funeral that Gary has ever seen.

Joe's casket being honored through the city of Gary
on a draped fire engine. May 23, 1957

United States Atlantic Fleet
Boxing Tournament

Guest of Honor

Tony Zale

Middleweight Boxing Champion
1940~1948

United States Naval Amphibious Base
Little Creek,
Norfolk, Virginia

1~3 April, 1964

Tony with Journalist Seaman Fred McMane, Lieutenant Commander John A. Widder, Jr., Chief Journalist Bruce Keith, all from the Atlantic Fleet Amphibious Force Public Information Office. McMane traveled to Chicago to escort Tony on his return to Norfolk.

Dinner at the CPO Club - (left to right) CPO Robert Archibald, President of the CPO Club Advisory Board; Lieutenant (junior grade) Dean Radtke, Amphibious Force Athletic Officer; Lieutenant Commander Ray McLerran, Atlantic Fleet Athletic Officer; Lieutenant Commander John A. Widder, Jr., Amphibious Force Public Information Officer; Tony; Lieutenant G. W. Gilbert, Tournament Director; Hugh Johnson, Amphibious Base Civilian Athletic Director; Chief Journalist Bruce Keith, Amphibious Force Public Information Office; and Master Archibald.

Tony squares off with Doug Amicone, Virginia Light-Middleweight Golden Gloves champion. Amicone captured the Atlantic Fleet light middleweight crown the same night.

THE LAST HURRAH - The best of their weight divisions stand ready to receive championship trophies following the Atlantic Fleet Boxing Tournament, April 3, 1964. More than 3,000 people came to see the finals of the three-day tournament, drawn largely by a boxing immortal - TONY ZALE!!!

Tony on the aircraft carrier U.S.S. Antietam, Norfolk, Virginia.

Antietam was commissioned in January 1945, too late to actively serve in World War II. After serving a short time in the Far East, she was decommissioned in 1949. She was soon recommissioned for Korean War service, and in that conflict earned two battle stars. In the early 1950s, she was redesignated an attack carrier (CVA) and then an antisubmarine warfare carrier (CVS). After the Korean War she spent the rest of her career operating in the Atlantic, Caribbean, and Mediterranean. From 1957 until her deactivation, she was the Navy's training carrier, operating out of Florida. *Antietam* was fitted with a port sponson in 1952 to make her the world's first true angled-deck aircraft carrier. But she received no major modernizations other than this, and thus throughout her career largely retained the classic appearance of a World War II *Essex*-class ship. She was decommissioned in 1963, and sold for scrap in 1974.   Courtesy of Wikipedia

Tony reflecting back to his
1947 Graziano II fight at Chicago Stadium. 1968

Original autographed ticket for fights at
Madison Square Garden. March 9, 1973

Chicago's Soldier Field promo.

CYO Finals. December 3, 1976

TONY ZALE   3001 SOUTH KING DRIVE, APT. 809, CHICAGO, ILLINOIS 60616/312-842-0363

7-19-73

DROGI ZENONIE:

BARDZO MIŁO OTRZYMAĆ LIST OD CIEBIE, JAKO TEŻ, DOBRZE SŁYSZEĆ ZE JESTEM ZNA-NY W POZNANIU, W POLSCE. TAKŻE CIESZY MNIE GDY OTRZYMAM LISTY Z POLSKI, Z KTÓREGO KRAJU MOJE RODZICE POCHODZA, PONIEWAŻ JA JESTEM Z POLSKIEGO POCHODZENIA, I MAM WIELKI ZASCZYT Z TEGO.

Z TEM LISTEM TAKŻE POSYŁAM MOJĄ FOTOGRAFIE JAKO TEŻ I MÓJ AUTOGRAF.

ŻYCZĘ CI WSZYSTKIEGO DOBRA i POWO-DZENIA.

ZAWSZE,

Antoni Zaleski

Tony Zale

A handwritten letter from Tony and translated by Agnieszka (Agnes) Szumowska. She is a boxer and was a personal friend of Tony's best friend, Gus Latsis. 1973

Dear Zenon:

It is very nice to receive a letter from you, also, it is good to hear that I am known in Poznan, in Poland. It also makes me glad to receive letters from Poland, a country from which my parents are from, because I have Polish origin and I am proud of it.

With this letter I am also sending my photograph and also my autograph.

I wish you all the best and good luck.

Always,
Antoni Zaleski
Tony Zale

Tony Zale plants a right hand on
Cleveland Boxing Historian, Jerry Fitch.
Washington, D.C. October 1974.
Photo Courtesy of Jerry Fitch.

Key to the City of Amsterdam, New York.

Davey Day and others with Tony at the 1st Annual "Tony Zale
Boxing Tournament Awards." Chicago, Ilinois

Area recipients of the Silver Bell Club Hank Stram-Tony Zale Sports Award include (from left)—Stan Woszczynski, EC Washington; Steve Kruszynski, Clark; Tim Puchley, Gavit; Mike Stanny, Morton; Mitch Skiba, Bishop Noll; Mark Kowal, EC Roosevelt; and Tim Strempka, Tech. Also pictured is Zale.

A young autograph fan.

Tony's oldest daughter Mary and her niece, Sharon.

Grandpa spending some fun time in California with
his daughters and grandchildren.

Grandaughter, Sharon.   Visits with Granddaughter Sophia Marie.

Tony and daughter Mary.   Sophia enjoyed their visits together.

Daughter Teresa with son Michael and daughter Sharon.

A future champ.

Aaron Mackenzie Wells.
Sophia's Son. Sydney, Australia.
Tony's great grandson he never met.

Tony enjoying the California sun.
Still at his fighting weight.

from the desk of

HENRY "HANK" STRAM

5/10/92

Dear Tony and Philomene —
Please accept my most sincere thanks and appreciation for your kind and thoughtful note. the autographed Picture. and the sentiments expressed. I thoroughly enjoyed being with you in Gary and hope that you will have an opportunity to visit Kansas City for a Game this fall. Will look forward to seeing you again soon.

Warm regards

KANSAS CITY CHIEFS FOOTBALL CLUB

Hank Stram had much love and admiration for Tony
and expressed it often. The feeling was mutual.

Tony and Philomena were frequent guests at the Wrigley family's
Arabian Horse Farm in Lake Geneva. They loved their
visits with these beautiful animals.

The family always made sure Tony and Philomena
attended any Zale family reunions. They both enjoyed being in
the company of the children. Here, the author's daughter Haley
and her Uncle Tony are having a one on one moment.
He lovingly called her "Miss America." 1989

Ready for a big night out.
What a handsome guy he was.

Lew Jenkins – Lightweight Champion of the World.

Tony and Davey Day – Lightweight and Welterweight contender and stablemate of Tony's. Friends from beginning to end.

A Polish Welfare Association Fundraiser.

HALLS OF FAME

Induction to the Steel City Hall of Fame. 1987
www.garypubliclibrary.org/steel-city-hall-of-fame/
Inductees: Rev. Julius James, Orval J. Kincade, Andre A. Means,
Barbara Leek Wesson and Tony Zale.

Tony's family members always proudly supported
him by attending special events.

National Polish-American Sports Hall of Fame. 1986
Hamtramck, Michigan. www.polishsportshof.com

Rev. Ted Blazczyk

Dear Father Ted; inductees, and guests:

Having looked forward to this year's
Polish American Hall of Fame Festivities
color, I find myself getting over an
unexpected illness which makes it impossible
at this time.

Much as I would like to be there to
share the joy with the new inductees as well as all the
doctors orders are negative.

Congratulations to new inductees, And
all concerned; I will be looking forward
to next years Polish American Hall of Fame
Festivities. I pray to God we are all
around and well to attend.

Sincerely, Tony Zale

Tony's induction to the Chicago Sports Hall of Fame
www.chicagolandsportshalloffame.com

Tony enjoyed his years with the City of Chicago's Parks District.

The Champ with Chicago Mayor Richard J. Daley.
Tony was jokingly cautioned by Ed Kelly not to hurt him.

Chicago Sportscaster
Ben Bentley

Ben Bentley introduces former world
middleweight champion Tony Zale to
an admiring Chicago crowd.

Illinois State Rep. and Senator Dan Rostenkowski.
Ed Kelly - Chicago Parks District. Tony.

THE ED KELLY SPORTS PROGRAM, INC.

AN ILLINOIS NOT FOR PROFIT CORPORATION

1951 WEST LAWRENCE AVENUE

CHICAGO, ILLINOIS 60640

Telephone: 728-6300

July 9, 1990

Mrs. Tony Zale
3001 S. King Dr.
Apt. 809
Chicago, IL 60616

Dear Philomena,

The following is the agenda for Tony's night at the Excalibur restaurant, 632 N. Dearborn, on Thursday, July 19th.

I will host a private dinner for you and Tony at 5:30 P.M. at the second floor restaurant of the Excalibur. The dinner will include the news media and some of Tony's friends. Mayor Daley will also be invited to this dinner.

The smoker will start at 6:00 P.M., with food and drinks being served from 6:30 to 7:30 P.M. The program will begin at 7:30 P.M. Just before the program starts I will make a special presentation to Tony. The entire program will be over by 9:00 P.M., but the bar will stay open until 10:00 P.M.

Enclosed are the tickets you requested, and I hope this evening will be the beginning of good things for the future of you and Tony.

Sincerely yours,

Ed

P.S. If you need me please call.

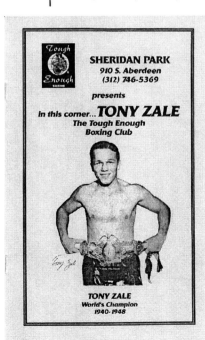

SHERIDAN PARK
910 S. Aberdeen
(312) 746-5369

presents

In this corner... **TONY ZALE**
The Tough Enough
Boxing Club

TONY ZALE
World's Champion
1940-1948

THANK YOU FOR BRINGING THE NY POLICE DEPARTMENT TO OUR BENEFIT

N.Y.P.D.
Patrolmans Benevolent Association
Boxing Team
260 Woodbury Road
Hicksville NY 1801

Jack Fitzgerald, Lee Packtor, Robert Papa, Bill Higgins, John Puglisi, Richie Frazier, Fred Corritone, Mickey Rosario

Interested in Tony Zale's Tough Enough Boxing Classes?

Monday • Wednesday • Friday
4:00-6:00 p.m.
at Sheridan Park

**Contact
Tony Martinez, Lou Ballo
or Marshall Christopher
(312) 746-5369**

Another Chicago publicity event included Walter Payton.

National Convention for the American Legion. Chicago. 1982

Tony loved Chicago…and Chicago loved Tony.

Tony with Chicago Mayor Michael Bilandic.

Tony out for a night in Chicago. Seen here with broadcaster and long-time announcer for the Chicago Cubs, Jack Brickhouse.

Curt Gowdy. "The Way It Was" taping. 1977

BOXERS   FIGHTERS   PUGILISTS

Tony and Jimmy Bivins

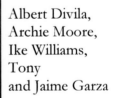

Tony, Archie Moore,
Jersey Joe Walcott, Ike Williams
Jimmy McLarnin

Albert Divila,
Archie Moore,
Ike Williams,
Tony
and Jaime Garza

Archie Moore,
Ike Williams
and Tony

Tony and Al Silvani
Boxing Trainer
and Actor

Kid Gavilan,
Sandy Saddler,
Rocky and Tony

Tony and
Tony DeMarco

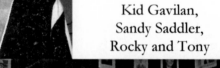

Billy Martin,
Whitey Ford
Rocky and Tony

Sunset Carson
Noble "Kid" Chissell

Jimmy Lennon Sr.

Floyd Patterson   Gene Fullmer

Fritzie Zivic

A National Polish-American Hall of Fame event.

Harry Duffy, an Irishman from Scotland, returns to Gary. He is visiting old Gary friends he hasn't seen in 33 years. They met the other night and talked over their boxing experiences at Zale's Tap, 35th and Broadway. From left to right, John Navicky, Frank Zale, Tony Zale (former World's Middleweight Champion), Charles Duffy (Harry's brother), Harry Duffy (the Irishman receiving trophy), Cy O'Bara, Matt Milligan, Mel Beckham, Mike Dudak, and Harry Coplen.

7-28-66

Tony and the Irishmen.

THE CAVALCADE OF CHAMPIONS
Calgary Convention Centre
November 14, 1977

Carmen Basilio, Angelo Dundee and Jake LaMotta with Tony.

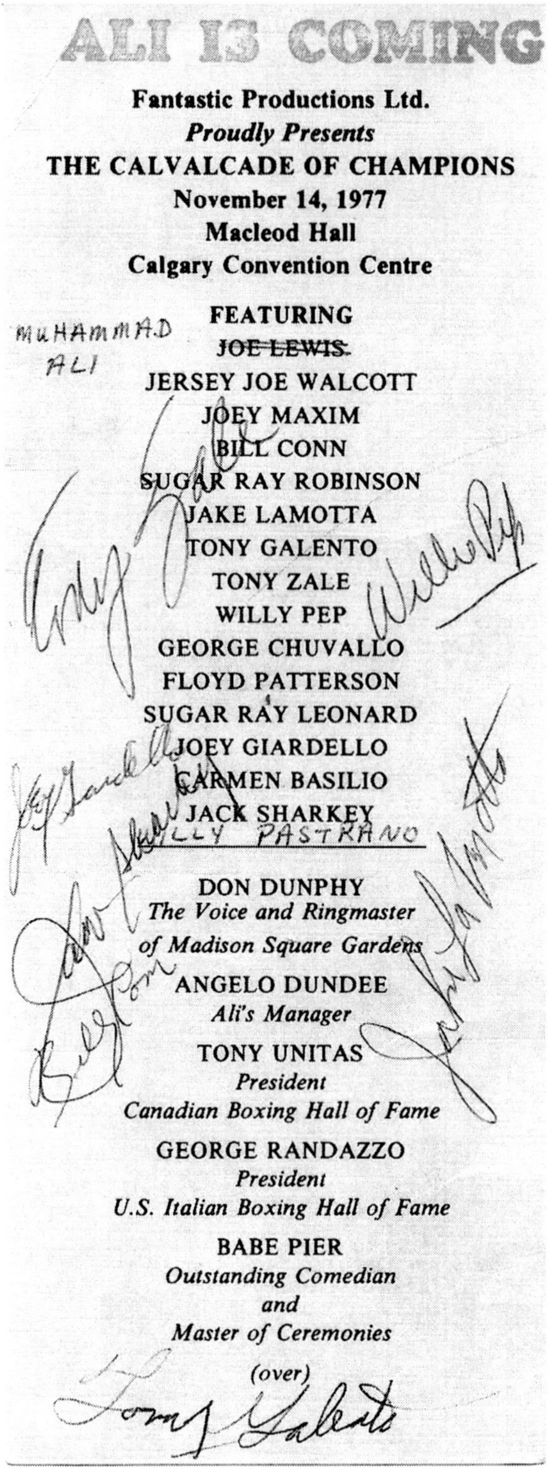

ALI IS COMING

Fantastic Productions Ltd.
Proudly Presents
THE CALVALCADE OF CHAMPIONS
November 14, 1977
Macleod Hall
Calgary Convention Centre

FEATURING

MuHAMMAD ALI

~~JOE LEWIS~~

JERSEY JOE WALCOTT

JOEY MAXIM

BILL CONN

SUGAR RAY ROBINSON

JAKE LAMOTTA

TONY GALENTO

TONY ZALE

WILLY PEP

GEORGE CHUVALLO

FLOYD PATTERSON

SUGAR RAY LEONARD

JOEY GIARDELLO

CARMEN BASILIO

JACK SHARKEY

WILLY PASTRANO

DON DUNPHY
*The Voice and Ringmaster
of Madison Square Gardens*

ANGELO DUNDEE
Ali's Manager

TONY UNITAS
*President
Canadian Boxing Hall of Fame*

GEORGE RANDAZZO
*President
U.S. Italian Boxing Hall of Fame*

BABE PIER
*Outstanding Comedian
and
Master of Ceremonies*

(over)

428

Don Dunphy   Jack Sharkey   Jake LaMotta   Carmen Basilio

Joey Giardello   Jake LaMotta

We wonder who won this card "match."

Tony and Floyd Patterson

Front: Angelo Dundee, Sugar Ray Leonard
Tony, Willie Pastrano,

Tony and Jake LaMotta

Jake LaMotta, Jersey Joe Walcott, Joey Giardello, Willie Pep

SAL BARTOLO-SOLLY ZALTER-TONY ZALE
"INTERNATIONAL CAVALCADE OF CHAMPIONS 78"
FIGHT NIGHT FOR CHARITY-SPONSORED BY
"THE OLD-TIMERS BOXERS GROUP INC."
MONTREAL, CANADA- NOV. 11th, 1978.

Tony, you may not have this in your collection — you do now. Jimmy Carter upstaged me.

Your pal Noble "Kid" Chissell

CAULIFLOWER ALLEY CLUB INDUCTS TWO TIME WORLD LIGHTWEIGHT BOXING CHAMP LOU AMBERS INTO INTERNATIONAL BOXING SHRINE at COCKATOO INN, HAWTHORNE, CALIF. JAN. 25, 1978 Left to Right: LAURO SALAS, former lightweight champ. AMBERS receives "MICKEY" Award from former great welter champ JIMMY McLARNIN. NOBLE "KID"CHISSELL, Master of Ceremonies/U.S.N. Middle champ 1932 and JIMMY CARTER, 3 time lightweight champ.

GOLD EAR AWARD presented by Club's Director MARSHALL WRIGHT and PRES. MIKE MAZURKI to ex-World Middle Boxing Champ TONY ZALE, observed by Ex- World welter Champ JIMMY McLARNIN and Ex-Navy Middle Champ NOBLE "KID" CHISSELL, seated. CAULIFLOWER ALLEY CLUB. 5-30-79. Foto Cr. Neporadny

To Philomena and Tony your pal Noble "Kid" Chissell

Cauliflower Alley Club Gold Ear Award
Marshall Wright, President Mike Mazurki, Tony,
Jimmy McLarnin, Noble "Kid" Chissell (sitting)
1979

For a Great Pal and Friend and the Worlds Greatest Middleweight Champion Tony Zale and his wonderful wife Filomena. Best wishes for Good Health and Happiness. God Bless Them Always. Your Friends Forever. Tony Messina - Abe Feldman - Joe Pope Cassillo.

The Champ's friends at the National Veteran Boxing Association.

Tony Messina, Abe Feldman, Joe Cassillo,
Sammy Angott and Lou Ambers

Congressman Ed Beard (Rhode Island) waiting
for his autograph from the Champ. 1979

An American Heart Association event with Bishop Grutka who
was the first bishop of the new Diocese of Gary, Indiana.

Senior Citizens Polka Fest. 1979
Former Mayor Gomulka of Amsterdam, New York.
Guests of Honor Tony and Philomena

Recorder Photo by Diane Tuman

Baseball Hall of Famer and Chicago Sportscaster, Bob Elson, held his last interview with Tony Zale.

CHICAGO PARKS DISTRICT FRIENDS

THE POLISH NATIONAL ALLIANCE OF NORTH AMERICA
An organization very near and dear to their hearts.

Lou Holtz's autograph hoping for the author's son,
Tony, to attend Notre Dame. 1993

For more information on the
Polish National Alliance please visit www.pna-znp.org

THE SILVER BELL CLUB

Twenty-six (26) young sports minded men banded together in 1925 to form an athletic club which became the Silver Bell Club. These men were exclusively a neighborhood group who lived in the densely populated area of the City of Gary east of Broadway between 11th and 21st Avenue. The center of this community was St. Hedwig Parish, whose residents were predominantly of Polish and Slavic origin. The club's primary objective at the time was to participate in various competitive sports of which boxing, baseball, and basketball were the major ones.

To assure themselves of lasting unity, the club became affiliated with the Polish National Alliance of North America, the largest Polish fraternal organization in America. The club became very popular and its membership continued to grow and its activities expanded to golf and bowling. For years the club's participants excelled in practically every competitive sport. The club, during this period, was incorporated and its by-laws provide for the following purposes: "To promote the welfare of our brothers and our fellow men; to participate in civic, athletic, social, and fraternal activities in our community."

In conforming with its purposes, the club earmarks thousands of dollars annually to scholarships and to the various charitable organizations and purposes as well as man power. The club sponsored the International Senior League World Series for years while at Gary and currently sponsors the Hank Stram-Tony Zale Sports Awards Banquet for outstanding school athletes of Polish-Slavic descent in Lake County, various little league teams, softball teams, a bowling team, and Polish Heritage Award.

Among the intra-club activities are: Installation Banquet, Memorial Service, a bowling league, sports outings, golf and bowling tournaments, Children's Christmas Party, picnics, and academic scholarships each year to deserving club members or their childern.

A NOTE FROM THE CHAIRMAN

I would like to welcome you to the 18th Annual Hank Stram-Tony Zale Sports Award Banquet, along with each member of the Committee. We offer our sincerest appreciation for your interest and participation in this great event.

As you can realize, there are many individuals who should be recognized for helping make this evening a success. We would especially like to thank the patrons for their continued financial support in helping us produce this program book. Their donations will make a significant contribution to our scholarship fund.

Our special gratitude to Club Members Hank Stram and Tony Zale for their incentives to continue promoting the recognition of academic and athletic achievements of young athletes we are honoring tonight.

Proceeds from this affair are used for scholarships awarded to those students who are members of our organization, as well as children whose fathers are members of the Silver Bell Club.

We are very grateful to have Hall of Famer Terry Bradshaw as our featured speaker, and fortunate his schedule could accommodate our invitation. His words of knowledge will be beneficial to our recipients tonight.

I would like to thank Wayne Larrivee, the Voice of the Chicago Bears and WGN Radio for taking on the duties of Master of Ceremonies for tonight's banquet.

To Ed McCaskey, we thank you for your participation and words of wisdom to our young people this evening.

To Mike Tomczak, Tom Thayer and Doug Buffone whose personal accomplishments have drawn the acclaim of fans and admirers alike, our thanks for your inspiration to our honorees.

A Special Thanks to Steve Buha for his continued support in coordinating and playing in the Celebrity Golf Outing along with the other Golfers, Bob Buha, Fred VanSenus, Sr., and Al Miza.

We thank Edward and Leslee Kirk for their continued support in promoting the Silver Bell Club.

Again, I sincerely thank my Bosses, Don and Fred VanSenus for their support, patience and understanding with me in the planning of this affair.

The Silver Bell Club would like to thank Mike and Diana Ditka for their donation of the Chicago Bears SkyBox tickets.

And finally, to members of my committee for their cooperation and dedication in making this one of the most memorable events in the history of the Silver Bell Club. The final product of their energetic teamwork is what you are witnessing here tonight.

Most sincerely,

Ed Hojnacki

Ed Hojnacki, Chairman

1993

PROGRAM

Welcome .... Edward Hojnacki
Master of Ceremonies .... Wayne Larrivee
Pledge of Allegiance .... Wayne Larrivee
Invocation .... Father Charles Niblick

Dinner

Remarks .... Tony Zale
Mike Tomzak
Tom Thayer
Doug Buffone
Ed McCaskey
Presentation of Certificates to Athletes .... James Barcinski
Special Award .... Joseph T. Sanok
Remarks .... Hank Stram
Featured Speaker .... Terry Bradshaw

Auction
Chicago Bears Skybox Tickets
Donated By
Mike & Diana Ditka

Raffle Prize

An Autographed
Football By
Super Bowl Champions
New York Giants

An Autographed
Football By
Central Division Champion
Chicago Bears

HANK STRAM

Hank Stram, one of the most successful coaches in the History of Professional Football is now a television and radio analyst on CBS for National Football League Games. On the CBS radio sports side, Stram has been paired up with his partner Iack Buck as the network's primary announce team since 1978. Their coverage of Monday Night Games has reached an audience of approximately 7.5 million,while the pair's Super Bowl Broadcasts reach approximately 12 million listeners. His pride of his hometown is evident in his broadcasts by frequent reference to Gary, Indiana.

Stram, who grew up in Gary, graduated from Lew Wallace High School where he played halfback and his senior year was the Captain of the football team. He held titles for All City, All Conference and All State and was also the scoring champion.

Stram attended Purdue University in 1941 and was invited to play in the College All-Star Game in 1943, but had to miss it because he enlisted in the Army Reserves and was called to active duty two months before the game. After three years in the Service, Stram returned to Purdue and graduated with a B.S. in Physical Education in 1948. While at Purdue, Stram won seven letters, four in baseball and three in football. In his Senior Year, he received the coveted Big Ten Medal which is awarded to the conference athlete who best combines athletics with academics.

After graduation, he served 12 years as an assistant coach at the collegiate level; Purdue, SMU, Notre Dame and Miami of Florida. Then in 1960, he was named Head Coach of the Dallas Texans in the American Football League and guided them to the AFL Championship in 1962, after which the team moved to Kansas City and became the Chiefs. In 1966, the Chiefs played in the first Super Bowl losing to the Green Bay Packers. Four years later, Stram took the Chiefs to Super Bowl IV defeating the Minnesota Vikings 23 to 7. The Chiefs were four games away from being the winningest team in football during Stram's 15 years as coach.

Stram coached 17 years in Professional Football and had a lifetime record of 131-97-10. He ended his career with two seasons (1976 and 1977) as the Head Coach of the New Orleans Saints.

Selected four times as "Pro Football Coach of the Year", Stram was also named on Pam Stanton's list of "Ten Best Dressed Men in Football". Stram has been inducted in the Polish Hall of Fame in Michigan; Indiana Hall of Fame, City of Gary; and the Kansas City Hall of Fame. Recently, Hank wrote a Book entitled "They're Playing My Game", and was the recipient of The Bert Bell Award in recognition for services offered in Professional Football. In March of 1990, Stram was the recipient of The March of Dimes NFL Press Box Awards in St. Louis, as the Radio Color Analyst of the Year. On March 9, 1991, Hank received The Lifetime Achievement Award from the Totino's National Quarterback Club in Washington, D.C.

Hank and wife Phyllis have six children and reside in Covington, LA., his mother Nellie and sister Dolly still live here in Lake County.

BANQUET COMMITTEES

Banquet Chairman .... Edward Hojnacki
Co-Chairman .... Hank Stram & Tony Zale
Decorations .... Andrew Gadzala
High School Athletes .... James Barcinski
Publicity... Edward Hojnacki
Raffle .... Thomas Hecker
Tickets.. John Muraida
Program Book .... Edward Hojnacki

Joe Samreta	Pete Ogiego
Gary Kalmas	Joe Sanok
John Sobczak	Bob Mazur
Harold Feneck	Marc Malczewski
Chester Klaja	Walter Baran

Seating .... Ben Frankowski
John Subart
Michael Feryo
Ed Persin

LODGE #2365 ADMINISTRATION

President .... Joseph T. Sanok
Vice President .... John Muraida
Treasurer... Henry Nawrocki
Financial Secretary.. Edward Frankiewicz
Recording Secretary... Jim Barcinski
Sergeant At Arms .... Casey Koss
Inner Door Guard .... Pete Ogiego
Chaplain .... Chester Klaja
P.N.A. Sales Representative .... Anthony Dziuba

Hank, Philomena and Tony

Tony and Philomena with
Hank Stram and his mother, Nellie. 1975

24TH ANNUAL

SILVER BELL CLUB

P.N.A. Lodge 2365

Hank Stram - Tony Zale

SPORTS AWARD BANQUET

Monday, May 19, 1997

Radisson Hotel • Grand Metropolitan Ballroom • 2nd Floor Convention Center

Featured Speaker

Former Major Leaguer

JOE GARAGIOLA

№ 726

Cocktails 5:30 p.m.
Donation $35.00

Dinner 7:00 p.m.
Proceeds to Scholarship Fund

Joe Garagiola   Angel Manfredy
Ed Hojnacki   Hank Stram   Tom Dreesen
The first banquet after Tony's death in 1997.

Tony Zale and Hank Stram. The Polish National Alliance
Silver Bell Club Annual Sports Award Banquet. 1975

SPORTS AWARDS COMMITTEE

Pete Ogiego
Conrad Serwatka
Mitch Serwatka
Ben Frankowski
Michael Feryo
Steve Tokarski
Ed Hojnacki
Ed Krieger
John Subart
John Muraida, Sr.
Chris Anton
Ted Wallace

BEST OF LUCK
FROM
Nicholas J. Schiralli
Judge of Lake County Court
Division #1

VERY BEST WISHES
To Silver Bell Club and to
Outstanding Athletes
Frank Stodola

CONGRATULATIONS
To the Silver Bell Club
Mr. & Mrs. Frank B. Roman

CONGRATULATIONS
To Silver Bell Sports
Award Committee From
Mr. and Mrs. Chris Anton

COMPLIMENTS FROM
Lorenzo Arrendondo
Judge of Lake County Court
Division #2

CONTINUED SUCCESS
To Silver Bell Sports Award
Committee From Rudy Bartolomei
Lake Co. Commissioner 3rd District

** PROGRAM **

Address of Welcome.........................Conrad Serwatka

Master of Ceremony..........................Walter Gembala

Pledge of Allegiance..................Dr. Joseph E. Kopcha

SONG: GOD BLESS AMERICA............Audience Participation

INVOCATION

DINNER

INTRODUCTION OF OFFICIALS AND DIGNITARIES...Conrad Serwatka

HISTORY OF SPORTS AWARDS PROGRAM............Walter Gembala

FILM..............................Tony Zale-Rocky Graziano
                                         Championship Fight

MAIN SPEAKER.....................................Tony Zale

REMARKS....................................Edward Swiss
          Former Professional Hockey Player and Trainer

                                              Al Pilarcik
          Former Professional Baseball Player

PRESENTATION OF CERTIFICATES.................Michael Feryo

MAIN SPEAKER....................................Hank Stram

GREETINGS................................Aloysius Mazewski
          National President, Polish National Alliance

CLOSING REMARKS..........................Walter Gembala

Conrad Serwatka

Dr. Joseph Kopcha

L – R   Ed Hojnacki, Tony, Chris Anton,
Hank, Pete Ogiego

TONY'S PAL ROCKY ET AL.

Tony and Rocky could never do enough PR.

Philomena Zale dies at 68

By Randy Shirey

Staff writer

Philomena Zale, the wife of former Gary resident and world middleweight boxing champion Tony Zale, died Saturday at Michael Reese Hospital in Chicago.

Philomena Zale, 68, a former professional baseball player and Chicago schoolteacher, died of cancer.

While Tony Zale ruled the middleweight division during the World War II years, Philomena Gianfrancisco was a star right fielder in the All American Girls Baseball League. She played for teams in Moline, Ill., and Grand Rapids, Mich., during her career.

A movie starring Madonna entitled "A League of Their Own" will focus on that women's fast-pitch baseball league. The movie is still in production.

Philomena Zale was honored by the Hall of Fame in Cooperstown during a special ceremony in 1988. A baseball traveling exhibit features some of her memorabilia.

Vivacious and outspoken, Philomena Zale had a tremendous impact on her husband's life, a driving force who helped the former world champion stay active the past few years. Tony Zale was frequently honored at area boxing shows, including the annual Chicago Golden Gloves Tournament.

She accompanied Tony Zale to a special presentation in Glen Ellyn last year when President Bush awarded her husband the Presidential Citizenship Medal.

"President Bush was a lot better looking in person than on TV," she told this reporter after that ceremony.

Tony Zale, 78, was inducted into the national Boxing Hall of Fame last summer.

Philomena Zale was his second wife.

Visits with the Champ after Philomena died.

At Warren Barr Pavilion in Chicago when Ted was
showing Tony what he had written for his life's story.
Tony suggested some changes and corrections.

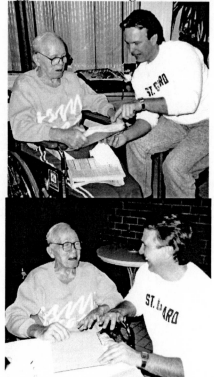

Author Ted and his uncle enjoying some family time.

Warren Barr Pavilion. Chicago, Illinois
Matt Phillips, Tony Zale, Deb Zale
Uncle Tony
1992

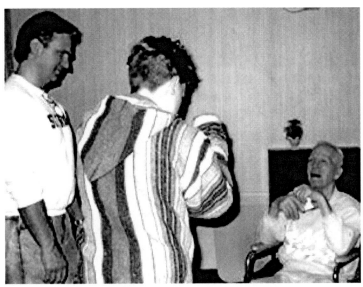

The Champ checking out young Tony's form.

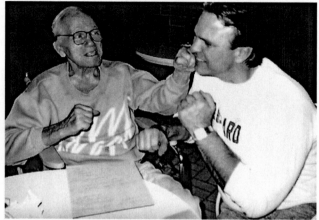

You can take the Champ out of the ring, but you
can't take the ring out of the Champ.

Handprints of famous Chicago sports figures.
Sports Authority, 620 N. LaSalle. Chicago. 1991

The author's sons, Patrick Zale and Tony Zale, with the Champ.
Fountainview in Portage, Indiana. 1994

NOWENNA

DO

MATKI BOSKIEJ

BOLESNEJ

✦

Ułożył
dla użytku publicznego
KS. JAKÓB R. KEANE, O. S. M.

przetłumaczył na język polski
KS. FRANCISZEK A. KULIŃSKI

Tony's personal Polish Prayer Book from 1955.

STACJA SZÓSTA

**MARIA PRZYJMUJE MARTWE
CIAŁO JEZUSA W RAMIONA
SWOJE**

Wszyscy wstają, gdy kapłan odmawia rozmyślanie:

Rozważ, jak gorzki smutek przeniknął duszę Marii, gdy zmarłego Syna, ranami okrytego, krwią zbroczonego, złożono na Jej łonie. O żałosna Matko, któżby się nad Tobą nie litował? Któreż serce się nie wzruszy na widok boleści Twoich? Nie pociesza Ją w tej chwili ani płacz Jana, ani Marii Magdaleny, ani Nikodema. Pocieszmy Ją w tym smutku, wołając do Niej:

Wszyscy klękają i odmawiają z kapłanem:

O Królowo Męczenników! * Kiedyż zdołam pojąć boleści Twoje? * Wyznaję, iż jestem grzesznikiem zatwardziałym! * Spraw, O droga Matko, * aby serce moje przeszyte zostało * tym samym mieczem boleści, * który przeszył zbolałe serce Twoje, * i abym dniem i nocą * opłakiwał grzechy moje, * które były przyczyną boleści Twoich.

Kap.: Zdrowaś Mario. Lud: święta Mario,
Kap.: Panno Bolesna, Lud: Módl się za nami.

1943
(US NAVY)

1971

To a great fight fan, Rinze Van Der Meer, too a great fan of mine. Best wishes and success, always Tony Zale

I'll Slap You Down!

♔ *TONY ZALE* ♔
WORLD'S CHAMPION··1940-1948◦
TONY-HELD THE MIDDLEWEIGHT CHAMPIONSHIP LONGER THAN ANY···
· · ·OTHER BOXER IN THE WORLD·
· · · ·

Rinze Van Der Meer sent the author this autographed photo that he is so proud of so we could use it in this book.

Tony appreciated his international boxing fans very much.
Thank you for being a loyal fan, Rinze.

TWO FISTEDLY YOURS — TONY ZALE

Photo Courtesy of Rinze Van Der Meer.

CELEBRITIES

Frank Stallone and Tony struck up a friendship during one of his visits in California. In 2011, the author Ted Zale presented this Riviera Hall of Fame Golf Classic polo shirt, one of Tony's favorites, to Frank for his personal boxing memorabilia collection. Frank is a boxer, collector and historian. Photo Courtesy of Frank Stallone.

John Ritter

Jackie Cooper

Joe DiMaggio

Tony, Eddie Albert, Robert Wagner, Charlie Callas

Vic Damone

Jack Carter

Jack Carter   Vic Damone   Ida Lupino

Jack Klugman   Bob Newhart

Pat Cooper   Robert Conrad

Robert Conrad   Larry Manetti

Marcello Mastroianni 1971

Having some fun with Jimmy Durante.

Anthony Quinn   Oprah Winfrey

Vincent Gardenia

Sandy Dennis

Rocky Graziano - Mike Douglas

Getting Smart with Don Adams

Chicago Mayor Kennelly - Jimmy Durante and Cast

John Forsythe

Frank Sinatra Jr.

Dennis James

Joking around with The Riddler.
Frank Gorshin   POWWW!!!

Mickey Rooney

Rose Marie

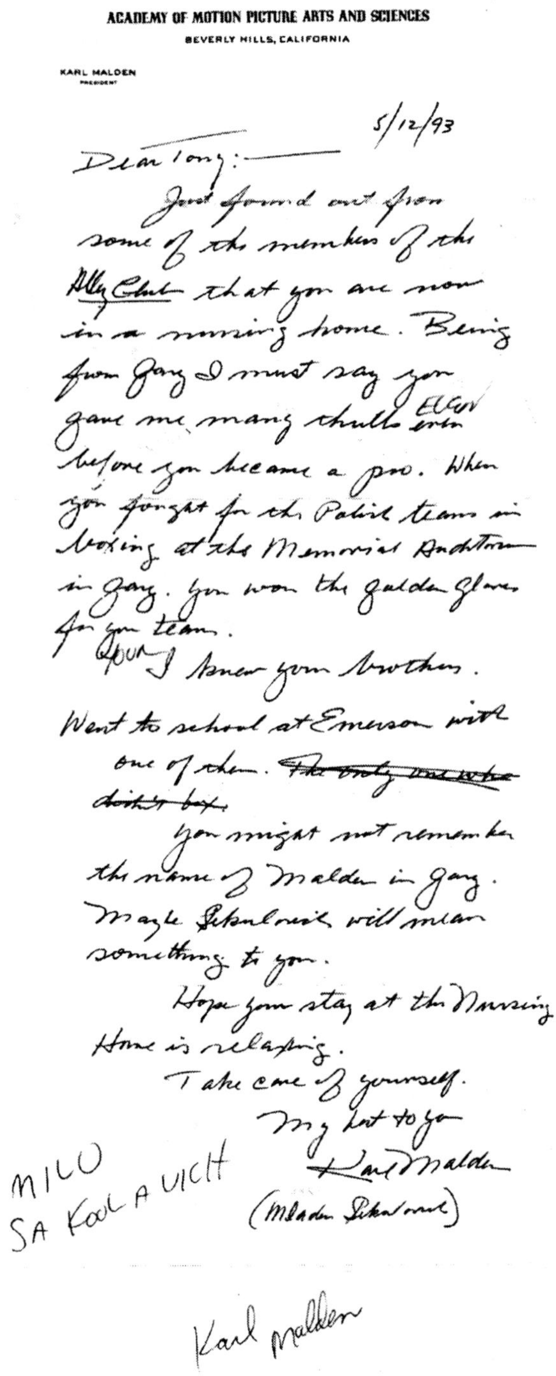

ACADEMY OF MOTION PICTURE ARTS AND SCIENCES
BEVERLY HILLS, CALIFORNIA

KARL MALDEN
PRESIDENT

5/12/93

Dear Tony:—

Just found out from some of the members of the Ally Club that you are now in a nursing home. Being from Gary I must say you gave me many thrills even before you became a pro. When you fought for the Polish team in boxing at the Memorial Auditorium in Gary. You won the golden gloves for your team.

Your I knew your brothers. Went to school at Emerson with one of them. ~~The only one who didn't box.~~

You might not remember the name of Malden in Gary. Maybe Sekulovich will mean something to you.

Hope your stay at the Nursing Home is relaxing.

Take care of yourself.

My best to you

Karl Malden

(Mladen Sekulovich)

MILO
SA Kool A VICH

Karl Malden

Karl Malden's fan letter to Tony Zale. May 12, 1993

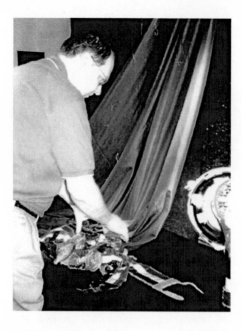

Tom Nakielski of Lights On Studio in Lansing, Michigan, is shown prepping Tony's championship belts and some other personal items. They were professionally photographed by Tom before being enshrined into the International Boxing Hall of Fame Museum in Canastota, New York. 1998

Photo Courtesy of Lights On Studio

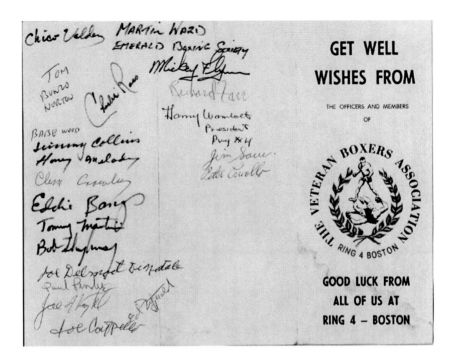

Brother:

All of us at Ring 4 are praying for you and hoping you will be feeling well real soon and will be back with us.

FIGHT ONE MORE ROUND

FIGHT ONE MORE ROUND!
When your feet are so tired you have to shuffle back to the center of the ring —

FIGHT ONE MORE ROUND!
When your arms are so tired that you can hardly lift your hands to come on guard —

FIGHT ONE MORE ROUND!
When your nose is bleeding and your eyes are black and your head is dizzy and the ring is rolling around and around —

FIGHT ONE MORE ROUND!
When you are so tired that you wish your opponent would crack you one on the jaw and put you to sleep —

FIGHT ONE MORE ROUND!
REMEMBERING — in your pain —
THAT THE MAN WHO ALWAYS FIGHTS
ONE MORE ROUND IS NEVER WHIPPED!
James J. Corbett

The whereabouts of Tony's 3rd championship belt
(top) is still unknown.

A TRIBUTE TO TONY ZALE

THE MAN OF STEEL - A CHAMP

May 29, 1913 - March 20, 1997

In the Boxing Ring, Tony Zale was an outstanding Boxer. As a person, Tony was a smiling, calm, pleasant, down-to-earth friendly man who would talk with anyone at any time - and who guided hundreds, possibly thousands, of young men in physical fitness, and to walk in God's ways. People were so enthralled by Tony Zale's boxing many didn't know his stature as a humanitarian.

Above and beside Tony Zale's coffin were his Gold Belt, his Nine Hall of Fame awards, the President's Citizen Medal, his Boxing Shoes, a large display of Tony Zale's accomplishments, family and friends and a multitude of beautiful flowers. Tony Zale merited all of these.

As Hank Stram said in his Eulogy to Tony Zale - "Tony accomplished everything he did on his own - no one could help him with what he did, and all thru the years Tony won thousands of people who love and admired him. He was a Champ! It was evident how all of Tony's family members cooperated with love, to handle the multiple arrangements that were necessary - people flying in to attend Tony's funeral - the nice large display of Tony's accomplishments and life - graciously introducing themselves and talking with each person - and sharing memories of a beloved down-to-earth fine man.

From the hundreds of people who came to the services of Tony Zale, these comments were heard: "Tony put me on the right track" - a crying young man said, "Tony was like a Father to me" - "Tony was such a fine and honorable man" - "Tony kept in shape in between his bouts and all his life" - "Tony wasn't a bit egotistical, he was a smiling, friendly man to everyone" - "Tony was a down-to-earth man, kind and gracious to everyone - "During his career, and after, Tony helped hundreds, possibly thousands of young men get on the right path to God in their lives".

Perhaps drivers who were detained by the Funeral procession on the 17 mile route to the Cemetery, counted over 100 cars. Along the route, a young boy 12 or 14 years old, patiently held up a large sign "Rest in Peace my Buddy Tony Zale".

For those of us who worked at the Catholic Youth Organization and appreciated Tony Zale's friendship and sending us Christmas cards, Tony Zale will always be remembered as our gracious, down-to-earth, smiling Dear Friend - who never gave up on his dedication of directing hundreds of young men to lead clean, wholesome lives, maintain physical fitness, and to follow God's pathway in Life.

Eugene and Shirley Magner

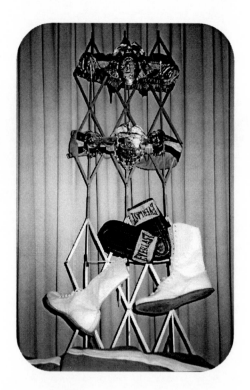

Two of Tony's three Championship belts,
workout shoes and gloves.

The Joseph Zale(ski) Family.   March 24, 1997
L-R: Ray, Ted, Lucille Izak, Joe, Gene and Bernie.

George Latsis. Best friend Gus Latsis
Tony Martinez

Kristofer Foster

Shirley Kordys-Bobin

Jim Krecik

Danny Zale

Friends came to pay their respects.

Robert Zale

George Foster, Deb Zale's father,
proudly played the bagpipes for his friend's funeral.

The Champ had full military honors for his service
with the U.S. Navy, U.S. Navy Reserves
and U.S. Army Reserves.

Tony would usually compose a rough draft before
penning a final copy of any handwritten note.
He wrote this poem.

If you are a boxing fan whatsoever, please visit the International Boxing Hall of Fame Museum located in Canastota, New York.
www.ibhof.com

October 16, 1990

The Presidential Citizens medal is awarded by the President of the United States. It is the second highest civilian award in the United States, second only to the Presidential Medal of Freedom. Established by executive order on November 13, 1969, by president Richard Nixon, it recognizes individuals "who [have] performed exemplary deeds or services for his or her country or fellow citizens." The award is only eligible to United States citizens, and may be awarded posthumously.

The medal is a disc of gilt and enamel, based on the Seal of the President of the United States, with the eagle surrounded by a wreath of leaves. The medal is suspended on a ribbon, dark blue with a light blue central stripe and white edge stripes. Courtesy of Wikipedia

The Man of Steel's medal is proudly on display at the International Boxing Hall of Fame Museum in Canastota, New York, located near Syracuse.

Thank you, President Bush.

Jack Sandner is one of Tony's former boxing students. He was such an inspiration to Jack that several years later, Jack played a large role in Tony receiving the Presidential Citizens Medal in October of 1990. Thank you, Jack.

TONY ZALE   3001 SOUTH KING DRIVE, APT. 809, CHICAGO, ILLINOIS 60616/312-842-0363

March 26, 1980

Tony Zale
Former two-time
Middleweight Boxing
Champion of the
World

Presently

Head Coach-Boxing
Chicago Park District

Member

Board of Directors
Second Federal
Savings & Loan Ass'n.

Jack Sandner

[   ]

Dear Jack:

I had been called the other day by phone, as
to whether I remembered you from the C.Y.O,
and if I had coached you. You were a pretty
good fight prospect at the time and I did remember, as you were outstanding enough to be
remembered, due to your ardent desire and application.

I was very happy to hear that one of my fight
students had reached the height you have, and
will continue on. I had always advised and
stressed schooling to all, if you remember. As
a matter of fact, another boy who took my advice
was a "professor at Georgetown University and
is now head of the department of philosophy at
the University of Chio. I think he was a little
after you, at the C.Y.O.. His name is Karl Kordig.
He was a light heavy.

It truly gives one a good feeling of satis-
faction, to hear his advice was taken the right
way, and followed through to success. There
are other boys who had heeded my advice, whom
I have not as yet heard about. It is truly
gratifying.

Nice to hear of your success, and I wish you
a continuation of it.

AWARDS

New York Boxing
HALL OF FAME

Edward J. Neil
Outstanding Boxer

RING MAGAZINE
Boxing's most
valuable man

GOOD AMERICAN AWARD
Greatest middleweight
Champion of World

BELTS

RING MAGAZINE
1941 Title Belt
Geo. Abrams—

NATIONAL BOXING ASS'N.
Defending Title Mematos

RING MAGAZINE
Rocky Graziano
1948

EVERLAST SPORTSMANSHIP
award
Outstanding service to
Boxing

Gary Indiana Sports
HALL OF FAME
Jr. Chamber of
Commerce

CATHOLIC ATHLETIC ASS'N.
as Outstanding Service
to Youth

ALWAYS

Tony Zale

TFZ/cbs

Tony wrote this letter to Jack Sandner in 1980. Little did he
know that Jack's admiration for him would result in Tony
receiving, just ten years later, the most treasured award of his
life, the Presidential Citizens Medal.

Thank you for purchasing *Tony Zale The Man of Steel*.
A portion of the proceeds from the sale of this book is being
donated by the authors to the Polish National Alliance
for the specific use of granting educational
scholarships in memory of Tony Zale.
The Champ was very proud of his Polish heritage and
his Catholic faith. We hope you have enjoyed his story.

PHOTO CREDITS AND PERMISSIONS

p. 3   Tony Zale's personal collection
p. 6   Kansas City Chiefs, Tony Zale's personal collection
p. 8   Thad Zale's personal collection
p. 16   Tony Zale's personal collection
p. 19-25 Wikipedia
p. 28   Thad Zale's personal collection
p. 29-32 Tony Zale's personal collection
p. 35   St. Hedwig – The Polish Community of Gary
p. 36-43 Tony Zale's personal collection
p. 44   Calumet Regional Archives
p. 45-57 Tony Zale's personal collection
p. 60   Associated Press Wire Photo
p. 61-67 Tony Zale's personal collection
p. 74   International News Photo
p. 75-76 Tony Zale's personal collection
p. 77   Chicago Daily Times, Tony Zale's personal collection
p. 83-86 Tony Zale's personal collection
p. 87   International News Photo, Tony Zale's personal collection
p. 88   Tony Zale's personal collection
p. 97   Clay Moyle's personal collection
p. 100   Official Photo U.S. Navy, Tony Zale's personal collection
p. 101-10 Tony Zale's personal collection
p. 122   Google Images
p. 123   Tony Zale's personal collection
p. 125   News Photo by Engels, Tony Zale's personal collection
p. 126   Associated Press Wire Photo, Tony Zale's personal collection
p. 129   Tony Zale's personal collection
p. 132   Associated Press Wire Photo, Tony Zale's personal collection
p. 134   Tony Zale's personal collection
p. 135   Associated Press Wire Photo, Tony Zale's personal collection
p. 136   Associated Press Wire Photo, Tony Zale's personal collection
p. 137-40 Tony Zale's personal collection
p. 141   The Ring Magazine, Tony Zale's personal collection
p. 142   Tony Zale's personal collection
p. 149   International News Photo, Tony Zale's personal collection
p. 155-57 Tony Zale's personal collection
p. 166   United Press International, Tony Zale's personal collection
p. 167-69 Associated Press Wire Photo, Tony Zale's personal collection
p. 176   Tony Zale's personal collection
p. 180   The Ring Magazine, Tony Zale's personal collection
p. 191   Tony Zale's personal collection
p. 192   Associated Press Wire Photo, Tony Zale's personal collection
p. 193-96 United Press International, Tony Zale's personal collection
p. 197   United Press International, Tony Zale's personal collection
         Journal –American Photo by Frank Rine and George Miller,
         Tony Zale's personal collection

Tony Zale's personal collection
p. 402-03   Tony Zale's personal collection
Compass, Tony Zale's personal collection
p. 404-07   Tony Zale's personal collection
Sophia Marie Well's personal collection
p. 408-32   Tony Zale's personal collection
p. 433   Photo by Neporadny, Tony Zale's personal collection
p. 434-35   Tony Zale's personal collection
p. 436   Photo Courtesy of Diane Tuman, Tony Zale's personal collection
p. 437-53   Tony Zale's personal collection
p. 454-56   Thad Zale's personal collection
p. 457   The Servite Fathers, Tony Zale's personal collection
p. 458-59   Photos Courtesy of Rinze Van Der Meer, Tony Zale's personal
            collection
p. 460   Photo Courtesy of Frank Stallone
p. 461-67   Tony Zale's personal collection
p .468   Thad Zale's personal collection
            Photo Courtesy of Lights On Studio, Tom Nakielski
p. 469-71   Tony Zale's personal collection
p. 472-74   Thad Zale's personal collection
p. 475   Tony Zale's personal collection
p. 476   Thad Zale's personal collection
p. 477   Tony Zale's personal collection
p. 478   Tony Zale's personal collection
            Thad Zale's personal collection
p. 479   Tony Zale's personal collection
p. 480   Photo by Frank Goodman, Tony Zale's personal collection

Other Photo Credits to:
Ed Kelly
Seattle News
Sandy Bertog Photo
MCS Photo
Jackson Photo Service
Bill Rand Promotions
K. Jewell
Ralph A. Newman
Times
Photo Ideas, Inc.
Milwaukee Sentinel
Top Ten Greatest Fights of All Time
The Knockout Photo
Angelo Prospero, Jr.
Boxing News Photo
Western Electric
Cameo Candids
News Photo by Engels
Tribune Photos by Nancy Stone and Larry Levin

INDEX

Continued luck
and success,

always

Tony Zale

Lightning Source UK Ltd.
Milton Keynes UK
UKOW04n0352061215

264168UK00002B/19/P